THE LAST NAHDAWI

THE LAST NAHDAWI

Taha Hussein and Institution Building in Egypt

HUSSAM R. AHMED

STANFORD UNIVERSITY PRESS
Stanford, California

STANFORD UNIVERSITY PRESS
Stanford, California

© 2021 by the Board of Trustees of the Leland Stanford Junior University. All rights reserved.

No part of this book may be reproduced or transmitted in any form or by any means, electronic or mechanical, including photocopying and recording, or in any information storage or retrieval system without the prior written permission of Stanford University Press.

Printed in the United States of America on acid-free, archival-quality paper

Library of Congress Cataloging-in-Publication Data

Names: Ahmed, Hussam R., author.

Title: The last nahdawi : Taha Hussein and institution building in Egypt / Hussam R. Ahmed.

Description: Stanford, California : Stanford University Press, 2021. | Includes bibliographical references and index.

Identifiers: LCCN 2021011024 (print) | LCCN 2021011025 (ebook) | ISBN 9781503615342 (cloth) | ISBN 9781503627956 (paperback) | ISBN 9781503627963 (epub)

Subjects: LCSH: Ḥusayn, Ṭāhā, 1889-1973—Political and social views. | Education ministers—Egypt—Biography. | Intellectuals—Egypt—Biography. | Education and state—Egypt—History—20th century. | Egypt—Cultural policy—History—20th century. | Egypt—Politics and government—1919-1952.

Classification: LCC DT107.2.T3 A46 2021 (print) | LCC DT107.2.T3 (ebook) | DDC 962.05/2092 [B]—dc23

LC record available at https://lccn.loc.gov/2021011024

LC ebook record available at https://lccn.loc.gov/2021011025

Cover design and illustration: Rob Ehle

Typeset by Kevin Barrett Kane in 10/14 Minion Pro

For my mother, Naglaa.

CONTENTS

Illustrations ix
Acknowledgments xi
Note on Translation and Transliteration xv

INTRODUCTION 1

1 Egyptian Cultural Expansionism
 Taha Hussein Confronts the French in North Africa 42

2 *Nahda* Goes to University
 Taha Hussein and the Mission of the Private Egyptian University 73

3 Democratizing Education
 Taha Hussein, Institutions, and Unstable Parliamentary Politics 104

4 Democratizing the Language
 Taha Hussein and Diversifying Authority over Classical Arabic 136

5 Winds of Change
 Taha Hussein and the End of a Political Project 168

CONCLUSION 206

Notes 215
Bibliography 259
Index 277

ILLUSTRATIONS

Figure 1	Sketch for the redesign of Ismailiyya (Tahrir) Square	3
Figure 2	Taha Hussein's family	6
Figure 3	Taha Hussein's desk in the Museum of Education in Cairo	9
Figure 4	Inauguration of Farouk I (Alexandria) University, 1943	48
Figure 5	Taha Hussein's trip to Tunis, 1957	49
Figure 6	Taha Hussein's trip to Nice, 1950	52
Figure 7	Inauguration of the Egyptian University, 1908	78
Figure 8	Faculty members at the Egyptian University, 1925	80
Figure 9	Al-Azhar, 1906	91
Figure 10	Taha Hussein in his study	97
Figure 11	Postcard photo of the New University Campus from the 1930s or 1940s	102
Figure 12	Amina Taha Hussein's Wedding, 1948	111
Figure 13	Suhayr al-Qalamawi	115
Figure 14	Meeting at the Arabic Language Academy, 1934	149
Figure 15	Taha Hussein at an Arabic Language Academy meeting, shortly before his death	164
Figure 16	Taha Hussein being carried from the Arabic Language Academy, shortly before his death	165
Figure 17	Nasser decorating Taha Hussein, 1959	203
Figure 18	Taha Hussein's grave under a mimosa planted by his wife	213

ACKNOWLEDGMENTS

Taha Hussein is a familiar household name in Egypt and much of the Arab world. Many first editions of his books were available in my late grandfather's personal library with its many shelves of hardbound volumes by al-Isfahani, al-Jahiz, and al-Zamakhshari along with other classics that reflected my grandfather's scholarly interest in the Arabic language, sciences, and literature in which he was trained and which were his passion. Like many people in our region, I also watched the television series and the film depicting Hussein's life. In Cairo, I repeatedly walked down a street bearing his name, and as a teenager I read his autobiography, probably because I felt that I should. Today, we are still overwhelmed by references to Hussein in school, public life, and the media. Such proximity is informative in its own way, but it is also challenging to work with (and against), as it forcibly nurtures the misleading feeling that we know the man or that we have figured him out. Working on this book has introduced me to a different Taha Hussein, however. There was the famous writer and critic, of course. But I slowly came to see him as someone who not only wanted to change the existing order but also proposed an alternative, which he labored to build under unpropitious circumstances. In the aftermath of the Egyptian Revolution of 2011 and its pressing question of "where do we go from here," Hussein's project became a thought-provoking precedent as I realized that many questions that he struggled with were still pertinent.

Researching and writing this book has taken me to a variety of places and allowed me to meet and work closely with many dear people, whom I wish to thank here.

I am especially grateful to the family of Taha Hussein in Egypt and France: Amina Taha Hussein-Okada, Sawsan El Zayyat, Hassan El Zayyat, and especially Maha Aon. They received me kindly, and graciously answered all my questions about Taha Hussein. They generously provided me with Hussein's private papers, which have been immensely helpful in navigating his life and giving me a better sense of the official and family man that he was. Moreover, many of the photographs in this book come from their family collection, which they shared with me and amiably allowed me to publish. They know they have all my gratitude.

Thanks are also due to the helpful and hardworking archivists and librarians at the Egyptian National Archives (Dar al-Watha'iq al-Qawmiyya), the Egyptian Registry and Property Records Archive (Dar al-Mahfuzat al-'Umumiyya), the Egyptian National Library (Dar al-Kutub), the Faculty of Arts at Cairo University, the Museum of Education in the Egyptian Ministry of Education, the library of the American University in Cairo, and the library of the Dominican Institute for Oriental Studies. In France, I would like to thank the staff at the Centre des Archives Diplomatiques du Ministère des Affaires Étrangères in La Courneuve, and at the Bibliothèque Sainte Geneviève in Paris. In Montreal, I would like to thank the amazing staff in the Islamic Studies Library and the McLennan Library at McGill University.

The researching and writing of this book has benefited from the facilities and support I received at McGill University, KU Leuven, the University of Cambridge, and Maynooth University. Financial support came from several institutions: the Social Sciences and Humanities Research Council of Canada (SSHRC), through the Joseph Armand Bombardier Fellowship and the Michael Smith Foreign Study Supplement; the Fonds de Recherche du Québec—Société et Culture (FRQSC), with a postdoctoral fellowship; the European Research Council, through a grant associated with the project Muslims in Interwar Europe at KU Leuven; and the History Department and the Faculty of Arts at McGill University, in the form of several fellowships.

I feel tremendous gratitude for having had the support of many mentors, colleagues, and friends over the past years. I thank my mentor Laila Parsons for her thoughtful guidance and unmistakable enthusiasm for this project. She gave me confidence and encouraged me to take an interest in the genre of social biography and in Taha Hussein. Her scholarship, attention to detail, and commitment to her colleagues and students will always inspire me. She has been incredibly generous with her knowledge and her time. She pushed me to think in new and deep ways about my project, and always encouraged me to try to do justice to the complexity of people's lives and their choices. Laila has changed the way I think about, write, and teach history, and without her I could not have completed this work. I am forever grateful.

I am fortunate to have had Khaled Fahmy as a mentor for many years now. His deep knowledge and supportive advice have informed all stages of the researching and writing of this book. In Cairo, he helped me gain access to and make sense of state and university archival documents. Then our numerous discussions on Egyptian history and present-day concerns have been a wonderful guide and a constant reminder to always keep my work relevant to Egyptians and people in the region. He knows how much I appreciate and value his scholarship, public engagement, and friendship.

Zachary Lockman, Tassos Anastassiadis, Will Hanley, and Lorenz Lüthi have read earlier versions of this work and their insightful comments, suggestions, and critiques have been invaluable. In addition to his feedback and our many cheerful conversations, Tassos offered me the opportunity to go on a research trip funded by the Fonds Québécois de Recherche Société et Culture, which allowed me to visit the archives of the French Ministry of Foreign Affairs in Paris and retrieve valuable material for my research. Likewise, my discussions with Will have been important, informative, and much fun. I am also indebted to him for the title of this book.

I would also like to thank Michelle Hartman and Nancy Partner for many memorable discussions on the history of Arabic literature, historiography, and biography writing. Special thanks are due to Orit Bashkin, who showed hearty enthusiasm for the project from the start, supported me with her thoughtful comments, and eventually helped me find a publisher. Dyala Hamzah and Yoav Di-Capua made key observations that forced me to think in new ways about Taha Hussein and his world, and I have learned a lot from them. Over the years, I have also benefited from discussions with various scholars and friends in Egypt, Canada, the United States, and the United Kingdom. I am especially grateful to the late Madiha Doss and to Robert Wisnovsky, Jens Hanssen, Anthony Gorman, Malika Zeghal, William Granara, Israel Gershoni, Sherene Seikaly, Ilham Khuri-Makdisi, Elizabeth Kassab, Hosam Aboul-Ela, Malek Abisaab, Brian Lewis, Setrag Manoukian, Paul Sedra, Khalid Medani, Richard Jacquemond, Donald Reid, Joel Gordon, Umar Ryad, Anaïs Salamon, Vincent Romani, Shokri Gohar, Mark Sanagan, Prashant Keshavmurthy, Aslıhan Gürbüzel, Jessica Winegar, Angela Giordani, Sean Swanick, Hussein Omar, and Raphael Cormack for all their encouragement, insightful comments, and suggestions.

Audiences at various conferences and workshops provided valuable feedback, and I would like to thank the organizers of the annual meetings of the Middle East Studies Association, the American Historical Association, the British Society for Middle Eastern Studies, the Institute of Islamic Studies Graduate Students Symposium at McGill University, and the Middle East History and Theory Workshop at the University of Chicago. I am also grateful to William Granara, Ari Schriber, Youssef Ben Ismail, and Chloe Bordewich, and the organizers of the

2017 Middle East Beyond Borders Workshop at the Center for Middle Eastern Studies at Harvard University, not only for having invited me to share my research with them but also for their constructive feedback and suggestions. Similarly, I would like to thank Khaled Fahmy, Hazem Kandil, Assef Ashraf, Charis Olszok, and Hana Sleiman, and the organizers of the Modern Middle East Reading Group at the University of Cambridge in 2019, for inviting me to discuss my work and for the thoughtful questions and suggestions I received from them.

I would like to thank Kate Wahl, editor-in-chief at Stanford University Press, for her support of this book project from the very initial contact and her gracious, smooth guidance as the book made its way to press. It has been a great pleasure working with her and the entire staff at Stanford. My thanks also to the two anonymous readers for their encouragement and invaluable commentary on the manuscript.

I am eternally grateful for many friends and their support over the years, both intellectual and emotional, especially Kathryn Kalemkerian, Steve Paugh, Araxi Kalemkerian-Paugh, Vilelmini Tsagaraki, Shirin Radjavi, Pascale Graham, Pascal Abidor, Sarah Ghabrial, Jimmy Leiser, Pierre Portier, François Riquebourg, Véronique Samson, Éric Martinet, Ludovic Fouquet, and Maxime Philippe.

Finally, I would like to thank Kevin Jones for his unfailing support and critical reading of my work over the years. His intelligence, knowledge, and encouragement are an endless source of inspiration. I thank my sisters, Sarah and Hend, for their love, kindness, thoughtfulness, wisdom, and humor. I am proud to be their brother. My deepest gratitude goes to my mother, Naglaa, who insisted, despite the distance and time difference, on being there every step of the way with her love, grace, reassurance, and support. Without her, none of this work would have been possible, and I dedicate it to her, together with my deep love and appreciation.

NOTE ON TRANSLATION AND TRANSLITERATION

All translations from Arabic and French into English, including the titles and descriptions of archival materials cited in the notes, are mine, unless otherwise indicated. In my translations from Arabic, especially of Taha Hussein's writings, I have opted for resistant translation, to give the reader a better sense of Hussein's style and sentence structure.

I have transcribed Arabic words and proper names according to a simplified system based on the *International Journal of Middle East Studies* (IJMES) style guidelines, whereby all diacritical marks have been omitted except for the *ayn* (ʿ) and the *hamza* (ʾ). I have used accepted English spellings for place names like Cairo and Beirut as well as familiar English spellings for famous people like Taha Hussein, Fouad I, and Nasser.

THE LAST NAHDAWI

INTRODUCTION

ON JANUARY 25, 2011, thousands of young Egyptians took to the streets in peaceful protests demanding freedom, justice, and human dignity. Escalating events marred by state violence quickly fixed the world's eyes on Tahrir Square, lying at the heart of modern Cairo, on the east bank of the River Nile. Tahrir Square quickly became the symbol of the Egyptian Revolution that was to topple President Husni Mubarak's regime on February 11, 2011, after thirty years in power. Until General ʿAbd al-Fattah al-Sisi deposed the democratically elected President Muhammad Mursi on July 3, 2013, the square continued to attract protesters angry with successive military and civilian governments. Ruling the country with an iron fist, Sisi reclaimed the square in the name of stability, as he skillfully diverted attention from citizens' demands for justice to the survival of the Egyptian state during the so-called Arab Spring, arguably the most devastating period in modern Arab history, with millions of casualties and displacements.

Historian Leyla Dakhli has described how the protesters in Tunisia who triggered the Arab Spring in late 2010 drew upon a legacy of Tunisian social movements. She remarks that only some of those protestors saw a continuity with earlier battles fought by their parents. In the absence of what she describes as "handbooks of the struggles of 1968, 1978, or 1983," protesters waved old combat flags and chanted fiery slogans without realizing their historical meaning.[1] Similarly, most Egyptians in Tahrir Square saw the 2011 revolution as an unprecedented protest, and not as one in a series of historical moments in which generations of Egyptians had demanded freedom and accountability. Such moments are often obscured by a potent nationalist narrative pitting the nation against conspiring foreign powers and their local collaborators while infantilizing citizens and dismissing their ability to fathom, let alone deal with, challenges facing the country.

Ironically, as protesters gathered in the square in front of the headquarters of the Arab League and the square's five-star hotel, demanding involvement in decision making, they did not realize they were standing in front of the site where there should have been a new Egyptian Parliament building. The story of that unrealized project goes back to the massive demonstrations that broke out in 1946 demanding an end to British occupation. In the aftermath of those demonstrations, Britain returned Qasr al-Nil barracks, an all-time constant symbol of British occupation in the heart of the capital, to Egypt in 1947. In the same year, Muhammad Dhulfiqar proposed revamping the square to be the showpiece of modern Egypt's state and cultural prowess, and a constant reminder of the supremacy of the people over the executive. He proposed building new headquarters for the Council of Ministers, Cairo Municipality, the Ministry of Foreign Affairs, and several museums, which would adjoin the already existing Museum for Egyptian Antiquities. In his sketch shown here, Dhulfiqar assigned this prime location on the Nile to a new parliament, a gigantic neoclassical design inspired by the Capitol building, to be dedicated to the sovereignty of the people.[2] The post-1952 regime discarded the proposal, however, and the Egyptian Parliament remains tucked away between Qasr al-'Aini and Sheikh Rihan Streets, impossible to see from the square.

Demonstrators in front of the British barracks in 1946 would have recognized the iconic writer and educator Dr. Taha Hussein (1889–1973). By the mid-1940s, he had written dozens of literary classics and hundreds of articles. His stature as the "Dean of Arabic Literature" and leading intellectual in the modern Arab world was, and still is, beyond dispute. Yet, these demonstrators would have also known him as a fearless public voice calling for full independence, sound democracy, and social justice. The well-respected academic was also a senior civil servant and an active politician associated with Egypt's most popular nationalist party, the Wafd. In 1950, his decision as the Wafd's minister of public instruction to introduce universal free secondary education would go down in history as one of his greatest achievements. As this study will show, this famous executive decision was one of many such that he made and was the culmination of a much

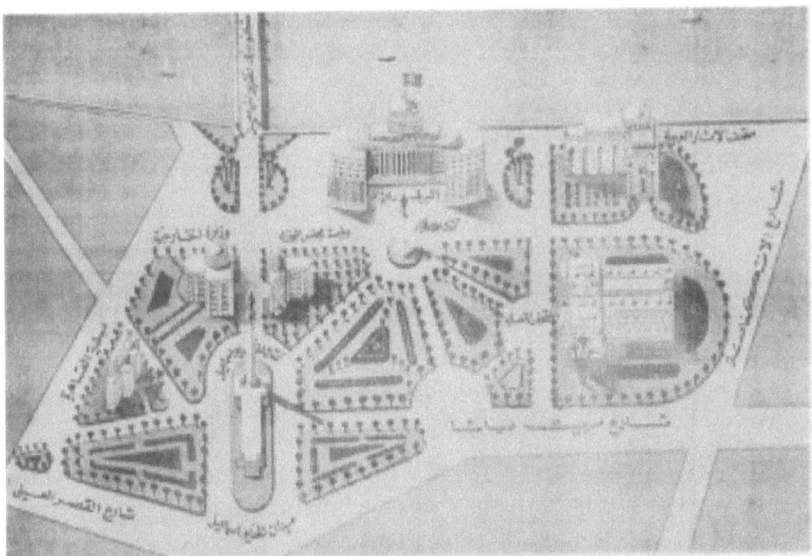

FIGURE 1. Sketch for the redesign of Ismailiyya (Tahrir) Square. Source: *Al-Musawwar*, no. 1173 (April 4, 1947): 8. (Creative Commons - CC BY-NC-SA 4.0.)

larger, coherent three-decade project of institution building, the implementation of which mocked clear-cut distinctions between thought and action, and between culture and politics, despite Hussein's public claims that art and culture should remain above political motives.

Hussein restructured and built the institutions he believed were necessary to engage with both the Arab-Islamic classical tradition and new western ideas, produce the knowledge required to achieve intellectual parity with Europe, and force European powers to recognize Egypt's full independence. All these institutions, including universities, a language academy, and several technical councils, persisted under the postcolonial state, pointing to significant continuities between parliamentary and Nasserite Egypt. After Hussein's exclusion from decision-making circles in the 1950s, critics and scholars considering the earlier period focused exclusively on his thought, and his reception today continues to be overdetermined by passages in some of his published work in which he pushed for a deep intellectual cooperation with Europe while idealizing culture as more noble and more enduring than politics. This book shifts the focus to Hussein's action and his role in building Egypt's educational and cultural institutional infrastructure within a challenging colonial context. Understanding his political career is essential not only to making proper sense of his extended and often controversial legacy but also to opening up an important moment in modern Egyptian history, a pertinent precursor to 2011.

That important moment was Egypt's parliamentary period, between its nominal independence from Great Britain in 1922 and the army coup in 1952, which ended the rule of the Muhammad Ali dynasty (1805–1953). As it ushered in Gamal Abdel Nasser's authoritarian rule (1954–1970), the coup betokened the end of serious attempts to configure a durable Egyptian democracy. An overly familiar colonial trope describing Egypt's soil as inhospitable to democracy then became an enduring postcolonial one. In an interview with Christiane Amanpour in 2011, 'Umar Sulayman, Mubarak's chief intelligence officer and vice president, warned that Egyptians did not have what he called "the culture of democracy" and cautioned that chaos might arise if Mubarak were to make a hasty departure (despite his thirty years in power).[3] The military coup in 2013 and the toppling of Muhammad Mursi seemed only to confirm that democracy was foreign to Egyptian society. International media, using what veteran historian Thomas Philipp has described as "hyperbole," sensationalized these events by describing Mursi as "Egypt's first freely elected president in 5,000 years," ignoring, as Philipp points out, that "the rule of law and constitutionalism have been debated, developed, and even temporarily implemented in the Middle East for over 200 years," and that in the 1920s and '30s, "Egypt established a fully-functioning freely elected parliament with well-organized parties."[4] Taha Hussein was actively involved in this parliamentary system. To develop his projects and ensure the efficient operation of various institutions and policies, he successfully won voters to his views and insisted all governments must be held accountable to parliament, the legitimate representative of the Egyptian people. This book is the story of institutions of culture and education and their ties to emergent democratic practices in Egypt's parliamentary period, viewed through the life and work of Taha Hussein.

Taha Hussein

Taha Hussein was born on November 15, 1889, in the village of 'Izbat al-Kilu, near the town of Maghagha in the Upper Egyptian province of al-Miniya. He lost his eyesight at the age of three, due to a maltreated ophthalmia. While his blindness caused him much distress throughout his life, it also added an aura of heroism and even genius to his exceptional intellectual accomplishments. His disability did not stop him from pursuing his studies at the village *kuttab* (elementary school), in a traditional educational system that had long accommodated the blind. He had memorized the Qur'an by the age of nine, and in 1902, went to continue his studies at the prestigious mosque-university of al-Azhar in Cairo, where, mostly through his brother Ahmad and Ahmad's friends, he came under the influence of the religious scholar and modernist reformer Sheikh Muhammad ʿAbduh. It was also at al-Azhar that he was introduced to the classics of Arabic literature by Sheikh Sayyid ʿAli al-Marsafi (1862–1931). Disappointed with al-Azhar's teaching methods emphasizing memorization and verbal analysis, however, he was among the first students to register at the new Egyptian University, which opened its doors in 1908. He was also the first to earn a doctoral degree from the new university, in 1914, with a dissertation on the blind Abbasid poet and philosopher Abu al-ʿAla' al-Maʿarri (973–1057), famous for his pessimism and for having described himself as "a double prisoner" of blindness and solitude. Hussein then went on a scholarship to France, first to Montpellier then to Paris, where he earned a doctorate from the Sorbonne, writing his thesis on the social philosophy of Ibn Khaldun. While in France, he also met and married Suzanne Bresseau, and in 1919, she returned with him to Egypt, where she lived until her death in 1989. The family photograph displayed on the next page shows them with their two children, Amina-Marguerite and Moenis-Claude. Back in Cairo, Hussein started teaching ancient history and then Arabic literature in the Faculty of Arts at the Egyptian University. His long academic career overlapped with a steadfast commitment to writing as he authored dozens of books and articles on Islamic history and Arabic literature. His work enjoyed wide readership throughout the Arab world, and his readers followed his avid participation in the intense and often controversial debates animating a lively Egyptian literary scene in the first half of the twentieth century.

A few months after Hussein's death on October 28, 1973, the Egyptian Marxist critic Ghali Shukri (1935–1998) wrote:

> I do not believe there is a single intellectual in the last four decades in Egypt, or in the Arab world in general, who has not been influenced by Taha Hussein. This was, and will continue to be, what sets him apart from the rest of his generation. Some will say they have been influenced by al-ʿAqqad, Salama Musa, or al-Mazini, but in addition to their favorite writer, you will find that they have all been influenced by Taha Hussein.[5]

FIGURE 2. Taha Hussein's family. Courtesy of the Taha Hussein family.

This laudatory remark from Shukri stands out against the background of intense debates that had pitted Hussein against many young leftist intellectuals in the 1950s and '60s. These debates echoed across the Arab world and distanced Hussein from younger intellectuals like Shukri, Mahmud Amin al-'Alim, 'Abd al-'Azim Anis, Ra'if Khuri, and others. Faced with a new generation of writers who promoted "committed literature," Hussein defended his views calling for the total freedom of writers to choose both the literary form and the content of their work. Hussein, by then a veteran who had championed the cause for social justice under the monarchy in his literary works and political chronicles, disheartened the enthusiastic leftist writers, who had expected his encouragement and blessings. Believing that literature must support the new anti-colonial struggle and become a vehicle for decolonization and social change, they saw Hussein as a "bourgeois and liberal" intellectual, a defender of "art for art's sake," and a representative of an older generation of writers that failed to grasp the new role literature had to play in society. Their critique of Hussein was part of their overall discontent with Egypt's parliamentary experiment between 1922 and 1952. In support of the new regime, these leftist critics argued that a corrupt monarchy and petty partisan politics had destroyed the potential of Egypt's 1919 revolution and failed to achieve full independence or the necessary social reforms.[6] Nevertheless, during and after the debate, Shukri, Amin, Khuri, and others never hid their admiration and respect for Hussein. Shukri, for example, emphasized the impact Hussein had had on the intellectual formation of several generations of writers and critics, including the younger ones who were now challenging him. Shukri even credited Hussein's famous periodical *al-Katib al-Misri* (1945–1948) with having introduced Shukri's generation to Jean-Paul Sartre, Albert Camus, and Franz Kafka in the first place.[7] In Shukri's view, the influence of Hussein's ideas, and his long fight for intellectual freedom and critical scholarship, could not be denied.[8]

Yet, promoting critical thinking and subjecting the canonical works of the Arab-Islamic tradition to academic scrutiny earned Hussein many enemies over the years. Decades after his death, he is glorified by some and vilified by others as if he were still alive and as if his work had just been published. In November 2016, for example, the media reported that al-Azhar had suspended the scholar Yusri Ja'far, professor of philosophy and theology in the college of the principles of religion, for three months. Among several other allegations, he was accused of "adopting Taha Hussein's critique of al-Azhar's curriculum and reviving Muhammad 'Abduh's thought."[9] The media did not elaborate on what the critique and the thought in question were. Yet, readers implicitly understood that if Ja'far's work was associated with 'Abduh and Hussein then it must have been deemed unorthodox and controversial. Ironically, around the same time, the Grand Sheikh of al-Azhar, Ahmad al-Tayyib, praised Hussein, saying that he was "extremely polite with the Islamic heritage, with the Prophet, and [with his companions] Abu Bakr, 'Umar and 'Uthman."[10] Al-Tayyib's measured statement, however, does not reflect the opinion of other religious groups and their followers. As I explain later, they blame Hussein for having westernized Egyptian thought and for having collaborated with Orientalists and missionaries. Some go even further and accuse him of having secretly converted to Christianity and of undermining Islam from within.

Hussein also has his ardent supporters in these debates. One of the many protests that paved the way to the 2011 revolution was the peaceful demonstration organized by the Writers and Artists for Change Movement in downtown Cairo in August 2005, in which the protesters held banners calling for political change. Some of these banners carried images of Hussein as the symbol of a long and still unfinished battle for freedom of thought and expression.[11] In addition, following Mubarak's overthrow, some leftists forgot the "art for art's sake" debate and appealed to other aspects of Hussein's legacy as they addressed Egypt's volatile political situation. For example, writing in 2012, during the battle that raged between religious and non-religious political parties over drafting a new Egyptian constitution, leftist Nasserist journalist Majida al-Jindi argued that the road Hussein had charted for freedom, culture, and education in his classic book *The Future of Culture in Egypt* (*Mustaqbal al-Thaqafa fi Misr*, 1938) was more relevant now than ever.[12] In a more recent statement, the poet Muhammad Ibrahim Abu Sinna called for adopting that book in its entirety as the official program for reforming the country's ailing educational system.[13]

Abu Sinna's statement speaks to another heated debate on the economic viability of free education in Egypt. In recent years, free education has come under sharp criticism. Recent local and international reports on the declining quality of Egyptian public schooling are fueling debates over the utility of costly state support for these schools and universities. Leftists use Hussein's name and his famous view of education as a fundamental right for every citizen to counter arguments by neoliberals who insist education is a commodity for which people must pay.[14] References to Hussein abound in Egyptian public life, and the passage of time has so far denied him the dispassionate debates granted to most intellectuals of his generation.

But Hussein's legacy does not stop with the intellectual disputes it continues to stir. Visitors to Cairo University and Egypt's Ministry of Education are visually reminded that Hussein, more than any other intellectual in Egypt's modern history, is associated with the country's modern secular educational system. Visitors see busts of the Dean of Arabic Literature, in his familiar glasses, sternly scrutinizing both institutions whose names remain invariably tied to his. Students and employees attend classes and hold meetings in various classrooms and conference halls bearing his name, not only at the university and the ministry but also at the National Council for Translation. His ministerial oak desk (shown in the photo here) is the only desk on public display at the museum of the Ministry of Education, a statement to his long career as Cairo University's Dean of Arts (1928, 1930–1932, and 1936–1939), a senior civil servant in the Ministry of Public Instruction—first as controller of general culture (1939–1942), then as technical advisor to the minister of public instruction (1942–1944), and finally as minister of public instruction himself (1950–1952)—and also a member and then president of the Arabic Language Academy until his death (1940–1973).

In these polarized and passionate debates, Hussein's political career and the context in which he wrote his books are usually absent. Compared to his

FIGURE 3. Taha Hussein's desk in the Museum of Education in Cairo. Source: Hussam R. Ahmed.

better-known career as a writer and critic, Hussein's role as a statesman, politician, and civil servant has received little attention. Unlike many intellectuals who were active between the two revolutions, such as Salama Musa (1887–1958), Ibrahim al-Mazini (1889–1949), or Tawfiq al-Hakim (1898–1987), Hussein had a long and dynamic political career. The 1919 revolution had triggered Great Britain's unilateral declaration of Egypt's nominal independence in 1922, followed by the adoption of the nation's constitution in 1923, and the beginning of its parliamentary life in 1924. While the independence of 1922 was famously hampered by four reservations maintaining Great Britain's political and military control over Egypt, education was one of the areas over which the Egyptian government reassumed full control.[15] This period thus became dominated by reform efforts and by political debates on how to turn nominal liberty into full independence, and Hussein became actively involved. For him, the real battle for full independence was about building strong institutions of learning and knowledge production. His political activities began in a serious way when he aligned himself with the popular Wafd Party in the 1930s and used the Wafd as a platform to pitch his ideas on culture and education while responding to his adversaries on the pages of widely read journals and periodicals. In this book, Hussein's under-studied public career becomes a lens for understanding not only the history of the institutions he fought for, which exist to this day, but also the history of the parliamentary era in which he was a main player.

A Social Biography

Using the life and work of Taha Hussein to examine various social, political, and cultural transformations in Egypt in the first half of the twentieth century makes this book a *social biography*, which is not a biography in the usual sense. Historian Nick Salvatore sums up nicely the various reservations historians have had about traditional biographies, and how a social biography, when rigorously done, may address those concerns. Biography, he argues, has traditionally been seen as a lesser form of history, a genre in which the historian's main task of periodization is predetermined by the birth and death of the biographical subject.[16] Another concern is that a strong focus on individual agency may obscure the wider historical context and flatten other forces at play.[17] Historians who contributed to the American Historical Association's forum on biography in 2009, for example, take these criticisms seriously. Their papers all start by explaining the ways in which their biographies and methodologies differ from the usual biographical approaches, leading David Nasaw, the well-known

American historian and biographer, to remark on the "apologetic tone" in these essays.[18] Yet, all these historians agree that there has been a recent revived interest in biography and a turn toward examining the capacity of an individual life to enhance our understanding of broader historical changes.[19]

A good social biography, therefore, does not take the individual alone as its subject but focuses on that individual within a particular historical context.[20] This double focus, as Salvatore argues, results in a valuable perspective by allowing the historian to ask this question: "How, in what ways, with what success, does an individual interact with, create life from, and possibly alter a culture and a society not of their own making, one which they largely inherit?"[21] Such an approach turns the historian's attention away from romanticizing and applauding the ways in which the biographical subject rose above various societal challenges, and focuses instead on an individual's response to the choices available to them and the transformations happening around them. This "broad and deep agenda allows the biographer to explore the particular response of one individual who occupies a specific social and cultural space without losing perspective on those transformations. Indeed, it is precisely the play between the two that is the crux of the matter."[22] In this way, and similar to microhistory and memory studies, a social biography helps us gain a greater understanding of particular institutions and forms of social change by analyzing how they have been understood and negotiated by particular individuals, allowing us to work with and against the grand narratives that usually fail to match the experience of individuals on the ground.

The extent to which biographical subjects can be said to be representative of their context becomes critical here. Taking Taha Hussein as an example of his times might be tempting in order to justify the focus on one individual. Yet, as Salvatore, Hans Renders, and Sigurdur Magnusson show, such "representativeness" can be misleading. These historians all agree that an agenda that sees a subject as representative will inevitably try to fit that subject into a general picture of history, thus suppressing the many contradictions and inconsistencies that we all experience in our daily lives as individuals. Magnusson goes even further to say that this leads to manipulating the subject matter into an already known outcome.[23] Renders also believes that a good biography or microhistory should always question such representativeness, look for breaking points in this larger narrative, and see the subject not as an example but as a "point of reference" in a complex context.[24]

In Middle East history, the need for such social biographies is particularly acute. While working on her recent monograph on Fawzi al-Qawuqji and the struggle for Arab independence between 1914 and 1948, historian Laila Parsons has reflected on the huge shortage in biographies in particular, and complex narrative histories in general, in the field.[25] As a result of this shortage, Parsons argues that descriptions of daily life, professional networks, schools, public disputes, and other immediate concerns, such as money, family, and friendship, tend to go missing. Parsons notes that since Edward Said's *Orientalism*, the field has been dominated by three main themes: colonialism, nationalism, and modernity. As a result, instead of using sources to build a narrative, historians in the field are more drawn to analyzing their sources as texts in which unequal power relations in colonial and postcolonial contexts are manifest.[26] To overcome this lacuna and provide her students with examples of accounts of complex, intimately drawn individuals, Parsons finds herself obliged to assign literary works in her history classes. This is "fraught," she admits, given that novels cannot replace narrative histories and should be analyzed as works of art from the perspective of form, plot construction, voice, and so on.[27]

Why Taha Hussein, and What Can He Tell Us?

Besides the curious lack of single studies on Taha Hussein in English or French, which I address below, why is Taha Hussein a good candidate for a social biography? At the turn of the twentieth century, Egypt was witnessing many changes. These changes included the nation's new independence, the introduction of a secular university system, the development of the Arabic novel, a burgeoning press, active literary salons, and intense public debates over nationalism and social reform, in addition to discussions on the role of religion, women, and knowledge and education in society. Hussein was involved in all of these debates and experienced all these transformations firsthand. Moreover, Hussein's French education and his university position in Cairo gave him access to the vibrant francophone cultural scene in Cairo and Alexandria with its many literary and artistic groups that were particularly active during the interwar period. Hussein circulated in all those circles with such ease that the literary scholar Richard Jaquemond remarks on how Hussein was "parfaitement à l'aise dans sa double culture, actif sur tous les fronts."[28]

It is therefore not surprising that references to Taha Hussein, the Dean of Arabic Literature, abound in scholarly studies of the period. As Roger Allen points out, there is hardly a single work on the history of the modern Arabic novel that does not refer to Hussein's masterpiece, *al-Ayyam* (*The Days*).[29] Yet, surprisingly, single studies on this iconic figure are extremely limited. Donald

Reid regrets that the main source on Hussein in English remains *The Days*, which is both novel and autobiography.[30] In one of the few studies dedicated to Hussein's thought, *Taha Husain's Education from the Azhar to the Sorbonne*, the intellectual Abdelrashid Mahmoudi laments how "at a time when interest in Taha Husain should be at its highest, there is a scarcity of good books on this great Egyptian writer."[31] The main scholarly work on Hussein's life in English remains Pierre Cachia's *Taha Husayn: His Place in the Egyptian Literary Renaissance*, published in 1956—a revised version of Cachia's doctoral dissertation submitted in 1951.[32] Considered a pioneer for choosing an Arab subject at the time, Cachia focuses mostly on Hussein's literary works and reformist ideas. An important work of literary criticism is Fedwa Malti-Douglas' structural analysis of *al-Ayyam*, in which she reads Hussein's autobiography as a struggle against blindness, both as a personal and social handicap.[33]

Mahmoudi's work and three earlier works—Meftah Tahar's *Taha Husain: Sa Critique Littéraire et Ses Sources Françaises* (1976), Jabir 'Usfur's *al-Maraya al-Mutajawira* (1983), and Ahmad Buhasan's *al-Khitab al-Naqdi 'inda Taha Husayn* (1985)—are valuable scholarly contributions to Hussein's intellectual biography.[34] These scholars and others have engaged with Hussein's critical thought and analyzed his widely acclaimed innovation in the field of Arabic literary studies. To varying degrees, these critics have studied Hussein's application of French rationalist and positivist research methods in his study of Arabic literature and its history. While recognizing the French influence on Hussein, Mahmoudi emphasizes the enduring influence of Hussein's earlier training in Egypt on his literary career, first at al-Azhar under the mentorship of Sheikh Sayyid 'Ali al-Marsafi, a protégé of Muhammad 'Abduh, and then at the Egyptian University where Hussein studied with the Orientalist scholar Carlo Alfonso Nallino. Marsafi and Nallino introduced Hussein to classical Arabic literature, its history and methods of literary criticism, and Hussein himself recognized their influence on him, when, in his preface to the second edition of Nallino's *Tarikh al-Adab al-'Arabiyya*, he wrote that he "owed his entire intellectual life to these two great professors."[35] Other literary studies in Arabic include al-Badrawi Zahran's *Uslub Taha Husayn fi Daw' al-Dars al-Lughawi al-Hadith*, in which Zahran analyzes the phonology, morphology, and syntax of Hussein's style in *al-Ayyam*.[36] Likewise, Rashida Mahran studies, in *Taha Husayn bayna al-Sira wa-l-Tarjama al-Dhatiyya*, how Hussein wrote about himself in his autobiography and how he wrote about various Islamic subjects in his other books. She also compares Hussein with other intellectuals of his generation who wrote autobiographies and biographies, discussing the ways in which she believes he surpassed them in his storytelling technique.[37]

References to Hussein and his work are not limited to literary scholarship. In her study of the development of the social sciences in Egypt, for example, Omnia El Shakry describes him as "Egypt's premier literary intellectual."[38] She looks at him and other social reformers as case studies of intellectuals who were deeply influenced by their western education but who were extremely conscious of the historical specificity of their own culture and thus were grappling with what they clearly saw as a tension between the universal and the particular. Yoav Di-Capua, in his study of Egyptian historiography, is critical of the nationalist framework that has defined, and continues to dominate, the historiographical field in Egypt since the nineteenth century. He sees Hussein as an exception to this rule. He hails him as the "intellectual giant of the Egyptian *nahda*" and presents him as someone who saw the danger inherent in the post-1952 historical discourse and its adoption of a simplistic linear historical narrative that celebrates the revolutionary moment as the culmination of a series of Egyptian nationalist triumphs. Di-Capua shows how, in response to this threat, Hussein with some of his friends edited a schoolbook so that it featured fragmented primary sources from various eras, and thus, "rather than presenting one familiar story (modernistic transition under European tutelage or revolutionary struggle), [the editors] presented history as a confusing, yet beautifully rich and colorful, experience," inviting students to actively engage with the material and form their own opinions.[39] Likewise, scholars refer repeatedly to Hussein's famous 1926 book *On Pre-Islamic Poetry* (*Fi al-Shiʻr al-Jahili*), in which he doubted the authenticity of this poetry as well as the historical existence of Abraham and Ishmael. As is well known, the book triggered a huge public debate, and a court case was brought against Hussein. He was forced to revise the book and republish it in 1927 under a different title: *On Pre-Islamic Literature* (*Fi al-Adab al-Jahili*). Richard Jacquemond argues that this case of intimidation and censorship set the stage for a pattern all too familiar for Arab authors to this day.[40]

Despite their astonishing dearth in English, books on Hussein abound in Arabic. Most, however, tend to see Hussein either as hero or villain, leading to frustration among critics like Mahmoudi, who dismisses authors of Arabic books on Hussein altogether, saying they make no serious attempt to read him critically.[41] Mahmoudi is probably referring to Islamist writers who slander Hussein, and their enemies who glorify him. The Tunisian literary scholar Munji al-Shimli, however, is somewhat less harsh in his criticism. He remarks that while many studies have been written on Hussein in Arabic, they are of varying degrees of quality. He says some are good, others are shallow, while many should never have been published.[42] On this shallow scholarship, he writes elsewhere that he is always surprised at the number of writers who neither read Hussein's work critically nor try to make connections between his books.[43] To this uncritical scholarship, one could add the mass appropriation of Hussein's works by the Egyptian postcolonial state, which republishes his books regularly and distributes them widely at affordable prices. In its complex and ambiguous relationship with Islamists, the state likes to portray itself as the defender of certain liberal values espoused by Hussein and his generation. Instead of promoting those values in the present, the state republishes the classics.

In the abundant Islamist literature on Hussein, he comes across as a dangerous scholar. Islamist authors claim in one way or another that Hussein was a "traitor" to his religion and community.[44] Their underlying criticism is that he combined his traditional training and perfect command of classical Arabic with his western knowledge to undermine Islam. They argue that he accomplished this by promoting Orientalist scholarship, which questioned the integrity of the tradition, and by calling for an uncritical appropriation of European culture. An example of such literature is *Taha Husayn: Al-Jarima wa-l-Idana*, with Hussein drawn on the front cover standing behind bars in a prison uniform. The author, Jabir Rizq, collected various articles that more or less summarize the list of (mostly undocumented) accusations made against Hussein over the years. In the introduction, Rizq states with satisfaction: "I was very happy because, with success from God, I was able to participate in stripping one of those who conspired against the Egyptian Muslim mind. [Hussein] worked to destroy it and empty it of its Islamic bases in collaboration with the colonial plan."[45]

The various authors in Rizq's volume accuse Hussein of having plagiarized some of his books from other Egyptian and foreign writers, of being a political opportunist who ingratiated himself with all political parties, of having been created by the university as a "black Orientalist" in order to serve the western colonial project intent on promoting missionary activities and conversion from Islam, of having secretly converted to Christianity himself in a French village, of actually being an atheist, and so on. These and other accusations still circulate, not only in printed material but also on social media when articles about Hussein or photographs of him appear: for example, celebrating his anniversary or discussing his books. In these accusations, like the one by the Islamist scholar and literary critic Muhammad Najib al-Bahtiti, Hussein's marriage to a French woman and his children's compound Arabic-French names only reinforce the suspicions:

> Taha Hussein spent his long life, which exceeded ninety years as far as I know, except twenty something years in the beginning, in an iron cast between a Christian woman and a Christian secretary delegated by the Jesuits. [This secretary] always had his eyes on Hussein, which were the eyes of the Jesuits. [Hussein's] two children, Claude and Marguerite, were called only by those names by their father, mother, the secretary and the servant. I swear, I never heard any Muslim name called in this house except Taha Hussein and Muhammad, the black servant.[46]

Another example is *al-Zur wa-l-Buhtan fima Katabuh Taha Husayn fi al-Shaykhan wa-Mu'alafat Ukhra Lahu*, published in 1991 as part of a series titled Saving Education: The Islamic Solution. The authors criticize Hussein's 1960 book *al-Shaykhan*—on the first two Muslim caliphs, Abu Bakr and 'Umar—calling on the Ministry of Education to stop teaching it in public schools. The authors accuse Hussein of doubting the authenticity of some of the sayings of the Prophet, and thus "destroying the second source of the religion after the Qur'an." They also argue that by questioning the transmission of some these sayings, Hussein was "questioning Islam itself, because the transmitters of the hadith are the carriers of the religion who delivered it to us." In their view: "Hussein's methodology is the farthest from proper scientific investigation. For we see that he investigates with his mind issues on which the texts have been proven, and then he goes against them. This, despite how he himself has described his mind as contradictory and confused in his autobiography, *al-Ayyam*."[47] The authors then summarize accusations by other Islamist thinkers, like Anwar al-Jindi, in his book *Taha Husayn: Hayatuhu wa-Fikruhu fi Mizan al-Islam*, in which he claims that Hussein supported Zionism, that he wanted to destroy al-Azhar, that he promoted pornography (*ibahiyya*) through his study of certain Abbasid poets like Abu Nuwwas, and so on.[48]

Interestingly, this Islamist critique of Hussein has been paralleled by postcolonial literary scholars in the West who draw on select passages in public writings by Hussein and his generation to create an image of these authors as uncritical intellectuals who were "seduced" by European culture. This self-Orientalization was analyzed and criticized by, for example, the literary scholar Stephen Sheehi in *The Foundations of Modern Arab Identity*.[49] By analyzing some key *nahdawi* texts, Sheehi has skillfully shown that while these intellectuals critiqued colonial discourses, they also appropriated colonial assumptions in their writings, developing a language of binaries to help them make persuasive arguments. These binaries include rise and decline, East and West, backwardness and civilization, and so on. Sheehi concludes that the reform they championed became inherently paradoxical, because it made the re-creation of the Arab subject conditional on accepting the existence of a certain "lack" as inherent to his subjectivity. Building on Sheehi's argument, literary scholar Shaden Tageldin argues that the *nahda*, the Arab reform movement discussed later in this chapter, was first and foremost a translation project that translated not only English and French texts into Arabic but was also translating Arabic and Arab subjectivity itself in the process. She reproaches *nahdawis* for having given in too easily to the charms of western knowledge disguised as the universal, and argues they were not suspicious enough of what the translation process entailed. She attributes their lack of caution to their seduction by the colonial project, in the figure of the knowledgeable Orientalist, who appreciated the old Arab-Islamic glory and promised *nahdawis* the return of this glory through this dubious translation project.[50]

In *Desiring Arabs*, Joseph Massad has argued that the *nahda* never managed to revive classical Arab-Islamic thought because *nahdawis* censored and suppressed aspects of that tradition, fearing what bourgeois European critics at the time would find decadent or degenerate in that tradition, such as Abu Nuwwas' homoerotic poetry.[51] Massad then takes this thought further, and argues that by accepting certain western critiques of Islam (especially those pertaining to the condition of women and queer Arabs), current Arab liberals and social activists are effectively colluding with the neo-imperialist project and justifying its intervention in the Arab-Islamic world. In response to Massad's critique, Tarek El-Ariss has recently decried the way in which postcolonial studies often overlook the aesthetics of Arabic texts, treating them instead "as sites of resistance to or deployment of Western cultural models, thereby engaging modernity as a narrative of complicity with the hegemonic West, which suppresses, one way or another, Arab-Islamic tradition and practices."[52] In *Trials of Modernity*, El-Ariss unsettles our understanding of the Arab encounter with European modernity by using affect theory to reexamine some Arabic texts, including ones by canonical *nahdawi* figures like Rifaʿa al-Tahtawi and Butrus al-Bustani. As he shifts the focus from intellectual to embodied encounters, El-Ariss shows how Arab authors were not only deeply conscious of their own culture but also viewed Europe critically, often with aversion.

Contrary to the Islamist and postcolonial critique, laudatory literature on Hussein tends to glorify him as a stubborn secularist, who heroically rose above his physical disability to become a staunch defender of liberal values in the Arab world. These studies include, for example, Kamal al-Mallakh's *Taha Husayn: Qahir al-Zalam*, in which Mallakh sees Hussein's life as a long struggle against darkness, whether his physical blindness or the conservative forces that had encaged free thinking in the country.[53] Likewise, Mahmud al-Samra published a recent study on Hussein describing him as the "Arab Prometheus," who stole fire from the gods to give to humans.[54] In *Taha Husayn wa-Sikulujiyyat al-Mukhalafa*, Misri Hannura analyzes what he argues was the "creative genius" that crystalized in Hussein's "consciousness, will-power and action toward the future."[55]

On the more critical side, the Tunisian academy has recently produced rigorous studies on Hussein. Munji al-Shimli and his students have organized conferences and produced important works on Hussein's literary and historical texts. While emphasizing Hussein's strong influence on generations of Tunisian writers and educators, these Tunisian academics agree there needs to be a more careful examination of the variegations in Hussein's thought. To address this lacuna, al-Shimli's student 'Umar al-Jumni, for example, wrote his 1989 doctoral dissertation on Hussein's historical work. Published in two volumes, under the title *Taha Husayn Mu'arrikhan*, this work was well received by the Egyptian academy, and was republished in Cairo with a preface by the chair of the history department at Cairo University, Muhammad 'Afifi.[56] Al-Jumni examines Hussein's training as a historian in Egypt and France, discusses the influence of Ibn Khaldun and the French positivist school on the way Hussein understood history and its philosophy, and analyzes Hussein's methodology through a careful reading of his historical works such as *al-Fitna al-Kubra*.

As far as Taha Hussein's political career is concerned, there is an even more remarkable dearth in scholarship. In *Taha Husayn wa-l-Siyasa*, Mustafa 'Abd al-Ghani was one of the first to engage with Hussein's involvement in politics before 1952.[57] Later, he also wrote *Taha Husayn wa-Thawrat Yuliu: Su'ud al-Muthaqqaf wa-Suqutuh*, dealing specifically with the relationship between Hussein and Nasser's regime. In both works, 'Abd al-Ghani reproaches Hussein for not having criticized King Farouk enough and for not having publicly denounced Nasser's policies. In 'Abd al-Ghani's reading of Hussein, he sees him first and foremost as an intellectual who should always have been at odds with the state. Such analysis overlooks how Hussein was a member of government at times and could not have been part of the opposition at the same time. Regarding Hussein's silence during Nasser's reign, 'Abd al-Ghani wrote years later that he might have been too harsh on Hussein, given the suppression of all political opposition under Nasser, and Hussein's old age at the time.[58]

More recently, another of Munji al-Shimli's students, Rashid al-Qarquri, published *Taha Husayn: Mufakirran Siyasiyyan*, a work based on his doctoral dissertation in Arabic literature, analyzing Hussein's political thought, which he ultimately summarized in four words: "people, homeland, democracy and culture."[59] Likewise, the historian Ahmad Zakariya al-Shalq has recently published *Taha Husayn: Jadal al-Fikr wa-l-Siyasa*.[60] Both works offer more measured views on Hussein's politics. They use published material to analyze Hussein's relationship with various political parties before 1952, especially the Liberal Constitutionalists in the 1920s, and then his cooperation with the Wafd Party from the 1930s onward. Al-Qarquri relies mainly on Hussein's books to trace his views on Egyptian politics from his early days at al-Azhar, and explores the role played by various people, such as Ahmad Lutfi al-Sayyid, and by Hussein's education at the Egyptian University and the Sorbonne in forming his views on democracy and constitutionalism. Al-Qarquri analyzes in detail how key events, such as the publication of *On Pre-Islamic Poetry*, were politicized and debated in parliament. In a similar vein, Al-Shalq uses articles by Hussein from the Nasserite period to demonstrate Hussein's initial excitement about the 1952 revolution, followed by his silence over most of Nasser's policies, which al-Shalq interprets as a disapproval of these policies.

Such limited scholarship on Taha Hussein's politics, according to 'Abd al-Ghani, is due primarily to the difficulty of locating and finding the political articles Hussein wrote for dozens of periodicals over many decades.[61] Al-Qarquri says the shortage exists because Hussein did not write explicitly on politics.[62] While it is true that Hussein did not write theoretical works in which he neatly laid out his project for educational reform and its intersection with politics, this does not mean that such theory does not exist, for his ideas are available even though dispersed across several books and in hundreds of articles. As I explain later, this book also draws on state archival material to illuminate Hussein's political career as an institution builder during the parliamentary period and to investigate the impact of Nasser's revolution on Hussein's project for culture and education.

Taha Hussein's Anti-Colonial Project

A useful starting point for thinking about Taha Hussein as an institution builder is his famous 1938 book *The Future of Culture in Egypt*, in which he proposed a series of practical steps to reform Egypt's educational system. In this section, I show how that book fits within his larger reform project. I argue that taking Hussein's institutional focus into account allows us to read this iconic work differently, especially as some of the views he expressed here on Egypt's cultural identity—contending it was intimately tied to Europe and the Mediterranean—remain controversial to this day. Initially, Hussein was supposed to report on two conferences that he had attended in Paris on education and culture. Instead of submitting a traditional report to the Ministry of Public Instruction, where he feared it would be simply stored away with other reports, he decided to go public. He published this now-famous book instead, and addressed it explicitly to the university students who had been asking him and other intellectuals about concrete steps Egypt should take after signing the 1936 Anglo-Egyptian Treaty.[63]

Egyptian university students have a long history of political activism.[64] In the immediate context that saw the publication of *The Future of Culture in Egypt*, students had managed, after effective demonstrations in 1935, to force the government to abolish the 1930 constitution, which had given sweeping powers to King Fouad, and they also forced it to restore the more liberal 1923 constitution. Adding to the euphoria was the Anglo-Egyptian Treaty signed the following year. While the treaty did not give Egypt the full independence the public had been demanding, it was seen as a major step forward. As Egyptian historian ʿAbd al-ʿAzim Ramadan explains, even though the treaty did not end the occupation, it restricted British military presence to the Suez Canal Zone and gave the Egyptian government control over the Egyptian army. The treaty also paved the way to ending the Capitulations, which Ramadan describes as having been "an obstacle in the way of the progress of the country, and a tangible affront to its sovereignty." He explains that removing the Capitulations, which had accorded foreigners living in Egypt extraterritorial fiscal and legal privileges, allowed the Egyptian government to impose its laws and legislation equally on all people living in the country, to raise taxes in a fair manner, and to prepare the annual budget accordingly. In that way, Ramadan argues, the treaty managed to "achieve equality between Egyptians and foreigners [in Egypt] for the first time since the nineteenth century."[65] On the negative side, however, the treaty bound Egypt to Great Britain in a twenty-year military alliance giving the British the right to impose martial law and press censorship in an international emergency. The British argued that in their view Egypt was not strong enough to protect the Suez Canal, which was vital for British interests. In *The Future of Culture in Egypt*, Hussein addressed this weakness and explained that his purpose in writing the book was to propose solutions to overcome the obstacles that stood between the country and its full independence. He argued that Egypt had to become a strong nation by developing the kind of strength Europe understood and respected. He contended that only then would Europe recognize Egypt as an equal and see it as fit to protect its own interests. Then the British would have no reason to keep their army in the country.

The thick book that resulted from this effort is painstakingly technical, with several hundred pages of suggestions on how to improve Egypt's educational system, including pre-university education, higher education, teachers' training, and so on. Most debates over the book since its publication, however, ignore its context and the proposed reform program and focus instead on the introduction, in which Hussein stated provocatively that Egypt had no path to follow but the one Europe had taken. He insisted that there was no way for Egyptians to become strong and independent but "to follow in the path of Europeans, to become their equals, and to be their partners in civilization, in its good and its bad, its sweetness and its bitterness. . . . Anyone who claims otherwise is deluding or deluded."[66] Such a path was inevitable, he insisted, and it was the only way by which Egypt could create the strong army it needed to protect its wealth and privileged geographical location. If that army was to be taken seriously and entrusted with protecting the canal, then it must be reorganized along European lines, and its soldiers and leaders educated in the European ways. Only then, Hussein went on, could Egyptians tell the English, "You can go, for we can protect the canal ourselves now. For he who seeks an end must seek the means, and he who seeks power must seek the grounds for power."[67] He then made similar arguments for economic and cultural independence.

Hussein reasoned that Egypt's safety and stability mattered so much to European interests that if Egypt could not protect itself, then Britain would always step in to provide that protection. More concretely, he insisted that the way to achieve independence "was one without second: building [a system of] education on solid basis."[68] Egyptians, he went on, were under the watchful eyes of Europe, which was a warning to them not to take the 1936 independence for granted but to see how fragile it was. "They are monitoring us, the Europeans in general, and our friends the English in particular. They keep a watchful eye on everything we do, they count our every step, and they hold us accountable for everything, be it minor or major."[69] Hussein's readers at the time would have understood that by mentioning Europeans and not just the English, he was referring to European powers' agreeing to abolish the Capitulations and inviting Egypt to join the League of Nations in 1937. Egyptians, therefore, had to prove themselves not only to the English but also to the Europeans, who were scrutinizing how Egyptians were handling the responsibilities of their independence. Hussein was using a language all too familiar at the time, and Europe's "watchful eye" was not a metaphor. The League of Nations had decided the level of control each Mandatory power would have over each of its mandates, based on a mandate's presumed readiness to govern itself. In this view, some nations were promising while others were less so. Western powers decided who was fit for self-governance and who was not.[70]

In 1939, Hussein became the nation's controller of general culture. This was the beginning of his career as a senior civil servant in the Ministry of Public Instruction, a position that allowed him to implement many of his reforms. His appointment came right after the publication of his book. showing that its message resonated within official circles and that it was well-received by those in power. Hussein was a man with a project, responding to a particular need at a specific moment in time, and he himself was aware of that. Years later, he confided to his secretary that he wished to update the book so it would be a more accurate reflection of the country's current system of education and its needs, but he never got to that task.[71] Those calling for adopting his book today as a valid program for educational reform tend to ignore the immediate context in which it was written. Moreover, their objective is usually educational reform, whereas for Hussein, the battle for democracy and the battle for education were one and the same. He pushed for both simultaneously, in the hope of creating a modern, politically active citizenry firmly rooted in the Arab-Islamic tradition and confident in its contributions to western knowledge. Moreover, as this study analyzes, Hussein predicated the proper functioning of his institutions on the presence of a strong parliamentary system that held government officials accountable.

In a symposium organized in Tunisia in 1990, dedicated to Arab reformist thought, the scholar Muhammad al-Marakishi took issue with Hussein's call for Egyptians to follow Europe and accused Hussein of not having constructed a sound argument. Al-Marakishi first deconstructed Hussein's introduction by showing how, elsewhere in the book, Hussein contradicted himself by calling for a selective and not a total appropriation of European culture. He quoted Hussein's statement that he was not calling for adopting Europeans' "sins and bad deeds," but only "what is useful and good in their lives."[72] Or again, he noted that Hussein said: "I do not call for us to forget who we are, be ungrateful to our past, or to dissolve in Europe. How could this be possible, when I am calling to stand up to Europe, protect our independence from its aggression and tyranny and prevent it from consuming us?"⁷³ Al-Marakishi concluded that such internal inconsistencies undermined the integrity of Hussein's overall argument, leading him to believe that Hussein's call for following Europe was "excessive," triggered by what he described as Hussein's "emotional enthusiasm toward Europe and the West, rather than a fruit of serious rational scientific research."⁷⁴ Like most critics of Hussein's book, al-Marakishi focuses almost entirely on the introduction, without mentioning Hussein's constant calls, in this book and elsewhere, for engaging with the Arab-Islamic tradition and preserving classical Arabic. This fascination with the introduction of *The Future of Culture in Egypt* has led al-Marakishi and others, like the historian Meftah Tahar, to conclude that Hussein "wanted Egypt to become part of Europe, culturally."⁷⁵

Ironically, Hussein did not specify what he meant by "culture" in the title of his book. This did not go unnoticed by the Marxist critic and philosopher Mahmud Amin al-ʿAlim. He remarks in his own book, *On Egyptian Culture*, that in *The Future of Culture in Egypt*, "Taha Hussein did not define what Egyptian culture was, except in a few lines at the end of his book. But it still remains vague and mysterious."⁷⁶ Indeed, without properly identifying what he meant by culture, Hussein, near the end of his book, referred to a "distinct Egyptian culture," saying it was composed of three elements: "an ancient Egyptian artistic heritage, an Arab-Islamic heritage, and what Egypt has acquired from the European civilization."⁷⁷ In the absence of any clearer definition of culture, it is not a surprise that someone reading Hussein's book for the first time would be struck by the lack of explicit literary, artistic, or linguistic examples referencing those three historical periods. A possible explanation for the absence of these references in that book is that it is concerned not with consuming culture but producing it. During the same Tunisian symposium, scholar Muniya al-Hamami responded to al-Marakishi's critique. In her response, she warns against trying, in her words, "to impose [our] current anthropological, philosophical or sociological understandings of the term culture on Hussein's use of the word in *The Future of Culture in Egypt*." Her understanding of Hussein's book as a whole has led her to believe that for Hussein, the word *culture* stood for a "comprehensive intellectual production" that takes Egypt away from "intellectual consumption to production," so that the country could achieve what she describes as a "cultural parity" (*al-niddiyya al-thaqafiyya*) with Europe.⁷⁸

By shifting the focus to institution building, my study supports al-Hamami's understanding of Hussein's book. Considering that work as a call for building structures of knowledge production requires a less literal reading of its controversial introduction. Al-Marakishi is not wrong to take issue with the book's internal inconsistencies over what to take from Europe and what to leave. The famous nationalist Satiʿ al-Husri, for example, had pointed out many of these inconsistencies, elaborately, in an article published in *al-Risala* in 1939.[79] Nor is al-Marakishi wrong to highlight Hussein's excitement over his reform program. Hussein used this excitement to persuade his readers—whether university students who were anxious to hear his thoughts on the way forward, or policymakers who were expecting his official report on what Europe was doing in the fields of culture and education—that the only possible action, according to his assessment of the political situation, was to build modern institutions along European lines. He believed such an endeavor was feasible, and if these institutions worked well in Europe, then nothing should stop them from working successfully in Egypt. In his view, these institutions, with their state-of-the-art research methodologies, would engage with the Arab-Islamic tradition, keeping it and the language alive, and thus providing the best possible protection against "dissolving" into Europe.

Besides ignoring the actual reform program in favor of analyzing the introduction, most debates involving *The Future of Culture in Egypt* overlook the exceptional political circumstances to which Hussein was responding. His work should be read in the context of the interwar period and the euphoria surrounding the signing of the Anglo-Egyptian Treaty in 1936, the ending of the Capitulations, and joining the League of Nations in 1937, the hallmark of independence at the time.[80] While Egyptians successfully wrestled these concessions from European powers, the continued presence of British forces in Egypt was a constant reminder of the deeply rooted presumption among colonial powers of colonized peoples' inability to rule themselves. Hussein's book was an intervention calling on Egyptians to vindicate themselves and to prove they could handle the responsibilities of their independence. Much like David Scott's thoughtful reading of C.L.R. James' account of Toussaint Louverture's revolutionary struggle against the French in *Black Jacobins* (also written in 1938), Hussein's call for vindication took the form of a "romantic" story of an anti-colonial liberation struggle that was supposed to end in victory and enlightenment.[81] Unlike Louverture's armed struggle, however, Hussein's solution was institutional, and he proposed building an integrated Egyptian system of knowledge production that was to achieve intellectual parity with Europe and place Egypt on equal standing with the more "advanced" nations of the world. This romantic mode of history writing, in which Hussein drew on Egypt's long historical interaction with the Mediterranean world and on Greek philosophy's influence on Islamic thought, was triggered by a political necessity, and was a mode of writing he deemed necessary to shatter notions of inherent incompatibility between Egyptians and Europeans, and thus assert Egypt's right to self-determination. In our reading of works by anti-colonial figures such as James and Hussein, Scott reminds us that they were writing at a "present" triggered by a different "horizon of expectation," and that their political thought was governed by a "problem-space" animated by different disputes and questions, the understanding of which becomes necessary to make sense of their intellectual production and political maneuvers, especially in what Scott sees as our "postcolonial nightmares," in which cynicism has replaced the optimism of "anticolonial utopias."[82] Independence was one of the most pressing concerns at the time, and as Elizabeth Thompson's recent research has shown, in the Middle East, "sovereignty was viewed as the primary prerequisite for justice and rule of law."[83] For Hussein, independence was the priority, and with independence came the—now defunct—assumption that once the colonizers left, everything would fall into place.

Our sinister postcolonial present impacts the way we understand Hussein's project and leads us to find his excitement in 1938 naïve and even off-putting. Readers today are often suspicious or even dismissive of Hussein's firm belief in democracy and institutions. Many readers have been desensitized to the discourse on democracy, people's rights, and the state's responsibility toward the people, because for decades, postcolonial states in the region and imperial powers have used the same discourse to legitimize their repressive agendas while suppressing the same rights they claim to defend. Even western democracies are currently facing a dire moment with the rise of right-wing populism. It takes much effort on the part of today's reader to go beyond what could come across as futile clichés and to read Hussein carefully and critically, and understand that, in Hussein's present in the interwar period, "promoting true democracy," "respecting the constitution," "holding the state accountable," and "achieving full independence" were all feasible and interdependent goals.

Hussein understood that Europe was setting the terms, and if Egypt were to maintain its nominal independence and turn it into a fuller one, then it had to be practical and play by the rules Europe recognized and imposed on the world. In his thought and action, Hussein accepted the premises informing those European rules: the nation-state, progress, and reason. In recognizing the obligation to build his project in terms set by the modern West, Hussein can be seen as a *conscript* of western modernity, a term David Scott borrows from Talal Asad and uses to describe Louverture and other colonial subjects who believed they were resisting European colonialism but who were, often unconsciously, obliged to think and act in conditions determined by European modernity. While Asad is more interested in the power differential between colonizer and colonized and how power transforms colonial subjects, this study focuses on Hussein's agency and creative efforts within that colonial context.[84] Moreover, Hussein was conscious of modernity's transformative power when he provocatively stated, decades before postcolonial studies, that Egyptians were already leading a European life in both its physical and intellectual aspects.[85] Hussein was in the middle of a battle of emancipatory politics, in which immediate political action was required and in which tough decisions and compromises had to be made regarding the direction in which the country was headed. In his understanding of the way forward after 1936, knowledge-producing institutions had to be implemented along European lines so Egyptian researchers, planners, and policymakers could master the dominant language, the language Europe understood and enforced elsewhere. In that sense of being "conscripted" and having "no choice," Hussein's comment that those who preached otherwise were either "deluding or deluded" makes more sense.

This constant negotiation between the universal and the particular informs Hussein's project for culture and education in Egypt. As this study shows, he did not begin working on institutions in 1938, with *The Future of Culture in Egypt*, but earlier, in 1922, right after Egypt achieved nominal independence. He repeatedly expressed his view that it was his duty as an intellectual and an academic to explain to the public the importance of reforming Egypt's educational system, which he believed had suffered under the British administration and was in serious need of reform. Immediately after independence, he called for reforming the Ministry of Public Instruction and ridding it of all British influence, which he believed had been responsible for reducing the number of schools, introducing tuition fees, and favoring the *kuttab* over higher education. Higher education, and especially the Egyptian University's Faculty of Arts, quickly became the cornerstone of Hussein's project, as he hoped the university would create the nation's much-needed "thinking elite." Besides the university and the ministry, a third key institution in which Hussein was especially active as member and president (1940–1973) was the Arabic Language Academy. The academy brought together experts, from Egypt and abroad, to work to protect the language and respond to the modern challenges it was facing. Besides his work with these three key institutions, as minister of public instruction (1950–1952),

Hussein created several institutes and university chairs for Arabic and Islamic studies around the Mediterranean, hoping to extend Egypt's "awakening" and its cultural influence beyond its borders. To ensure the proper operation of all these institutions, he created or restructured what he called "technical councils," bodies that he believed would empower technocrats and shield them from divisive partisan politics. These technical councils included the Supreme Council of Education, the Supreme Council of the Universities, and the technical office of the language academy, all of which still exist today.

So, while *The Future of Culture in Egypt* is an important document, I see it more as a snapshot of the condition of the educational system at the time Hussein wrote about it. Various chapters of this study explore how Hussein's project developed over the years leading to the publication of his book, and how his official duties (from 1939 to 1944 and again from 1950 to 1952) helped him implement some of his ideas after its publication. Over those years, Hussein responded to various transformations happening around him, and he was in constant dialogue with the public and his adversaries through public statements, parliamentary discussions, and the pages of widely read journals and periodicals. Even when he was not in power, he still shared his thoughts in many published articles and was involved in debates as a public opinion maker. His views and debates when he was out of office (from 1944 to 1950) not only shed light on how he defended his project and what his opponents had against it but also provide valuable understanding of how the institutions he nurtured evolved during this period.

This book also explores the end of Taha Hussein's institutional project and his inability in the 1950s and '60s to continue promoting critical thinking and academic freedom. The Second World War and the ongoing British occupation showed the futility of the 1936 Anglo-Egyptian Treaty and quickly put an end to his interwar euphoria. His resentment of the ensuing corrupt politics and the failure of successive governments to address the three famous societal ills of poverty, ignorance, and disease became clear in the series of books and articles he published in the 1940s. His support for patient, peaceful, and long-term negotiations with the British came to an end with his full endorsement of Prime Minister Mustafa al-Nahhas' decision to abrogate the Anglo-Egyptian Treaty in 1951, authorizing armed combat against British forces in the Suez Canal Zone. He then supported the Free Officers' coup on July 23, 1952, and initially saw Gamal Abdel Nasser as a heroic figure who could break the political deadlock and achieve full independence. But to Hussein's dismay, the sixth principle of the 1952 coup, calling for creating a healthy democratic life, was put on hold.

Then the era of decolonization and state authoritarianism in the 1950s and '60s dealt heavy blows to his project and his institutions. He was also horrified by the crimes committed by the French in North Africa and these colonizers' double standards, and he was disheartened by young Arab intellectuals whom he accused of having turned literature into a propaganda machine for the state and willingly giving up their freedom in the name of social realism and committed literature. Increasingly isolated, he found it impossible to advocate his project of natural synthesis between the old and the new, and he died shortly after having confided to Ghali Shukri that he was leaving with "much pain and little hope."[86] By accepting David Scott's invitation to read the legacy of anti-colonial figures as tragedies instead of romances, this present study tells the tragic story of the life and death of an alternative Egyptian history, the story of what modern Egypt could have become.

The *Nahda* in Parliamentary Egypt

Taha Hussein firmly believed in creating the institutional infrastructure necessary to foster a critical scholarly engagement with both the old Arab-Islamic cultural tradition and the new ideas, institutions, and social practices coming from Europe. This synthesis of the old and the new was the defining formula and one of the central tenets of the Arab *nahda* of the long nineteenth century. Often translated as the Arab "Renaissance," "Revival," "Awakening," or "Rising up," the Arabic term *nahda* came into circulation in the mid-nineteenth century, and it initially denoted the cultural revival then spreading from Egypt and Lebanon to other parts of the Arab world.[87] It was a period of intense intellectual activity animated by heated debates over rupture with and/or return to the cultural foundations of Arab-Islamic thought. These debates were dominated by what Ilham Khuri-Makdisi has described as a "mantra of reform." Through social, religious, political, economic, and educational reforms, *nahdawis*, according to Khuri-Makdisi, wanted to create strong states, institutions, and individuals and healthy social bodies capable of facing Europe's colonial project.[88] Such a "renaissance," as Kamran Rastegar argues, was not a concept peculiar to the Arab world, for "this notion of rebirth is common to the ways by which non-western societies have conceptualized their entry into the historical stage of modernity."[89] While the "beginning" and the "end" of the *nahda*, as well as its regional scope, are subject to debate, Samah Selim contends that "the region's 'enlightenment' [*tanwir*] is understood to have been initiated, for better or worse, by the colonial project."[90]

For Hussein, this critical engagement with the old and the new and standing up to the colonial project required a solid institutional infrastructure capable of taking the *nahda* forward and going beyond discussions among intellectuals and individual publications. His larger project, to which he devoted most of his adult life, focused on building institutions of knowledge production—like the university, the Arabic Language Academy, and various technical councils—and the dissemination of this knowledge through universal education. These institutions would train scholars, fund their research, connect them with scholars working in other countries, and make the Arab-Islamic tradition physically and intellectually accessible by locating and publishing critical editions of old manuscripts as well as making classical Arabic easier to teach and to learn. Hussein understood that a project of such a magnitude required steady support from and formal recognition by the state, which he saw as the ultimate force of modernity capable of bringing about the required change, but which had to be scrutinized and held accountable by a modern politically active citizenry at all times. To translate his holistic vision from abstract thought into coherent policies, Hussein the academic-writer turned into a clever bureaucrat proposing feasible projects within budget. To ensure the steady operation of these institutions, Hussein the intellectual also functioned as an astute statesman maneuvering a complex parliamentary system, itself undermined by an ongoing British occupation and divisive partisan politics.

In his classic *Arabic Thought in the Liberal Age*, Albert Hourani famously periodizes the *nahda* from 1798, the year of the Napoleonic invasion of Egypt, to 1939, the year that has traditionally marked the death of "liberalism." He ends his discussion with a chapter on Hussein the intellectual, whom he describes as "primarily a man of letters" and "the most systematic thinker" of all the writers active in the 1920s and '30s.[91] Hourani devotes much of this chapter to his reading of *The Future of Culture in Egypt* and sees Hussein's ideas as the logical culmination of a system of liberal thought that inspired three generations of Arabs.[92] Curiously, Hourani disregards Hussein's insistence that the independence given in 1936 was incomplete and precarious, which, as I argued earlier, is crucial to understanding why Hussein wrote this text the way he did. Instead, Hourani introduces *The Future of Culture* as Hussein's plan for an independent Egypt now that the "goal to which public life had been directed for a whole generation had been attained."[93] Hussein's call to follow in Europe's footsteps fits comfortably into Hourani's overall thesis foregrounding the provenance of liberal ideas from Europe. Although Hourani mentions that as a public servant Hussein managed to implement some of his ideas, this does not take away from the strength or the coherence of Hourani's overall argument, which is structured around the liberal thinkers' struggle—and eventual inability—to apply their ideas in ways that could ensure the creation of enduring democratic institutions. He argues that Hussein's years of greatest activity were those between 1919 and 1939.[94] Because of his method, sources, periodization, and overall argument, Hourani does not discuss Hussein's efforts at the Ministry of Public Instruction, which he joined, ironically, in 1939.[95] Twenty years after the publication of the first edition of his book, however, Hourani reflected on his methodology and how he would write the book differently after all those years. On the one hand, he would still choose to write about the same thinkers whose ideas he had analyzed in the first edition. On the other hand, he said, the book was a product of its time, and he would now also consider "how and why the ideas of my writers had an influence on the minds of others." More importantly, he would be interested in other forms through which those ideas were mediated to the public.[96] Still, the practice of reducing Hussein's project and intellectual outlook to a decontextualized *Future of Culture in Egypt* has endured, enforcing a fairly common view in the field that Hussein had an uncritical infatuation with European culture.

Historian Dyala Hamzah builds on Hourani's self-criticism and also takes issue with his paradigm as a whole. In *The Making of the Arab Intellectual*, Hamzah argues that Hourani's approach, which has dominated the field since the appearance of his book, has undersold the contributions of various *nahdawis*. By constantly using Europe and its achievements as a yardstick against which their contributions are measured, it becomes difficult to see them as original or effective, having failed to achieve their predetermined objectives. Owing to Hourani's paradigm, Hamzah explains, "the *nahda* was enduringly locked within a dialectics of impact and reaction. [And it is within this paradigm] that the defining trope of [the *nahda*'s] historiography, imitation (and its corollary: failure), was engineered."[97] To break with Hourani, Hamzah proposes to look at various *nahdawis* and assess their contributions within their complex local context. She uses the framework of the public sphere to read the ways in which different *nahdawis* articulated their thoughts and under what conditions. Hamzah argues that by turning attention to the public sphere, "one is able to map the web of [the *nahdawis*'] relations, the space of their experiences, the horizon of their expectations, the ideational matrix in which they evolved, in their sustained endeavors to plot the coordinates of selfhood as against the coordinates of statehood."[98]

By focusing on these details, Hamzah believes historians can turn away from what she describes as "impact paradigms," such as the "Coming of the West," or the "Clash of Civilizations."[99] More importantly, such details allow Hazmah to make the larger claim that by constructing a public sphere promoting state accountability and constitutional governance, *nahdawis* successfully made a tangible contribution, and as a result, the *nahda* appears in a more positive light.

Other historians have similarly emphasized the need to (re)tell the story of the *nahdawis*. Leyla Dakhli, for example, calls for writing the history not of Arab thought but of Arab intellectuals, as a way to seriously consider their society and the social structures within which their thought was embedded.[100] She suggests paying attention to intellectual practices to eventually allow us to push back against what she describes as the "chain of oppositions" often used as a lens to understand the work of Arab intellectuals, such as reducing them to western intellectual influences or to their religious affiliation. In that way, Dakhli argues, we can reframe these intellectuals as complex "social actors" and not "mere knowledge transmitters."[101] Likewise, Yoav Di-Capua laments how scholars "end up portraying the persona of the Arab intellectual as a static signifier of an idea rather than as a contextualized and dynamic human being." Such a separation between "the person" and "the fruit of the mind," Di-Capua goes on, leads ultimately to the dehumanization of Arab intellectuals.[102] Echoing Laila Parsons' views, discussed previously, Di-Capua calls for rehumanizing Arab intellectuals by returning to narrative history, which he sees as part of a wider trend reaffirming the unique capacity of storytelling "to embed human subjectivity into the original social context in which the subject spoke, wrote, and acted."[103] While many scholars would prefer to see more engagement with critical theory instead of narrative histories, Di-Capua believes that "most Arab intellectuals benefit little from a theoretical approach that precedes their humanization. They need to be brought back to life first."[104]

Thus, by focusing on the complex details of Taha Hussein's local context, this social biography tells the story of how he acted in response to the problems facing his society. It is not simply an examination of the ways in which he articulated his ideas as an influential writer in various publications but also a means of seeing how he fought to implement those ideas in his interactions with others as an active civil servant. As I show in the section on sources that follows, given the scope of his public duties and the wealth of archival material his active engagement has left us, Hussein is an intellectual who lends himself to this kind of reading. This study shows that Hussein's political battles and societal debates shaped his conceptual work. As he tried to implement what he wrote and as he wrote about what he was trying to implement, Hussein was not working in an institutional vacuum; acting on his ideas implied practical compromises dictated by bureaucratic, institutional, and political constraints. Furthermore, by engaging the public in debates about the role of education and its design and dissemination, Hussein and others were defining the role of the institutions they were building, while rooting those institutions in the specific reality and needs of the country as they understood them. These institutions were not an abstract idea that Hussein and others imported wholesale from Europe. As Omnia El Shakry shows in her study of the institutional and discursive establishment of the Arab social sciences between 1870 and the 1960s, Egyptian intellectuals did not simply copy foreign knowledge. She argues that while they internalized some western premises, such as progressive temporality and the nation-state, these intellectuals relied on their society's historical specificity to push back against, and sometimes reverse, colonial forms of knowledge.[105] Moreover, the existence of a relatively free press and public conferences allowed Hussein, his supporters, and his adversaries to include the public in those debates. Such attention to the public goes beyond the usual *nahdawi* self-assigned task of educating the masses. Instead, the very existence of a parliamentary system implied that Hussein and others had to *persuade* the public of the soundness of their projects to gain the necessary votes. The battle over educational reform shows that in parliamentary Egypt, people and their opinions mattered. Hussein used his campaign for institutional reform and universal education as an attempt to renegotiate the social contract and to convince voters that the state was there to serve them and provide the education and dignified life they demanded. The debates on education became thus infused with tangible ideas on democracy, proper governance, the role of state, and political accountability. An intellectual history that collapses Hussein's decades-long project—along with the society and social structures in which it developed and in which it was embedded—into a reading of *The Future of Culture in Egypt* and some of his other published work is reductive and only reinforces the "chain of oppositions" Dakhli warns against.

Likewise, the details of educational reform in parliamentary Egypt challenge the dominant historiographical paradigm that has dismissed this period as a failure. Afaf Lutfi al-Sayyid Marsot's *Egypt's Liberal Experiment* remains the classical reference on the topic.[106] In her work, al-Sayyid Marsot focuses on the infamous triangular struggle over power between the Egyptian king, the British occupiers, and the Wafd Party. In her view, King Fouad's autocratic rule and the monarchy's subservience to the British set the stage for the divisive politics that made it impossible to build proper democratic institutions in this formative period of Egypt's modern history. Nevertheless, al-Sayyid Marsot is careful to point out in her introduction, albeit very briefly, that the liberal experiment was not a total failure:

> The liberal experiment was a partial success, and in fact saw the burgeoning of several elements that were vital to the future development of Egypt, such as the beginning of industrialization, the emancipation of women, the spread of education and of better hygiene, and the Anglo-Egyptian Treaty of Alliance of 1936—which for all its defects was a step in the right direction.[107]

This partial success of the experiment is not the focus of al-Sayyid Marsot's important work, however, and that work, much like Hourani's *Liberal Thought*, has dominated the field since its appearance in 1977. Al-Sayyid Marsot wants to pin down the political and social reasons that stopped the 1919 nationalist revolution from responding to long-standing demands for more grassroots social measures, such as land reform. Seeking British tacit or explicit approval before appointing cabinets, the incessant shuffling of those cabinets, King Fouad's attempts to circumvent the constitution, and constant bickering among elitist political parties made it impossible, in al-Sayyid Marsot's view, to enact any real change.[108] In unpacking those political reasons, al-Sayyid Marsot's aim is to explain what made the flourishing of democratic institutions difficult:

> That period of Egyptian political life has generally been regarded as an experiment in constitutional life which failed. When the Nasir era in mid-century ushered in a more extreme period of repression than [Prime Minister Isma'il] Sidqi's, it accentuated the belief that constitutional institutions were incapable of taking hold in so hostile a political soil as Egypt seemed to be. The Egyptians have therefore been described as servile, unaccustomed to self-government, and incapable of appreciating it.[109]

Arguing that the period between 1919 and 1952 "continues to receive insufficient scholarly attention" and that its "cultural vibrancy, societal dynamism, and intellectual-political legacy [require] a renewed intensity of focus,"[110] Arthur Goldschmidt, Barak Salmoni, and the late Amy Johnson edited a volume in 2005 in which several scholars reexamined various political, social, and cultural transformations that took place before 1952. These scholars try to flesh out both the challenges and the accomplishments of this period, including a general commitment to the constitution, lively parliamentary debates, a growing judicial efficacy, and a thriving intellectual life. They also argue that examining the period before 1952 is essential to understanding the period that followed, as the postcolonial state adopted and built on many of the policies and trends already set before 1952, including those in the areas of foreign policy, social reform, and democratizing army admissions.[111] They identify the history of education in this period as one of the areas requiring further attention and study.

> Perhaps because of its manifest shortcomings in the past thirty years, some of the more under-studied achievements of the 1919–1952 years relate to education. After decades of British neglect, state educational efforts underwent a gradual revolution under the constitutional monarchy. This included an expansion in numbers of schools, their geographic distribution, and the provision of female education.[112]

In the conclusion to this volume, the late Roger Owen gives several reasons for the scholarly disinterest and the general dismissal of the pre-1952 period as one rampant with decay and failure. He mentions Nasser's own views emphasizing the corruption of the monarchy. These views, according to Owen, were taught in school and continue to shape the way Egyptians, including "most of Egypt's own historians," see the constitutional period.[113] Joel Gordon remarks something similar, when he says that the new regime promoted the inevitability of the fall of the monarchy, and then foreign scholars propagated this official history uncritically.[114] Another reason, according to Owen, is the nationalist emphasis on defining Egyptian history in terms of a series of struggles against foreign forces, which, as far as the pre-1952 period is concerned, translated into an emphasis on the triangular struggle between the British, the king, and the Wafd.[115] Referring specifically to al-Sayyid Marsot's and Hourani's works, Owen criticizes them for their teleological reading of the period in question—al-Sayyid Marsot for reading the liberal experiment as a failure and Hourani for choosing to end the liberal age with the year 1939. In a much earlier piece, Owen warns that too much focus on the triangular struggle oversimplifies the complex relationship between these main political actors and overlooks the role played by other historical agents in challenging and influencing government policies and political events.[116] Taha Hussein, as this study shows, was one such historical agent, and the way he carried out his reforms indicates that Egyptian voters were a fourth key political player in the parliamentary period. Once free education was introduced in 1950, Hussein defended it against its detractors, insisting that it was a right Egyptians had won and that should not be taken away from them.[117] Here, he was not being merely rhetorical, because voters had brought the Wafd Party back into power, which enabled him to introduce his policy. It is overly simplistic to see free education as a decision imposed from above.

Owen also stresses the difficulty of accessing the Egyptian National Archives as an important factor hampering any serious study of this period. Instead, journalistic accounts, like those of Muhammad Hasanayn Haykal and nostalgic writings on Egypt's *belle époque* have become the main sources of information on this period.[118] Finally, Owen blames, what he calls "a particularly short supply" of scholarly biographies on the important political actors of the parliamentary period, including those who helped overthrow the monarchy, like Nasser himself.[119] Much work needs to be done, he insists; while of the work done so far, he says, "Illuminating though [all these works] are, they just touch the tip of an iceberg consisting of all the institutions, relationships, practices and processes which make the monarchical period so important, interesting and, in its own special way, unique."[120] The Egyptian academy has long dismissed the pre-Nasser years as corrupt as well. Historian Yunan Labib Rizq, for example, discusses pre-1952 events in a piece titled "The fall of the liberal experiment in Egypt," in which he accuses the political parties of having accommodated, if not collaborated with, an autocratic palace.[121] Yet, some voices have questioned the prevalent accepted wisdom on the pre-1952 years. 'Abd al-'Azim Ramadan is one such historian, and he calls for rewriting the history of Wafdist leader and Sa'd Zaghlul's successor Mustafa al-Nahhas (1879–1965). Ramadan argues that since 1952, the role played by al-Nahhas in the earlier national struggle has been systematically ignored and deliberately dismissed as part of a larger effort to discredit any accomplishments that happened before the Free Officers' coup.[122] He also states that the official historiography taught in schools and universities has completely adopted Nasser's view on the pre-1952 period, which dismissed all political parties as corrupt and inept.[123]

Similarly, after Nasser's death, the well-known intellectual Luwis 'Awad spoke out in favor of revising the historiography of the pre-1952 period. He argued that the 1952 revolution denigrated the period between the 1919 and 1952 revolutions, and as a result, generations of Egyptians could no longer distinguish between the popular Sa'd Zaghlul and Mustafa al-Nahhas on the one hand and the autocratic Muhammad Mahmud and Isma'il Sidqi on the other.[124] In his own assessment of that period, he wonders if the political parties at the time could have forced real change, succeeded in toppling the monarchy, or resisted feudalism and capitalism. "Highly unlikely," he concludes, because in his view the

British would never have let it happen, comfortable as they were with a regime they knew all too well how to manipulate.[125]

Likewise, the philosopher Fu'ad Zakariya wrote in the early 1980s that an entire generation of Egyptians ignored what happened during the monarchical period as it "was written about by its opponents," and as such, it needs further study and analysis.[126] For example, he accuses the journalist Muhammad Hasanayn Haykal of having obliterated the differences between the various political parties active during that period by claiming that they all "betrayed, failed and disavowed the national struggle."[127] He describes the last two years of Wafdist rule between 1950 and 1952 as the "culmination of the democratic experience that had developed over a period of seventy-five years," despite various forces that had opposed its development, including the palace, the occupation, and the army itself.[128] While Zakariya admits that the Wafd was never "a homogeneous perfect party," he says it understood that the popular vote was its source of power, and thus continued to support the constitution and people's demands until the end.[129] Interestingly, in Zakariya's view, Taha Hussein's decision to make education free was "the real beginning of social change."[130]

Sources: Looking beyond Taha Hussein's Published Work

This book relies mainly on archival documents from the Egyptian National Archives (Dar al-Watha'iq al-Qawmiyya), Cairo University, the Egyptian Ministry of Education, and the French Ministry of Foreign Affairs, in addition to dozens of periodicals and, importantly, Taha Hussein's private papers, which I was able to study through the kind authorization of his family. Regarding the actions proposed or the decisions made by Hussein during his time at the Ministry of Public Instruction, the archives of the Council of Ministers at the Egyptian National Archives hold records of the meetings and the various memoranda submitted to the council for approval. Each memorandum makes a case for a proposed project; explains its context, history, and justification; and gives the council's recommendations and final decision. The archives of the Faculty of Arts at Cairo University hold Hussein's employment record at the university, and the Egyptian Registry and Property Records Archive (Dar al-Mahfuzat al-'Umumiyya) has his pension dossier as a state employee. Together, both files clarify many of the duties that were assigned to him by the ministry and the university, supplying his promotions, assignments, and job descriptions. The archives of the Ministry of Education, housed in the Museum of Education, provide useful reports and information on the ministry itself.

Moreover, recently, in an initiative of Egypt's former Minister of Culture and Hussein's student Jabir 'Usfur, the Egyptian National Archives collected many of Hussein's articles from 1908 to 1967. At the time, 'Usfur was president of the National Library and Archives (Dar al-Kutub wa-l-Watha'iq al-Qawmiyya), and he tasked the Egyptian historian Ra'uf 'Abbas with supervising the project. Collecting the articles took four years, then editing and publishing them in six volumes took another four years. The first volume was published in 2002 and the sixth in 2006. 'Abbas found that out of the hundreds of articles, one hundred and forty-four, focusing on education, had never been published before.[131] These articles span more than forty years of Hussein's active involvement in the question of education and its ties to democracy, and are therefore crucial in unpacking how his project developed over time and how he tried to persuade the Egyptian public of the utility of his ideas. They also contextualize these developments within the overall debates and politics of the period between the two revolutions. The articles Hussein published from the time of the coup of 1952 to the mid-1960s help us understand his reaction to the revolution, how that change impacted his project, and what led to his eventual marginalization. Finally, the *Journal of the Arabic Language Academy* (*Majallat Majma' al-Lugha al-'Arabiyya*) offers a wealth of details on the structural changes Hussein introduced in the academy, the reasons for them, and the different ways in which he redrew the policies of the academy to focus on tasks he believed were necessary to protect classical Arabic and make it more accessible.

In France, the Ministry of Foreign Affairs keeps detailed records of that nation's cultural relations with Egypt in the nineteenth and twentieth centuries. After the Second World War and in preparation for the de facto end of the capitulatory privileges in 1949, hundreds of mostly confidential reports and telegrams document French concerns over the future of dozens of French educational establishments in Egypt. These reports also indicate how the French authorities dealt with Taha Hussein when he became minister of public instruction and give fascinating insights into Hussein the statesman and the politician, as he clashed with the French government over the expansion of Egyptian cultural influence in French-controlled North Africa.

Although I have relied mostly on archival material, I have read these documents with and against Hussein's more well-known published work. An engagement with both is necessary, not only to get a better sense of Hussein, his intellectual outlook, and the context in which he both worked and published but also to compare theoretical ideas with their implementation. Hussein's official letters, memoranda, and public decrees address statesmen and cabinet members to whom he reported or who were his colleagues. These official Egyptian documents and the French archival reports are precise, often with a reserved and dry tone. As they documented proposals addressed to decision makers, these reports provide the background information and cross-referencing necessary for every case at hand. Many documents from the Egyptian Council of Ministers, including memoranda and meeting agendas, exist in the original Arabic and in French translation. The minutes also recorded council discussions of unscheduled urgent events, like the violence that erupted in the Suez Canal Zone after Egypt abrogated the 1936 Anglo-Egyptian Treaty in October 1951.

Taha Hussein's published work on education, culture, and politics requires a different kind of reading, one that is broad and deep at the same time. Many scholars have noted the difficulty of reading Hussein, despite his beautiful and flowing writing style. The Tunisian scholar Muhi al-Din Hamdi, for example, has warned that "tracing [Taha Hussein's thought] requires long years."[132] Moreover, the sorts of internal contradictions noted earlier in *The Future of Culture in Egypt* are not unique to that work. Abdelrashid Mahmoudi points to the existence of "various sorts of tension and ambivalence, if not outright inconsistency" in Taha Hussein's thought as a whole.[133] The famous French Orientalist Jacques Berque finds Hussein's style, with its music, rhyme, and repetition, "seductive."[134] Miqdad al-Jumni has elaborated on Berque's observation, saying that the beauty of Hussein's style ends up diverting attention from the ideas themselves. Al-Jumni argues that for him, it is important to "understand the philosophy of [Hussein's] text from a psychological and emotional point of view, as well as rationally, and especially, culturally."[135] Likewise, the writer Shukri Faysal, who collected some of Hussein's radio broadcasts on Arabic poetry and published them under the title *Taqlid wa-Tajdid* (*Imitation and Renewal*), describes Hussein's style as "mysteriously clear, or clearly mysterious."[136] Faysal explains further that Hussein's deceptively clear sentences and their music cause the impatient reader to gloss over the details of Hussein's argument, retaining the overall idea at the expense of the subtle details.[137] Faysal thinks Hussein sets up his prose deliberately in such a way as to prevent the reader from losing sight of the main argument despite "a plethora of steps, turn of phrases and side points." When the reading is finished, Faysal explains, the main idea "continues to ring in the reader's ears against the backdrop of the musical rhythm generated by [Hussein's] particular style."[138] This claim that Hussein employed a captivating style as a literary device to keep his readers focused on the main idea could help us understand why some of the subtle arguments and internal inconsistencies in his texts sometimes go unnoticed.

Taha Hussein's particular way of writing, which was certainly influenced by his blindness, could also explain his dedicated focus on the main idea of a text. In 1934, he explained how the writing process was exceptionally burdensome for him. He said he always dictated his texts and never liked to be interrupted as he did so. Glad when the dictation was over, he never returned to the text after that. He could not, in his words, "bear the burden of re-reading what he had written."[139] In a much later interview, his son, Moenis, confirmed that as far as he knew, his father "never revised a single line that he had written."[140] While fact verification and cross-checking occurred in preparation for the dictation, the actual writing involved none or very little of that. It therefore seems safe to assume that focusing on the main idea was important for Hussein himself as he dictated his ideas, so he would not lose his line of thought and could keep the text coherent.

This book uses all the sources described here to drive a new narrative in which the focus shifts from Hussein the literary figure to Hussein the statesman and public servant building institutions of knowledge production. My aim is to understand not only the ways in which these institutions were conceived and restructured to face the colonial challenge but also how the builders of those institutions, Hussein and others, tried to overcome the shortcomings of Egypt's unstable parliamentary system, and how Hussein implicitly relied on that system as a framework within which these institutions were to operate efficiently. Moreover, I investigate how Hussein tried to use these institutions to expand Egypt's regional cultural influence, and how this brought him into conflicts with the French authorities in North Africa several years before Nasser's Pan-Arabism. Finally, I show how political events in Egypt and abroad in the 1950s and '60s made it impossible for Hussein to continue promoting his project of reform and led to his ultimate marginalization.

Two main questions thus animate this study. First, what was Taha Hussein's overall project for education and culture in Egypt, and second, what can Hussein's promotion and implementation of his project over the years tell us about what we refer to as "liberal" or "parliamentary" Egypt? These two large questions then lead to the following more specific questions. What were the contours of Hussein's public career as a politician and civil servant, and how can his understudied public career inform or change our understanding of his well-known career as writer and intellectual? In his approach to facing the colonial challenge, how does Hussein differ from earlier *nahdawis*? How can we reconcile Hussein's championing of academic and intellectual freedom with the central role he assigned to the state in his project? As a statesman and a civil servant, how did Hussein deal with partisan politics, which were undermining policymaking and the overall parliamentary system? Finally, in what ways can a focus on institutions of culture and education revise our understanding of the parliamentary period as a whole?

To answer these questions, this study follows two streams, which also dislodge several assumptions about both the man and the parliamentary period in which he worked. The first deals with Hussein, and explores his public career, duties, and responsibilities. Studies of Hussein have often been susceptible to a narrow focus on his published work and literary debates. In these studies, he comes across as an intellectual who idealizes a "pure" form of art and culture that he claims should transcend politics in order to enable a genuine understanding and cooperation between peoples and nations. As a result, he has been criticized for having overlooked the impact of the unequal power relations that existed between colonizers and colonized and that undergirded all cultural exchanges between them. By exploring Hussein's career as a politician and a decision maker with an urgent reform project, I contend that a different Taha Hussein emerges. His political conflicts with local adversaries (such as King Farouk and the Sa'dists who opposed his calls for free education) and, surprisingly, with France (which opposed his attempts to expand Egyptian cultural influence in North Africa despite his well-known cultural and family ties with France) can help us achieve a more rounded understanding of Hussein. Similarly, in his published work, he expressed his wish for Egypt to follow in Europe's path and repeatedly criticized al-Azhar and its educational system. This has led many scholars to categorize him as the archetypical "westernizer," "modernist," or "secularist," as opposed to other intellectuals who were "traditionalist" or "religious." By looking at Hussein's efforts in the Faculty of Arts and the Arabic Language Academy, I will show that such binaries do not help us account for his serious engagement with the Arab-Islamic tradition, nor his dedication to preserving classical Arabic. Moreover, studying the concrete steps he took to implement his project of critical thinking, including the reasons why he had to challenge the monopoly of the religious establishment over tradition and language, enriches our understanding of his complex intellectual outlook and clarifies his multilayered relationship with al-Azhar.[141]

The second stream of argumentation uses Taha Hussein's efforts toward the building of some of Egypt's key modern educational and cultural institutions to examine the history of these institutions, especially in terms of their development and operation during the parliamentary period. I will show that understanding Hussein's efforts requires investigating the links that tied these institutions, and him, to an earlier *nahdawi* discourse that proposed facing the western colonial challenge by reviving classical Arab-Islamic thought while also forging strong ties with modern Europe. I will show the ways in which Hussein's lifelong engagement with the university, the language academy, and the Ministry of Education reflected an unwavering commitment to this *nahdawi* mission. Furthermore, examining the ways in which Hussein responded to the challenges facing these institutions after the nominal independence achieved in 1922 sheds light on how institutional roles and responsibilities came to be defined within a new and volatile parliamentary system. To regulate the operation of these state-funded institutions, Hussein had to deal with partisan politics, and he tried to use the parliamentary system in place to keep the state in check. By telling the story of Taha Hussein's attempts to maneuver this system into introducing free universal education and expanding Egypt's cultural influence beyond its borders, this book deepens our understanding of this period and challenges scholarship focused mainly on the failures leading to the end of the parliamentary era in 1952.

1 EGYPTIAN CULTURAL EXPANSIONISM

Taha Hussein Confronts the French in North Africa

> His Excellency Moustapha El Nahas Pacha,
> President of the Council [of Ministers],
> Cairo
>
> Farouk I Institute for Islamic Studies was inaugurated today at noon in a grandiose ceremony worthy of Egypt and its great king worthy also of great and proud Spain STOP On this occasion I would like to express to your Excellency my deep and sincere affection and my faithful friendship to all the other colleagues STOP Leaving tomorrow Sunday for Paris
>
> Taha Hussein[1]

ON NOVEMBER 7, 1950, Taha Hussein, Egypt's minister of public instruction, arrived in Madrid on a six-day official trip to Spain. Awaiting Hussein and his wife, Suzanne, at the train station were Spain's minister of national education, the deputies for the Spanish ministers of foreign affairs and national education, the Spanish Arabist Emilio García Gómez (Hussein's old student and a future ambassador), students from the Egyptian educational mission in Spain, and members of the Egyptian diplomatic corps. Spanish newspapers, interested in the visit, focused on Hussein's literary accomplishments and the reason for his visit: the inauguration of the Farouk I Institute for Islamic Studies. In his confidential report to Cairo, Egyptian Ambassador Muhammad Husni 'Umar described the event as a great victory for Egyptian cultural diplomacy. In his words, Spain's extremely positive reaction was a "wonderful showcase proving to the world Egypt's scientific standing and cultural influence."[2]

For Taha Hussein, then at the peak of his career, taking Egypt's "scientific standing and cultural influence" to a regional level was integral to what he called "Egypt's mission." In his view, this mission was predominantly cultural, and the nation's modern awakening, or *nahda*, had qualified the country for resuming what he believed to be its historical role of leading the Arab-Islamic world in what he described as "the advancement of civilization and the consolidation of peace."[3] As minister of public instruction in the last Wafd government (1950–1952), Hussein took this regional agenda forward, especially in the Mediterranean world. He created the Farouk I Institute for Islamic Studies in Madrid, the Muhammad Ali al-Kabir Chair for Arabic Language and Literature in Nice, and a similar chair at the University of Athens. When he tried to create Egyptian Institutes for Arabic and Islamic Studies in Tangier, Rabat, Tunis, and Algiers, however, Hussein collided head-on with the French authorities, who feared and opposed any official Egyptian presence in North Africa. This conflict came after the signing of the Anglo-Egyptian Treaty (1936) and the abolition of the Capitulations (1937), which returned to Egypt control over its foreign policy and over hundreds of foreign establishments operating in the country.[4] The rich details of this conflict reflected Egypt's growing confidence in its educational and cultural institutions, signaled its expanding cultural influence in Europe and North Africa, and represented a major shift in its foreign policy, which until then had focused on the Arab Mashriq and had avoided any tampering with what was considered to be a traditional Franco-Egyptian friendship.

Mentioned only in passing in a few secondary sources, this dispute remains largely unknown even among scholars. In analyzing it, I argue for an important continuity between Egypt's so-called liberal age and the Nasserite era that followed, in which Egypt's political involvement in North Africa, especially Algeria, became more vocal. While scholars have shown that Egyptian Pan-Arabism started under the constitutional monarchy, they have focused on the Egyptian involvement in the Mashriq. This chapter, however, shows that Egyptian interest also extended to the Maghrib in the 1940s and early 1950s. By insisting on having an official Egyptian presence in North Africa, Hussein forced both the French and Egyptian authorities to articulate their cultural policies in the region. His projects reveal a conscious and systematic effort to enforce an official cultural role in Europe and North Africa. This cultural diplomacy started before Nasser came to power, and it established important channels of communication between Egypt and the Maghrib. Faced with staunch French resistance to his plans, however, Hussein retaliated by suspending French archaeological digs in Egypt and by threatening to take serious action against long-standing French cultural establishments in the country. These unprecedented threats and retaliatory measures against French influence in Egypt, an influence to which Hussein was intimately tied, reveal that these establishments had come to a precarious position long before the Suez Crisis in 1956, which led to the ultimate nationalization of many of them.

This chapter also delves into the workings of Egypt's multiparty system. In this conflict with France, the British did not play any role, and King Farouk (r. 1936–1952) was largely absent. The French considered involving the king to reverse Hussein's measures but eventually decided Farouk's relationship with the popular Wafd cabinet was too tense to allow any intervention in their favor. Pressured by Hussein into accepting the creation of cultural institutes in North Africa, the French authorities took into consideration that he was member of a popular elected government. They followed his press conferences closely and feared his influential statements would turn public opinion against them, especially as many Egyptian journals and periodicals found their way to French-controlled North Africa, often without French permission. Instead of direct confrontation, the French government stalled on meeting Hussein's demands, hoping for the election of a less nationalist government for which the cultural institutes would be less important.

As far as Hussein himself is concerned, by turning attention to his actions and negotiations with the French, I show that far from his image as a man of letters disinterested in politics, he was extremely conscious of the political nature and the long-term anti-colonial goal of the institutes he was trying to build. Accordingly, I begin the next section of this chapter by examining some of his published ideas on expanding Egypt's cultural role in the region, and the ways in which they illustrate his (now controversial) belief that culture is "universal" and should transcend narrow political motives. Then, using primary sources from the Egyptian National Archives (DWQ) and the French Ministry of Foreign Affairs (AMAE), as well as from Taha Hussein's private papers (PP), I turn to his efforts as minister of public instruction to create cultural institutes and university chairs in the region. Next, I explore the reaction of the French authorities to a changing cultural landscape in which Egypt sought to position itself as the guardian of Arabic and Islamic studies. I end with Hussein's unprecedented measures against French cultural influence in Egypt a few weeks before the dismissal of the Wafd government in January 1952.

Taha Hussein Calls for an "Apolitical" Egyptian Cultural Mission

Scholars have explored Egypt's interest in the Arab Mashriq before 1952, demonstrating that Nasser's Pan-Arabism had its roots in the monarchical period. Israel Gershoni and James Jankowski, for example, discuss the ways in which Pan-Arab thought had started to develop in the early 1930s, and how the question of Palestine in the 1930s and '40s increased Pan-Arab feeling among

Egyptians, forcing politicians to take events in Palestine and the Mashriq in general more seriously.[5] As a result, Wafdist leader Mustafa al-Nahhas, for example, began in 1942 and '43 to pursue an Arab-oriented foreign policy. According to Gershoni, by championing Egypt's leadership of the Arab world, al-Nahhas hoped to increase his own popularity at home, and these policies culminated in the coming together of, initially, seven nations in the Arab League, agreed upon in Cairo in 1945.[6] After the Second World War, successive Egyptian governments used Pan-Arab policies to increase Egypt's influence in the Mashriq, hoping to use this growing influence to pressure the British into leaving their country.[7]

After the army coup of July 1952, Nasser shifted Egypt's foreign policy toward more direct state involvement in arming anti-colonial resistance movements, especially in Algeria, while deploying a more radical rhetoric, most notably on the frequencies of the radio station Sawt al-ʿArab, which began broadcasting in 1953.[8] In one of the few pieces of scholarship on the role Egyptian educational missions played in promoting Pan-Arabism, Gerasimos Tsourapas points out how Nasser used these missions to promote his influence in the Arab world by supplying them with Egyptian textbooks and choosing politically minded teachers, a move often leading to friction with host countries, such as Libya and Algeria, that feared radicalization of their students.[9]

While Tsourapas has stated that it was only under Nasser that "the expansion and politicization of educational missions abroad occurred within a distinct foreign policy agenda,"[10] my research has found that the Wafd had implemented Pan-Arab cultural diplomacy in North Africa before Nasser came to power. David Stenner has also shown that Cairo attracted many members of the various North African opposition movements before 1952, including future Tunisian and Algerian presidents Habib Bourguiba (1903–2000) and Ahmed Ben Bella (1916–2012).[11] In 1947, these opposition members sought to organize their efforts through the creation of the Maktab al-Maghrib al-ʿArabi (Bureau of the Arab Maghrib), which became the headquarters for North African nationalist movements promoting the independence of Tunisia, Algeria, and Morocco through various events and publications.[12] Yet, these were not the only reasons why the French authorities came to regard Cairo as a possible threat to their well-established influence in North Africa. As this chapter demonstrates, Taha Hussein's conflict with the French reveals that Egypt was not only harboring North African nationalists but also taking concrete steps to introduce an official Egyptian cultural presence into the Maghrib by building institutes of Arabic and Islamic studies.

Even though Taha Hussein remained opposed to any rushed political unity between Egypt and other Arab countries, he insisted from the 1930s on that knowledge produced in Egypt must be shared with Arab neighbors.[13] In a chapter in *The Future of Culture in Egypt* focusing on what he believed was Egypt's duty toward Arab countries, Hussein called for making Egyptian publications more accessible to other Arabs. He also pushed for sending more teachers to Arab countries, receiving Arab students in Egyptian schools and universities, and making sure the Egyptian government did everything possible to facilitate their stay in Egypt. In response to longstanding European educational missions in the Mashriq, such as those in Syria, Lebanon, and Palestine, he suggested using Egypt's new freedom in matters of foreign policy after the 1936 treaty to build Egyptian schools in these countries in order to provide a more appropriate "eastern Arab culture" to students there. He insisted that these Egyptian schools should teach Arab students in the Mashriq their own history and geography, and avoid what foreign schools had done in Egypt, which was to teach the history and geography of their respective countries. "Arab students should be raised for their countries, not for Egypt," he clarified.[14] Furthermore, given the sophistication of Egypt's higher education, which attracted students from a variety of Arab countries, Hussein suggested unifying all educational systems in Arab countries to prepare Arab students for Egyptian academic life. By assuming its cultural responsibilities toward other Arabs, Egypt, he believed, would become an important center of intellectual cooperation in the world, and the cultural link between "East" and "West." With its "geographical location and modern *nahda*," Egypt, according to Hussein, was particularly suited for taking on this cultural role and assuming a leadership position.[15] Such a tangible role would be powered by the country's cultural and educational institutions, in dialogue with similar institutions abroad, allowing Egypt to participate in building what he called "the human civilization."[16]

Most of the cultural institutes and university chairs that Minister of Public Instruction Taha Hussein established were in the Mediterranean—Spain, France, Greece, and North Africa. He also encouraged the Greek government to create a chair for Hellenic Studies at Farouk I (later Alexandria) University, which he had founded in 1942 and whose seal carries a representation of Pharos, the city's Hellenic lighthouse and one of the seven wonders of the ancient world. Hussein was that university's first president and can be seen in the photo on page 48 giving the inauguration speech. He also planned to build an institute in North Africa, along the lines of the French research institutes already active in Cairo,

Athens, and Rome, to facilitate scholarly cooperation and exchange. In *The Future of Culture in Egypt*, Hussein had argued that Egypt's ties to the Mediterranean were ancient and that Egyptian influence on the Near East, especially Greece, was undeniable. Likewise, he went on, Egyptian culture was marked and influenced by its extensive contact with the Mediterranean region, and Egypt's current *nahda* only revived those old connections.[17] With its modern institutions, wealth, and influence on Arab-Islamic countries, Egypt, he believed, was in a strong position to contribute intellectually and financially to initiatives fostering intellectual cooperation between Mediterranean countries and to promote studies examining the region's civilizations, interactions, history, and geography. He embraced a form of scholarly cooperation in which Egypt was to become an active and equal partner, setting forth a rigorous and well-financed research agenda. As we will see, this Mediterraneanism in Hussein's vision for Egypt's regional role coexisted with a cultural form of Pan-Arabism and strong Egyptian leadership in the field of Arabic and Islamic studies.[18]

Taha Hussein idealized culture and believed it transcended the complex web of unequal power relations that existed between colonizers and colonized. For this, he has been subjected to much criticism. Some work grounded in postcolonial studies, like Shaden Tageldin's *Disarming Words: Empire and the Seductions of Translation in Egypt*, argues that Egyptian intellectuals, including Hussein, surrendered too easily to the charms of western knowledge, which she contends was often presented by western scholars as "universal knowledge." She considers Hussein's claim that culture should transcend politics, and carefully analyzes the impact of that claim on translation. She examines one of Hussein's published debates with another famous Egyptian intellectual, 'Abbas al-'Aqqad (1889–1964), in which Hussein argued that all nations translated texts in foreign languages into their own language out of social and intellectual needs. He even provided historical examples to prove that at times the colonizer needed the culture of the colonized more than the other way around: for example, when Romans translated from Greek texts, and Arabs translated from Greek and Persian texts.[19] In her analysis, Tageldin takes issue with Hussein's belief in a "universal need" to translate, which in her view implies a natural willingness to exchange and presumes an "innate predisposition of all human beings to think and feel alike."[20] Tageldin's concern is that such universalization apoliticizes the act of translation, removes it from its imperial context, and masks the complex web of unequal power relations that undergird the translation process.[21]

The lack of overt political action from Taha Hussein also disappointed many

FIGURE 4. Inauguration of Farouk I (Alexandria) University, 1943. Courtesy of the Taha Hussein family.

North African intellectuals. The literary scholar Abu al-Qasim Muhammad Karru states that North African writers have reproached Hussein for not having been outspoken enough about French colonialism in North Africa, especially in Algeria. Karru refers to Hussein's visit to Tunisia in 1957—documented in the photograph on the next page—at the height of the Algerian war of independence against France, and how he disappointed his audience by choosing a purely literary topic and not mentioning Algeria at all. This irritated many intellectuals at the time, and some received his visit coldly.[22] Without giving details, Karru believes Hussein's clash with the French over the institute in Algiers indicates Hussein had thought about the "Arabness" of Algeria when he was minister of education.

Yet, Karru argues, it was not until Hussein left office, and was encouraged by Egypt's regime change in 1952, that he publicly denounced French colonialism. This signaled, in Karru's opinion, Hussein's shift from the silence and courtesy that characterized his time as minister to a more blunt and forceful approach under Nasser. While recognizing what he describes as Hussein's honorable record against British colonialism in Egypt, Karru states that prior to Hussein's articles against French colonialism under Nasser, "no stand against French colonialism was either known or read about him."[23]

The detail-rich historical context provided in this chapter reveals how Hussein negotiated his cultural projects with the French, allows us to explore the extent to which Hussein was successful in separating the cultural from the political, and shows that he was extremely conscious of the political impact of the cultural institutes he was trying to build. He also understood the political opposition these institutes provoked in French circles. In his public statements,

FIGURE 5. Taha Hussein's trip to Tunis, 1957. Courtesy of the Taha Hussein family.

he held to his opinion that culture was universal and should not be motivated by politics.[24] But the main theme of most of the correspondence and reports relating to his projects is the extent to which the cultural was indeed political. On arriving in Madrid, Hussein gave a speech on the local radio carrying his unmistakable imprint: "Cultural relations are the right foundation for bringing nations together because they are free from political motives. This is the aim of what Egypt has done here in Spain."[25] For Hussein, precisely because of his awareness of the unequal power relations thwarting his efforts in spreading Egypt's cultural influence abroad, capitalizing on the cultural and downplaying the political became the cornerstone of his negotiations.

Egypt Situates Itself as the Guardian of Arabic and Islamic Studies

In January 1950, a few days before the instatement of a new Wafd government under Prime Minister Mustafa al-Nahhas, the Council of Ministers approved a request by then Minister of Public Instruction Muhammad al-'Ashmawi to create an Institute for Islamic Studies in Madrid.[26] Behind that idea was Taha Hussein who, during a visit to Spain with other Egyptian intellectuals in 1949, had raised the issue with Spanish officials and discussed the possibility of opening an Egyptian Institute in Madrid similar to the ones already operating in London and Washington. His idea was positively received.[27]

'Ashmawi's request traced the interest in creating cultural centers abroad back to 1943, when Taha Hussein was technical advisor to Najib al-Hilali, at that time the Wafdist minister of public instruction. 'Ashmawi argued that given Egypt's independence under the Anglo-Egyptian Treaty of 1936, the country should have a proper policy for cultural representation abroad. Such representation, he explained, should reflect Egypt's advanced position on the world cultural scene and build on what had begun in 1943 with the creation of Egyptian institutes in London and Washington. These institutes were built to keep Egyptians informed about recent scientific and administrative innovations, and to celebrate Egypt's modern *nahda* and its accomplishments in both countries. Considering their success, 'Ashmawi continued, there would be a great benefit in fostering similar ties with Spain because of the impact this could have on the study of Arab history. Given the Arab legacy in Spain, the minister explained, such a center would facilitate the task of researchers in the West and the East by copying and publishing the Arabic manuscripts existing in Spain, in the fields of literature, philosophy, language, and religion.

Egypt, said 'Ashmawi, was especially fit for taking on such a task. Historically, he went on, Egypt had enjoyed a privileged cultural exchange with Muslim Spain, as many Andalusian ulama had come to Egypt, and their works were still being taught at al-Azhar. Such an old tie could benefit from Egypt's modern institutions, such as the Islamic Monuments Institute, the Arab Monuments Institute, the School of Fine Arts, and Egypt's recent interest in studying the Mediterranean culture, especially where it overlapped with Islamic civilization. The minister referred to two French institutes for art and culture already operating in Spain and told his colleagues that European countries should not monopolize such institutes, especially in a country that mattered so much to the Arab-Islamic world. The Council of Ministers approved the request.[28]

On becoming minister of public instruction in 1950, Taha Hussein made the Madrid institute a priority. He informed the Ministry of Finance that all required studies for the creation of the institute had been undertaken. He requested 30,000 Egyptian pounds (LE) for the Madrid institute and also the one he intended to open in Tangier. The money was provided and used for rent, furnishings, salaries, and other expenses, and he inaugurated the Madrid institute on November 11, 1950.[29] Mustafa al-Nahhas replied to Hussein's telegram, quoted at the start of this chapter, expressing his pleasure with the successful opening of the institute and his wish to see it fostering cultural ties between Egypt and Spain. He also sent his personal wishes for Hussein's safe return. Both telegrams were forwarded to King Farouk's court.[30]

Likewise, in April 1950, after a few months in office, Hussein informed the Council of Ministers that the Institut d'Études Méditerranéennes, affiliated with the Université d'Aix-Marseille, had been created in Nice. It was devoted to literary studies and to the natural and social sciences related to the Mediterranean region and its civilizations. French and non-French lecturers gave public talks, funded by various organizations and governments. In his memorandum, Hussein also wrote that "given Egypt's status in the Mediterranean and its close ties with its civilization, it should participate in the efforts of such an institute, and the institute itself is worthy of Egypt's support in carrying out its mission in the best way." His ministry proposed funding a series of lectures titled Conférences Commémoratives de Muhammad Ali El Kébir (The Grand Muhammad Ali Annual Memorial Lectures), as Egypt was celebrating the centennial anniversary of Muhammad Ali's death at the time. Moreover, as the ministry's report said, Muhammad Ali had "renewed Egypt's ties with the West, established its modern Renaissance, and was one of those who had revived the Mediterranean Sea, politically, militarily, and economically, paving the way for its return as an artery for world trade and a vital center of international relations." The Egyptian

FIGURE 6. Taha Hussein's trip to Nice, 1950. Courtesy of the Taha Hussein family.

government would provide funding in the amount of LE 1,200 a year and invite Egyptian and non-Egyptian lecturers to give talks in the series.[31] Hussein himself went to Nice to represent the Egyptian government during the inauguration of the Muhammad Ali Chair, as shown in the photograph here, accompanied by his son, Moenis, to his left.[32]

A year later, in March 1951, the council approved another official trip for Taha Hussein, this time to Greece, from March 22 to April 3, 1951, to receive an honorary doctorate from the University of Athens.[33] The council also supported his request to provide the funds necessary for the creation of a chair for Arabic language and literature at the University of Athens.[34] In his memorandum to the council, Hussein explained that to strengthen cultural cooperation between Egypt and Greece, and given his upcoming visit to Athens, he thought the time was convenient for creating such a chair, which would cost LE 1,200 a year. He told the council that he had already consulted with his colleague the minister of finance, who had given his approval. Hussein asked the council to decide quickly on the matter so he could announce the news during his visit to Greece. He expected the Greek government to reciprocate and announce the creation of a chair for Hellenic studies at the Farouk I University in Alexandria.[35]

Two months later, in May 1951, King Farouk's private secretariat submitted a special report from Taha Hussein to the king in which Hussein proposed to create a Farouk I Institute for Arabic Studies in Istanbul. In line with the Wafdist reconciliatory attempts at the time to pacify the young king and win him over to Wafdist views by getting him involved in policymaking, Hussein conveyed to Farouk an official Turkish invitation to have Egypt create an institute in Turkey like those established elsewhere.[36] The Turkish ambassador had expressed this wish to Hussein over dinner, saying such an institute would have the best impact in Turkey, and Hussein promised he would think about it. He informed the king that he was in favor of such an institute, not only for the prestige that would come with it but also for the major benefit of copying and transferring the Arabic manuscripts that the Turks had moved from Egypt to Istanbul following the Ottoman conquest in 1517, and which filled thirty-two libraries there.[37] Hussein proposed immediate action, since he had the funds necessary to get the institute ready in time for the meeting of the International Congress of Orientalists expected to be held in Istanbul in September 1951. The inauguration of the institute would thus benefit from the presence of key scholars in the field. Well-versed in government bureaucracy and having developed ways of handling the exigencies of the Ministry of Finance over the years, Hussein explained that he had at his disposal the 32,000 Egyptian pounds assigned to the Madrid Institute, and a similar amount for the Tangier Institute. He said he would negotiate with the Ministry of Finance to reassign part of this budget to Istanbul until more funds were made available the next financial year. Yet, Farouk, who was not on good terms with Hussein, whom he repeatedly accused of being a communist, denied the request. Without giving details, a comment in red said: "No need to create an institute in Istanbul."[38]

Failing to bring Farouk on board with his ambitious project of creating as many Egyptian cultural centers abroad as possible, Hussein addressed his next request, to create a center in London, directly to the Council of Ministers. In September 1951, Hussein wrote to the council explaining that a Center for Islamic Culture had been created in London during the Second World War, financed by various Islamic governments. The funds for the center had dwindled, however, and the capital put aside for the construction of the center's mosque was being used for the daily operations of the center. Consequently, that center could no longer provide the necessary teachers and researchers capable of representing Islamic culture in the best light. The ministry, he wrote, conscious of Egypt's responsibilities and duties in the field of international cooperation, as dictated by Egypt's status as "leader and guardian of Islamic studies," was willing to take on all the center's expenses. Such support would be conditional on the full Egyptianization of the center's administration, and on naming the center the Farouk I Institute for Islamic Culture.³⁹ In support of Hussein's ambitious cultural diplomacy, the council approved his new request.⁴⁰

Taha Hussein Opens an Institute in Spain

By this time in his career, Taha Hussein was a man of fame and many accomplishments, accustomed to receiving honors in Egypt and abroad. Soon after his return to Cairo from Europe, he would learn that King Farouk had granted him the prestigious title of Pasha in December 1950.⁴¹ The Egyptian ambassador had reported on Hussein's busy schedule in Madrid and listed the Spanish officials and dignitaries with whom he had met, giving us a snapshot of his activities. His scheduled lunches and dinners had him meeting with the ministers of foreign affairs and national education, the deputy of the minister of foreign affairs, the general director of cultural relations at the Ministry of Foreign Affairs, and the Arabist García Gómez. He also met the president of the Spanish Academy of History, who organized a session at the academy in Hussein's honor, presided over by the Spanish minister of national education. García Gómez introduced Hussein, in Spanish and in French, and Hussein presented a lecture titled "Fictional Prose in the Islamic East and West," comparing Abu al-ʿAlaʾ al-Maʿarri's *Risalat al-Ghufran* and Abu ʿAmir Ahmad al-Andalusi's *Risalat al-Tawabiʿ wa-l-Zawabiʿ*. The Spanish minister then awarded Hussein the academy's medallion and appointed him a correspondent member. The Spanish government also awarded him an honorary doctorate, in recognition of his "exceptional talents."⁴²

The inauguration ceremony for the Farouk I Institute for Islamic Studies began at noon on November 11, 1950, with the ministers of foreign affairs and national education among the invited Spanish officials. A newsletter in Arabic and Spanish highlighting the mission of the institute was distributed to the guests. In his opening speech, which he delivered in French, Hussein thanked the Spanish government and the Egyptian king for their support. Arabs and Spaniards had created a civilization together, despite all the wars that had taken place between them, Hussein said. Now humanity had progressed, and the institute represented the renunciation of violence, for "relations between people are now based on culture." He called on the Spanish government to authorize using a printing press at the institute to reproduce the Arabic manuscripts held in Spain, expressing his hope that the institute would become a place for "innocent scientific cooperation between the two countries." In the Spanish minister of national education's response, he referred to the historical relations that tied Spain to the Arab World, especially Egypt, saying that the new institute would work hand in hand with two Spanish institutes: the Asín Palacios Institute in Madrid and the Institute for Arabic Studies in Granada. Subsequently, he awarded Hussein the Civil Order of Alfonso the Wise.[43]

France Fears the Changing Cultural Landscape

Colonial powers, especially France, were uncomfortable with these Egyptian cultural activities. Present at the event organized by the Spanish Academy of History in honor of Taha Hussein was Bernard Hardion, the chargé of the French delegation to Spain, who congratulated the Egyptian ambassador on Hussein's knowledge, his mastery of the French language, the clarity of his presentation, and his methodology. He also communicated to the Egyptian ambassador the wish of the French minister of public instruction to receive Hussein and his wife as his guests during their upcoming trip in France. Hardion also relayed the wish of the director of the University of Paris to have Hussein give a lecture at the Sorbonne and be present in Paris on December 2, 1950, to attend the official celebration of the beginning of the school year at the university. Hussein accepted the invitation.[44]

Yet, in his reports to Paris, Hardion focused almost entirely on the political implications of Hussein's visit to Spain, and on Hussein's astute awareness of these implications. Hardion explained that the creation of the institute posed problems for the Spanish, who were worried about possible political repercussions in Spanish-controlled Morocco. He revealed that the Spanish approval resulted from the personal initiative of Martin Artajo, the Spanish minister of foreign affairs, despite serious opposition from Artajo's own ministry. Furthermore, Hardion specified that the reserve shown by the Spanish Directorate of Cultural Relations with regard to opening an Egyptian school in Tangier was another indication of Spanish concerns over possible expressions of nationalism that the authorities in Cairo might be tempted to undertake. He concluded that, like France, Spain was uncomfortable with an expanding Egyptian cultural influence.

In this report, Hardion also tried to explain the lavish attention that Taha Hussein received from the Spanish government, for in the chargé's words, "during his stay, Dr. Taha Hussein Bey was the object of the most distinct attentions from the Spanish authorities." Hardion thought that this attention was perhaps an attempt by the Franco regime to give the impression that Hussein's visit was motivated by an interest in stronger political ties between Madrid and Cairo. Yet throughout this visit, the Egyptian statesman had insisted on the apolitical nature of his endeavor. Hardion even quoted Hussein as having said: "We only want one thing, and that is to deepen culture and spread knowledge. Our relations with Spain, based on this pure and healthy concept, are only interested in the sciences." If the Spanish government had hoped to draw some political benefits from the visit, Hardion concluded, they were certainly disappointed because, in his words, "the Egyptian minister knew skillfully how to avoid the trap that was set for him."[45] Hussein's official message was clear. The institute was created for cultural reasons. It neither promoted political gains nor sought to stir nationalist sentiments in Spanish-controlled Morocco, or elsewhere.

In the preceding months, Taha Hussein had also been in close communication with the French authorities in Paris over the creation of a Farouk I Institute for Islamic Studies in North Africa. He insinuated to French officials that should France refuse, Egypt would reciprocate and close down the prized Institut Français d'Archéologie Orientale (IFAO) in Cairo. He also wrote to King Farouk asking for his support in case he had to make the threat official. The French sources show, however, that Farouk was opposed to taking any measures against French interests in Egypt. He opposed his minister's idea and wrote to tell him: "The relations [between Egypt and France] are still cold. This should wait until the situation has cleared."[46]

These cold relations had resulted from a political incident that had seriously undermined Taha Hussein's efforts to establish a cultural institute in the international city. A French official wrote to the French ambassador in Cairo that the creation of the institute would have to wait until relations between the two countries had returned to normal after they had been compromised by a visit made to Tangier by some Egyptian writers whom the French official described as "irresponsible." These writers were the journalists Mahmud Abu al-Fath and Sa'id Ramadan, who had spoken in favor of Moroccan nationalism in front of an audience of two thousand people. The French official complained that not only did they encourage people to adopt a hostile attitude toward France but Ramadan had also called on Muslims to consider "holy war" as a means of uniting all Muslims. The consequences were such that Moroccan officials had to intervene and close down the gathering. Employing a familiar colonial trope, the French official used this incident to claim that Egypt was not mature enough to handle its political responsibilities in North Africa, and that he doubted any Egyptian would respect the mission on which he was sent.⁴⁷ As the story of the Egyptian institute in North Africa unfolded, however, it became clear that France had other concerns about the project and had used the incident with the journalists as an excuse to stall negotiations.

French worries about Egypt's influence in North Africa were not new. The French had refused any official Egyptian presence in North Africa. Not only were they extremely sensitive to visits by Egyptian intellectuals and educators but they also inspected very closely Egyptian publications, films, and theater productions distributed in the Maghrib. After the expiry of the Capitulations in 1949, putting an end to the extraterritorial privileges enjoyed by European nationals and establishments in Egypt, the French knew it was only a matter of time before Egyptian officials would raise the question of cultural reciprocity. French reports reflect a genuine anxiety over the continued smooth operation of French establishments in Egypt—mainly cultural institutes, schools, the École Française de Droit, and hospitals—and they expected the question of Egyptian influence in North Africa to resurface at any moment. Ironically, given Hussein's well-known domestic and cultural ties to France, his appointment as minister of public instruction signaled the start of the first long, official political dispute between Egypt and France over North Africa.

Two years previously, in February 1948, Algeria's governor-general, Yves Chataigneau, had written to the French minister of foreign affairs, Georges Bidault, reminding him of a report Chataigneau had sent him several months earlier. The report endorsed a cultural exchange between Egypt and France that would also involve Algeria. Dr. Anne-Marie Goichon, the well-known specialist in Islamic philosophy, had submitted this report in 1946, after a trip to Egypt, commissioned by the French Ministry of National Education, to collect information on what the Egyptians needed and what they wanted, so that France would know what cards to play when the time came for negotiations over North Africa and the French establishments in Egypt.⁴⁸ Goichon proposed an intellectual cooperation in which any exchange involving Algeria would pass through Paris, ensuring France maintained the upper hand. She recommended the creation of a Franco-Oriental Center of Cooperation in Paris, where high-caliber professors would give a series of lectures. The governor-general of Algeria later wrote that he believed an exchange of professors among Cairo, Paris, and Algiers would only benefit France's "cultural and moral influence" in Muslim countries.⁴⁹ The Direction Générale de Relations Culturelles then forwarded the project to the Direction Afrique-Levant for its feedback, expressing real concerns over the project:

> The Direction Générale de Relations Culturelles would be grateful to know if the Direction Afrique-Levant thought such a project—so contrary to the usual policy of the North African administrations—would not have dangerous consequences, at least for Algeria, by setting precedents for our North African protectorates toward which the Egyptian authorities sometimes show an excessive concern.[50]

The Direction Générale said it would be happy to conclude an agreement with the Egyptians if the French residents-general in Morocco and Tunisia did not mind an Egyptian presence in Algeria and later on in their territories, as such an agreement would help to maintain the French institutions in Egypt after the expiry of the Capitulations in 1949. The Direction Générale warned, however, that the Egyptians would see in this, if not a weakness on the French part, then at least an opportunity to ask for the creation of more institutions in North Africa, and possibly even regular consular services, which had so far been denied them. The letter ended with a reminder that although such suggestions were very interesting on strictly cultural terms, they would cause "a serious inconvenience on the political level."[51]

France Readjusts Its Regional Cultural Policies

As requested, the Direction Afrique-Levant ran an investigation and updated Goichon's report before sending it back to the Direction Générale des Relations Culturelles. This document represents the French response to a shifting cultural landscape in North Africa, in which Egypt was pushing for a more active role in what the French report described as "the Arabization of North Africa and the spreading of the traditional Islamic culture."[52] While the investigators consulted with important leaders in the Maghrib, they turned to French North African administrators only for their opinion on the thorny question of introducing Egyptians to the scene.

The impending expiry of the Capitulations in 1949 was flagged in the report as a game changer, for the fate of all French educational facilities in Egypt depended on the cultural agreements that would follow. Egypt would not give these facilities the freedom they had enjoyed for decades without some measure of cultural reciprocity in North Africa, the absence of which Egypt considered humiliating. Important as French institutions were to the country, Egypt could invite other foreign teachers to run them under the direct control of the Egyptian government rather than continuing to have independent French educational systems on its soil. As for the institutes of higher learning, like the École Française de Droit, the degrees they gave were already facing strong competition from local institutes.[53] Egypt, having received no benefits from France in the past years, was now "playing the role of the protector of the oppressed Africa," bluntly speaking against the French presence in North Africa, whenever the occasion arose. The solution, according to this report, was to accept the principle of cultural reciprocity and allow Egyptian teachers to teach in North African schools.[54]

To reach its recommendations, the investigation had focused on the question, "Are we favorable to the potential arrival of Egyptians in North Africa, and in what form?"[55] Except for one official, the answer was a resounding no to having any Egyptian permanent presence in North Africa. "Better shut down all the French establishments in Egypt than allow the Egyptians to come to North Africa!" exclaimed an important but unnamed Parisian personality. Yet, the investigators warned against such hasty reactions, highlighting the need to appease the Egyptians. As the French presence in the Mashriq was primarily cultural, closing down the establishments in Egypt meant "abolishing what is left of the French influence in the Near East."[56] Not having the French institutions to remind Egyptians of France and its culture would thus have negative consequences in North Africa. Egypt was actively preparing for the abolition of foreign education within its borders, and excitement over the end of the French cultural presence in Egypt would only make the Egyptian press more antipathetic than it already was to the French presence in North Africa. As the ties between the Maghrib and Egypt were close, and Egyptian publications circulated secretly in the Maghrib, Egyptian professors banned from North Africa would find other ways of exerting their influence. The recommendation, therefore, was for Paris to accept and regulate this cultural reciprocity. Closing North Africa completely would not stop Egyptian influence or hinder Egyptians and North Africans from developing secret ties; whereas opening it completely would only lead to what was described in the report as "the most insane and false politics, because the Egyptians are full of prejudices against the French work [in North Africa]."[57]

To handle the Egyptian question, the recommendation was therefore to adopt a new cultural policy in the Near East, as the traditional French support in the arts was no longer enough for Egypt.[58] The benefits for Egypt had to be large enough to turn the Egyptian press away from its aggressiveness toward France.[59] Moreover, appeasing Egypt by allowing Egyptian professors to come to North Africa could weaken France in Egypt's eyes. To overcome these issues, France had to maintain the upper hand by helping Egypt and other countries in the Near East with their scientific development.[60] The impact of such scientific assistance would be felt immediately. If done properly, France could even count on Egyptian books and magazines, "read all over the Near East," to disseminate French thought in the form of positive propaganda, and as stressed in the report, "our thought would do so well to return by this route."[61] The recommendation, therefore, was to dismiss all arguments raised against providing French scientific assistance.

The proposed intellectual cooperation favoring the sciences was to be regulated through a center created for that purpose in Paris. The Centre de Coopération Intellectuelle would have a section for literature, philosophy, and history; one for society, economy, and law; and more importantly, a scientific section.[62] Egyptian lecturers would be carefully chosen for very short assignments organized through the cooperation center.[63] In what was referred to in the report as a "better solution that nobody had thought about before," scientists would be invited, but not politicians, literary people, theologians, or philosophers. Scientific cooperation was recommended as the ideal compromise to encourage the desired cultural reciprocity while keeping a political invasion at bay. "Personally, I would only reluctantly allow any Egyptian here, but if we really had to, then I would prefer scientists," said the director of education in Morocco. "I would receive an Egyptian geologist without any inconvenience, and he would leave after having acquired useful knowledge for him and his country," the director explained condescendingly. France, the director implied, did not enjoy the same power over Egyptian men of letters, journalists, or scholars of the humanities. Scientists, however, were described in the report as more likely to be impressed by the French advanced sciences:

> Scientists are more objective, more in touch with what is real, less saturated with local prejudices, and in general, the French leaders in North Africa prefer to see their work judged by scientists, even if they are of a low level, rather than men of letters imbued with politics, the way they all are in the East.[64]

Having such a cooperation center in Paris would also allow North Africans in France to meet their counterparts from the Mashriq under French supervision and in a framework of common work and preset tasks, without which they would inevitably drift to politics. The need for such a center would be even more pressing should Egypt manage to create its longed-for Institut Égyptien in Paris, which North Africans would surely frequent, and over which France would have no control at all.[65]

Interestingly, the report also said the French view was that North Africans' feelings about Egypt's rising cultural influence were "very nuanced." On the one hand, to feel left out from "the Egyptian development, the focal point of

Muslim thought," would be unbearable, as North Africans felt the need to be in touch with what was happening in the Mashriq. On the other hand, this did not imply being submissive to Egyptian directives. An influential Moroccan in Paris reiterated that as much as he desired more contact with Egypt, he was dreading Egyptian control, which he did not want to see replacing the French tutelage.[66] Whereas Egyptians thought Moroccans were outside the influence of the *nahda*, the Moroccans thought their closer contact with western knowledge and French methods put them ahead, and the report cited the case of a Moroccan student who went to write his philosophy thesis at al-Azhar, but being used to the French methods, he decided to continue his work in Paris. As the report put it, "Egyptians see Moroccans as wild, and Moroccans consider Egyptians to be oafs who would slow them down."[67]

Nevertheless, such fears do not appear in the direct communications between Egyptians and North Africans. In an official letter to Taha Hussein dated December 18, 1950, Tunisian Prime Minister Muhammad Shaniq (1889–1976) reiterated his government's wish to have Egyptian professors teach at the prestigious university of al-Zaytuna in Tunis, and informed Hussein that his government had decided to send four graduate students to finish their degrees in Egypt. The introductory paragraph had nothing but praise for Hussein, saying Egypt could not have chosen a better person to look after Egyptian culture, which, in Shaniq's words, was the culture of the whole Arab world: "Egypt is [the Arab world's] beating heart, thinking mind, and overflowing resource."[68]

Cairo Strengthens Ties with North Africa

Against the backdrop of these French fears, Charles Lucet, the French chargé d'affaires in Egypt, sent an urgent telegram on January 22, 1950. He informed Paris of *Zaman* magazine's report that a group of Moroccan intellectuals had asked the new Wafd government to open an Egyptian high school, a Lycée Farouk, in the Spanish-controlled zone in Morocco, or in Tangier, under international control since 1923. The magazine also said that the new minister of public instruction, Taha Hussein, had announced his wish to build Egyptian educational establishments in all the Arab capitals.[69] A few days later, Lucet sent a five-page report to the French minister of foreign affairs on the new Egyptian minister of public instruction. Lucet summarized Hussein's career and his strong ties with France, in terms of culture, education, and family, but warned: "If the knowledge of his deep thinking gives us the strongest hope for the future of our work here, the sensitiveness of his character and his political position with respect to the country mean that we should only approach him with the most prudent steps."[70] Hussein's plans would pose what Lucet described as "a thousand difficulties" to the French. Hussein wanted permission from the French and Spanish governments to send Egyptian professors to North Africa and to create Egyptian lycées in all its big cities. Egyptian newspapers highlighted, too, that Hussein would decide on the status of the French schools in Egypt only once the Egyptian requests had been addressed. Lucet added that he did not think Hussein would clash with the French government over this. Hussein had made these promises during the election campaign and, at least initially, he would have to position himself as an "intransigent nationalist." Lucet's recommendation was to wait and hope that, once Hussein was in power, his ideas would mellow.[71]

But Lucet was wrong. Two days after sending that report, the French resident-general in Tunis wrote to the French minister of foreign affairs, attaching a two-page intelligence report on the visit to Cairo of Sheikh Fadil ibn 'Ashur (1909–1970), the well-known Tunisian theologian and professor at al-Zaytuna. Ibn 'Ashur had put together a plan to bring a mission of Egyptian professors to Tunisia, an idea that was received enthusiastically by Taha Hussein, who started working on it immediately. According to the French ambassador in Cairo, Hussein even promised Ibn 'Ashur that he would intervene with the French authorities to get their approval. The resident-general proposed to refuse all these requests, or at least to postpone the decision on them. He argued that even though the worry over Egyptian visits to North Africa had been symbolic so far, this case was different and could present problems. According to the resident-general, not only would this plan put the Egyptians in touch with the staff and students of al-Zaytuna, known for their nationalist tendencies, but it would also interfere with a project proposed by the directorate of public instruction to establish a new high school diploma, the baccalauréat des territoires de la France d'outre-mer et de l'étranger, giving more weight to teaching Arabic and the history and geography of North Africa. Ibn 'Ashur, however, preferred the idea of a baccalauréat arabe, and sought Egypt's help to create one. Even though the director of public instruction in the Tunisian government had already explained the limitations of the proposed Arab degree to Ibn 'Ashur, once at al-Zaytuna the Egyptian mission would surely bring up the topic again and compromise the success of the new French baccalauréat.[72]

This intelligence report showed how closely the French authorities followed the movements of the Zaytuna emissary in Cairo and, more importantly, why

Cairo was seen as a source of political trouble, as it had become home to, and was regularly visited by, several leaders of North African nationalist movements, including Habib Bourguiba and Ahmed Ben Bella. Ibn ʿAshur met with the Tunisian scholar Sheikh Muhammad al-Khidr Husayn, who had moved to Egypt and cofounded the Front de Défense de l'Afrique du Nord in 1944.[73] The Algerian nationalist Chadli el Mekki, who had sought refuge in Cairo and created an office for the Algerian People's Party in 1945, was also eager to receive Ibn ʿAshur. Members of the Bureau of the Arab Maghrib, which coordinated action for the liberation of the three North African countries of Tunisia, Algeria, and Morocco, also invited Ibn ʿAshur and organized a press conference.[74] Some of his declarations at that conference were reported in the Tunisian daily *Ez-Zohra*:

> Tunisians feel that their attachment to their natural alliance, which is the Arab League, is the only way for the realization of their national aspirations for independence, which will protect them against the dangers threatening their national existence and will thwart the efforts done to push them toward a union that is foreign to them. Being the popular center of the Arab mind and the Arab League, Egypt is considered by Tunisians to be a refuge to which they turn to achieve their independence.[75]

Ibn ʿAshur spent most of his time in Cairo accompanied by his compatriot Hasan Husni ʿAbd al-Wahab (1884–1968), a member of the Arabic Language Academy and a longtime friend of Taha Hussein. In his meeting with Hussein, Ibn ʿAshur asked to have the diplomas from al-Zaytuna and al-Khalduniyya recognized as equivalent to those from al-Azhar, to encourage Tunisian students to come to al-Azhar for their graduate studies. An agreement on that issue was to be announced, and his wish to have Egypt send professors was quickly granted. On his return to Tunisia, he announced that three Egyptian professors would arrive at al-Zaytuna to teach philosophy, history, and geography. He also declared that an arrangement had been made with al-Azhar for an exchange of books between Tunis and Cairo. In a meeting with students, he expressed his wish to create an official bureau in Cairo that would represent al-Zaytuna throughout the entire Mashriq. It would support Tunisian students in Cairo and strengthen ties between al-Zaytuna and Egypt. Immediately following this visit, Tunisian students in Cairo announced the creation of the Association des Étudiants Nord-Africains.[76] Alarmed by these developments, the French minister of foreign affairs authorized the French resident-general in Tunis to delay issuing visas to the Egyptian professors in question.[77]

In the meantime, Taha Hussein was not wasting time. On January 28, 1951, the Egyptian Council of Ministers approved his request to send four professors to al-Zaytuna to teach science, mathematics, English, and geography. The Egyptian government doubled their salaries and added an inflation subsidy amounting to 40 percent of their basic salary. Egypt would also cover the expenses of their trips with their families to and from Tunis, as was customary with other Egyptian teachers on missions to Syria and Lebanon.[78] In his memorandum, Hussein stressed that the Ministry of Public Instruction was keen on promoting closer cultural cooperation between Egypt and Tunisia.[79]

Trying to make sense of Taha Hussein's agenda for North Africa, some French circles suspected Great Britain was encouraging him. In February 1950, the minister of France in Syria wrote to the French embassy in Egypt suggesting that Egypt was having problems establishing its influence over members of the Arab League, so it was now turning to the Maghrib. In his last visit to Cairo, Britain's then foreign secretary, Ernest Bevin, clarified that Great Britain would continue to run its own policies in the Mashriq and would keep its army in the Suez Canal Zone but would not mind if Egypt directed its influence westward. That could explain not only the demands made by Egypt's minister of public instruction for opening Egyptian schools in North Africa but also the Egyptian Freemasonry's request to the Masonic lodges in France to allow the creation of lodges in North Africa reporting directly to Egypt.[80] A stronger Egyptian economic influence in North Africa was expected too. With this policy, the British hoped Egypt would play a stronger role in defending the Mediterranean against any Bolshevik expansion.[81]

A few weeks into his ministerial position, Taha Hussein did not soften his demands as the French had hoped, and the official confrontation happened sooner than they had anticipated. On March 7, 1950, the French ambassador in Cairo wrote to Paris that "the step taken a few days ago by Dr. Taha Hussein, the minister of public instruction, with the advisor of this Embassy, raises for the first time, in an *official manner*, the question of an Egyptian presence in North Africa."[82] In his meeting with the ambassador, Hussein had insisted on more substantial cultural exchanges with Tunisia, Algeria, and Morocco, and he raised the question of the restrictions imposed by the French authorities on the circulation of Egyptian publications there. He also expressed his wish to open, by the following October, an Egyptian secondary school in Tangier, along with a cultural center and a library.[83] The ambassador predicted that Hussein would not stop at this and would soon ask for similar establishments in Algiers, Tunis, and Rabat: "The question currently being asked in a hesitant and limited manner could quickly escalate," he warned. Nothing, he continued, would stop Hussein from carrying out his project, for this had become a question of prestige to him, and he would not hesitate to deprive some local facilities of what they needed in order to ensure the success of his project in North Africa. With the Egyptian academic missions in the Arab Mashriq, and with specialists graduating from al-Azhar and from the Ministry of Public Instruction every year, the project, concluded the ambassador, was entirely feasible.

Continuing his assessment of the Egyptian position, the French ambassador explained that Egypt was experiencing what he described as "an intense intellectual life expanding with its growing population and accumulated wealth." He argued that although Egypt should focus first on the needs of its own population, being the center of the Arab world, it had a natural tendency, especially under the current government, to extend its influence outside its borders. When asked who these schools were for, as there were hardly any Egyptian students in Tangier, Hussein had replied: "If there are no Egyptians in Tangier, there are at least Arabs and Muslims, and it is our right to educate them." To speak of an "Egyptian right to educate" was a clear indication for the ambassador that Egypt's goal was to extend its influence over the entire Arab world. It was also a way for that nation to deal with what he described as an inferiority that the Egyptians felt with respect to France and other European countries operating prestigious schooling networks in Egypt while Egypt was denied a similar role in countries with which it shared both religion and language.

During the meeting, Taha Hussein made no open threats. On the contrary, the ambassador praised the subtlety and cleverness of Hussein's negotiating style, highlighting that Hussein's choice of Tangier was not haphazard. Given that Tangier was an international zone at the time, Egyptians hoped France would be more vulnerable there than elsewhere, and they favored a setting in which they could play one international power against another. The ambassador also described Hussein's approach as very courteous but precise. That Hussein negotiated in place of the Egyptian minister of foreign affairs (known for his impulsiveness) also did not go unnoticed by the French. Furthermore, given Hussein's famous ties with France, the Egyptians were tugging the cord of traditional Franco-Egyptian friendship. Several Wafdist ministers repeated to the French ambassador on many occasions that choosing Hussein as minister of public instruction was proof of the friendship the Wafd felt for France.

The ambassador stressed that Taha Hussein did not want to use the proposed institute to stir political unrest in North Africa, nor was he under the influence of

North African nationalists in Cairo.[84] This became clear later during the second Arab Conference on Culture, held in Alexandria in August 1950. No delegations from North Africa were invited, and when North Africans present in other capacities tried to raise the issue of sending Egyptian cultural missions to countries under French control, Hussein stopped the discussion, saying it was not on the agenda, and adding that from his experience with what he called "the French mentality," it would be easier to accomplish this through diplomacy rather than a series of resolutions.[85] The French ambassador believed the French government might be able to buy some time, but eventually it would have to deal with Hussein's initiatives. "We are facing a well thought-out and precise move from the Egyptian government," he concluded.[86]

The French Disagree over Where to Host an Egyptian Institute

On learning that the Egyptian government had allocated LE 20,000 for the creation of the Egyptian institute in Tangier, the authorities in Spanish-Morocco and the French protectorate in Morocco decided to act.[87] They feared that Egypt wanted this institute to become a de facto center for the Arab League in Morocco, and a hub for nationalist agitation led by Emir Muhammad Ibn ʿAbd al-Karim al-Khattabi, the well-known Moroccan political and military leader. ʿAbd al-Karim had fought the Spanish and French forces in northern Morocco in the early 1920s and achieved some remarkable victories. After his defeat by the French, he was exiled and eventually sought political asylum in Egypt in 1947. Consequently, the two governments asked the comité du contrôle for Tangier, chaired by the United States, to deny Egypt permission to create such an institute, on the grounds that existing treaties forbade any political or social agitation in the international zone. The Egyptians had also expressed their wish to open a consulate in Tangier, which required permission from both Sultan Muhammad V and the French resident-general of Morocco, Alphonse-Pierre Juin. The refusal of the latter would surely have damaged Franco-Egyptian relations, at a time when Egypt was threatening to close the French establishments in Egypt in response.[88] The French authorities therefore decided to stall and wait for an opportunity to shift the project away from Tangier to the regions they controlled more directly in North Africa. That moment came with the incident mentioned earlier of the Egyptian journalists whom the French accused of political agitation.

Sensing the difficulty of establishing his institute in Tangier, Hussein turned his attention to Morocco's capital, Rabat. In May 1951, Resident-General Juin declared his firm opposition to Hussein's request. Juin argued that having an

Egyptian institute in Rabat in the way proposed by Hussein meant Egyptian citizens would be given permission to stay and move around freely in the French-controlled zone of Morocco. This implied granting Egypt undeniable privileges, making the continued refusal of Egyptian consular services in that zone increasingly difficult. Juin informed Paris that the local press in Morocco had republished an interview with Hussein in which he had declared that Egypt would retaliate against the French establishments in Egypt if the French government did not authorize the Egyptian institute in Rabat. Juin expressed his discomfort and wanted to know how to confront what he described as Hussein's "blackmail."[89] His own suggestion was to shift Hussein's idea to Algeria, which, unlike the protectorates of Tunisia and Morocco, was then considered French soil, "a sovereign land," as the resident-general described it in his report.[90] However, having shifted the location of the future institute away from internationally administered Tangier to French-controlled territories, the French then disagreed among themselves as to where they could have more control over the institute.

Sensing the French elusiveness, Taha Hussein made a statement on June 7, 1951, that was duly communicated the next day to Paris. He wanted to redefine the nature of Franco-Egyptian cultural relations.

> It is time that the cultural relations between France and Egypt become based on reciprocity. The two countries are joined together by a traditional friendship. Yet, by nature, friendship is reciprocal. Its outcomes need to be, too. That is why I asked for and received in May last year France's support to create a Farouk I Institute for Arab Culture in Tangier. . . . Seeing that Tangier had become a center for political activity and wanting to raise culture above any suspicion, I asked that our Institute be founded in Rabat. I have not yet been told no, nor have I been told yes. That is why I have approached our French friends, informing them that the Institut Français d'Archéologie Orientale and all the excavations currently being undertaken by the French learned societies could suffer from this ambiguity.[91]

Four months later, in September 1951, the French Council of Ministers approved the creation of an Egyptian institute in Algiers. The institute would, however, neither provide education nor become a space for public discussions; it would be a place only for scholars or archaeologists to engage in scientific research, like the IFAO or the French institutes in Rome and Athens. The number of visiting scholars would be limited to four at a time. A library would be created, but it would be restricted to the visiting guests.[92] To minimize any inconvenience, the institute would not be authorized to carry out any public activity. The Egyptian government agreed to these conditions and requested copies of the regulations governing the roles of the French archaeological institutes in Cairo, Rome, and Athens to help with writing the statutes of the Egyptian one in Algiers. Taha Hussein assured the French embassy in Cairo that once ready, these statutes would be communicated to the French government for its approval.[93]

Yet, the Egyptians continued to sense French reluctance to move forward with their promises, especially when they stalled on issuing a visa for Yahya al-Khashshab, nominated by Taha Hussein to become the future director of the Egyptian institute in Algiers. Speaking to the French ambassador, Hussein reiterated Egypt's commitment not to stir political unrest in North Africa or directly threaten French interests in Egypt. He informed him, however, that al-Khashshab would not go to Paris, as requested by the French government, without a complete understanding of the French intentions toward the institute. Hussein, according to the French ambassador in his report to Paris, was mistrustful, and nothing would make him change his mind. The ambassador suggested that the French government stall the project by other means, rather than directly refusing al-Khashshab's visa, which Hussein would surely interpret as putting the entire project on hold.[94]

This time, it was the governor-general of Algeria, Marcel-Edmond Naegelen, who refused categorically to have al-Khashshab on his territory. He believed the institute was a threat, and he preferred to have it situated in Tunisia instead. He believed the French position there was weaker, whereas in Algeria there was still hope for what he described as "a definitive assimilation" of the local population. The director of the Africa Division in the French Ministry of Foreign Affairs was opposed to the position of the governor-general, arguing that anything happening in Morocco or Tunisia would have immediate repercussions in Algeria and that it would be easier to control such an institute in a "large, very French city, like Algiers." As a result of these internal squabbles among the French, the issue was pushed up to the French Council of Ministers.[95]

Al-Khashshab, according to a French intelligence report, was the ideal man for the position, and if creating the institute had been strictly cultural, he would have had no problem getting his visa. Al-Khashshab was Professor of Persian at Fouad I University and had obtained his doctorate from the Sorbonne. His friendship with many renowned French scholars, such as Henri Massé, Louis Massignon, and Évariste Lévi-Provençal, was certainly expected to facilitate his task in Algiers. French professors and the Dominicans working in Egypt

Taha Hussein Strikes Back

Finally, Hussein took what the French ambassador described as "shocking measures" against French excavations in Egypt.[97] In November 1951, he suspended all permits for scientific work given to the French missions working in Egypt, and Egyptian representatives abroad were instructed to refuse the majority of visa applications by French personalities coming to Egypt on cultural missions. These measures impacted the work done by the IFAO as well as the excavations committee, stopping the missions working in Dayr al-Madina and Karnak. Moreover, the heads of these missions were evicted from the houses they occupied on the archaeological sites. The arrival in Egypt of other French archaeologists was cancelled, and intended work in Tanis, Saqqara, and Darat Manfalut was suspended. Similarly, an important medical team planning to come to Egypt saw their trip cancelled as the Egyptian authorities refused to grant them entry visas.[98] In December, Hussein told the daily *al-Ahram* that he was doing his best to ensure that France stopped obstructing the creation of the institute in Algiers, warning that "if France persists in its attitude, [he would] adopt a similar attitude toward the French Institute in Cairo and the French teachers in Egypt."[99] He gave similar statements to the daily *Le Progrès Egyptien*, signaling the escalation of his dispute with France by using the Egyptian press to involve the public.

After Hussein's actions, the French ambassador considered speaking to King Farouk. Although the ambassador knew the king disapproved of Hussein's measures, he was unsure whether Farouk could intervene in France's favor, owing to the tension between the king and the Wafd government. The ambassador believed addressing French concerns with the Egyptian minister of foreign affairs would not help either, finally concluding that the problem could only be resolved with Hussein himself.[100]

Following the events of what came to be known as Black Saturday, on January 26, 1952, during which riots and fire destroyed much of downtown Cairo's commercial center, King Farouk dismissed the Wafd cabinet, and Taha Hussein left office.[101] After his exit, however, the cabinets that followed were unwilling to revoke any of the measures he had taken. The Algiers institute had become

Endorsed his deep attachment to France, describing him as a loyal Muslim without "fanaticism." More importantly, they confirmed that al-Khashshab "always kept himself away from any political activity."[96] Hussein had nominated a director whose credentials the French could not fault.

a matter of Egyptian prestige, and successive ministers could not lose face. On May 2, 1952, *al-Ahram* announced that the Egyptian Ministry of Public Instruction had asked the Egyptian embassy in Paris to stop giving visas to French teachers and professors until the French government had issued the entry visas to Algeria required by the future director of the Egyptian institute and other personnel.[102] In June 1952, the Egyptian minister of foreign affairs explained to the French ambassador that the current government was not inclined to reverse any of the measures taken by the previous Wafd government, because they were sure Taha Hussein would attack them heavily in the press and turn public opinion against them. The minister insisted the problem of the Algiers institute had to be resolved. The French ambassador reported to Paris that "the case of the Algiers institute continues to embarrass our relationship with Egypt. The return to power of a more nationalist government risks changing this embarrassment into tension."[103] However, following the Egyptian army coup on July 23, 1952, the French Ministry of Foreign Affairs decided to wait for the Egyptian government to raise the issue again, as those who had envisaged the creation of the Egyptian cultural institute in North Africa were no longer in power.[104]

Conclusion

Taha Hussein's conflict with the French authorities over the establishment of Egyptian institutes in the Maghrib shows that Egypt's interest in the Arab world before Nasser came to power was not limited to the Mashriq. Going beyond the influence of periodicals, films, and theater productions, the Egyptian government pushed for a more official presence in French-controlled North Africa in the form of cultural institutes. Confident in the expertise of its scholars, and proud of its educational and cultural institutions—not only al-Azhar but also modern institutions like the Arabic Language Academy and Egyptian universities—Egypt considered it had the wealth and technical expertise necessary to position itself as the guardian of Arabic and Islamic studies. After signing the Anglo-Egyptian Treaty in 1936, Egyptian officials like Taha Hussein developed an expansive cultural diplomacy and saw it as integral to what they believed was Egypt's leadership in the Arab world.

The French authorities feared that Egypt's cultural institutes would undermine their control of the Maghrib. While they wanted their long-standing cultural mission in Egypt to continue uninterrupted after the ending of their capitulatory privileges, they also saw Egypt's rising cultural influence as a threat, and they therefore opposed any official Egyptian presence in North Africa. They considered shifting their cooperation with Egypt to science, a field in which they believed Egyptians would appreciate their support and in return be dissuaded from pursuing a North African agenda. In their dealings with Hussein, the French took into account his popularity and that of the Wafd government, and therefore decided to stall his projects instead of directly refusing them. As Hussein resorted to the press, the conflict escalated and became a matter of public concern. Neither King Farouk nor the subsequent cabinets could reverse Hussein's measures against the French without losing face.

On the surface, Hussein's insistence that his projects were only cultural seems to agree with his published ideas about the "universality of culture," and how it should transcend political gains. This does not mean, however, that Hussein's decisions as minister were not political. For him, the promotion of culture over politics was a supremely political strategy. He was aware that Egypt, not yet fully independent, could not stand up to the colonial powers. His framing of Egypt's wish to exercise a stronger role in North Africa in terms of scientific exchange and cultural reciprocity allowed a request the French could not dismiss out of hand. It was a language they understood, and which they used themselves to justify the operation of their own schools and cultural institutions in Egypt and elsewhere. As a result, Hussein's careful and precise demands caused confusion among French decision makers in Paris, Rabat, Tunis, and Algiers. The French could not resort to their usual tactic—of claiming they were protecting North Africa from political agitators—once Hussein insisted that the proposed North African institute was for cultural purposes only and that it would be built along the lines of the French institutes already operating in Athens, Rome, and Cairo.

Yet, culture was never *strictly* cultural. Faithful to a career-long tradition of resigning whenever he felt his judgment was questioned, after another minister challenged the utility of these cultural institutes and antagonizing the French, Hussein submitted his resignation to the prime minister on October 1, 1951. In this resignation, which Mustafa al-Nahhas immediately refused, the indignant Hussein wrote:

> It is my honor to send to your Excellency my resignation from my post in the ministry after the valuable lesson that I learned from one of my colleagues. He taught me humility and convinced me I was not fit for my position as minister, for I am only good at trivialities like the creation of useless institutes.
>
> I see no harm if the council listened to the opinion of my honorable colleague and stopped the plans for the Institute in Algiers, as well as shut down

the Madrid Institute, the Muhammad Ali Chair in the Institut d'Études Méditerranéennes in Nice, and the Arabic Language Chair at the University of Athens. These are all trivialities that can neither fight off colonialism nor achieve the independence of the Arab nations.[105]

Hussein, with his usual sarcasm, thus revealed in his resignation letter the long-term anti-colonial goal of his institutes, in which the line between the cultural and the political fades completely.

Hussein's published work has led many scholars to believe he was interested only in culture and that this (supposed) exclusive attention to culture was an indication of his having been "seduced" by what scholars have assumed he considered to be a "superior French culture." Yet, this hitherto unstudied conflict with the French authorities reveals that Hussein was very conscious of the political impact of the culture he was trying to promote, and of the unequal power relations dominating these cultural exchanges. It is only through closely examining the details of his disputes with the French over the establishment of the Egyptian institute in the Maghrib that this very political Hussein emerges. In other words, it is important to look carefully at what he tried to do, rather than relying on assumptions drawn from his published work about what he believed. That published work can be read quite differently when examined alongside his actions.

2 *NAHDA* GOES TO UNIVERSITY

Taha Hussein and the Mission
of the Private Egyptian University

> Egypt will not rise and attain the modern civilization it seeks, while preserving its character and dignity, unless it knows its past, revives it and connects it to its present. From the past and the present, it can then adopt the right disposition, which becomes the basis for a good life that neither dissolves in the old and ossifies, nor dissolves in the new and strays....
> Only the Faculty of Arts can lead Egypt to achieving these goals.
>
> Taha Hussein[1]

ALTHOUGH TAHA HUSSEIN did not participate in the early stages of the *nahda*, he shared many *nahdawi* concerns with the Arabic language, classical *adab*, and the importance of a humanist education. Early *nahdawi* intellectuals believed that cultural reform was necessary to face what they perceived to be a more advanced civilization in the west, and one with an active colonialist agenda. Hussein was convinced that the secular university was the only institution capable of undertaking such a task. He had returned from France with his doctoral degree in the aftermath of the 1919 revolution and immediately started teaching in the Faculty of Arts at the private Egyptian University. A key moment in modern Egyptian history, the revolution triggered a series of events culminating in Egypt's nominal independence from Great Britain in 1922. For Hussein, the university was to lead the way toward a proper democratic life and full independence. Chapter 3 unpacks Hussein's project for culture and education in more detail; this chapter shows first how that project intersected with the *nahda* and was a continuation of its legacy.

To explain this continuity, I turn to the history of the private Egyptian University that existed from 1908 to 1925. While most historical accounts have focused on celebrating the transformation of the private university into a full-fledged state institution in 1925, this chapter shifts the focus back to the early years of the university, when it was completely independent from the state. Those early years were more than a passing phase that found its conclusion in the creation of the state university. The private university was a crucial endeavor in and of itself, and it left an unmistakable mark on the future of Egypt's higher education. During those early days, the founders of the university raised important questions about the role of a university education, why a new humanities program was essential to the nation, the steps required to create such a program of studies, and how to teach it. These early discussions determined the intellectual mission not only of the private university but also of the future state university, which later became the leading university in Egypt and the model for other Egyptian and Arab state universities.[2] I show how these decisions internalized some of the *nahda*'s central tenets prescribing cultural reform in terms of two interrelated tasks: reviving classical *adab* humanism and at the same time integrating the sophisticated accomplishments of western civilization. The university founders believed the institution's role was to "revive" the Arab scholar, who had once impressed the west with his knowledge and abilities. Taha Hussein would not only become the prime example of such a scholar but would also remain committed to this mission throughout his long career as an intellectual, a university professor, and a senior civil servant. Recognizing this commitment helps us to better understand the complexity of his intellectual outlook and his actions.

Furthermore, I argue that the private university was not only the institution where Hussein received his secular education and where he started teaching upon his return from France but also where he formed his views on the quintessential role he felt the state had to play in the fields of culture and education. While most historical accounts have focused on the financial difficulties the university faced, and that led to its acquisition by the state, these accounts have paid little attention to the challenges posed by the new type of education the university was offering. Students were unfamiliar with studying the humanities as a program in and of themselves, and in the absence of official government recognition of university diplomas, such a program of studies proved unattractive. The short turbulent life of the private university convinced Hussein that the humanist education advocated by *nahdawis* was not an economically viable project and could not survive without state support. The question of how to regulate the state role in culture and education posed a serious challenge for him and became an integral part of his project, as the next chapter illustrates in more detail.

In the Footsteps of Early *Nahdawis*

Taha Hussein's calls for a stronger institutional role in the fields of public instruction and culture were in the tradition of the early *nahdawis*. In his recent work on the Arab *nahda*, intellectual historian Abdulrazzak Patel examines the leading reformers of the nineteenth century and stresses their agreement on the importance of education and learning for any proposed reform—whether social, cultural, or political. Patel shows how Azharite scholars like Rifaʿa al-Tahtawi, Husayn al-Marsafi, Husayn al-Jisr, and Muhammad ʿAbduh not only advocated the introduction of modern secular knowledge in schools but also promoted teaching the classical *adab* tradition and the Islamic sciences. Through this humanist education, Patel argues:

> [These reformers wanted to] reproduce the literary legacy and moral philosophy of the Arab classical period in an attempt to foster the virtues of character suitable for an active life of public service among their subjects. They wanted to produce citizens who would not only be able to speak and write with eloquence and clarity, but also possess wisdom and learning and who would be endowed with a sense of duty to the community and state.[3]

To accomplish these goals, all four of these reformers were active in educational institutions, although these schools eventually closed down or resisted the proposed reform: al-Tahtawi in the School of Languages, al-Jisr in al-Madrasa al-Wataniyya al-Islamiyya in Tripoli, ʿAbduh in al-Azhar, and al-Marsafi in al-Azhar and Dar al-ʿUlum.[4]

In his discussion, Patel proposes using humanism as a way of considering *nahdawi* legacies. Using scholarly work on humanism by Paul Oskar Kristeller, George Makdisi, Edward Said, and others, Patel concludes that *adab* humanism, in which all these reformers were interested, "was a characteristic and pervasive intellectual current of medieval Arab-Islamic culture."[5] Kristeller had defined humanism as a program of studies centered on grammar, rhetoric, poetry, history, and moral philosophy. Although Kristeller and others argued that humanism originated in Renaissance Italy, George Makdisi demonstrated that practices of humanism started in the Muslim world two centuries earlier—debunking the idea that Arab-Islamic scholarship was only a passive link between antiquity and the renaissance. He showed that the major fields of humanism defined by Kristeller as *studia humanitatis* were all included within the term *adab*, and Makdisi argued that they could therefore be referred to as *studia adabiyya*. These fields include grammar (*nahw*) and lexicography (*lugha*), poetry (*shiʿr*), rhetoric (*khataba*), history (*tarikh, akhbar*), and moral philosophy (*ʿilm al-akhlaq*).[6] Patel then contends that to acquire a deeper understanding of humanism within the context of the *nahda*, scholars should consider elements of the European

Renaissance and *adab* humanism together.⁷ He identifies some of these essential humanist elements as follows: "The underlying motive [of humanism] must be preservation and purity of language from external influence; the concept of eloquence, seeking substance in the classical or distant past, derivative methodology, and eclecticism and many-sidedness."⁸ These issues, as discussed in the next chapter, were of prime concern to Taha Hussein, and employing this humanist lens allows us to consider Hussein's complex intellectual outlook in a different light. The usual binary of modernist/traditionalist, for example, accounts for neither his serious engagement with classical *adab* and his fierce defense of classical Arabic against colloquial usage nor his work at the university creating chairs; locating, editing, and publishing old Arab-Islamic manuscripts; and also trying to render classical *adab* more accessible to his contemporaries. Ibrahim Abu Rabiʿ is an example of a scholar who uses this misleading binary to classify Hussein and other intellectuals, such as ʿAli ʿAbd al-Raziq, Farah Antun, Yaʿqub Sarruf, and Salama Musa, as Arab modernists focused on the future and content to forgo tradition. Similarly, Zaki Badawi has described Muslim secularists, such as Hussein, as willing to follow the European path in nearly all aspects of life.⁹ But as Patel rightly points out, these intellectuals held a variety of views on a range of issues and cannot be reduced to these simplistic categories.¹⁰

Furthermore, the lens of humanism allows us to see important continuities between Hussein and earlier *nahdawi* figures, such as Husayn al-Marsafi (1815–1890) and Muhammad ʿAbduh (1849–1905). Many years before Hussein, both of these scholars wanted to disseminate humanist education, believing it was necessary for the "revival" of the Arabic language and literature. Marsafi, in particular, is mostly remembered as the first teacher of Arabic rhetoric and literature. Like Hussein, he received a solid religious education, first at the *kuttab* then at al-Azhar, where he started working as a teacher of the Arabic language. Then in 1872, he moved to the newly opened school of Dar al-ʿUlum, where he taught the Arabic linguistic disciplines.¹¹ Marsafi is famous for having promoted the study of Arabic literature by gathering the lectures he gave at Dar al-ʿUlum and publishing them in his masterpiece, *al-Wasila al-Adabiyya ila al-ʿUlum al-ʿArabiyya*, which influenced generations of Egyptian poets and a new generation of Azharite scholars.¹² He was able to lecture on literature more freely at Dar al-ʿUlum than at al-Azhar, which, despite offering courses on rhetoric, provided no courses on literature, considering them frivolous.¹³

Similarly, Muhammad ʿAbduh in attending to educational reform proposed courses that combined *adab* humanism with existing religious instruction and called for the inclusion of modern history, sciences, and languages in the curriculum.[14] However, his attempts to reform the curriculum at al-Azhar were met with fierce opposition from both Azharites and Khedive Abbas II, who accused him of "wanting to turn al-Azhar into an institution of philosophy and literary education bent on extinguishing the light of Islam," an accusation in response to which 'Abduh resigned in 1905.[15] It is not surprising, therefore, that 'Abduh supported the idea of creating a national secular university more open to humanist education.[16] His students, Sa'd Zaghlul (1859–1927), Lutfi al-Sayyid (1872–1963), and Qasim Amin (1863–1908), took on his call after his death, and created Egypt's first university that was entirely devoted to studying the humanities.

Patel concludes his study by making a distinction between those whom he refers to as "*nahda* humanists," like Sa'id and Rashid al-Shartuni, who engaged with their immediate past, and other *nahdawi* humanists who did not, like Ibrahim al-Yaziji, Muhammad 'Abduh, and others. He argues that the latter faced a different reality in which they had to confront not only ideas of "civilization and progress" coming from the west but also western nations' colonialist agenda. Their solution was to prescribe a reform based on "assimilating, through translation and adaptation, the great learning and achievements of western civilization, while simultaneously reviving the classical Arab culture that preceded the so-called centuries of 'decadence' and foreign domination."[17] Decades later, Taha Hussein took this call forward and insisted that only the secular university possessed the know-how required to engage seriously with implementing this solution.

A *Nahdawi* Institution: Creating a National Secular University

> "For strengthening the nation, the victory of the truth and the dignity of mankind."[18]

Scholars have recognized the impact of Cairo University on Egyptian society and its significant role in the making of modern Egypt. In his work of reference on the university, Donald Reid claims that the Universities of Paris, Harvard, Cambridge, and Oxford were never as vital on their national scenes as was the Egyptian University (later renamed to Fouad I University in 1940, and then Cairo University in 1953).[19] The early phase from 1908 to 1925, when the university was a private institution, stands out as a formative, experimental period. While historians see this period as having successfully prepared the ground for the new institution to develop into a mature state-owned institution, it was also rife with struggle and attempts by the university founders to enlist state recognition of the university without jeopardizing its independence. Their acquiescence to state acquisition was a last resort, accepted to avoid bankruptcy and the collapse of the entire project.

After an initial successful nationwide fundraising campaign, spearheaded by key nationalists and intellectuals, the private university was inaugurated in December 1908 in a grand ceremony attended by Prince Fouad surrounded by other dignitaries, commemorated in the photograph displayed here.[20] Convinced the university would produce Egyptian nationalists harboring anti-British sentiments, Britain's consul-general in Egypt, Lord Earl Cromer, had been opposed to the project, but his opposition only turned the struggle for building it into a national cause.[21] Yet, even after its creation, the university continued to be a hotbed of contestation among various political players in the country including political parties, the palace, and European powers. Frustrated with the overt politicization of students and the continued disruption of university life, Ahmad Lutfi al-Sayyid, president of the university (from 1925 to 1932 and from 1935 to 1941), resigned briefly from his post in 1937. In his resignation letter, he recorded his objection to the constant attempts by politicians to mobilize students along partisan lines, which, in his words, "damaged the bonds of fraternity among university students."[22] Moreover, within the walls of the university, Britain, initially

FIGURE 7. Inauguration of the Egyptian University, 1908.

opposed to the project, quickly started competing with France and Italy over programs of study, creation of chairs, and appointment of deans. The university quickly became a key political player in the country.

Historians have focused on how the university developed against this backdrop of political struggle. In their accounts, the private university figures as an inchoate structure, a rudimentary step on the road toward a mature university. As the private university faced severe financial and administrative problems, these historical accounts consider its acquisition by the Ministry of Public Instruction in 1925 as a laudable moment in the overall history of the university. Promises of stable funding, expansion of faculties, and recognition of diplomas were hailed as the necessary steps to save the university and help it fulfill its national mission. Historians have echoed what seemed to be a genuine relief at the time that state intervention had rescued the floundering institution, together with all the national hopes that had been placed on its success. For example, in his autobiography, *Qissat Hayati*, Ahmad Lutfi al-Sayyid (shown in a 1925 photograph on the next page, surrounded by faculty members, including Taha Hussein standing behind him) divided the history of the university into three phases: the "publicity phase" (*dawr al-diʿaya*), starting with the fundraising campaign; "the preparation phase" (*dawr al-tamhid*), in which the university sent educational missions to Europe and offered general lectures; and finally, the phase of "completeness" (*dawr al-tamam*), to be celebrated for the transformation of the private university into a state university.[23]

Although the university started off as an independent, private initiative, the seeds of government control had already been planted in those early days. The university founders saw no inherent contradiction in framing its intellectual mission as "seeking knowledge for knowledge's sake" while simultaneously trying to fulfill "the needs of the nation" for progress and independence. They identified one objective with the other, presumably because at this early stage the university alone was interpreting what it meant to be seeking knowledge for knowledge's sake. By emerging as the embodiment of a national cause, however, the university was placing itself in an uncomfortable relationship with the state. The decision in 1925 to appoint the minister of public instruction as the higher president and ultimate authority of the university was one in a series of steps that reflected the state's vested interest in defining what the "nation's needs" were and how the university was to fulfill those needs, especially as the university became financially dependent on the state. Over the years, state involvement became

FIGURE 8. Faculty members at the Egyptian University, 1925.

more pronounced, culminating in the creation of the Supreme Council of the Universities in 1954 and the Ministry of Higher Education in 1961.

Egyptian nationalists and academics hailed the creation of the national university as a cornerstone of the modern Egyptian nation-state. The famous Egyptian nationalist historian, Shafiq Ghurbal, for example, called for a reperiodization of the national movement so it would start with the creation of the university in 1908 and not with the 1919 revolution. Writing in 1950, he argued that the fight for the creation of the university had marked the beginning of the real fight for independence. Such a fight, he continued, initiated Egyptians into an education that had been foreclosed to them (by the British occupation), forcing them to search for it abroad. The university opened the "gates of knowledge" to Egyptians in Egypt, marking a revolution against a form of "slavery" that had been forced upon them and laying the proper groundwork for independence.[24]

Like Ghurbal, contemporary Egyptian historians continue to pay tribute to the role played by the university in the national struggle. Most accounts of the university start by taking a position in the battle over origins, that is, over whose idea it was first and who should get credit for it. This debate is important as it shows that most of the university's founders were either *nahdawi* figures or people who had direct connections with leading *nahdawi* reformers, such as Muhammad 'Abduh and Jirji Zaydan. Nationalist historians like Ahmad 'Abd al-Fattah Budayr, 'Abd al-Mun'im Ibrahim al-Dusuqi al-Jumay'i, and Yunan Labib Rizq start with Jirji Zaydan (1861–1914) as the first to have called for the creation of the university, followed by the Egyptian nationalist Mustafa Kamil (1874–1908). According to their accounts, students of Muhammad 'Abduh, like Sa'd Zaghlul, Lutfi al-Sayyid, and Qasim Amin, then took on the idea and implemented it. Contemporary historians, like Samia Ibrahim and Amina Hijazi, go further back in time to Yacoub Artin (1842–1919), who had an idea for creating a college-university when he was minister of public instruction, which he advocated in his 1893 book on education in Egypt.[25] Artin's idea was to appoint an academic president for the existing higher schools of medicine, engineering, and others, in order to transition them into colleges.[26] Historian 'Ali Barakat, however, credits 'Ali Mubarak (1823–1893) with creating something akin to a university by grouping all higher schools of education in the palace of Darb al-Jamamiz when he became head of Diwan al-Madaris, in 1868.[27] Hasan Nasr al-Din and Amina Hijazi trace all these attempts to Muhammad Ali's changes and the creation of a modern state to serve his army following the French campaign of 1798. The road to the university, Nasr al-Din concludes, took a hundred years.[28] Despite minor differences, these accounts agree that the *real* university took off and started to reach its potential with the creation of the state university in 1925.

The university's origins and the role it was expected to play in the fight for independence were the subject of much political debate among the university founders themselves. Mustafa Kamil, for example, objected during a trip to Europe that the first administrative meeting under the leadership of Sa'd Zaghlul had taken place in his absence, as Kamil saw himself as the initiator of the idea and thought its implementation should have happened under his supervision.[29] Kamil was sidestepped to appease the British, who feared his radical nationalist politics. He had created a club for students of the higher colleges in 1905, and this could have antagonized the British even further. Kamil and his National Party openly refused to deal with the British until Egypt's full independence, and Kamil was in favor of realigning Egypt with the Ottomans.[30] In 1906, *The Times* was glad Kamil did not get credit for the idea, and *The Globe* was worried he might find a way of controlling the university and subjecting it to the influence of his National Party.[31]

Muhammad 'Abduh's students were equally keen on realizing their mentor's idea for the creation of a secular university. One of those students, the well-known journalist Muhammad Rashid Rida, wrote that 'Abduh's students decided that creating a college associated with his name would be the best means of keeping his memory alive.[32] Rida was interested in the project but wanted the university to offer courses on religion.[33] Sa'd Zaghlul and other 'Abduh students started a fundraising campaign of which Zaghlul was in charge, and he hosted the first university committee meeting in his house on October 12, 1906. The committee was composed of twenty-six members, including Zaghlul and Qasim Amin, who were joined by Muhammad Farid from the National Party.[34]

Jirji Zaydan's *al-Hilal* supported the fundraisers and reminded readers that Zaydan had been the first to call for the creation of a national university, out of his belief that "creating such a university would be an important milestone in the history of the *nahda*." In the style of the day, the article went on to say that "hopes are tied to [the university] and eyes are fixed on it."[35] While western Orientalists were invited to teach at the new university without hesitation, Zaydan was denied the teaching of a course on Islamic history in 1910 because the University Council was worried about the public reaction to having an Arab Christian teaching Islamic history. Zaydan, who had already prepared his course lectures, was utterly disappointed.[36]

When Sa'd Zaghlul resigned as head of the committee in 1906—to accept his new appointment by Cromer as minister of public instruction—another of 'Abduh's students, Qasim Amin, took over that role.[37] Predicting that the university would run into political and financial obstacles, the founders hoped royal patronage would give the university more political weight and open locked doors. The university committee (which gave way to the administrative council in 1908) thus intentionally left the president's position empty, hoping a member of the Royal Family would agree to occupy it. The committee wrote to Prince Fouad on December 22, 1907, asking if he would accept the position, which he did.[38]

The choice of Prince, later King, Fouad (r. 1917–1936), made sense given his connections and his wish to be seen as an enlightened patron carrying on the legacy of his father, Khedive Ismail (r. 1863–1879). Until the declaration of the Republic in 1953, Fouad was considered the patron-father of the university, and it was by official decree in 1940 that the university was renamed Fouad I University. Fouad used his friendship with European dignitaries, like Italy's Victor Emmanuel and others, to recruit some of Europe's most famous Orientalists to teach at the new university. The Egyptian National Archives (Dar al-Watha'iq al-Qawmiyya) have a folder of correspondence between the prince and various Orientalists and universities in Europe, in French and Italian, arranging the details of their teaching assignments in Cairo. In a speech he gave to the University Council on March 15, 1911, Fouad reminded the council how he had managed to recruit the Orientalists Ignazio Guidi (1834–1935) and Carlo Nellino (1872–1938), and how he had written to the government of the German Emperor William II requesting that the Orientalist Enno Littman (1875–1958) teach in Cairo: "With this, we managed to bring to the first literary college created in our days in the Muslim World a professor whose worth scientists know, [and who is] versed in the origins of Semitic languages."[39] Fouad's name and connections also helped the university receive sizeable donations from the governments of France, Italy, Germany, Russia, and Romania.[40] He personally supervised the educational missions and the organization of student life in Europe, strengthened cooperation with several European universities and made sure the new Egyptian University was invited to participate in some of the events organized by other universities in Europe.[41] During his term, donations and waqfs (endowments) from rich Egyptians were made, and they dwindled after his resignation from the post on May 20, 1913. Fouad's connections also ensured that the university library received thousands of books donated by various universities and governments in Europe, in addition to books from the private collections of members of the royal family and others in Egypt.[42]

Although the difficult political and financial contexts in which the university was created pushed the university founders to seek royal patronage, the royal weight came at a price. The future king, as time would reveal, was tough-minded and impatient with opposition, even within the University Council, forcing two of the council members, Ahmad Zaki and Ibrahim Najib, to resign due to their disagreement with his policies.[43] More importantly, despite his early reassurances that the university would remain independent, when Fouad became king of the newly independent Egypt (1922), he did not try to help the struggling private university get back on its feet so it could work on its own terms. Instead, he encouraged the creation of a state university, under the presidency of the minister of public instruction, signaling the end of the private initiative. As historian Yunan Labib Rizq argues, when the intention of the government to build a state university, including a new Faculty of Arts, was announced, the existing university knew it could never compete, and in Rizq's words, it raised "the white flag."[44]

Studying the Humanities: Knowledge for Knowledge's Sake?

Despite the tense political context in which the private university was born, all the inauguration speeches and official communiqués stressed that the mission of the new university was the pursuit of "knowledge for knowledge's sake." The university was to focus on teaching the humanities, to compensate for the dedication of the existing higher colleges to the practical sciences, such as medicine and engineering. The university founders argued that just as the country needed doctors and engineers, it also needed thinkers and intellectuals.

During the official inauguration of the Egyptian University in 1908, Prince Fouad had announced that the purpose of building the university was "to have, in Cairo itself, a center of high culture that would spare young Egyptians the trouble of going abroad to complete their intellectual training."[45] The university was to be the institution responsible for defining this high culture and providing the training necessary for acquiring it. Members of the University Council echoed the same vision for the university. For a sumptuous dinner on April 18, 1908, given by Hasan Bey Zayid in honor of the new university, the guests were taken on the Nile in two steamboats from downtown Cairo to Zayid's large estate in Munufiyya. There were one hundred and sixty guests in total, including Prince Fouad, members of the University Council, journalists, and lawyers.[46] Qasim Amin gave a speech in which he argued that Egypt desperately needed such a project to address the huge shortage in thinkers, whom the nation required to lead public opinion, especially since the current system of education was tailored to produce only government employees. He called on Egyptians to support this new initiative.

> We hope to see among our compatriots a community that seeks knowledge out of love for the truth, and out of eagerness to discover the unknown, a community whose principle would be to learn for the sake of learning. We wish to see among the children of Egypt, as we see in other countries, a scientist who is aware of all human sciences, and a specialist who has specialized in a specific branch of science dedicating himself to cover everything that is associated with it. [We wish to see] a philosopher who has earned a wide fame, a writer whose name has become known to the whole world, and a scientist whose opinion is sought and who becomes an authority to turn to when solving problems. These are the leaders of public opinion in other nations, who guide [these nations'] success, and direct their progress. In their absence, they are replaced by ignorant advisors and humbugs.[47]

Similarly, to explain to the public the mission of the new university and the importance of the humanities, a communiqué from the university was distributed to several newspapers explaining that existing higher education in Egypt—in law, medicine, and mathematics—had so far targeted practical subjects, and its graduates sought this type of education only to secure jobs as lawyers, doctors, or engineers. "Given that the purpose of a university," the communiqué went on, "is much more noble than this practical need," the university committee decided that the university would do its best to instill in people the desire to "seek knowledge for knowledge's sake."[48]

Trying to legitimize "seeking knowledge for knowledge's sake," the university founders argued that such had been the approach to learning in the early days of Islam (*sadr al-Islam*) and was still the approach followed by the "more advanced" nations of Japan and the west. They believed that for Egypt to revive its "old glory" and attain the desired "civilization," the university must introduce types of knowledge that had not yet received enough attention in the country, such as history, art, literature, and the higher sciences. According to the communiqué, these were the subjects that had helped the advanced nations of Europe, America, and Japan rise to "glory and power." Therefore, the university founders reasoned, if Egypt were to become an advanced nation, the path was clear:

> All nations, when they decide to adopt the means necessary for their awakening (*nahda*), have no option but to do the same as the peoples that have acquired the most advanced civilization. History has shown the result of such an approach: the Greeks have taken from the ancient Egyptians, and the Arabs from the Greeks during the Abbasid era, and the Europeans from the Arabs during their renaissance, and the Americans and the Japanese took from the Europeans.[49]

In terms of logistics, creating connections with European universities was to start by hiring European professors and training Egyptian ones. The priority was therefore to train qualified professors who had to be prepared to teach in Arabic, and the first step was to send them on educational missions to Europe. There, they could spend all the time necessary to "receive the highest degree in the branch of knowledge in which they are to specialize." The regulations indicated that half the students on missions would study the arts, and the other half would study the sciences.[50] As for destinations, the inauguration communiqué stated that these students would learn the literary arts from "the two great nations whose languages have spread the most among Egyptians": that is to say, France and Britain. Such training, the communiqué went on, was the only means by which students could become "saturated with modern methods." After receiving sufficient training, they would then apply these modern methods to "dig into the treasures written in the Arabic language."[51]

As for the internal organization of the university, Fouad was ambitious. Unsatisfied with general courses, he wanted a proper Faculty of Arts. Due to budgetary and logistical reasons, such as not having enough trained professors or textbooks in Arabic, the university started with a few mandatory courses: History of the Ancient East, Philology of Semitic Languages, Geography and Ethnography, History of Philosophical Doctrines, Arab Philosophy, History of the Muslim Peoples, and Arabic Literature. Students were also given their choice of a course on English literature or a course on French literature.[52] Then, in 1910, the Faculty of Arts was officially created. Addressing the University Council on March 15, 1911, Fouad expressed his pleasure with this step. He reiterated that general lectures were not enough and that the development of the Faculty of Arts along the lines of its western counterparts must continue.[53] The country, he argued, had been deprived of this kind of education that focused on the arts, when it needed "writers, wise people, historians and the like." Such an education, he added, must be offered in Arabic, within a system compatible with "the modern scientific spirit." He declared that he wanted this new institution to "become unique in the east."[54]

Over the course of several speeches to the University Council, Fouad explained his vision for the new faculty. A Faculty of Arts, Fouad believed, would give more coherence to the individual lectures and courses offered at the university. In his view, this faculty would "revive the scholar of the Arabic arts [*daris al-adab al-'arabiyya*] so he is on par with his counterparts in European and American countries." Using modern research methods, he went on, the faculty would revive the early Arab accomplishments in the literary, scientific, and artistic fields, accomplishments that, Fouad argued, had impressed the west in medieval times but that contemporary Arabs had forgotten. This revived knowledge would then trickle down from the top to the bottom, that is to say, from the scholars at the university to schoolteachers and the general public, or in Fouad's words, "the light of the literary and intellectual renaissance will flow from the peaks of education to its foundations, bit by bit, until it illuminates the entire Egyptian world."[55] To address the question of knowledge provenance and to encourage intellectual cooperation with western institutions, Fouad turned to another familiar *nahdawi* trope, saying that the faculty would "bring back the treasures of the old Arabic sciences, which we are now taking from the west."[56]

Fouad declared he was proud the country finally had the kind of institution that offered the education of which it had been deprived.[57]

At this key moment in the history of the Egyptian-Arab academy, basic *nahdawi* tenets were inscribed into the mission statement of the Faculty of Arts, the core of the new university. The faculty was a *nahdawi* institution, tasked with the "revival" of the "glorious" classical Arab-Islamic thought, once appreciated by the west and now forgotten by contemporary Arabs. This discourse was not new. It had developed during the Arab *nahda* as a solution to what *nahdawis* perceived as Arab cultural "backwardness" facing a strong western "civilization." Stephen Sheehi has shown in the *Foundations of Modern Arab Identity* that while these intellectuals critiqued colonial discourses, they also appropriated colonial assumptions in their writings. They developed a language of binaries to make persuasive arguments: rise and decline, east and west, backwardness and civilization, and the like. By analyzing some major *nahdawi* texts—for example, Butrus al-Bustani's (1810–1883) magnum opus *Khutba fi Adab al-'Arab* (1859)—Sheehi argues that Arab subjectivity was constructed in such a way as to include both a "knowing self," corresponding to the "enlightened Abbasid" (mentioned explicitly in the university communiqué to the press just described), and an "unknowing self," corresponding not only to present-day Arabs but also to the "ignorant Umayyads." This binary, in Sheehi's words, finds its "dialectical resolution in the 'representation of the third term,' which might be, for instance, the literary figure of a European humanist or a wise Arab ruler or good government." Sheehi concludes that the required reform is inherently paradoxical because it made the re-creation of the Arab subject conditional on accepting the existence of a certain "lack" as inherent to his subjectivity.[58]

Yet, the university founders were not thinking in those terms, but rather expressing their hope that the university would become the powerful engine of the *nahda*. They understood there was a power discrepancy between the "advanced" and the "less advanced" nations and saw the university as a practical solution for redressing this weakness and pushing back against the colonialist threat. For them, the required cultural reform would be carried out by a generation of new scholars trained in the modern research and teaching methods already used by Orientalists exploring the Arab-Islamic classical tradition. These university founders were thrilled by the available research possibilities and were excited to embark on a project of natural synthesis, which they did with circumspection and confidence. They were neither intimidated by western scholarship nor feeling threatened by what it could bring. For them, building a secular university along western lines was a means of creating scholars comfortable with both the old and the new.

In those early days, the running of the university involved not only Prince Fouad, who liked to be seen as an enlightened patron and a wise ruler, but also the European humanists Sheehi refers to. Several Orientalists were hired by Fouad to teach in the Faculty of Arts, and there were new administrators as well, such as Gaston Maspero (1846–1916), whom Fouad entrusted with organizing the new Faculty of Arts. A renowned Egyptologist, professor at the Collège de France, and member of the French Académie des Inscriptions et Belles-lettres, Maspero was also a member of the University's Administrative Council. Fouad had turned to him to draw the blueprints for the new faculty.[59] Maspero had submitted a detailed report of ten typed pages a year earlier, on February 26, 1910, with his design for the new faculty. While not all of its suggestions and courses were implemented, due to financial restraints, the document is particularly useful for explaining the logic that went into the organization of the faculty.

Maspero made a case for dividing the nascent faculty along several binaries: ancient and modern sections first, each of which was subsequently divided into eastern and western subsections.[60] He stated that European and Islamic civilizations had roots in the Greek and Roman civilizations and that in Europe classical studies had become an important part of mainstream education and were no longer limited to amateur erudition. Egypt, too, needed to make classical studies the basis of its literary education, he argued. The western subsection of the ancient studies would include the Greek and Latin languages, philology, literature, philosophy, archaeology, and history. The eastern subsection would include courses on ancient Egyptian language and history, the Semitic languages and their history, and also the Persian language and its history.

For the western subsection of the modern studies, Maspero did not hide his preference for giving more attention to French literature.[61] Course design should reflect the status of each European language in Egypt, he reasoned. While admitting that English language and literature had become important in Egypt since the British occupation, Maspero believed preference should still be given to the Romance languages, especially French. Maspero proudly credited France with having initiated Egypt's contact with modern European life. Since then, he argued, French language and literature had become more important than other European languages and literatures in Egypt.[62] He recommended that this subsection start with French and English language and literature. In the long run, however, courses should also cover the philology of the Romance and Germanic languages; the history of French, English, Italian, and German literatures; the history of modern Europe since the fall of the western Roman

Empire; contemporary European history; and also the history of European art and philosophy.

For the eastern subsection under the modern section, Maspero clarified that by eastern he was referring to the Islamic East (l'Orient Musulman) and not the Far East (l'Extrême-Orient): "not because there is no interest in knowing [the Far East], but because Egypt has always had such a little interaction with it, that it could, without much inconvenience, hold off studying it." The focus would be on the largest three Muslim populations: Arabs, Turks, and Persians. The courses he proposed, therefore, were Arabic, Turkish, and Persian philology; the history of the Arabic, Turkish, and Persian literatures; and the history of Arabs, Muslims, and Muslim Egypt as well as of Islamic art and philosophy. To confer legitimacy on his propositions, Maspero framed his design for the Faculty of Arts as responding to the present "needs of the country."[63]

Maspero also discussed the diplomas to be awarded to those who successfully completed their undergraduate and graduate studies. The faculty would give two degrees: the equivalent of the French *license ès lettres* (bachelor of arts) and the *doctorat ès lettres* (doctor of arts) of European universities. The former would be granted based on the student's achievement in chosen subjects. The bachelor's degree exam would "allow the University Council to determine whether the candidate had acquired the knowledge necessary or simply useful for the exercise of what is referred to as a 'liberal career.'" The doctoral exam, however, would be "purely scientific," allowing students who wanted to dedicate their studies to aspects of literature or history to demonstrate their mastery of the field. In his report, Maspero raised the issue of the university's lack of official ties to the country's public and private secondary educational institutions. More importantly, he predicted the conundrum that would trouble the private university for years to come, and that eventually resulted in turning it over to the Ministry of Public Instruction in 1925. Both degrees, warned Maspero, would have no official value unless the government recognized them and gave their holders access to public careers. He therefore suggested inviting the government to assess the abilities and competencies of university graduates.[64] He proposed the creation of an examination committee; half of which would be appointed by the government, while the other half would be academics from the university.[65]

From Azhar to University

The new Faculty of Arts quickly made an impact, especially on new and curious students. These students came mostly from al-Azhar, Dar al-'Ulum, and the

School of Judges. Those who had transferred from al-Azhar, like Taha Hussein, Ahmad Amin (1886–1954), and ʿAbd al-Wahab ʿAzzam (1895–1959), had no problem absorbing the new sciences. These Azharites were even praised by the university administration as the most "hardworking and engaged students."[66] Many of them took up academic careers later and became leading intellectuals in the country, just as the university founders had hoped. These students were conscious of the novelty of the humanist education to which the new university dedicated itself and were impressed by a different learning experience. Not only were the subjects new and the teaching methods unfamiliar, but also foreign Orientalists were teaching Egyptian students about Arab and Islamic history, although not without friction.[67]

Hussein, Amin, and others had been frustrated with their learning experience at al-Azhar and were eager to try something different. Hussein compared his experiences at al-Azhar and the secular university in his autobiography, *The Days*. Initially, he had been excited about leaving his village to go to Cairo and start his studies at the prestigious mosque, shown here in a photograph from 1906. Referring to himself in the third person, he wrote: "It was [at al-Azhar] that he found rest and security. The fresh breeze that blew across the court of al-Azhar at the hour of morning prayer met him with a welcome and inspired him with a sense of security and hope."[68] Yet, excitement quickly gave way to disappointment. Hussein was frustrated with the teaching method at al-Azhar. Studying any text at the time implied memorizing a superstructure of texts and interpretations. The sheikh would explain the main text (*matn*) in great detail with a strong focus on linguistic and rhetorical analyses, which Hussein believed distracted students from the main ideas. When done with the main text, the sheikh would move on to the commentary on the text (*sharh*), then the glosses (*hashiya*), and finally the supercommentary (*taqrir*), with the underlying assumption that students would memorize and comment on all these texts. Like Muhammad ʿAbduh, who had called without success for bypassing this superstructure of texts, Hussein wanted to go back to the primary sources.

> The boy sat beside the pillar, toying with the chat and listening to the sheikh on tradition. He understood him perfectly and found nothing to criticize in his lesson except the cascade of names which he poured forth on his listeners in giving the source and authorities for each tradition. It was always "so-and-so tells us" or "according to so-and-so." The boy could not see the point of these endless chains of names, or this tedious tracing of sources. He longed for the sheikh to have done with all this and come down to the tradition itself.[69]

Nahda *Goes to University* 91

FIGURE 9. Al-Azhar, 1906. Source: Travelers in the Middle East Archive (TIMEA). Original source: A. B. de Guerville, *New Egypt* (New York: Dutton, 1906), 158a. (Creative Commons - CC BY-2.5.)

In the midst of his frustration, Hussein applied to study at the new university and was worried he would not get accepted because of his blindness.[70] While al-Azhar had always admitted blind students (and even had a special *riwaq*, or portico, for the blind), the rules at the new institution were not clear. He was eventually admitted, but he expressed his surprise that students had to pay fees, had to buy an education. Students did not pay tuition fees at al-Azhar, and it was even customary to hand out free bread to poor students.[71] With regard to his blindness, the new university was not as flexible as al-Azhar. For example, to better regulate access to lectures, which had become popular and crowded, the university administration decided to let in only students with registration cards. As a result, Hussein was allowed in, but not his assistant, who normally helped him to his seat and then waited for him outside the classroom to take him back home when the lecture was over. In *The Days*, Hussein remarked that had it not been for the help of his classmates, this small incident would have been the end of his studies.[72]

These initial frustrations aside, Hussein was ecstatic with his new learning experience at the secular university. He described it as a constant celebration, a "knowledge feast." While he and other students found their European professors' Arabic accent peculiar, they were impressed by their command of the language and their knowledge of the subject matter. These European and Egyptian professors dealt with the subject at hand directly, without referring to commentaries, supercommentaries, or glosses.

> It impressed the newcomer, too, that the professor did not say when the study began: "The author—God have mercy on him—said . . ." He broached the subject by speaking for himself, not reading from a book. What he said was clear and needed no explanation, being straightforward and lucid, and free of qanqalah [sic], or citation and counter-citation, obviating mere contention. How altogether strange and new it all was, exciting my mind and revolutionizing my whole way of thinking.[73]

And again:

> There were Egyptian professors too, who added to [the university's] appeal and its fascination enormously. Imprinted on my memory are recollections of a group of such men, who exercised a profound and long-standing influence on my career. They gave me a new awareness of life, a new zest for it, and a new awareness of the old and the new together. They turned my outlook round towards the future, to days ahead. They strengthened and established my Arab, Egyptian personality, in the context of all the wide learning brought to me by the orientalists which could easily have engrossed me totally in European values. But these Egyptian teachers enabled me to cling to a strong element of authentic eastern culture, and to hold together congenially a balanced harmony in the learning of both east and west.[74]

He expressed his fascination with the new courses and showed off his knowledge of ancient Egyptian history, for example, in front of his cousin studying at Dar al-'Ulum. Such a course had never been taught in Egypt before, and he was proud to be at the place that gave him access to topics students in other institutions, like al-Azhar, had not heard about. He found the whole approach stimulating and refreshing.[75]

Years later, in 1958, Hussein gave a eulogy for his old teacher, the famous Orientalist Enno Littman, who had been member of the Arabic Language Academy since its creation in 1932. In this eulogy, Hussein remembered Littman's classes and how he managed to win his students' admiration and full attention. Hussein credited Littman with having introduced the study of Semitic languages to Egypt, which students at the time saw as a major innovation in the field of Arabic literary studies.

> It was unprecedented in the entire history of the Arabic language, since scientific study started in the late first hijri century until Littman arrived in Cairo to teach at the old Egyptian University, that an Arabist studied the old Semitic languages and compared between those languages and the Arabic language.[76]

Hussein remembered how Littman first taught the basics of some of these Semitic languages, like Hebrew, Aramaic, and Abyssinian, so students could understand the comparisons he was going to make. Students responded favorably, Hussein went on, so much so that in Littman's farewell reception, some of his students composed a farewell poem entirely in Syriac and read it out to him. Through linguistic comparisons that Littman made between Arabic and various Semitic languages, Hussein said that students could finally understand many of the "secrets of the Arabic language." As an example, he said that during his studies at al-Azhar, he had learned that the letter *alif* in the past tense verb *qala*, as in many other verbs, changed to the letter *waw* in the present tense verb *yaqulu* (*alif munqaliba 'ala al-waw*). He said he had never understood why this was the case until Littman taught them about the Abyssinian language, and how *qala* in that language is pronounced *qwl*, with a *waw*. Only then could Hussein connect what he had learned at al-Azhar with what Littman had just explained to them, solving the riddle of why the *alif* changed to a *waw*. Similarly, many of the references in Syriac, which Hussein's sheikhs at al-Azhar had casually made without explaining what they meant, made sense to him only after Littman's classes. These classes were even more interesting in Hussein's view, because they were interactive. Littman would say a word from one of the Semitic languages and then ask students to suggest the closest Arabic word to it. Hussein said he was one of the fastest students to make these linguistic connections.[77] In Littman's classes, Hussein felt he was learning something new, and he enjoyed Littman's active teaching method.

Other intellectuals and future professors at the university, such as 'Abd al-Wahab 'Azzam and Ahmad Amin, had similar reactions to the new system. When Thomas Arnold lectured at the university, 'Azzam praised him for his willingness to admit to not having the answers to some of the students' questions, and for asking for their feedback on his lectures.[78] Similarly, Amin remembered his Azharite sheikh and expressed his dislike of the Azharite method of teaching: "[The sheikh] read the text, then the commentary, and I understood them. But then he soared, offering comments on and objections to the wording and answers to the objections, of which I understood nothing."[79] For Amin, the way the subject matter was approached and periodized at the secular university was exciting. He remarked how organizing Arabic literature into periods and then examining these periods and authors' lives was all new and had been unknown in Egypt before Arabic literature courses started at the university.[80] Donald Reid quotes Amin on his appreciation of university education and how he understood from his experience there that the mission of a university was to engage critically with existing knowledge and produce new knowledge:

> I saw [at the university] a new kind of education, which I had not known: thoroughness in research, depth in study, patience in referring to various sources, comparisons between what the Arabs and the Europeans said, and quite serious deductions from all that.
>
> The difference between the university and the school lay in research.... The school teaches the latest achievements in learning, while the university tries to discover the unknown, criticizes the achievements in learning, introduces arguments, replaces the old by the new, destroys one viewpoint and builds up another.... This was what I understood in the first year I taught at the university ... from foreign professors who had undertaken serious new researches in the individual fields; I understood from my association with some Orientalists at the university as I came to know what they were doing, and I understood from a few Egyptian professors who had adopted their plans and used their methods.[81]

Despite Hussein's critique of the teaching method at al-Azhar, it was there that he came under the influence of Sheikh Muhammad 'Abduh and was introduced to Arabic literature and literary methods by Sheikh Sayyid 'Ali al-Marsafi. In his work on Hussein's education, Abdelrashid Mahmoudi has rightly warned against dismissing the training Hussein received at al-Azhar. Mahmoudi argues that despite all the commentaries, supercommentaries, and glosses that frustrated Hussein, it was through this rigorous training that he discovered the "primary sources of Arab creativity."[82] He had started his studies at al-Azhar in 1902, only a few years before 'Abduh resigned in 1905. Although Hussein attended only two of 'Abduh's lectures, he was introduced to 'Abduh's ideas in more detail through his readings and through Ahmad, his Azharite brother, and Ahmad's friends, who were close followers of 'Abduh.[83] Writing years later for one of Egypt's francophone periodicals, *Un Effort*, in 1934, Hussein talked about 'Abduh, his teaching method, and the strong impact his lectures had on his followers and his opponents alike. He described how students discussed 'Abduh's lecture repeatedly during the evening and the following day:

> ['Abduh] used the most ancient and the most venerated of the classics as the basis of his teaching. The method was on the other hand quite new, representing a complete break with the Azharite scholastic tradition. He was deliberately and sometimes exaggeratedly negligent as regards everything connected with words, and extremely meticulous as regards everything connected with ideas. He took a close interest in anything which stimulated thought and reflection. He questioned his pupils and encouraged them to ask him questions, and then tried to make them answer, discussed their replies and in so doing opened up new horizons for them. He instilled in them an appreciation of reading and discussion, he made them love freedom of thought and taught them to express their opinions.[84]

Such a teaching method, giving pride of place to classical texts, along with professors who encouraged critical engagement with the tradition while developing ideas in dialogue with their students, was what Hussein experienced later at the secular university. For Hussein, 'Abduh had legitimized this approach to learning. "There is no doubt," Hussein went on, "that it was Sheikh Muhammad 'Abduh who gave Egypt its intellectual freedom."[85]

It was also at al-Azhar that Hussein came to study with Sayyid 'Ali al-Marsafi, a figure whose intellectual influence Hussein continued to praise until the end of his life. Marsafi was a close follower of 'Abduh and taught Arabic literature, then considered an optional elective.[86] Mahmoudi devotes a chapter to Hussein's discovery of literature and literary methods in Marsafi's classes, an experience Hussein described in *The Days*. Like 'Abduh, Marsafi returned to the early primary sources, especially the pre-Islamic *jahili* poetry, and used Abu Tammam's *al-Hamasa* and other classics as the main study texts. Marsafi engaged directly with these classics and criticized other Azharite sheikhs for their teaching methods and choice of textbooks.[87] Mahmoudi argues that Marsafi not only encouraged students to participate in class discussions but, for Hussein, also represented the free outspoken scholar. In Mahmoudi's view, Hussein made a connection between literature and freedom through the figure of Marsafi, who showed Hussein that freedom for men of letters was a freedom based on "the possession of such moral and intellectual qualities as courage, breadth of culture, versatility, and fluency."[88] In his description of Marsafi's teaching method, Hussein leaves no doubt to the impact the sheikh had on him.

> I know of nothing in the world which can exert so strong an influence for freedom, especially on the young, as literature, and above all literature as Sheikh Marsafi taught it when he was explaining *al-Hamasa* and later the *al-Kamil* to his class. What then did this study consist in? Unfettered criticism of the poet, anthologist and commentator, not to mention the various philologists. Then the testing and exercise of taste by inquiry into the elements of beauty in literature: in prose and poetry, in general drift and detailed meaning, in rhyme and rhythm, and in the combination of individual words. Then experience of the up-to-date sensibility which was part of the atmosphere of his circle, and a constant sense of contrast between the gross taste and jaded wits of the Azhar and the delicacy and penetration of the ancients.[89]

By reclaiming freedom to critically engage with the canon, Marsafi was following the example of the ancient *udaba'*, and his message resonated deeply with Hussein, marking his own intellectual trajectory.

Yet, as already discussed, 'Abduh's calls for the inclusion of a humanist education at al-Azhar were met with fierce opposition, leading to his resignation in 1905. Marsafi was marginalized after the death of his mentor, and his optional literature courses were not taken seriously. Learning at al-Azhar, as Timothy Mitchell has shown, was organized around the study of law, which can help us understand why Arabic literature was taken lightly at the time.[90] Other subjects as well, such as Arabic grammar and morphology, were learned only as tools for understanding the main subjects required for the study and practice of law.[91] So while al-Azhar seemed set in its proven ways and was resistant to the kind of education 'Abduh and Marsafi were hoping to introduce, the secular university was built specifically to provide such an education. For Hussein, 'Abduh and Marsafi were exceptional figures. Their ideas and teaching methods left their mark on him and other students. The authority and knowledge of these two important Azharite scholars legitimized humanist education and helped Hussein to make the transition when the new university offered an education in which *adab* was to be studied for its own sake.

As he showed in the passages I have quoted from *The Days*, Hussein embarked on his education at the university with excitement and enthusiasm. He went on to become the first student to receive a doctorate from the university, in 1914. He then went on a scholarship to the Sorbonne for another doctorate, after which, in 1919, he was hired at the Egyptian University as a professor to teach classical Greek and Roman history. He was also the first Egyptian to become dean of arts there, briefly in 1928 and then in 1930 and again in 1936. For Hussein's large reading public, he was more than a famous writer and intellectual: he was professor at the university. Tellingly, he was always referred to as "Doctor Taha Hussein" and the university's "eldest son."[92] Although Hussein was given the honorific titles of Bey in 1936 and Pasha in 1950, he was still referred to as Doctor Taha Hussein Bey or Doctor Taha Hussein Pasha. When titles were abolished after the regime change in 1952, he remained Doctor Taha Hussein. He can be seen here in his study wearing his academic gown. As I show in the following chapters, he continued to defend seeking knowledge for knowledge's sake and the role of the Faculty of Arts until the very end.

FIGURE 10. Taha Hussein in his study. Courtesy of the Taha Hussein family.

From Private to State University

As we have seen, in practice the ambitious private initiative stumbled, and the government eventually took over. Although the contractual agreement between the private university and the Ministry of Public Instruction was supposed to guarantee the university's independence, future conflicts—most notably in Taha Hussein's case in 1932, when he was forced to retire temporarily from the university because, as dean of arts, he had refused the ministry's request to grant honorary doctorates to government supporters—proved that this independence was not real.[93] Following his forced retirement, Hussein himself wrote that "the university was somewhat independent, and now this independence has been erased. Education at the university was somewhat free, decided by faculty councils and the University Council, but now everything is decided by the Ministry of Public Instruction." He even wrote that he missed a time when academics could refuse to go to the undersecretary's office at the ministry to discuss matters related to their university.[94] Appointing the minister of public instruction as the higher president of the university made the institution part of the ministry's administration and rendered it vulnerable to ministerial politics. Whereas initially it was up to the private university to interpret what it meant by "seeking knowledge for knowledge's sake" and to run its affairs as it saw fit, the takeover reinforced a model started by Muhammad Ali, in which the state had control over all Egyptian institutions of higher learning. Furthermore, while historical accounts have focused on the financial difficulties the university had to face, the details of this struggle indicate that another major problem was the marketability of the new degrees. How was the university to recruit students interested in its mission of "seeking knowledge for knowledge's sake" when they were unfamiliar with the humanist education the university was offering and its diplomas were not recognized by the state?

The inability of the private university to continue on its own must have shaped Taha Hussein's outlook on the role the state had to play in supporting humanist education. Hussein witnessed this struggle firsthand: first as a student in Cairo (1908–1914), then as a doctoral student in France (1914–1918)—a mission from which he had to return briefly due to the severe financial crisis facing the university—then as a professor from 1919 on. More importantly, he was the first faculty member to join the University Council, in 1922, at a crucial moment when the council was debating the future of the entire project. This challenge must have confirmed his belief that strong state involvement was necessary to take culture and a humanist education forward in any serious institutional way.

Reports from the Administrative Council on the private university reflect genuine anxiety over these concerns early on. In the annual report for the academic year 1910–1911, for example, the Faculty of Arts was concerned that the number of students had declined considerably that year, for reasons that were both financial and intellectual. University administrators explained that the Faculty of Arts was the first institution of its kind in the Islamic world, which meant that its program of studies was new and demanded an intellectual effort that students were neither used to nor adequately prepared for in secondary schools. Most students in Egypt, the report went on, still considered the high school certificate as the fastest means to securing employment in the public or the private sector. Even though the government had agreed in principle to recognize the degrees offered by the university, the main worry was still that the Faculty of Arts was offering a different kind of education. Even though the faculty thought highly of its humanist education that "addresses the ideal needs of the mind," the faculty was also aware that it could not compete with other higher colleges offering a more practical education in an area like medicine or engineering, which promised a lucrative career.[95] The annual report for the following academic year, 1911–1912, tried to remain positive with regard to improved organization, courses, and the hiring of professors. Yet again, dwindling numbers were a major concern that could be addressed only by state recognition of the degrees offered by university.[96]

After the government agreed to grant the university an annual subsidy, the University Council seized the opportunity to thank the Ministry of Public Instruction and requested, again, formal recognition of the university's degrees. The letter explained that the university was ready, with its qualified staff and organized faculties, to offer studies far superior to those offered by other schools already recognized by the ministry. The council stressed that their students acquired thorough knowledge at the university, making them better qualified for filling government positions, so priority should be given to them over other applicants. The university admitted that a fairly large number of students were not entirely dedicated "to [studying] science for the sake of science," as most students expected that the knowledge acquired at the university would help them secure future employment. A legal value, the council concluded, must be conferred upon the university's degrees, otherwise students would lose interest in pursuing higher studies altogether, "to the great loss of the country."[97]

Yet, the Ministry of Public Instruction remained reluctant. In the parliamentary session on April 19, 1924, the ministry turned down another request by the university to officially recognize its degrees. The ministry stated that it "could not acknowledge the degrees offered by the university to its graduates in the desired way as long as the ministry was not involved in the supervision of studies there."[98] Furthermore, poor student enrollment encouraged voices skeptical about the utility of the project all together, and the university had to defend itself. For example, the pro-British *Egyptian Gazette* criticized the university and Fouad's autocratic management of the Administrative Council. The newspaper wondered whether the entire project amounted to anything more than a "high school," especially with the dwindling number of students, as enrollment had fallen from 201 in the academic year 1910–1911 to 103 in 1911–1912. The *Gazette* concluded:

> Whatever takes place the government will have to assume control. Private initiative is too weak, the sense of personal responsibility too underdeveloped, the social sense, if the term may be used, of Egyptians not sufficiently advanced to permit of individuals conducting an institution of this kind with success.[99]

The university condemned the newspaper's assessment and pushed for more support of what it described as "the first enterprise in which Egypt has exhibited its enlightened patriotism." There was reason for continued optimism, the university's response to *The Gazette* went on. It reminded readers that the university was founded under the patronage of Khedive Abbas II and in response to a "patriotic impulse on the part of the whole Egyptian nation." Moreover, to reassure the public, the university explained that it received funds from waqfs and generous donations, in addition to an annual subsidy of LE 2,000 from the Egyptian government, which the university cited as proof of government commitment to the success of the project.[100] To reassure university benefactors, the response included a detailed budget for the university that refuted *The Gazette*'s claim that a large sum of money was lumped under "miscellaneous" in the annual budget report. The private university was fighting to show that its humanist education could survive independently of the state. In what sounded like an appeal for support, the university insisted that for the project to succeed, it had to remain independent from the government.

> The university must remain the independent national institution that its founders intended. It has not failed its task and it will continue to progress on the ways

that are open to it. . . . But its friends must understand that such a work cannot be improvised. They must remember that, even in the countries of the highest culture and unlimited resources, a university does not come into existence all at once. Years and steady growth are necessary everywhere, and in Egypt the conditions are especially difficult.[101]

Funding was a major challenge for the private university. Historian 'Abd al-Mun'im al-Jumay'i argues that in retrospect, the private university could never have survived with its poor financial situation. He explains that the university was forced to cut its expenditures due to the eruption of the First World War, citing as evidence the need in 1915 to shift the campus from the old Gianaclis palace (now the old main campus of the American University in Cairo in Tahrir Square) to the smaller Muhammad Sidqi palace on Falaki Street in order to save on annual rent.[102] Because of the war, the Ministry of Waqfs reduced its support from LE 5,000 to 2,000, then to LE 1,800, and finally to LE 700 in 1916. The Ministry of Public Instruction, however, continued to pay its annual LE 2,000. Due to worsening economic conditions in the country, only members of the University Council continued to pay their subscriptions and donations.[103] The University Council then had to decide on the fate of the educational missions to Europe. Having to choose between stopping the courses at the university and recalling students from Europe, the council opted for the latter. The council reasoned that stopping classes or shutting down university divisions would imply the end of the university itself.[104] Al-Jumay'i also finds that the private university had little success owing to poor funding from the government and diminishing donations from the nation's notables, who turned away from supporting it, and that it was in light of this worsening situation that university professors and the University Council eventually decided to hand the university over to the Ministry of Public Instruction.[105]

Despite these problems, the university had become a symbol for the national struggle. On the eve of the 1919 revolution, the University Council counted among its members the following prestigious public figures: Sa'd Zaghlul (vice-president and general secretary), Lutfi al-Sayyid, 'Abd al-'Aziz Fahmi, and Husayn Rushdi (president and future prime minister), as well as four more future prime ministers: Zaghlul, 'Abd al-Khaliq Tharwat, Isma'il Sidqi, and Muhammad Mahmud. Reid accurately concludes that "the council's distinguished membership reflected the importance of the struggling university as a national symbol."[106] The solution was to preserve the symbol by rebranding it as a state university, which would mean the end of its financial difficulties and automatic state recognition of its degrees. The old private university thus became the Faculty of Arts of the new university. The minister of public instruction's explicatory memorandum on the proposed law for the creation of the new state university said:

> There existed in the country a university called the "Egyptian University," created about fifteen years ago by subscriptions and donations from benefactors. As it has become an educational establishment not to be overlooked when studying the creation of a State University, the directors [of the private university] have agreed to transfer the existing university, with all its properties and equipment [to the state] in order to become the core of the Faculty of Arts of the new university, provided that the latter has an autonomous management as is the case with other universities.

At the new university, the humanities would be taught next to the more practical sciences, medicine and law. To remain faithful to the initial design of the university founders, all these faculties "would focus on theoretical and philosophical studies." The minister then reiterated the importance of the independence of the university: "No university can grow and prosper if it does not have the freedom to organize its own educational system and if it is not independent of any outside management."[107] Yet from that moment on, the minister was the

FIGURE 11. Postcard photo of the New University Campus, undated but from the 1930s or 1940s.

university's higher president, and over the years, the university would have to negotiate its independence vis-à-vis the ministry. In 1928, the university moved to a luxurious, new neoclassical campus (shown here in a postcard photo), but the total independence the university founders had planned for their institution now belonged to the past.

Conclusion

The private secular Egyptian University was created to provide a humanist education to Egyptians in Egypt, so they would not have to search for such an education abroad. The institution, celebrated by its founders as the first of its kind in the east, assigned itself the *nahdawi* task of "reviving" the glorious classical Arab-Islamic *adab* by creating the modern Arab scholar, trained in cutting-edge research and teaching methods. The university founders believed that acquiring such modern training was essential to simultaneously engage with the classical tradition and the accomplishments of the western culture. The private university was built explicitly to fulfill this mission, a mission that had already been an integral part of the *nahdawi* discourse.

Taha Hussein became the prime example of the Arab humanist scholar the university founders had hoped for. He embarked on a lifelong engagement with classical *adab*—as a prolific writer, an academic, and a member and then president of the Arabic Language Academy. In his overall reform vision, "the university's eldest son," as Hussein was repeatedly called, positioned the university as the mastermind behind the changes he advocated for culture and education and that he believed were necessary to achieve full independence and create a sound democratic life. He insisted the university was the only institution capable of producing the intellectual leaders who were comfortable in both the old and the new and who were trained to diagnose the country's problems and offer adequate solutions. Yet, as the private university stumbled in its early years, it became clear that the humanist education the university provided required substantial and stable support from the state. How Hussein sought to regulate that state role while guaranteeing academic freedom and ensuring the stable operation of the university and other institutions of culture and education in Egypt's volatile multiparty system is the topic of the next chapter.

3 DEMOCRATIZING EDUCATION
Taha Hussein, Institutions, and Unstable Parliamentary Politics

> Democracy requires that people get an education, which it believes is their right, neither a gift nor a grant. Democracy considers that providing some level of education to the people is a duty, ignoring which brings no good to citizens. Democracy needs a long time, a huge effort, plenty of money and a stable comfortable peace necessary to build the required schools, prepare teachers, and build education on a solid basis that meets the standards specified by experts of proper upbringing and philosophers of pedagogy.
>
> Taha Hussein[1]

TAHA HUSSEIN BELIEVED that the secular university was the only institution capable of designing, implementing, and providing the primary and secondary education systems Egypt needed. He argued that without such educational systems, no democracy or real independence could be achieved. Through modern research and teaching methods, the university would create the intellectual leaders trained to critically engage with the past and face the challenges of the present. Using their acquired skills and knowledge, these leaders, according to Hussein, could articulate the problems facing the nation in precise terms and offer adequate solutions, which would be reflected in the national education they designed. In Hussein's vision, free primary and secondary education prepared Egyptians to become what he described as "soldiers," or educated citizens, aware of their rights and responsibilities and capable of leading a democratic life.

Understandably, the press was an important arena for Hussein's battle for reform. Whether he was acting as a member of government or as a critic of government policies, he expressed his ideas and responded to his critics on the pages of widely read journals and periodicals. These debates raised serious questions about the purpose of the humanities, the kind of role the state should play in culture and education, and even why and how people should get an education. Examining these debates on education and institutions gives us fresh insights into Egypt's multiparty political system between 1922 and 1952 and how it functioned. By turning attention away from the constant struggle over power between the British, the palace, and the political parties, these public debates show how Hussein and others used the relatively free public sphere and the existing political parties as platforms from which they pitched their ideas on education and tried to convince the voting public of their feasibility. This helps us account for important achievements in education during the parliamentary period, which scholars often dismiss. Egyptian bureaucrats developed new knowledge production structures through intense social debates, fierce political battles, and serious scholarly engagement with both classical Arab-Islamic thought and contemporary European pedagogical and research methodologies.

In this battle for reform, Hussein saw Egypt's parliament as the means that could further the *nahda* project by rebuilding the country's education system on a solid basis. He denounced the colonial legacy of meager state school funding and lack of interest in building universities. He argued that the government must reverse British policies, make education free for all Egyptians, and focus on building state-funded knowledge production institutions, such as the Egyptian University's Faculty of Arts and the Arabic Language Academy. Drawing on his experience in the Ministry of Public Instruction, he used documents and statistics to show that people wanted free education for their children. In parliament, instead of focusing solely on education's benefits, he argued that it was the duty of any democratically elected government to respond to people's needs. In public, he presented the Wafd as the only party the people could entrust with these demands.

This chapter shifts our focus from Taha Hussein the intellectual and university professor to Taha Hussein the civil servant actively negotiating and implementing his ideas for education and culture in Egypt. By turning to the sociopolitical context in which he tried to implement his project, I show his efforts to transform his vision into a coherent policy proposal and ensure educational institutions' stable operation in a volatile political system, crippled by partisan politics and Britain's ongoing occupation. Hussein wanted to give these institutions as much autonomy as possible, but he also understood that such huge projects demanded orderly state funding and regulation. My study of official state documents reveals that Hussein sought to resolve this tension between university autonomy and regulation by creating technical councils run by knowledgeable technocrats elected by their respective institutions. He believed these councils would allow educational experts to focus on long-term planning by sheltering them from the rapid political turnover at the ministerial level.

I argue that despite Hussein's many frustrations with the multiparty system, that system was an essential component of his vision for reform. His plan was to use the democratic system in place, flawed as it was, to fix itself through education. Analyzing his debates shows that while he called for a stronger state role in culture and education, he implicitly expected the democratic system to regulate that role. The checks and balances that he had in mind included an active and relatively free press through which policymakers addressed and attempted to persuade the public, a commitment to transparency on the part of government officials, electoral campaigns that diagnosed and offered solutions to problems, a turnover of power among political parties, accountability, and more importantly, a democratically elected parliament that represented the Egyptian people, to whom all governments had to answer.

Taha Hussein and the Supreme Council of the Universities

In June 1950, the Egyptian Council of Ministers convened in the government headquarters in Alexandria, as was customary during the summer months. During this meeting, the council approved a request from Taha Hussein, the minister of public instruction, to create the Supreme Council of the Universities (SCU, al-Majlis al-A'la li-l-Jami'at).[2] In his memorandum explaining the need for such a council, Hussein called for better coordination between the existing Egyptian universities: Fouad I (later Cairo) University, Farouk I (later Alexandria) University, Ibrahim Pasha (later Ain Shams) University, and Muhammad Ali (later Assiut) University.[3] With the recent rise in the number of universities (Farouk I had been created in 1942, Muhammad Ali in 1949, and Ibrahim Pasha in 1950), Hussein anticipated discrepancies would arise between their policies, as each University Council was handling its own affairs separately. Such affairs included programs of study, examinations, the evaluation and awarding of diplomas, the creation of various chairs, and the appointment of faculty members. He argued that such lack of coordination would eventually result in a disparity in the value of the degrees the universities offered when these degrees were all issued by the same authority, which was the Ministry of Public Instruction. In terms of faculty members, Hussein warned that if each university evaluated professors' credentials differently, then this could disrupt their seniority and affect their promotions when they were transferred from one university to another. The SCU would therefore become responsible for the overall standardization of these policies and procedures.

Hussein proposed that the SCU be composed of the minister of public instruction (as its president), the presidents of all universities, and their undersecretaries, while deans would be invited to attend meetings related to their faculties. To maintain the existing power hierarchy—that is to say the minister as the higher president of all universities and the ultimate arbiter of policy—the SCU would act only as a consulting body, mediating between each University Council and the minister. Under the new law, each University Council had to seek the opinion of the SCU on all its decisions before these decisions could be submitted to the minister. The SCU had the authority to ask a University Council to reconsider one or more of its decisions, provided that there were justifications for such a request. The University Council, however, was under no obligation to accept the SCU recommendations and could forward its decisions to the minister anyway, explaining why the SCU recommendations were not taken into consideration.[4]

Less than a year later, however, Hussein wrote an urgent memorandum to the Council of Ministers, addressed to Prime Minister Mustafa al-Nahhas, requesting the annulment of the council's earlier decision to create the SCU. The universities of Fouad I and Farouk I had informed Hussein that they were opposed to reporting to such a council. In his letter to al-Nahhas, Hussein said that he decided to abide by the rule of the majority and abolish the council.[5] In his own defense, Hussein insisted that the Supreme Council of the Universities would not have posed any threat to the independence of the universities, "from near or far," as he said. He had created the SCU, he argued, out of his interest in coordination among the existing universities, which received their budget from the state. He added that the State Council (Majlis al-Dawla) had examined the text of his proposed law and confirmed that it did not infringe on any of the existing laws regulating the work of the universities. In this rare instance of Hussein backing down, he asked the prime minister to personally expedite the annulment of the SCU by passing the motion around the members of the Council of Ministers instead of waiting for the next scheduled meeting. Clearly vexed, he nevertheless said the SCU should be abolished so that "the universities can focus on their work and students, and not worry about a debate that serves nobody."[6]

The resistance to Hussein's initiative did not come only from the universities. The press, too, were involved in the debate. Bahiy al-Din Barakat, previously a professor of law and twice minister of public instruction in the 1930s, tactfully expressed his disappointment with Hussein's initiative.[7] In an article in *al-Hilal*, Barakat started by praising Hussein, calling him the "university's eldest son" and added that Hussein's "genius, open mindedness and imagination" had had a most positive impact on the Faculty of Arts. Yet, Barakat expressed his surprise that Hussein could propose such a council that jeopardized the independence of the universities, when Hussein himself had suffered greatly in 1932 at the hands of the Ministry of Public Instruction when it imposed its will and had him transferred despite objections from the university.

That notorious incident had happened when the government, under the firm hand of Prime Minister Isma'il Sidqi (famous for having replaced the 1923 constitution in 1930 with an autocratic one giving sweeping powers to the king), wanted the Faculty of Arts to confer honorary doctorates on some government supporters. Hussein, then dean of arts, refused and said it was up to the Faculty Council alone to decide on such matters. Although the government eventually got what it wanted through the Faculty of Law, the ceremony on February 27, 1932, did not go as planned. Sensing that most of the honorary degrees were being awarded to supporters of the current and unpopular government, and not to any members of the opposition parties (the Wafd or the Liberal Constitutionalists), students did not applaud. King Fouad and Sidqi were furious and blamed what had happened on Hussein.

Hilmi 'Issa, Sidqi's minister of public instruction, retaliated in March 1932 by transferring Hussein from the university to a junior position in the Directorate of Elementary Education. Hussein agreed to leave the office of dean but refused to take on his new responsibilities. The government ignored the strong objections from the council of the Faculty of Arts and paid no attention to students' demonstrations demanding the reinstatement of their dean. Ahmad Lutfi al-Sayyid, then president of the university, submitted his resignation protesting the ministry's decision, which he qualified as a serious onslaught on the independence of the university.[8] A month into this conflict, Hussein was fired, leaving him and his family in serious financial difficulties. It was not until the end of 1934, that Najib al-Hilali, minister of public instruction in the cabinet of Prime Minister Muhammad Nassim, asked Hussein to return to the university, and students carried him on their shoulders back to his office.[9] The incident turned Hussein and Lutfi al-Sayyid into symbols of the autonomy of the university and its resistance to government autocracy.[10]

Barakat, in what appeared to be an appeal to Taha Hussein (the minister) to remember the hardships Taha Hussein (the professor) had faced, called on

Hussein to implement more measures ensuring the independence of the universities. Each university, argued Barakat, should have its own regulations, develop its own traditions, and earn an academic standing among all other universities in Egypt and abroad based on its own merit and academic rigor. The SCU, Barakat warned, put the universities at the heart of the administration of the Ministry of Public Instruction, rendering their own systems and administration vulnerable to political influence. Barakat also, in an attempt to explain Hussein's initiative, and possibly to give him an opportunity to reverse his decision without losing face, attributed Hussein's decision to his strong sense of social justice. Hussein, in Barakat's words, was a "leader of social reform," who always sensed people's need for justice and felt their suffering. A "revolutionary man," Hussein wanted to impose his social reform and implement as many measures as possible to spread equality among people while he was in power as minister. Yet, Barakat was worried that Hussein preferred "reforms that were wider in scope rather than deep in impact." Each approach, Barakat concluded, had its merits, and only time would tell which approach was better suited for the needs of the country.[11]

Even though Barakat was surprised Hussein had proposed the creation of an organization that could jeopardize the autonomy of the universities, this chapter shows that Hussein's initiative was in line with his larger plan for educational reform in Egypt. Since the acquisition of the private university by the state in 1925, all universities received their budget from the state and reported to the minister of public instruction as their higher president. Hussein anticipated that, sooner or later, all state universities would have to coordinate and standardize their policies. Worried that this coordination would be imposed from above by the Ministry of Public Instruction, he proposed the creation of the Supreme Council to allow universities to organize themselves internally and submit their collective recommendations to the ministry. Recognizing the already-existing involvement of the state in running the universities, Hussein had hoped such a council would help academics remain in charge of all technical matters pertinent to their universities.

Taha Hussein: A Career in Civil Service

By 1950, when Taha Hussein proposed the creation of the Supreme Council of the Universities, he had gained wide experience in working for the Ministry of Public Instruction. For years, he had navigated a cumbersome and complex state bureaucracy and was seriously involved in policymaking. He was at the heart of the decision-making circles, and his official duties, through his alliance with the popular Wafd Party since the early 1930s, gave him the opportunity to negotiate and implement his ideas. As mentioned earlier, his career in government began in December 1939, when the Ministry of Public Instruction created a new division to organize all cultural matters. As well as supervising education at its various stages, the ministry wanted to oversee "the dissemination of culture in the country."[12] It named the new division the Directorate of General Culture (Muraqabat al-Thaqafa al-'Amma) and made it officially responsible for

> organizing the ministry's cultural efforts outside of the walls of schools; finding the means to encourage and supervise these [cultural] efforts; creating an intellectual cooperation within the country and abroad, studying matters related to scientific, literary and artistic conferences as well as supervising the [cultural] efforts of private associations concerned with the propagation of culture in the country.[13]

The ministry stipulated that the person leading this division must possess "high academic qualifications and long practical experience in such matters." They chose Hussein, then dean of arts, to head the new division, effectively appointing him Egypt's first minister of culture.[14] The reference to Hussein's "long experience in cultural matters" spoke to his career not only as a writer but also as an influential critic in matters of education and culture. At the time of his appointment, he was one of Egypt's most prominent intellectuals. He had written dozens of literary classics and hundreds of widely read articles. He had also served as the first Egyptian dean of arts at the Egyptian University for several terms between 1928 and 1939. In 1938, Hussein had published *The Future of Culture in Egypt*, his detailed report on the state of Egypt's educational system and his suggested improvements. The book confirmed Hussein's deep knowledge of the system and made clear that his reform project aligned with the ministry's objectives. It was his blueprint for the steps he believed Egypt should take to develop a strong cultural and educational system capable of protecting the nation's newly acquired independence following the Anglo-Egyptian Treaty (1936) and turning that qualified independence into a fuller one.

Hussein continued as controller of general culture until May 1942, when the ministry promoted him to technical advisor to the minister (*al-mustashar al-fanni li-wazir al-ma'arif*).[15] As advisor, he became responsible for the directorates of general culture, fine arts, and higher education. He advised committees and technical projects for education planning, curricula, school systems, textbooks, and educational missions abroad.[16] Among Hussein's important achievements

FIGURE 12. Amina Taha Hussein's Wedding, 1948. Courtesy of the Taha Hussein family.

in this role was his 1944 collaboration with the Wafdist minister Najib al-Hilali to make primary education free. When the Wafd won a parliamentary majority in January 1950, party leader Mustafa al-Nahhas asked Hussein to become his minister of public instruction, even though Hussein was not a party member. The two men saw eye to eye and were close friends. They can be seen in the photograph here, sitting on either side of Ahmad Lutfi al-Sayyid, during the wedding of Hussein's daughter, Amina-Marguerite, in 1948. Hussein was happy to work with the Wafd as he needed a political platform from which he could officially promote his ideas and implement them. So he agreed, on the condition that the government would immediately make secondary and technical education free.[17] He then served as minister of public instruction until the January 1952 Cairo fire, when King Farouk dismissed the Wafd cabinet.

The Faculty of Arts: Here to Stay

Important as free education was for Taha Hussein, his larger project for educational reform depended on the secular university, and in particular the Faculty of Arts. As we saw in the previous chapter, the years from 1908 to 1925, when the university was private, saw the active formulation of the institution's mission, long-term goals, and overall organization. The university founders recruited new students and professors and sent several educational missions to Europe. They even asked experts to write new textbooks suitable for the new courses. Though it was relatively easy to find textbooks for English and French literature courses, for example, the university needed similar textbooks for teaching Arabic literature. In the academic year 1909–1910, the university announced in the local newspapers that it was organizing a "textbook writing competition," and invited literary scholars to write a textbook specifically on Arabic literature, covering its main topics in some detail. Competitors had two years to submit their manuscripts, and the winning author was to receive a prize of LE 200. The university was to publish the winning manuscript and give the author two hundred copies. Owing, no doubt, to the project's novelty, the university expected complications and also announced that "if nobody wins the competition, it starts again for another period of two years. The monetary value of the prize stays the same, until the book has been created in the desired style."[18]

At the same time, the university needed to acquaint the public with its mission and make a name for itself. It organized public lectures on various topics, some of which were open to women.[19] It also encouraged publishing the coursework of its professors and making these works accessible in public bookshops. In 1929, Robert Blum, one of Egypt's francophone journalists, attributed the rising number of lectures and of literary and artistic clubs in the capital to the university and its staff, and in his view, the university shifted the cultural weight in Egypt from Alexandria to Cairo.[20] Deans, professors, and students animated and were regularly invited to important cultural events taking place in Cairo, including those organized by the elitist francophone literary and artistic circles, such as the Amis de la Culture Française en Égypte and the Essayistes.

Interestingly, for people at the time, the university came to mean the Faculty of Arts. In 1932, Dean of Arts Hussein gave an interview to the weekly magazine *al-Musawwar* in which he explained that when the old Egyptian University was created, its only area of study was the Faculty of Arts, and people still retained that connection. Such an association, he went on, continued in their minds due to the faculty's long tradition of giving public lectures, accepting classroom auditors, and being actively involved in the cultural life of the country through professors' books and articles.[21] For many people, he was proud to say, the university *was* the Faculty of Arts.

Hussein was outspoken about the role the Faculty of Arts was playing in the country, insisting that only this faculty was capable of leading Egypt along the path to its proper awakening (*nahda*). In the *Musawwar* interview, he expressed his disappointment with those who did not take the faculty and its mission seriously. Although its impact on Egyptians had been huge, he argued that its message remained largely misunderstood. People were still confused over what the Faculty of Arts was about, he said. Some, he continued, questioned the overall worth of the faculty. These people argued that compared to other faculties like medicine and science, the Faculty of Arts was a luxury, concerned with matters that "people only need in their free time." Such a critique, he lamented, could even be heard in the corridors of the Ministry of Public Instruction and the Ministry of Finance. Critics from both ministries, he said were "always ready to cut the wings of the Faculty of Arts and belittle it."[22] Other people, he went on, had unrealistic expectations and were disappointed that so far the Faculty of Arts had not "turned Egyptian life upside down and created miracles." These critics, he argued, never expected such miracles from the Faculties of Medicine, Science, or Law, but when it came to the Faculty of Arts everybody was an expert.[23] Everyone, Hussein emphasized, needed to understand that the Faculty of Arts was as rigorous and methodical as any other faculty: "What is taught at the Faculty of Arts is not a common venture accessible to everyone. It is a science, like any other science, which has its proper methodology and doctrine." Such methods and approaches required proper training, Hussein insisted: "If you were a poet or a writer, this would not make you a professor of literature, just as understanding a history book would not be enough to make you a historian. Even if you were a historian, that would not be enough to make you a professor of history. Being a philosopher does not make you a professor of philosophy."[24]

Perhaps Egypt's historian Shafiq Ghurbal (1894–1961) was a good example of the credentialed and well-trained professional arts academic Hussein had in mind. Graduating from the Higher Teachers' College in 1915, Ghurbal went to England on a scholarship and studied under the supervision of Arnold Toynbee. He began teaching at the Egyptian University in 1928 and became the first Egyptian professor of modern history, before being promoted to dean of arts. Historian Anthony Gorman describes Ghurbal as "the key figure in putting modern Egyptian history on a firm academic footing."[25] Similarly, historian Yoav Di-Capua shows how Ghurbal and his students were the first Egyptian researchers to explore the Egyptian archives seriously. They showed their professionalism by cooperating with archivists, scrutinizing primary sources, and extensively footnoting their research.[26] Their rigorous methods distinguished them from contemporaries such as the renowned nationalist historian 'Abd al-Rahman al-Rafiʿi (1889–1966), who did not cite sources or document how he arrived at his findings. Despite his fame, al-Rafiʿi lacked the new academic credentials, and in Ghurbal's view, he relied too much on secondary sources, especially periodicals. Due to their profound disagreement over how to write history, Ghurbal and his students banned al-Rafiʿi from the Royal Historical Society.[27] "By the early 1940s," Di-Capua concludes, "Ghurbal and his disciples had vouchsafed to themselves the task of gatekeepers, ensuring that no despised amateur historian would ever inadvertently slip in."[28] While Di-Capua and others rightly agree that Ghurbal was the "doyen of Egyptian historiography," Ghurbal's efforts should not be dissociated from the institutional commitment at the Faculty of Arts to teaching modern methods. It was at the Faculty of Arts that history students were prepared for their role as gatekeepers of the Arab past.

Hussein did not exclude women from the rigorous intellectual training at the Faculty of Arts.[29] His student and protégée Suhayr al-Qalamawi (1911–1997) had been denied admission into the Faculty of Science by its British dean. Hussein, however, famously set a precedent by allowing Qalamawi and other female students into his Faculty of Arts in 1929.[30] In his decision, Hussein relied on a university regulation that allowed the admission of Egyptians into various faculties. He interpreted this law to mean all Egyptians, whether male or female.[31] Moreover, as Qalamawi explained later, Hussein had set certain rules for the admission of students into the Arabic Language Department, rules that he manipulated later to allow her and others into the faculty. He had stipulated that students needed the Egyptian high school certificate, "or its equivalent," to be admitted. When Hussein wrote down this condition, he had in mind the Azharite certificate, as he wanted to allow Azharite students into the faculty, but he left the rule intentionally vague so it would not irritate al-Azhar. He was then later able to use this condition to accept Qalamawi into the department, given that she did not have the Egyptian high school certificate but had graduated from the American College for Girls in Cairo.[32] Qalamawi, shown in the photograph displayed here, was among the first women to graduate from the university, in 1933, with a degree in Arabic literature. She then became a graduate assistant in 1937, and upon finishing her PhD degree in 1941, she was made an assistant professor. A few years later, Qalamawi became head of the Arabic Language Department.[33]

Upon her graduation in 1933, Hussein wrote an article to congratulate her and mentioned the other first female graduates by name: Fatima Salim (who had majored in Greek and Roman literature), Zuhaira ʿAbd al-ʿAziz and Fatima Fahmi (philosophy and sociology), and Naʿima al-Ayubi (law). He congratulated

FIGURE 13. Suhayr al-Qalamawi.

Egypt and the Egyptian woman for what he described as a "victory," and congratulated the Egyptian University for having made this victory possible.

> What a major event this is for our Egyptian intellectual and social life. What a great victory it is for those who promote our awakening and those who work for the liberation of the Egyptian woman and making her equal to the Egyptian man in rights and duties. What a great hope this event inspires in Egyptians, allowing them to see themselves as equals to other advanced nations, in which knowledge is not assigned to one group and not another, in which culture is not monopolized by one gender and not another, and in which man does not monopolize the means to excellence and power.[34]

Moreover, in 1937, Hussein stood firmly in support of continued coeducation at the university. A crisis erupted when some students from the Faculty of Law wrote to Ahmad Lutfi al-Sayyid requesting the separation of male and female students and forcing female students to wear uniforms. Azharite scholars led by Sheikh al-Azhar Muhammad Mustafa al-Maraghi supported these law students, and Azharite students threatened to march on the Egyptian University if these demands were not met. While Lutfi al-Sayyid was cautious and said in his statement to the press that he was studying the memo, Hussein, then dean of arts, came out in defense of coeducation at the university. He said he did not know of any text in the Qur'an or in the Sunna of the Prophet that forbade boys and girls from attending classes together in the presence of their professor who taught them science, literature, or art. In his view, the university therefore was not overstepping any boundaries or rules. He went on to say that nothing happened at the university to justify such a polemic at a time when professors, families, and university administrators were all pleased with the way classes and social life at the university were going. Life in Egypt had changed, he continued, and even if boys and girls were separated at the university, they would continue to see each other in other venues. The implication of the calls to end coeducation would be to build universities dedicated for girls, an idea he dismissed as impractical on account of not only the time and the complicated logistics such a project entailed but also the lack of funds, which even if they were available could be put to better use.[35] In another article, he accused politicians of fueling this debate to undermine the Wafd government, which was actively negotiating the end of the Capitulations and joining the League of Nations.[36] A few days later, crowds of students from the Faculties of Arts and Law organized a demonstration in support of Hussein. They carried him on their shoulders and cheered: "Long live the free dean! Long live freedom of expression! With Taha to the end! The law school salutes you, Taha!" The students asked Hussein to address them, and he improvised a speech, which he ended with advice for students to return calmly to their work as the academic year was coming to an end and he would not want to see their year-long efforts wasted:

> Let our rules be as follows: the Faculty of Arts wants to be the source of good taste and proper behavior, and to be the mind that transcends petty problems. We want to honor our past and make use of our present, to preserve our dignity and protect our independence, so return blessed to your studies.[37]

By admitting female students into the Faculty of Arts and defending their right to coeducation, Hussein, as historian Latifa Salim argues, was able to ensure that the university remained open to female students once and for all.[38]

In the same *Musawwar* interview previously mentioned, Hussein reiterated the *nahdawi* mission embraced by the university's founders, the purpose for which the Faculty of Arts was created: "to revive the Egyptian mind and give it the fertile power necessary to live, love life and understand it. . . . This [revival] will happen when we have Egyptians who understand, appreciate and love what distinguishes us as human beings: the aspiration to the highest ideals of literature, science and art." He repeated that if Egypt were to become a modern nation, only the Faculty of Arts could achieve this transformation: "Egypt will rise if the mental differences between its sons are gone, so they can understand things in a closer way, judge them in a similar manner, and share a sense of feeling and appreciation."[39] Only the Faculty of Arts and the people it trained could design the education required to achieve such a goal.

Five years later, again as dean of arts, Hussein gave another interview, to *al-Muqtataf*, in which he reiterated the same goals he understood to be the purpose for which the Faculty of Arts was created in the first place:

> What I hope and what I am working on is for the Faculty of Arts to accomplish three goals. First: the revival of our Egyptian and Arab past; second: to strengthen a clear and strong connection between us and western civilization; third: to show Europe what it needs to know about our right predisposition for rich intellectual life and to contribute to the advancement of human civilization.[40]

In this interview, he was especially proud of his faculty and its accomplishments in Egyptian intellectual life. Referring to the knowledge produced by the faculty, he said, "I am yet to see any other school in the entire east that has accomplished as much as we did in such a short period of time." As an example, he cited Ahmad Amin's *Fajr al-Islam* (1928) and *Duha al-Islam* (1933–1936), works on the Islamic intellectual life in the first and second hijri centuries. Hussein described Amin's work as the best history ever written on the topic. "Had Amin not worked in the Faculty of Arts," Hussein continued, "he would not have written such a masterpiece that the previous centuries were unable to produce."[41] The list of such works was long, according to Hussein. The faculty, he went on, was also the first institution to translate Goethe's *Faust* and *Hermann and Dorothea* into Arabic directly from German. Moreover, the faculty had participated actively in the general literary movement in Egypt: for example, during the millennial celebration of the Abbasid poet al-Mutannabi, the faculty dedicated a week of events to him and produced two books about him, one by 'Abd al-Wahab 'Azzam

(*Dhikra Abi al-Tayyib ba'd Alf 'Am*, 1936) and another by Taha Hussein himself (*Ma'a al-Mutanabbi*, 1936).[42] Referring to 'Azzam's other famous work, a revised translation of the Persian poet Ferdowsi's masterpiece, the *Shahnameh* (*Book of Kings*), Hussein went on to say that the faculty was perhaps the first to introduce Egyptians to that epic poem. The faculty had also represented Egypt abroad in various academic conferences, including the Orientalists' conferences, and conferences centered on the history of religions as well as geography and populations. This was in addition to all the books, articles, and dissertations produced by professors and students. All of these accomplishments, concluded Hussein, were having a tremendous impact on intellectual life in Egypt, especially "in matters of perception and judgement."[43]

Furthermore, Hussein was particularly proud that the faculty was responsible for having involved Egyptians for the first time in the field of archaeology and excavations.[44] As dean, he had created the Institute of Egyptian and Islamic Archaeology during the 1930–1931 academic year to train Egyptian students in a field once monopolized by western scholars, and in this way he was able to expand the existing archaeology section created by the Ministry of Public Instruction when it took over the university in 1925.[45] The institute offered bachelor's, master's, and doctoral degrees in Egyptian and Islamic archaeology. In the 1933–1934 faculty report, the institute was credited for having undertaken important digs in the Guizah area as well as in Touna el Goubal, yielding "real treasures" that were being thoroughly studied at the institute and on which several theses were being written. A fourth pyramid built in the honor of Queen Khent Kawes was discovered in Guizah, and an old Greek city at Tounet el Goubal was discovered as well.[46]

As dean of arts, Hussein also created the Institute of Oriental Languages and Literatures. The institute had three sections: Semitic languages, Islamic languages, and Arabic dialects. The Semitic languages included Acadian, Canaanite, Aramaic, and southern Semitic. The Islamic languages included Persian, Turkish, and Urdu, along with other Islamic languages not classified as Semitic. The Arabic dialects were both old and modern dialects found in the various regions and provinces. Hussein believed studying these languages facilitated better comprehension of classical Arabic, which would allow scholars to find ways of making Arabic more straightforward to teach and to learn.[47] Moreover, Hussein credited the Geography Department for having written the first scientific works in Arabic on geography.[48] The department had also carried out research in a prehistoric site discovered in Maadi, south of Cairo, with the hope of shedding more light on ancient Egyptian civilization.[49] The Faculty of Arts was also the first to organize student trips to Iraq, Greater Syria, and Iran. A mission to Yemen had yielded important geological studies and brought back a hundred and fifty carvings that were to become the thesis topic of one of the doctoral students, in addition to recordings of the various dialects used in southern Yemen.[50]

Later, in a 1959 article, Hussein reminisced, almost nostalgically, about his early days at the university. He reminded younger generations of what the Faculty of Arts stood for and why it was important to support. It was not a surprise that he repeated, again and again, the mission of the old private university. He said that in those early days it was a dream to see Egypt freed from colonialism, and such freedom was never going to happen until people's minds had been freed as well. Creating the university, he explained, replaced the limited education designed by the British only to prepare Egyptians for administrative work in government offices with an institution that offered students a new kind of knowledge that opened new horizons for them. They could learn about the old Egyptian civilization and its great monuments. They also found ways to study the origins of the Arab civilization and foreign literatures. He claimed that this early period of the university—with its anxious excited students, missions to Europe, young professors, and new subject matter—successfully produced a new generation of Egyptians, who, with the 1919 revolution, became responsible for what he described as an intellectual awakening Egypt had never experienced before.[51]

Backlash against the Faculty of Arts

Hussein understood this awakening to mean a spirit of intellectual freedom that encouraged thinkers and writers to apply modern methods of critical scholarship unhindered by either "highly conservative restrictions or fear of the oppression of the powerful."[52] For example, he claimed that the university fostered the spirit of intellectual freedom that had encouraged 'Ali 'Abd al-Raziq (1888–1966) to write *al-Islam wa-Usul al-Hukm* (*Islam and the Principles of Governing*) in 1925, in which he argued that Islam does not advocate the caliphate or any other particular form of government, and that Muslims are free to choose a form of government that suits their needs.[53] As is well known, 'Abd al-Raziq's colleagues at al-Azhar were so offended by the book that they stripped him of his position as a scholar and jurist. Hussein's landmark 1926 contribution to this new and controversial body of scholarship, *On Pre-Islamic Poetry*, also famously sparked an outcry. The book began as a collection of Hussein's lectures at the Faculty of Arts, in which he challenged the authenticity of the pre-Islamic canon and subjected these works to more rigorous scrutiny than previous scholars. In line with the faculty's tradition, he published these lectures in book form. Al-Azhar responded by demanding Hussein's dismissal from the university, and parliament debated the affair. Although the university supported Hussein's academic freedom, he had to withdraw the book, delete the passages deemed offensive, and republish the book a year later under a different title: *Fi al-Adab al-Jahili* (*On Pre-Islamic Literature*).

Hussein believed the hostile reception that met both his and al-Raziq's books was not simply a reaction to the specific arguments of each work. In his view, this hostility was above all a condemnation of the Faculty of Arts, a rejection of its methodology, and a repudiation of this new scholarship and its circulation among the public. The writer Mustafa Sadiq al-Rafi'i (1880–1937) provided evidence for Hussein's perspective in his belligerent response to Hussein's work, a long article in which he questioned the future of the entire university. He accused the university of providing a platform for Hussein and his ilk to attack the "constants of the tradition" (*al-thawabit*), and he asked the university's president, Ahmad Lutfi al-Sayyid, rhetorically:

> Don't you know . . . that even after all the 'ulama' have complained and the public has been dismayed, that Taha Hussein has informed his students that literature classes the following year will focus on "studying the Qur'an as a literary text?" Could the likes of Taha Hussein [be allowed to] study the Qur'an except in this despicable university [*al-jami'a al-mamquta*]?[54]

Years later, the Marxist critic Ghali Shukri interviewed Hussein, shortly before his death, and asked him whether choosing to write about such Islamic topics reflected a "crisis of liberalism" in the 1930s. Hussein did not hide his surprise that his books on pre-Islamic poetry and the Islamiyyat in general had been interpreted as such. "Was it our holy duty to leave [these topics] to the Orientalists?" he asked. "There are distinguished scholars among the Orientalists, but science is not their monopoly and is not limited to them. We should have the priority over them when [studying] our own history [*nahnu awla bi-tarikhina minhum*]." He saw himself and his generation as having broken into the scholars' den by applying modern research methods to the history of the heroes of Islam.[55] For Hussein, the institution with the know-how that encouraged and showed the way to producing such critical scholarship was the Faculty of Arts.

The Faculty of Arts held out against the attacks. Writing in 1959, Hussein was proud to note that the Egyptian University had weathered all storms and became an integral part of Egyptian intellectual life. Neither the people nor the state, he said, could now imagine modern Egypt without it. The university had expanded to include all the other higher schools and within fifty years of its creation, Egypt had three other universities, in Alexandria, Ain Shams, and Assiut. "The alumni from these universities now control all aspects of Egyptian life.... And can you find a single Arab country in the east or the west which does not have an Egyptian university graduate doing some kind of rich work there?" he asked.[56] In time, the responsibility of university professors grew and their expertise was solicited, not only by the Ministry of Public Instruction but also by other institutions in Egypt and the Arab world. These professors sat on the committees assembled by the Ministry of Public Instruction to oversee educational policies throughout the entire country, in addition to writing and approving textbooks and curricula for secondary schools.[57] They were also regularly asked to write high school examinations for the Arabic language.[58] Al-Azhar itself was requesting professors from the university to teach on its premises. For example, in 1938, al-Azhar needed professors from the Faculty of Arts to teach logic, hadith, history, and pedagogy in the Faculty of the Principles of Religion, as well as a professor to teach philology in the Faculty of Arabic Language.[59] Fearing a disruption of its own classes as a result of delegating all these professors, the Faculty of Arts proposed to assist al-Azhar with its hiring process.[60]

Holding the State Accountable: Checks and Balances in Hussein's Project

Taha Hussein believed all these intellectual achievements fitted within a larger reform project. He believed that a successful democracy required a sound educational system. In a 1944 speech, he argued that democracy enabled people to understand and articulate their need for justice, truth, and a better life. But for people to come to this awareness, education was essential.[61] This section focuses on the attention Hussein paid to educational reform as a means of creating a proper democratic life in Egypt. This analysis supports Elizabeth Kassab's observation that the "centrality of political accountability, the rule of law, and the importance of political representation in *nahda* thought is not acknowledged enough, yet these principles are among its leitmotivs." Without referring to Hussein in particular, she explains that this political critique, which runs through *nahda* writings and which continued in Arab thought as a whole during the twentieth century, was eclipsed by a major anxiety over "cultural authenticity," especially in the 1960s and '70s.⁶² In line with Kassab's findings, I argue that for Taha Hussein, the battle for education and the battle for democracy were one and the same.

When the first parliament began its deliberations in 1924, Hussein was aware that the assembly faced difficult circumstances. Not only was Egypt's independence incomplete, but he believed the nation also had to demonstrate to colonial powers that it deserved independence. He warned later that Egypt was being watched, not only by "our friends" the English, as he joked bitterly, but also by other European powers judging whether Egypt could handle the responsibilities of independence.⁶³ Writing during a visit to France in 1924, Hussein compared France's parliamentary elections of that May to Egypt's four months earlier. He argued that both election campaigns were full of "beautiful promises" and "shiny hopes," but that the victorious parties in both countries had not considered the feasibility of those promises, setting themselves up for post-election confusion and disappointment.⁶⁴ If the winner in France had accomplished more than the winner in Egypt, the explanation was simple.

> France is truly independent. It is not occupied by the English and does not worry about foreign control. If the Egyptian parliament and government enjoyed the same independence and sovereignty enjoyed by the French parliament and government, then who knows what the Egyptian parliament and government would do with Egypt's friends and foes.⁶⁵

Inspired by the French opposition, which criticized the government and kept a watchful eye on its performance, Hussein considered it his duty to do the same in Egypt.⁶⁶ What the two countries shared, he went on, was that the majority in both parliaments did not have the knowledge necessary to diagnose problems and propose adequate solutions. Only higher education provided the tools necessary to acquire such knowledge, and he finished his article by warning: "Woe to a country governed by the semi-educated."⁶⁷

Hussein was also convinced that the Ministry of Public Instruction was in dire need of reform. In 1923, he wrote a series of articles about the problems facing the ministry and how to address them, and he described why, in his opinion, the ministry could not rid itself of British influence:

> The men of the [Ministry of] Public Instruction have undertaken a specific line of work and thought, which they cannot see beyond. They are used to a special educational policy charted by Dunlop, so it will not be easy or even possible

for them to replace this policy with another, no matter how much the circumstances and the times have changed.⁶⁸

Hussein was referring to the infamous educational policy ordered by the British Consul-General in Egypt, Evelyn Baring (Lord Cromer), and his inspector of education, Douglas Dunlop. Their policy restricted access to education by imposing fees, limiting educational institutions' mission to producing administrators for government offices, and concentrating on elementary education at higher education's expense. Hussein criticized the ministry for not rethinking its educational philosophy after independence and not reforming the system according to the needs of the nation. What was education, and what should education do to form the people? These were the key questions he hoped the ministry would consider.⁶⁹

Egypt, Hussein argued, had known two educational policies. The first was a national policy that had aimed to expand both elementary and higher education before the British occupation in 1882. The second policy was decreed by the British and favored elementary education only. The third and post-independence policy, he said, must be inspired by the first. In the middle of the problems facing the private university we saw in the previous chapter, Hussein insisted that there would be no reform without a solid investment in higher education. Only higher education, he said, could design and spread elementary education in the right way.

> Spreading elementary education does not mean spreading reading, writing, and arithmetic, but it is much more difficult and complicated. It needs minds that can understand and appreciate the Egyptian environment, its psychology, its needs and aspirations, and find a way of adapting all this to the elementary education that we want to spread in the country. It is not easy to understand all these matters. Only those who have received solid higher education—and managed, thanks to this kind of education, to understand the many groups of people and appreciate their different needs and aspirations—can imagine what elementary education should be like and how to disseminate it correctly. The basis of education in Egypt is not elementary education. Higher education is the basis of the entire Egyptian awakening [*assas al-nahda al-misriyya kuliha*]. A wise educational policy is one that ensures the university is created first and before anything else. . . . A democracy that stands on elementary education alone is standing on a weak basis and cannot deal with the calamities and the horrors which face political systems.⁷⁰

Hussein warned that the Ministry of Public Instruction itself lacked this necessary knowledge and was incapable of doing the required studies needed to address the problems facing the country. Even parliament, which he insisted should get involved in educational policies, lacked the technical knowledge required to make the right decisions.[71] From then on, he advocated the creation of technical councils to serve as resources the ministry could consult on policy and procedure. "Technical matters should be referred to technical people, and those who supervise education should be knowledgeable about education," he wrote.[72] In his view, these councils would decentralize the executive power that had been concentrated in the minister's hands since the British administration. Hussein complained that the ministry refused to allow input into decision making from anyone except the ministry's inspectors and high officials, who almost never had any direct engagement with teaching. He advocated committees composed of specialists, especially teachers, who were familiar with students' needs and could propose effective solutions. He insisted that officials abandon the thought that permitting teachers' involvement in policymaking would weaken the ministry.[73]

Hussein reminded his readers that Egypt had already known a Supreme Council of Education (Majlis al-Ma'arif al-A'la), which existed before the British occupation, and he called for creating a similar council, adapted to the needs of the present. He laid down his vision for such a council, a vision that he implemented later as minister in 1951. He believed the council should not rely on higher members of government but should include those who possessed the real, hands-on experience, that is, teachers. Teachers, he insisted, should feel involved in policy and decision making. With this would come the added advantage of empowering teachers, who "will feel their dignity, and they will know that they are not just employees, conscripts or tools run by a higher-ranking employee. They will become critical thinking minds that make decisions in the Supreme Council of Education."[74] In his view, all levels of education must be represented in this council: elementary, primary, secondary, and higher education. Interestingly, he called for benefiting from the experience of foreign schools operating in Egypt, and turning to their French, American, and Italian supervisors, whether in secular or missionary schools, for advice: the education offered in these schools "is an education that we do not doubt is good. Its excellence and utility are a result of the adeptness of those who run and supervise it."[75]

Convinced of the utility of these technical councils, as described earlier, Hussein created the Supreme Council of the Universities in 1950 to coordinate the functioning of Egyptian universities, whose number had increased in the 1940s. As minister of public instruction, he also reorganized the Supreme Council of Education in 1951. He explained that the council would continue to be consulted on all matters related to general educational policy: study plans, examinations, and other laws; the creation of educational institutes; and any educational matter on which the minister of public instruction wished to consult the council. In line with his earlier recommendations, he decided to appoint ten teachers of various subjects and eight representatives of the universities to the council (the four presidents of the existing Egyptian universities and four professors from these four universities, chosen by each University Council). He argued that teachers' experience made them better qualified than anyone to speak for students and the needs of the educational system as a whole.[76] While proposing these councils, Hussein specified that he was not challenging the authority of the minister of public instruction. "We are not asking the minister to give up some of his power to a person in particular, but to [give some of this power to] independent technical administrations. He would remain their supreme authority, and become the link between them and parliament," Hussein explained.[77]

Hussein also believed technical councils would ensure the educational system's stability and protect it from rapid government changeovers. He viewed partisan politics, particularly the tendency for the winning political party to reverse the outgoing party's policies, as a major obstacle to educational reform.[78] In 1932, he decried the way in which partisan politics pervaded the ministry in all "shapes and forms."[79] He gave the example that the ministry stage-managed the minister's visits to schools and institutes for the press in order to convince the public of the ruling party's popularity, rather than meaningfully engaging those institutions' needs. He warned that officials often intimidated and discriminated against employees based on their political affiliation.[80] In another article, he criticized the way the ministry was using teachers of the compulsory elementary education (*al-ta'lim al-ilzami*) as a source of political propaganda instead of offering real solutions to their problems and providing them with a stable, comfortable life. Caring for those teachers in a genuine way, he said, was to care for the entire Egyptian people, given the intimate relationship they have with the young generations that they bring up. "I am convinced," he went on, "that education, no matter its level, should remain above political parties and their political disputes."[81] He believed technical councils could shield policymakers from political exigencies and permit them to focus on short- and long-term planning.

Hussein remained optimistic despite all the problems facing the system, which he believed democracy would eventually fix. Democracy, in his view, was the basis for political life in Egypt and would be recognized as such sooner or later.[82] Excited about Egypt's new parliamentary life, he wrote in 1923 that Egyptians expected much good from parliament. For parliament to do its work, it was the duty of all Egyptians, he said, to voice their opinions about the problems they experienced and the reservations they had about the way the Ministry of Public Instruction was run. Once the country had a serious debate on educational reform and once parliament realized how deficient the ministry was in preparing the ground for "the life of an independent democratic nation," as he described it, Hussein was sure parliament would intervene and put the necessary pressure on the ministry to fix its ways.[83]

Likewise, after independence and the adoption of the 1923 constitution, Hussein wrote that he expected the minister to keep the public informed through clear communiqués about what the ministry was working on and what its plans for the future were. Such transparency would allow people to give their feedback and follow what the ministry was doing.[84] In a series of articles criticizing what Hussein described as the mystery surrounding a proposed plan to merge the School of Judges (Madrasat al-Qada' al-Shar'i)—with al-Azhar, he called on the government to issue a clear statement of its proposal, so that "the fears of Azharites, judges, and those who cared about them are laid to rest." Defending the right of the traditional educational institutions to the same transparency as the new institutions, he said the government should study and prepare the project, but not implement it until the Egyptian people had provided their thoughts via parliamentary debate. Reforming al-Azhar and the School of Judges was not a "state secret," Hussein said, but a matter that affected education. The clearer the plan and the more it was subjected to debate, the better. Thinking about reforming al-Azhar, closing the School of Judges, or narrowing the school's scope would have a huge impact on the entire justice system, he went on, and "people have the right to know. . . . The constitution has returned this right to them. . . . It is their right to worry, [it is their right] to demand an official statement from the government, and to wait for parliament [to have its say]."[85]

After the government made primary education free in 1944, Hussein gave an optimistic speech. He claimed that people's enthusiasm for education indicated growing support for democracy because democracy had inspired them to realize their need for education. Referring to the period between 1942 and 1944, when the Wafd Party was in power, he said:

> I would like to point your attention to the last two years. As soon as Egyptian democracy returned to its normal life, the people's conscience was revealed to them. They realized they needed an education, and they pushed their government to provide and expand this education, not infinitely, but to a great extent. I would have liked to say infinitely, for this is what we should aim for if we were to live a true democratic life.[86]

In making this explicit link between democracy and education, he also clarified how he believed the university was crucial in making the link viable.

> Democracy enables people to recognize their need for justice, truth and ambition. I don't think that people can discover any of that if they are ignorant. Therefore, I am not exaggerating when I say that democracy does not hate anything as much as it hates ignorance and does not like anything as much as it likes science and knowledge.[87]

He further identified the relation between the university and democracy as "the relation between mind and body, the relation between the mastermind [*al-'aql al-mudabbir*] and the material that needs to be managed." He was against the idea of limiting access to university education to a select few, as if higher education were a luxury that should be dispensed to the people cautiously, so it did not raise their expectations or give them wrong ideas. He said such thinking was dangerous for democracy, which called for equal opportunities for all citizens. Whether university education was good or bad, it should not be restricted to the privileged few, he insisted. "University education provides [the country with] the thinking minds capable of organizing other types of education and raising [education's] level." Calls to limit access to university education in order to give more support to primary and secondary education, he warned, were made by those who wanted their country to have "neither a head nor a mind." Access to a university education, he said, should be based on merit and not monopolized by those who had money or power.[88]

While these calls could be read as populist propaganda for his policies, Hussein was speaking out of professional experience. His career in the ministry granted him a bird's-eye view of school admissions. He had read the applications of children of poor parents who were turned away because they found the tuition fees prohibitive or because of a lack of classrooms. In 1942, he wrote about "thousands" of rejected scholarship applications each year.[89] In the ministry, he used these figures to illustrate the need to grant more scholarships and to build a case for free primary education, which was successfully implemented in 1944.⁹⁰ Considering the details of Hussein's project reveals that, unlike earlier nahdawis, he was not simply saying the intellectual class must educate the other classes. He was mobilizing figures and statistics to argue that "the people want to be educated [al-sha'b yurid an yata'allam]."⁹¹

A Democratic Debate on Education

Hussein saw the growing numbers of Egyptians seeking education as a healthy sign, and he sought to persuade the government that providing free education was an important basis for proper governance. In a 1944 speech at the Royal Geographical Society, he cited Plato's *Republic*, Aristotle's *Politics*, and Arab philosophers such as Ibn Khaldun to argue that none of these thinkers could imagine any reform without adequate attention to education. Providing education to the people, Hussein insisted, was the duty of the state.⁹²

Speaking in favor of teachers who had gone on strike demanding better salaries, Hussein argued three years later that the state was created to grant people their rights. If the state failed to deliver those rights, then "the state has no rights over the people and the people should no longer have to obey it."⁹³ He called on Egyptians to accept this principle as one of the cornerstones of their lives, without which their lives would never improve. "Egyptians will not be qualified for freedom, independence, or dignity unless these priorities have become part of their hearts and minds," he wrote.⁹⁴ Hussein was effectively calling for a new contract between state and people by urging Egyptians to see the state's raison d'être as attending to their needs. Education, from Hussein's perspective, not only made people aware of their duties and responsibilities, but also of their rights, especially their right to hold the state accountable and measure its performance by what it was doing to improve their lives.

Hussein's calls for free education did not go unchallenged. His nemesis in this debate was the pedagogue Ismai'l al-Qabbani (1898–1963), who feared that this policy's rapid implementation would diminish educational standards. Their conflict in the 1940s and early 1950s came to be known as the "quantity vs. quality" debate (*ma'rakat al-kamm wa-l-kayf*). Al-Qabbani, who would serve as minister of education from 1952 to 1954, based his position on a detailed analysis of the Ministry of Public Instruction's existing capacities in schools and qualified teachers. He opposed flooding the existing institutions with new students, citing pedagogical studies that advocated limited classroom sizes. He was against the rushed construction of new, substandard schools that did not meet the ministry's requirements in terms of buildings, playgrounds, and laboratories.[95] He also opposed the Wafd Party's attempts to make secondary education free, arguing that in a country like Egypt, with an illiteracy rate of 80 percent, the government should give more priority to elementary education than to secondary education.[96] Qabbani published and lectured widely, and his positions won the support of non-Wafdist officials, such as the Sa'dists.

But Hussein refused to let the number of schools and instructors stall his project. In opposing Qabbani, Hussein expressed an idealistic grand vision and did not linger on its practical restrictions. In this debate, he composed his well-known analogy, which continues to circulate to this day: "education is an absolute necessity, like water and air." He advocated rejecting Qabbani's "elegant pedagogy," which demanded that everything proceed according to strict instructions, on the grounds that it contradicted what Hussein believed the "Egyptian life wanted." What Egyptian life wanted, he thought, was for the entire Egyptian people to get an education.[97] When the Wafd left power in 1944, Hussein lost his position as technical advisor to the minister of public instruction. When interviewed in 1945, he defended the Wafdist policies that had made primary education free. He explained that complaints about the limited number of schools, large classrooms, and insufficient number of teachers were nothing new. The problem had started with independence, when the British were no longer limiting education, but people's new demand for it surpassed what the government could offer. What distinguished the Wafd from other parties, he argued, was that the Wafd refused to give in to these limitations.[98] In the same interview, Hussein voiced his discontent with the famous jurist 'Abd al-Razzaq al-Sanhuri (1895–1971), who became minister of public instruction after the Wafd left power in 1944. Sanhuri was drawing new policies to limit the number of students benefiting from free primary education.[99] Hussein warned Sanhuri against listening to Qabbani's pedagogical methods and going against the "spirit of the constitution" and fueling partisan politics:

> The current minister should realize that the Wafdist minister drew a policy that was approved by parliament. He was exercising his legitimate power when he was drawing his policy and parliament was exercising its constitutional power when it approved his policy. The constitutional way would be for the current minister to draw his new policy and present it to parliament so that parliament decides whether to put it in place of the Wafdist policy.[100]

Historian Misako Ikeda has shown that Hussein's criticism of non-Wafdist policies between 1944 and 1950 and his "water and air" discourse were effective in turning the public opinion against non-Wafd governments.¹⁰¹ Sanhuri tried to charge students for lunch and books, and the minister that followed him, Muhammad al-ʿAshmawi, wanted students to pay fees for stationery, health care, sports, activities, and exams. In this debate, Ikeda explains, others joined Hussein in denouncing the new policies, including the writer and educator Muhammad Farid Abu Hadid (1893–1967), who explained the impact of Hussein's discourse on public opinion this way:

> Some of my respected friends introduced a wonderful innovation about education in their writing and then in their speech: as with water and air, one should not deprive one who seeks education or shut the door in his face. If the Ministry of Education prevents one student, it would be just depriving him of water and leaving his stomach burned or keeping him from air and letting his breath stop. I truly believe that this innovation is novel, witty, amiable, and pleasant. One is pleased to listen to it and is delighted to speak about it. No sooner did people read what these respected friends wrote than they snatched it, reproduced it and repeated it over and over. It has become like a popular song or a beautiful story, or like a well-known proverb about which people do not ask where it is from or who is credited with creating it.¹⁰²

In the face of public pressure, the government was forced to modify its policy and exempt students unable to pay fees for books, exams, and stationery. Moreover, Sanhuri was questioned in parliament by the Wafdist deputy Muhammad Hanafi al-Sharif, who warned him against spreading the kind of confusion resulting from the ministry's indecision about tuition fees.¹⁰³ Given this resistance, the new fees were dropped altogether, except for an optional monthly ten piasters for extracurricular activities.¹⁰⁴

Several years later, in 1949, Hussein made a different case, drawing on his professional experience to resolve the funding problem and also referencing figures made available to the public that summer in *al-Ahram*, which allowed him to call for a better redistribution of the state's annual budget. Rejecting elegant, expensive western pedagogy, Hussein demanded that the Egyptian government adapt its budget to the people's needs and not the other way around. He questioned how the Ministry of Finance understood the term "budget." If the problem was insufficient resources, Hussein proposed raising taxes. "The budget," he argued, "should not be about the Ministry of Finance balancing figures every year, but it should be about balancing taxes and the facilities that people need."¹⁰⁵ He insisted that the government had sufficient resources and that the question was how to manage those resources. He had previously noted that the government had spent 12 million Egyptian pounds on the army alone, when it could have spent some of this money on public education.[106] After the 1948 war in Palestine, he again warned against designating millions of pounds for the army at the expense of education and other vital services. "Egypt has spent a lot of resources to have a strong army. Egypt should know, however, that a strong army needs to protect a strong nation and a strong nation is one that is made of educated and not ignorant people, healthy and not sick people."[107] In yet another article, he expressed the same concerns in these words: "What worries me here is that the military does not overshadow other facilities. Egypt's need to ward off enemy attacks is not more [urgent] than warding off the resident enemy of poverty, ignorance, and illness. Poor, ignorant, and ill people cannot build a strong army." And he used the budget figures published in *al-Ahram* to make his point. Commenting on the Ministry of Public Instruction's request for a million pounds to address the needs of its teachers and schools, he observed that the government promised this funding to the ministry in installments over five years, while simultaneously promising tens of millions of pounds to the military. "Is this serious or a joke [*Ajaddun hadha am muzah*]?" he exclaimed.[108] Hussein demanded nothing less than complete transparency in budget allocations.

Hussein continued to defend free education, despite attacks on the Wafdist policies of 1942–1944, until the Wafd was reelected in 1950. A couple of months before the elections, Hussein predicted the Wafd Party's landslide victory. He declared that if elected, the Wafd was ready to take on the task of free education, which it had started in 1944, and ready to enforce a new policy making secondary education free as well. He wrote that the Wafd was ready to bear the consequences of such policies in front of parliament and the Egyptian people. The Wafd was ready because it had a "magic wand": "The magic wand is that Wafdists love the people and the people love Wafdists. Wafdists speak and people listen. Wafdists call and people respond to their call. . . . Wafdists see themselves as servants to the people and not their masters."[109] When the Wafd returned to power in 1950, Hussein's first decision as minister of public instruction was to make secondary and technical education free. In a statement to *al-Nida'*, he warned that any school headmaster who sent a student home because he or she had not paid the fees, would be fired immediately for having refused to comply with a direct instruction from the ministry. "Gratuity is a commitment that the people's government [*al-hukuma al-sha'biyya*] has taken on in front of parliament, and it is now enforceable by law," he said.[110]

At the beginning of the 1950–1951 school year, Hussein was happy to report to the Council of Ministers that not a single applicant was turned away from the secondary or technical schools. The council duly recorded its appreciation.

> The council has decided to thank and congratulate His Excellency Dr. Taha Hussein Bey, the minister of public instruction, on the incredible effort that his Excellency has done concerning the admission of students into schools and universities and facilitating education to all Egyptians. This is to be published in the various newspapers and to be broadcast from [Cairo] Radio.[111]

To brief the public on his evaluation of the rolling out of free education, Hussein organized a press conference at the Supreme Council of Education in June 1951. He started by thanking the press for helping to make the task possible, and especially thanking the opposition press for its criticism, which forced the ministry to rethink its policies and avoid mistakes. "I hope the supporting press joins the opposition, for we need criticism much more than we need praise," he said. The gratuity was a success, declared the minister, "but I will not say it was an outstanding success, only that it was a good success," he continued. Although all students who applied to secondary and technical schools were accepted, the same could not be said for primary schools and kindergartens due to the limited number of schools.[112]

Throughout these debates, Hussein stressed that a democratic life was only a means to an end, the end being a better life for Egyptians. In a sarcastic article, he attacked intellectuals and politicians who, without shame as he said, blamed Egyptians for their ignorance that led to the spread of the cholera epidemic in 1947. He explained that those who blamed the people for ignorance and poverty should realize that independence, the constitution, and the power to rule were only the means of providing the people "with a happy life that has some grace, pride, and prosperity." He called yet again on political parties to change their methods and focus on eradicating ignorance, poverty, and illness from society, "when in power and when out of power."[113]

Now able to take a step back from being an adversary in the heated debate over free education, Hussein represented the Egyptian Ministry of Public Instruction before the Arab delegations to the second Arab Conference on Culture in Alexandria in the summer of 1950. He thanked the delegations for having elected him president of the conference and for having chosen to meet in Egypt. He did not need to welcome them to Egypt, he said, because nobody needed to be welcomed to his own home. He called on all delegations to address the educational and cultural needs of their countries, for no freedom or independence, he stressed, could be achieved without culture and education. Fortunately, he went on, the conference was taking place in Egypt where important changes were taking place and where free education had just been decreed for all educational stages, except higher education.[114] Despite all the difficulties and frustrations, these accomplishments happened through a democratic process that, he believed, responded to popular needs. He was proud of his ministry's accomplishments in democratizing education. Rejecting the notion that free education was a European innovation, he argued that it was a return to practices that had existed for centuries in the *kuttab* system and at al-Azhar:

> Differences over gratuity, its validity or invalidity, are differences based on sincerity and devotion and wanting what is best for Egypt. Each side of the debate has its reasons and proofs. Free education is not something we have learnt from Europe, but it is a return to our past in the early days of Islam, or even to the early days of modern Egypt. We did not come to know rented education [*al-taʿlim al-maʾjur*] until we came into contact with Europe.[115]

He described free education as a triumphant "Egyptian experiment" that he hoped would benefit other Arab countries in their fight for freedom and independence.[116]

Conclusion

For Taha Hussein, the battle for full independence was both cultural and political. He believed such a battle should be organized along the lines of strong, state-funded institutions that ensured, through free accessible education, that Egyptians understood their rights and responsibilities. The secular university, with its modern subject matter and teaching and research methods, was to provide the thinkers, the teachers, and the technocrats required for this project. Struggling against a British legacy that had centralized all power over the educational system in the hands of the minister of public instruction, and having to address the detrimental impact of the infamous partisan politics of the parliamentary era, Hussein called for the creation of supreme councils whose responsibility was to oversee the work of educational institutions and provide expert opinion for decision makers. Although these technical councils were to continue working under the authority of the minister of public instruction, they offered a more stable platform for the study, coordination, and recommendation of policies, with a firm eye on long-term goals and the interests of the country. Over time, Hussein hoped these councils would accumulate enough legitimacy to become important centers of power with which successive governments would have to reckon. Run by experienced technocrats with the right credentials and expertise, these councils would diagnose and offer solutions to the challenges culture and education were facing. Although final decisions rested with the minister of public instruction, the minister would have to take the recommendations of these councils seriously.

This chapter has also explored the conditions under which Hussein expected the system of free education to unfold and his institutions to run. Disappointed as he was with partisan politics, he believed a parliamentary system remained the best guarantor for the success of his ideas on the long run. Hussein remained optimistic that democracy would gain ground in Egypt, and that his project for educational reform would expedite this process. His critique of his adversaries and his frustrations with politics gave way to a sense of pride and accomplishment when speaking to Arab and foreign audiences about an "Egyptian experiment" that had managed, democratically, to democratize primary, secondary, and technical education and had made them accessible to all Egyptians irrespective of social class. His cooperation with the popular Wafd government that was in power from 1942 to 1944 and 1950 to 1952 marked the peak of this optimism, for he believed these were the periods in which the political party Egyptians trusted was ruling. He interpreted people's clamor for education as a demand for a better life, and he celebrated the election and reelection of the Wafd as the victory of the political party people knew would address their demands.

The fact that the technical councils and free education continued after the regime change in 1952 forces us to question the presumed rupture between parliamentary and Nasserite Egypt. This continuity shows that, in many ways, Nasserite Egypt was built on Hussein's reforms. But in his reforms, Hussein was also anticipating checks on power, including a free press, transparency from government officials, regular turnovers of political power, and governments accountable to the people. With these conditions in view, he did not think that creating the Supreme Council of the Universities compromised the autonomy of the universities. He designed it as a consultation body and hoped it would allow knowledgeable academics to debate and decide on policies affecting their universities before the minister of public instruction made his decisions. Yet, as the regime changed in 1952, the context in which this and other councils had developed changed considerably as well, as will be shown in Chapter 5.

Furthermore, the debate on education shows that Hussein and his colleagues negotiated their ideas and tried to *persuade* the public of the utility of their projects. They chose the political platforms that best supported their ideas, had access to state annual budget figures, and understood government revenues and expenditures, including army allocations. These informed debates helped to shape public opinion and election results, which in turn enforced some political accountability. At the same time, however, one wonders if Hussein was not too idealistic and uncompromising with his vision for universal free education. Even if he believed that the Egyptian state at the time had the financial means to invest in education, he must have known that money and grand statements alone were not enough, and that time, long-term planning, and committed support from the state were required to build the required schools and train the necessary teachers. His hope that a functioning parliamentary system would force the state to revise its priorities and see investment in education and research to be as important as investing in the military remains an unfulfilled dream.

4 DEMOCRATIZING THE LANGUAGE

Taha Hussein and Diversifying Authority over Classical Arabic

> I think you all agree that if there was one thing that should unite our true sincere efforts to elevate science and literature, and to accomplish Arab unity for real and not for mockery, it would be for the government, the Arabic Language Academy, and various organizations, to work together in order to make the writing of the language and the learning of its grammar easier, so that the Arabic language becomes more accessible, and becomes a language the youth can learn and teachers can teach.
>
> Taha Hussein[1]

SINCE THE EARLY *NAHDA*, language reform has been a main concern in the Arabic-speaking world. As the language of the holy Qur'an and the Prophet's sayings, classical Arabic is intimately tied to religion, and proposing changes to the language has always resulted in intense debate. Within a challenging colonial context, classical Arabic had come under attack and was accused of being incapable of keeping up with the scientific achievements taking place in Europe. While *nahdawis* agreed that something had to be done about the language so it could meet the challenges of modern times, they disagreed over the required reforms and how to implement them. Some *nahdawis* even called for the replacement of classical Arabic with the various spoken dialects, while others advocated Latinizing the Arabic script, following the example of the Turkish Republic in 1928.[2]

For Taha Hussein, doing away with classical Arabic was out of the question. Not only did he fiercely defend the language against its critics, praising its richness, precision, and potential for responding to the needs of the time, but he also refused to endorse any artistic or literary expression in colloquial Arabic. He insisted that new cultural contributions must be made in classical Arabic in order to build on and enrich the existing centuries-old heritage. As explained in the previous two chapters, engaging with classical Arab-Islamic thought was at the heart of his oeuvre, and keeping classical Arabic alive was essential for engaging with that tradition. He believed such critical engagement was necessary for "reviving" the classical culture and ensuring its continuity. Yet, like other *nahdawis*, he was also convinced the language was facing dire challenges. He repeatedly voiced his fear that if these challenges were ignored, then the classical language faced the danger of being relegated to religious matters and monopolized by "men of religion," as he described them.

To encourage access to the accomplishments of the classical period, which included not only the religious canon but also *adab*, and to build on them, Hussein called for making classical Arabic more accessible. As education was no longer limited to a select few, he argued that the language, too, had to be "democratized," and brought closer to the people. To reach this end, he insisted on simplifying the rules of grammar and finding ways of making Arabic writing a more accurate reflection of correct Arabic pronunciation. While he acknowledged al-Azhar's role in preserving the language and Arabic sciences over the centuries, he believed that the venerable mosque did not possess the expertise required to deal with the pressing tasks of coining new terminologies, engaging in comparative linguistic studies, creating modern dictionaries, designing new teaching methods, and training language teachers in these new ways. For Hussein, the Faculty of Arts was the only institution capable of providing such necessary training and taking on these serious responsibilities. Working closely with the university and created explicitly to attend to the dangers facing the language was the Arabic Language Academy. Founded in 1932, the academy was to become an authority over classical Arabic as it brought together language experts from Egypt and abroad. Unsurprisingly, Hussein became a full member and then president of the academy, and quickly made simplifying grammar and writing one of the academy's main tasks. He attended its meetings regularly until his death in 1973.

This chapter looks at Hussein's efforts to diversify authority over classical Arabic. In these endeavors, he did not try to marginalize al-Azhar, but he challenged its monopoly over the language. He insisted that the revered institution was too set in its ways to deal with what he considered to be serious challenges undermining the use of classical Arabic in modern times, especially as education became universal and more people were complaining about the difficulty of learning the language. As modern curricula became responsible for teaching classical Arabic in state schools, Hussein and others tried to change the way the language was taught, bringing it closer to the people and finding ways to bridge the gap between spoken and written Arabic.

Modern Times, a Modern Language?

Language reform was a central preoccupation of the *nahda*, and *nahdawi* debates over the role of the Arabic language—its history, capabilities, and suitability for undertaking what these intellectuals considered to be essential social and political reforms—were a defining feature of this movement. Beginning in the second half of the nineteenth century, many of the founders of widely read journals in Egypt and Lebanon were themselves *nahdawi* figures who discussed the status of the language and its syntax, semantics, and writing style on the pages of their periodicals. These included, for example, Butrus al-Bustani (*al-Jinan*), Jirji Zaydan (*al-Hilal*), Ya'qub Sarruf (*al-Muqtataf*), and others.[3] As anthropologist Niloofar Haeri points out, it is difficult to put an accurate date on when these efforts to modernize the language began. She believes modern Egyptian state institutions created under Muhammad Ali, the work of various Arab intellectuals, and numerous social movements and linguistic debates all contributed to these efforts.[4] Accelerated by a closer contact with Europe, many changes were taking place in the world of these *nahdawi* figures, and they were faced with a plethora of new European terms, ideas, and technologies that they believed were necessary for the Arab-Muslim world to understand and put into effective use. Understandably, integrating these terms into the language became a priority.

Scholars refer to Ibrahim al-Yaziji (1847–1906) as the archetype of the *nahdawi* language purist who was perturbed by the way the Arabic language was changing and being used in the new journalistic medium. He hailed language as "the mirror of the conditions of a community and the image of its civilization," and appointed himself the Arabic language watchdog.[5] He published many articles in his periodical *al-Diya'*, which he later collected in his book *Lughat al-Jara'id*, in which he fiercely attacked his colleagues for using inaccurate words, wrong meanings, and infelicitous writing styles. As journals and periodicals were increasing in number and claiming wide readership, he feared they were spreading linguistic mistakes that would lead to the eventual corruption of the language. He argued that his critiques of incorrect usage were the first step toward protecting Arabic's purity, and called for standardizing the language by referring to canonical classical works, such as the writings of al-Zamakhshari (1074–1144).[6]

In Egypt, European colonialism had an important impact on the perception of classical Arabic. Unlike the French who made aggressive efforts to impose the French language in North Africa, the British in Egypt did not try to eliminate classical Arabic. Yet, as Haeri points out, using English and French in higher education and in parts of the state bureaucracy became detrimental to the development of classical Arabic and undermined its image.

> Colonial rule and its consequences weakened the image of Arabic as a "perfect" language. It continued to be viewed as a "miracle" but also somewhat paradoxically as "backward" in comparison to English and French. Unlike the latter, Arabic was perceived as a language unfit and unequipped for dealing with the modern world, with the progress of science and advances in technology.[7]

Thus, intellectuals, educators, and bureaucrats became preoccupied with what they saw as "deficiencies" in classical Arabic, considering it to be "too literary and flowery."[8] The underlying assumption in these discussions was that the language had to become easier to use and more succinct in order to effectively disseminate the new ideas as well as the important scientific and technological terms coming from Europe. While most of these thinkers debated how to respond to these new challenges while simultaneously protecting the integrity of their language, some proposed more controversial measures, such as the adoption of the colloquial language or the Latinization of the Arabic alphabet.

Salama Musa was an influential intellectual who espoused both measures. In *al-Balagha al-'Asriyya wa-l-Lugha al-'Arabiyya*, he argued that "at the core of calling for [having] a modern language was the call for [living] a modern life."[9] Such a modern language, in his view, would never materialize as long as the written language remained separate from society and radically different from the spoken language.[10] He went on to describe the Arabic language as a "dead language" that could not express the ideas used in scientific fields, such as "biology, chemistry, psychology, and hygiene." He added that it was a dead language even as far as Arabic literature was concerned, since this literature was written in a language that millions of Egyptians could not understand. It was not a "people's literature."[11]

Famous for his Fabianism, Musa used socialist ideals to argue that the colloquial speech was the language of the people and should therefore be recognized as the language of the country. He reproached the famous intellectual 'Abbas Mahmud al-'Aqqad for criticizing what Musa believed were socialist calls for adopting the spoken language, or *'ammiyya*. Musa explained that such socialist calls emanated from a commitment to the people and a respect for the language they used in their daily lives, not that of the forefathers (*al-salaf*).[12] These socialists, as Musa called them, were forward looking (*mustaqbaliyun*), when al-'Aqqad and the great majority of Egyptian writers, Musa lamented, were only looking to the past (*salafiyun*).[13] He accused graduates from Dar al-ʿUlum of opposing calls for developing the language because of what he described as their "narrow-mindedness," in addition to their wish to maintain their economic situation, which depended on keeping the language in "its current ossified state."[14] Language and literature, Musa argued, were social phenomena that could be understood using a society's economic situation. As Europe was an industrial society, its language and literature were modern and forward-looking. Egypt, in contrast, was still an agrarian society, whose farming methods, had not changed in hundreds of years, and this was reflected in its language and literature. "Stability in the economic system resulted in the ossification of the linguistic and literary systems," Musa insisted.[15] He was unequivocal about his belief that Egypt's situation would not improve until the language problem had been resolved, even if that meant doing away with classical Arabic altogether.

Adopting colloquial Arabic was, and remains to this day, a highly controversial issue. Scholars—such as ʿAbd al-ʿAziz al-Kumi, Yusuf Qazma Khuri, Niloofar Haeri, and Yasir Suleiman—trace such calls back to the 1880s. Haeri refers to a debate that started when an article published in the periodical *al-Muqtataf* in November 1881 called for writing scientific literature in colloquial Arabic. *Al-Muqtataf* argued that the reason for the progress of Europeans was that the various sciences—for example, algebra, philosophy, and biology—were written in the languages Europeans spoke, while in Egypt the written and spoken languages were different, leading to Egypt's "backwardness." *Al-Ahram* quickly responded by warning against the negative impact of spoken languages, which the *al-Ahram* editors believed had been subjected to "distortion and decay" and warned that spoken languages were an imminent threat to classical Arabic, as dialects weakened the language and could even lead to its loss of form.[16]

Adding to the controversy was William Wilcox's support for using the colloquial. A British irrigation officer, Wilcox became an editor of a magazine called *al-Azhar* in 1893, and he encouraged Egyptian engineers to submit articles in Egyptian Arabic. He also gave speeches in which he praised the use of the spoken language.[17] Yasir Suleiman argues that Wilcox was one of several European thinkers who supported a shift from classical to colloquial Arabic and the adoption of the Latin alphabet. He claims that Wilcox took this editorial position for political reasons supporting the colonial agenda.[18] According to Suleiman, such Orientalists also included de Lacy Evans O'Leary in his work *Colloquial Arabic* (1872) and Seldon Willmore in *The Spoken Arabic of Egypt* (1901), among others.[19] As Haeri explains, this colonial encouragement of the colloquial led to an intense politicization of the debate. "To this day," she explains, "these and similar stories about Wilcox are mentioned as examples of how the 'invitation to 'ammiyya' was an explicit policy of British colonialism to weaken Egyptians and Arabs in general."[20]

Besides Salama Musa, reforming the language was a major concern for many other intellectuals. Qasim Amin and Ahmad Amin both called for doing away with the case endings (al-i'rab) and ignoring the short vowel associated with the last letter (taskin).[21] Although Lutfi al-Sayyid opposed using Egyptian Arabic in artistic and literary creation, he called for bringing classical Arabic closer to the spoken language, and referred to this kind of Arabic as the "Egyptian language."[22] Musa fully embraced a call by 'Abd al-'Aziz Fahmi for the adoption of the Latin alphabet, a move that, according to Musa, implied stopping the use of the case endings in order to simplify the spelling of Arabic words in Latin letters. Such a measure, Musa went on, if implemented "would take Egypt where Turkey is today, where the [Latin] script has closed the doors on the past and opened the gates to the future."[23]

Unthinkable as it may seem today, Latinizing the Arabic alphabet was a serious proposition. It came from 'Abd al-'Aziz Fahmi Pasha (1870–1951), who had all the credentials to be taken seriously. He was a prominent nationalist, judge, lawyer, and once president of the Court of Cassation, the highest judicial authority in the country. As a politician, his name was familiar and respected since he had accompanied Sa'd Zaghlul as part of the Egyptian delegation that went to London and Paris in 1919 to make Egypt's case for independence. He studied European constitutions and was on the committee that wrote Egypt's 1923 constitution after independence was granted in 1922. Furthermore, Fahmi was appointed as a full member of the Arabic Language Academy in 1940, and it was at the academy that he submitted his Latinization proposal so it could be examined by other academy members, including Taha Hussein.

Classical Arabic: Whose Is it?

In her work on the political and cultural implications of the divide between Egyptian and classical Arabic, Haeri probes into the efforts to "modernize" classical Arabic. She raises thought-provoking questions about how these efforts have intersected with politics and official policies, including the question of authority.[24] She asks who has the authority to make changes to the classical language, and whether Egyptians (who are the focus of her work), and Arabs in general, "own" the language or are just its "custodians."²⁵ She raises the question of state institutions and the role they play in challenging the authority of the religious establishment, which she sees as the traditional custodian of the language of the holy Qur'an and the rich religious canon. The state role, in her view, started when Muhammad Ali opened new institutions of learning associated with his modern army. Creating new textbooks and translating the required teaching material from European languages began to transform the way classical Arabic was being used. While state institutions continue to influence the contemporary usage of classical Arabic through college degrees, textbooks, publishing houses, and the overall control of the media, Haeri believes the state does not claim to have full authority over the language as these institutions themselves always evoke classical Arabic as the language of the Qur'an and Islam.²⁶

To give an example of where state authority over classical Arabic is lacking, Haeri refers to three language correctors (*musahihun*) whom she interviewed. They told her that instead of using grammar books written more recently by non-religious scholars, they still refer to classical texts on grammar from the fourteenth and fifteenth centuries, such as *Sharh Qatr al-Nada* by Ibn Hisham (1359), *Sharh Ibn 'Aqil* (1367), and *Sharh al-Ashmuni* (1494). For Haeri, continued reliance on such classical references, which enjoy a prestige that surpasses by far any of the new grammars, not only in al-Azhar but also in state universities, is an indication that the state does not have full authority over the language that is the official language of the country according to the constitution. Haeri concludes that the state never managed to claim complete authority over the language and still has to fight for it.²⁷ Yet, what the state has successfully managed to do, according to Haeri, is diversify the gatekeepers of the language through a form of mediation, or "appropriation."

> [These appropriations] take place at the level of institutions, in the figure of text regulators and on the level of the language itself. The diversification of the gatekeepers of a form, through a variety of means, including the changing curricula of study and control over the creation of different professionals, is a kind of appropriation. In this case, appropriation signifies processes that alter or diversify the legitimate gatekeepers of any given form, and of its domains of use.²⁸

Given the anthropological nature of her work, Haeri does not examine the history of these "appropriations" or how they have rolled out in detail. In fact, she reproaches historians and political scientists for paying only lip service to the role classical Arabic has played in the cultural and political life of the modern

Arab world and calls for undertaking historical research that examines the social and political processes that have influenced classical Arabic.[29]

While Haeri rightly points out the impact of Muhammad Ali's modern institutions of learning, such as schools of engineering, medicine, and law, on classical Arabic and its development, these were institutions that taught practical subjects. As shown in the previous chapters, another modern institution of learning that had an immediate and more direct impact on classical Arabic was the Faculty of Arts. The faculty was explicitly created for the study of the Arabic language, its sciences and literature, and other subjects. While Haeri's fieldwork and pertinent questions reveal how classical Arabic is strongly tied to religion, for the founders of the university, and for Taha Hussein after that, classical Arabic and the classical tradition were not limited to religion.[30] If the language was to be protected and adapted to modern times, that was because it was the language of the classical Arab-Islamic heritage in its entirety, including not only the religious canon but also *adab*.

In *The Future of Culture in Egypt*, Hussein called on the state to take the necessary measures for the proper training of Arabic language teachers and for relying on language experts to simplify the complex rules of grammar and make them more accessible. He advised against resisting these proposed reforms, for without them, he warned, "[we] face the dreadful prospect of classical Arabic becoming, whether we want it or not, a religious language, and the sole possession of the men of religion."[31] Haeri finds it ironic that Hussein put the verb "becoming" in the future, "as if," she explains, "in the preceding centuries this had not been the case."[32] Yet, given Hussein's larger understanding of the classical tradition, his fear should rather be understood as fear of a possible rupture with the Arab-Islamic heritage, access to which would then be restricted to men of religion, who, by training and vocation, would not necessarily wish to engage with other aspects of that tradition, like *adab*.

For Hussein, classical Arabic was not merely a language of religion. It belonged to those who used it, Muslims and non-Muslims alike: "[The Arabic language] belongs to all the nations and generations who speak it. Every individual from these people is free to use this language the way an owner uses it, as long as the conditions that govern this usage have been met."[33] He explained that he could not understand why al-Azhar wished to monopolize the language and resist reform efforts when, historically, the sciences of the Arabic language had been developed before the creation of al-Azhar itself. None of the grammarians who codified the rules of the language, he went on, were Azharites, and most were not men of religion to begin with.[34] He acknowledged, however, that al-Azhar had safeguarded the language and its sciences for centuries, and invited Azharites to participate in the efforts being made to develop these sciences. Yet, he warned against al-Azhar monopolizing such endeavors at the expense of other institutions.[35] He criticized specialists in education who were afraid to voice in public their belief that al-Azhar was ill-equipped to supervise the language or meet the challenges it was facing. He believed al-Azhar was not willing to branch out from its established canon, not willing even to consult other old references if they were not part of its curriculum.[36] For Hussein, simplifying the grammar and the writing, revising teaching methods, and choosing literary texts for schools demanded a certain level of knowledge of the history of other languages and of how foreign languages, ancient and modern, had developed, and also the ability to compare Arabic to other Semitic languages. He believed al-Azhar lacked such knowledge.[37] To make his argument, he reminded his readers about al-Azhar's resistance to the introduction of the study of Arabic literature, and how he and those who attended the lessons of Sheikh Marsafi were subjected to "criticism, ridicule, and mockery." He also reminded readers how Muhammad ʿAbduh was attacked and the sincerity of his beliefs questioned when he tried to introduce modern sciences into the curriculum.[38]

Keeping the classical language alive, relevant, and accessible was vital for the founders of the university and for Hussein. One of their contributions, born out of the *nahdawi* discourse for reform, was the creation of the Faculty of Arts. In their view, the faculty was to study the language not only as an instrumental subject required for the study of law, as was the case at al-Azhar, but as a subject in and of itself.[39] The faculty was to assess the problems facing the language and its needs, study its grammar, literature, and history, examine its origin and relationship to other Semitic languages, and think about its development, teaching, and learning in comparison to modern European languages, which Egyptian students were already learning in school. Compared to European languages, like English and French, teaching classical Arabic was difficult and challenging.

Another *Nahdawi* Institution: The Arabic Language Academy

If the Faculty of Arts was to provide the latest teaching and training methods, experts in the language from the university and elsewhere were to meet in another institution created explicitly for protecting the integrity of the language, as well as proposing and examining solutions for the challenges it was facing. The Arabic Language Academy was founded as the Royal Academy for the Arabic Language (al-Majmaʿ al-Malaki li-l-Lugha al-ʿArabiyya). Like the Egyptian University, the academy was born out of a *nahdawi* discourse that pushed for an active engagement with both the classical tradition and modern European methods to achieve what was considered to be a much-needed reform. Like the university, which was created on a private initiative and then became a state university, several individual attempts to build a language institution finally materialized in the creation of the Royal Academy for the Arabic Language, in 1932, which was under the supervision of the Ministry of Public Instruction. As with the university, the academy's first members included some Orientalists, who also lectured at the university, and similar to the university, the academy was renamed the Fouad I Academy for the Arabic Language in 1938. As soon as Taha Hussein joined the academy in 1940, he modified its mission, reprioritized its activities, and energetically participated in its discussions and activities until the end of his life. He was elected vice-president of the academy on October 10, 1960, and then president on May 13, 1963, after the death of Lutfi al-Sayyid. Hussein remained president until his own death on October 28, 1973.

Early members of the academy saw their institution as the latest addition to a long list of prestigious academies that had brought together like-minded scholars over the centuries to discuss knowledge and science. In one of the first academy meetings, Mansur Fahmi (1886–1959), dean of the Faculty of Arts, spoke to fellow members about the history of world academies and the many efforts to create an academy in Cairo in modern times.[40] He traced these circles of learning and thought, as he described them, back to Athens, Alexandria, Basra, Kufa, Baghdad, Fatimid Cairo, Arab Spain, Florence, and finally Paris, whose academy was constantly evoked by Fahmi and others as the role model for the academy in Cairo. "French academies whether scientific, literary, linguistic and artistic," he said, "have maintained the form in which they had been created in the late eighteenth century, and they remain the model to follow in the creation of academies in all countries."[41] By creating the Arabic Language Academy, Fahmi seemed to be proudly saying, modern Cairo was reclaiming its rightful place among these illustrious ancient and modern cities. Paying tribute to Khedive Ismail, King Fouad's father, Fahmi called the Khedive the first modern patron of the Arabic language. He had financially encouraged the Bustanis to write their encyclopedia and supported their chief, Butrus, so he could write his dictionary *Muhit al-Muhit*. Then in the late nineteenth century, several formal and informal discussions devoted to the Arabic language were organized in Cairo. Local dignitaries keen on *adab*, like Lutfi Salim and Sheikh al-Bakri, met informally to exchange ideas on philosophy, language, and literature.[42] Muhammad ʿAbduh was interested in the idea of establishing a language academy on the lines of the existing European academies, and in 1892, he joined the meetings taking place at Sheikh al-Bakri's.[43] Al-Bakri and his circle discussed the idea of writing a new dictionary for the language and creating an academy entirely devoted to the Arabic language.[44] A decade later, graduates from Dar al-ʿUlum, led by Hifni Nasif, who lectured later at the new university, created a group of their own in which they tried to find Arabic equivalents to the foreign words already in circulation, and they published their findings in their own journal.[45] In 1908, they also organized a seminar on Arabized and foreign words, which lasted for two weeks and ended with another call for the creation of an official language academy.[46] Other figures, like Ahmad Hishmat, Idris Raghib, and Ismaʿil ʿAsim, tried to create similar groups. ʿAsim's group met under the leadership of the Grand Imam of al-Azhar for almost two years, until the eruption of the 1919 revolution.[47]

According to another academy member, Ibrahim Bayumi Madkur (1902–1996), the key figure behind the creation of the official language academy was Ahmad Lutfi al-Sayyid. As discussed previously, al-Sayyid was Muhammad ʿAbduh's student and one of the founders of the Egyptian University.[48] In several articles in his journal, *al-Jarida*, al-Sayyid called for reforming the language and developing it so it reflected the changes taking place in society. He was worried about the differences between written and spoken Arabic and called for bringing them closer together by introducing colloquial words into written Arabic and simplifying the grammar and writing to make the written language more accessible to the general public. After he was appointed director of the National Library (Dar al-Kutub), he created an organization in 1916 to look into linguistic matters, which he called the Dar al-Kutub Academy (Majmaʿ Dar al-Kutub). When it was first established, he had hoped it would become a private institution, on the lines of the Académie Française. The academy met eleven times in the season of 1917–1918 and seven times in the following year before its meetings stopped due to the 1919 revolution. It met briefly again in 1925, and al-Sayyid tried to transform it into a state institution when he became minister of public instruction. He drafted a project for that purpose, which became the blueprint for the decree that was used later for the creation of the new, official Arabic Language Academy in 1932.[49]

Fouad I, patron of the Egyptian University as already discussed, also became the patron of the academy when he asked the Ministry of Public Instruction to create an institution entirely devoted to the Arabic language, its literature and sciences. The rhetoric used to celebrate the creation of the academy was predictably very similar to the one that had hailed the creation of the Egyptian University twenty-four years earlier. According to the founders of the academy, it would be another institution dedicated to seeking knowledge and bringing together people who had the interests of the Arabic language at heart. Mansur Fahmi, in his earlier speech to other academy members, commented on the explicit link between the academy and the university, saying it was a link that would not go unnoticed by the "perceptive observer." Both institutions, he said, shared the same "spirit" in the form of a belief that knowledge was a right for all people, regardless of their race or religion. This spirit, Fahmi explained, was encouraging the academy to invite both Arab and western scholars, who cared for the language and appreciated its *adab*, so they could share their knowledge and unite their efforts. Such scholars, he emphasized, understood the importance of the language and realized that "serving the language was to serve knowledge itself."[50]

The tone of the rhetoric was only one of many similarities between the academy and the Egyptian University. As was the case with the university, the mission of the academy, initially drafted by al-Sayyid, featured the *nahdawi* discourse that prized Arabic as the language of both the old and the new. It was the language of a glorious classical Arab-Islamic culture that modern society had to protect and in which it had to root itself. It was a rich, flexible language capable of responding to the many challenges taking place in a rapidly changing world. According to the royal decree, the academy was created explicitly to honor all these qualities:

> [to] maintain the integrity of the Arabic language; to adapt it to the demands of progress in the sciences and arts, and generally to make it suitable for the needs of life in modern times, and [to accomplish] this through deciding in dictionaries or special glossaries and other means, which words and structures should be used and which should be avoided.[51]

The academy would invite university professors, sheikhs from al-Azhar and Dar al-'Ulum, and well-established writers, journalists, and intellectuals from Egypt, the Arab world, and Europe to implement this mission. Using the familiar *nahdawi* tropes called upon for the creation of the Egyptian University, Muhammad Tawfiq Rif'at, the first president of the academy, reiterated in his opening speech the significant role Egypt's modern institutions, including the academy, were playing in the revival of classical culture: "The East is shaking off its dust of lethargy and is working to revive its immortal glory and recover its old honor, and has found in Egypt the best example.... The Arabic language is the strongest tie that has linked Egypt to these faraway peoples."[52]

More concretely, to carry out its mission, the academy was charged with replacing foreign and colloquial words with correct Arabic words, using the standard methods that had been used by grammarians for centuries like *qiyas* (analogy), *ishtiqaq* (derivation), and *majaz* (metaphor). If this process was unsuccessful, then *taʿrib* (Arabization) of foreign words could be used.[53] The academy was to produce a historical dictionary of the language, and regularly publish findings on the etymology of words as well as their changing meanings and connotations. It would also study the various dialects used in Egypt and other Arab countries. Like the state university, the academy was to receive systematic funding and support from the state. As a function of the Ministry of Public Instruction, the academy was also obliged to undertake any research necessary for the development of the language as decided by the minister of public instruction, who was the higher president of both the academy and the state university.[54] The minister was to approve the academy's annual budget and its acceptance of donations, as well as endorse its internal regulations. Officials from the ministry would manage the academy's finances and the Council of Ministers would decide on hiring the necessary employees, as well as the allowances and bonuses for academy members.[55] Contrary to Lutfi al-Sayyid's initial plans, the academy was born as a division of the ministry, tied to it both financially and politically.

Among the first academy members tasked with these duties were Mansur Fahmi, who was then dean of arts at the Egyptian University; Ahmad al-ʿAwamri and ʿAli al-Jarim, inspectors of the Arabic language at the Ministry of Public Instruction; and the well-known Orientalists H.A.R. Gibb (London School for Oriental Languages), A. Fischer (Leipzig University), A. Nallino (Rome University), L. Massignon (Paris University), A. J. Wensinck (Leiden University), and M. Littmann (Tubingen University). Nallino, Massignon, and Littmann had all taught at the Egyptian University. Al-Azhar was represented by Sheikh Ibrahim Hamrush, sheikh of the Faculty of the Arabic Language, and Sheikh Muhammad al-Khidr Husayn, professor in the Faculty of Religious Sciences. Sheikh Ahmad ʿAli al-Iskandari, a professor of Arabic, represented Dar al-ʿUlum. Other members included Egypt's chief rabbi Haim Nahum, the journalist Faris Nimr, the notable Syrian scholar Muhammad Kurd ʿAli, Father Anastase-Marie, a Carmelite, and the Tunisian scholar Hasan ʿAbd al-Wahab.[56] Muhammad Tawfiq Rifʿat was elected president of the academy on March 1, 1934, and can be seen in the photograph here, seated to the right of the minister of public instruction,

Democratizing the Language   149

FIGURE 14. Meeting at the Arabic Language Academy, 1934. Source: *Majallat Majmaʿ al-Lugha al-ʿArabiyya* 1 (October 1934).

Hilmi ʿIssa, and surrounded by other academy members in June 1934.[57] The Grand Sheikh of al-Azhar, Muhammad al-Maraghi, was invited to attend the inauguration ceremony for the academy's third and fourth sessions and joined the academy as a full member in 1940.[58]

In terms of provisions for disseminating the work of the academy, the decree stipulated that the Ministry of Public Instruction was to use its own printing houses to publish the academy periodical and other publications, like dictionaries. The academy's decisions were to be broadcast to the public, and its usage recommendations were to be applied in government offices, especially in educational materials and school textbooks.[59] As early as 1938, the academy sent a list of 2,400 new terms, recorded and approved by its various committees, to the Ministry of Public Instruction. The ministry was to publish and circulate these words among teachers and writers in order to standardize the spelling of these terms and put an end to the confusion arising from arbitrary usage.[60] To regulate its interactions with the public, the academy created a Committee for General Issues, responsible for interfacing with the public and circulating everyday terms approved by the academy to replace foreign and colloquial words.[61] The academy was also expected to contact various ministries and chambers of commerce, and send delegates to investigate incorrect usage of Arabic words and expressions in these organizations. To maximize the academy's reach, lists of correct words were also to be published in newspapers and magazines, and the owners of these newspapers would be encouraged to use these correct forms in their publications.[62]

Taha Hussein Joins the Academy

The political reasons that stopped Lutfi al-Sayyid from joining the academy when it first opened its doors may well have been the same reasons that delayed the appointment of Taha Hussein as a full member. When King Fouad and his minister of public instruction, Hilmi 'Issa, created the academy in December 1932, they were at the height of their university crisis with Hussein. As previously discussed, tensions had escalated when Hussein refused to comply with Fouad's and 'Issa's wishes to confer honorary degrees upon government supporters. Lutfi al-Sayyid, then president of the university, stood by Hussein, and submitted his resignation in protest of the ministry's decision to transfer Hussein from the university. It is very likely that both al-Sayyid and Hussein were excluded from the academy for that reason. Their appointment had to wait until Fouad's death and the issuance of a decree on November 25, 1940, inviting a new group of intellectuals to join the academy as full members. The new members included Taha Hussein (who was also the controller of general culture at the time), Lutfi al-Sayyid, Husayn Haykal, Mustafa 'Abd al-Raziq, 'Abd al-'Aziz Fahmi (who later proposed the Latinization of the alphabet), 'Abbas Mahmud al-'Aqqad, Ahmad Amin, and the Grand Imam of al-Azhar, Sheikh Muhammad Mustafa al-Maraghi.[63]

Hussein quickly put his mark on the academy's structure, mission, and activities. One of his first decisions was to revise the regulations of the academy and give it more autonomy. Academy president Muhammad Tawfiq Rif'at welcomed the new members in 1940, and explicitly thanked Taha Hussein and the jurist 'Abd al-Razzaq al-Sanhuri for the changes they had made to the academy regulations, which in Rif'at's view, allowed the academy to better carry out its mission.[64] Rif'at did not specify what the changes were. Yet, comparing the new regulations to the old ones of 1932 reveals that Hussein and Sanhuri tried to give more power to academy members. According to the new regulations, the number of members increased from twenty to thirty, and the Council of Ministers was no longer involved in hiring employees. Moreover, from then on, academy employees would report only to the academy president.

Another measure that was clearly Hussein's work involved new academy regulations stipulating the creation of what was called the Academy Office, which was in line with his idea for creating technical councils working as independently as possible from the minister of public instruction so they would be sheltered from the partisan politics at the ministerial level. The Academy Office was to be composed of the president of the academy, the undersecretary of the Ministry of Public Instruction, and four academy members chosen by the minister of public instruction from a list of eight members elected by the academy. The Academy Office became responsible for preparing the annual budget (done previously by the ministry), appointing academy employees and managing their supervision, promotion, and transfer, and attending to other tasks assigned to the office by members of the academy.[65]

In this way, while respecting that the academy was a state institution receiving its budget from the state and presided over by the minister of public instruction, Hussein used his authority as controller of general culture at the ministry to give more power to the academy members. Creating the Academy Office was in line with his vision that technocrats should be in charge of as much policy and budget planning as possible.[66] In his view, this enhanced the independence of the academy and its research, while keeping its members sheltered from ministry politics and from administrators who lacked the knowledge necessary to engage with the challenges facing the language.

In terms of academy activities, Hussein raised two issues that became the subject of much discussion and debate for years. He proposed that academy members, with their expertise and interest in the language, must find ways to promote *adab* and literary production, and they must also design ways to render classical Arabic more accessible to the general public. Upon Hussein's recommendations, Husayn Haykal, then minister of public instruction, issued a decree on February 6, 1941, assigning these two new tasks to the academy: simplifying the writing and the rules of the language, and encouraging modern literary production. According to this decree, the academy became responsible for encouraging writers to compete over "excellent literary production."[67] Hussein, as controller of general culture, then turned a literary competition, initially organized by the Ministry of Public Instruction, over to the academy, explaining that it was now the responsibility of the Arabic Language Academy to handle such kinds of competitions.[68] A special committee for literature was created to handle this assignment, and was tasked with finding ways to encourage literary production. Called the Literature Committee (Lajnat al-Adab), it included some of the most well-known literary names at the time: Lutfi al-Sayyid, Husayn Haykal, Taha Hussein, Ahmad Amin, 'Ali al-Jarim, 'Abbas Mahmud al-'Aqqad,

Mahmud Taymur, and Ibrahim al-Mazini.[69] For the first competition, Hussein forwarded sixty-six novels to the academy for the Literature Committee to review. Among the five eventually shortlisted for the prize were *Malak min Shuʿaʿ* by ʿAdil Kamil, *Kifah Tiba* by Naguib Mahfouz, and *Wa Islamah* by ʿAli Ahmad Bakathir. Although the committee decided that none of the novels deserved the first prize, it recommended the five novels for publication. But first, the authors had to fix what the committee described as "instances of incorrect language usage."[70]

Encouraged by the new literature competition, the famous Egyptian nationalist and leader of Egypt's feminist movement, Huda Shaʿrawi, created another competition, in 1943, which she placed under the supervision of the academy. She called it the Farouk I Prize for Arabic poetry and the Egyptian Story, and donated LE 100 annually for it. Similarly, the editor in chief of *al-Ahram*, Antun al-Jimayil, allocated LE 50 for a prize to be awarded by the academy for the best study on the history of translation in Egypt during the nineteenth century.[71] The awarding of literary prizes continued, and Hussein was happy to note that most awards for literary research were going to university graduates like Suhayr al-Qalamawi and Salim Hasan.[72] In the late 1950s, the academy started honoring some of the well-established names in the literary field, and Hussein was the first to receive the academy prize for literature. Lutfi al-Sayyid received the prize for the social sciences, and Mustafa Nazif for the sciences. The following year the prize for literature went to ʿAbbas Mahmud al-ʿAqqad.[73]

The second task for academy members was to consider how to make classical Arabic easier to teach and learn. They were to find ways to make writing Arabic easier and to simplify the rules of grammar and morphology. As discussed previously, Hussein had already talked about the importance of both measures in *The Future of Culture in Egypt*, and they became two of his main priorities when he joined the academy. Likewise, some ministers of public instruction, like Bahiy al-Din Barakat, had expressed their concern about the difficulties encountered by teachers and students in Arabic language classes. To deal with this task, the academy's Principles Committee (Lajnat al-Usul) was created to verify that none of the proposed solutions infringed in any way upon the well-established principles guiding the correct usage of the language.[74] A subcommittee for the simplification of grammar was chosen from the members of the Principles Committee, and included Taha Hussein, Ahmad Amin, and ʿAli al-Jarim. Barakat asked the committee to investigate possible solutions and indicate what changes were necessary to address this problem.[75]

It was in the context of the work done to simplify language rules and its writing that on May 3, 1943, ʿAbd al-ʿAziz Fahmi proposed Latinizing the Arabic alphabet. He argued such a measure would ensure the language was written and pronounced correctly. Fahmi's proposition was referred to the Principles Committee, and the academy decided to publish his suggestion in 1944 to get feedback from the public.[76] Hussein firmly opposed Fahmi's proposal from the start, both during academy meetings and openly in the press. Latinizing the alphabet would have dealt a blow to Hussein's project. A critical engagement with the classical tradition demanded an advanced command of classical Arabic. He believed that the integration of modern European accomplishments had to happen in classical Arabic as well so that the required continuity with the past would be preserved. In that way, European ideas would be integrated into the already rich tradition of Arab-Islamic culture without overwhelming that tradition. Moreover, changing the Arabic script would have alienated people and would have restricted future access to the classical tradition to a select few. In *The Future of Culture of Egypt*, Hussein explained that Egyptians taught and learned Arabic because it was their national language, by which he meant that Arabic was not only the language of religion, or merely a means for communication in society, or even just a tool for thinking and feeling, but that the Arabic language also "transfers the heritage of our forefathers to us, and it receives from us the heritage that it shall deliver to the future generations."[77] He could not accept the adoption of the Latin alphabet.

Democratizing Classical Arabic

Taha Hussein must have seen such radical propositions for language reform, such as Fahmi's Turkish example, as increasing the challenges facing the Arabic language. Moreover, as shown in Chapter 1, he was particularly aware of colonial attempts to undermine classical Arabic and France's aggressive efforts to make French the language of education and culture as well as politics and administration in North Africa, especially Algeria.[78] He was also responding to calls for the adoption of ʿammiyya by Salama Musa and others. We must read his condemnation of any literary or artistic creation in ʿammiyya and his fierce defense of classical Arabic in this context, and see them as reactions to what he considered to be a series of threats to the classical language, which was the cornerstone of his oeuvre.[79] As he specifically said:

> The Arabic language that I want taught at school in the best and most complete way is the classical language, and nothing else. It is the language of the holy

> Qur'an and the venerable hadith. It is the language of what the ancients have left us in poetry and prose, in science, literature, and philosophy. I would like the conservatives in general, and the Azharites in particular, to know that I am the farthest one could be from those who think that the colloquial could function as a tool for understanding or for communication, or as a means to accomplish what our intellectual life needs. Since my youth, I have resisted [such calls] as much as I could, and I think have been largely successful. I will continue to resist as long as I live and as long as I can resist. For I cannot imagine renouncing that great heritage that the classical Arabic language has preserved for us.[80]

Hussein's eye was always on the classical heritage, and his efforts focused on ensuring continued access to it. Men of religion, as he called them, would always be trained in the classical language, as it is the language of the Qur'an and the religious tradition. Yet, their training at al-Azhar was designed to help them understand the law, and studying the language or its literature was not a goal in itself. When Hussein warned against al-Azhar's monopoly of the language, his concern was the entire classical heritage, in which the religious establishment was only partially interested. As such, his concern was not driven by animosity toward men of religion, but rather his wish to ensure that the language and the tradition as a whole were made accessible to more people.

In one of Hussein's long and lesser-known public lectures, which he gave in January 1955 in front of various intellectuals and specialists from the academy and the university, Hussein reiterated his position on classical Arabic and the problems it was facing. In this lecture titled "The Problem of *al-Iʿrab*," that is, case endings, Hussein started by saying that the title of the lecture was forced upon him, and he feared it was confusing. He described the word *iʿrab* as a "very scary word" and reminded his audience that as students, all of them, including himself, feared that word. To lessen the psychological impact of the word *iʿrab*, he said, he preferred to return the word to its original meaning. As explained in dictionaries, *iʿrab* meant "to speak clearly and eloquently like the Arabs when they expressed [*yuʿribun ʿan*] themselves." Yet, as more people in various regions started speaking Arabic, they found it difficult to express themselves the way the Arabs did. As a result, many of them found refuge in colloquial speech, which according to Hussein, "did not require study, research, determining case endings, or any of the problems facing anybody trying to use classical Arabic." Calls for replacing classical Arabic with the colloquial, Hussein explained, were therefore not new. The academy, he added, was founded specifically to "preserve the integrity of classical Arabic, to allow it to adapt itself to the times in which it lives, and to face modern civilization without fear."⁸¹ The problem, in his view, was not the case endings, which were an integral part of the language and should be preserved, but the complex way in which existing grammar books explained the rules that governed the use of these case endings. He lamented that some Arabic speakers were turning their backs on the language and were even asking others to do the same. Such people were ignoring how strong and flexible the language was, how well it had adapted itself to the "cultures of Greece, Persia, and India," and how easily it was doing so also with "the culture and knowledge that the European and American civilizations were bringing." If members of the academy believed in the language, Hussein went on, and did not need to be convinced of its "power, flexibility, and capacity for resistance," their duty was to convince the others.⁸² Ultimately, the "challenges facing the language [today] are very dangerous, and are not devoid of difficulty, yet the difficulty does not come from the language itself, but from its owners."⁸³

Hussein had repeatedly warned that even educated people's command of the language was seriously lacking. Earlier, he had relayed this concern to the president of the Egyptian University. Students, he cautioned, were not benefiting from the huge efforts made to teach them the Arabic language and its literature.⁸⁴ Similarly, he wrote to the minister of public instruction expressing his dismay at the low level of fluency in classical Arabic among young men and women.

> Experiments have shown that our youths are the farthest they could be from an average command of the language, not to mention fluency in it, the fluency that allows them to maneuver it the way someone who owns a language can, [someone who] is in control of its intimate details. After a lot of effort spent on this language—four years in primary school and five years in secondary school, [they] reach university or the higher colleges and they are incapable of representing their views or their thoughts in the correct way—whether in writing, speech, or in conversation, not to mention representing these views and thoughts in wonderful poetry or beautiful artistic prose.⁸⁵

Although in the same report Hussein praised the younger generation for having introduced the art of the novel to Arabic literature, he remained disappointed with these young writers' command of the language. Despite what he described as their acute sense of observation and their attention to the details of this new art, he warned that they had to respect the language and the rules that governed its correct usage: "Without respecting the characteristics of the Arabic language and its literature, . . . the beautiful imagery, the exquisite style, and the correct language necessary for any literature, this new art will only be a colloquial art destined for mortality."⁸⁶

Softening his tone when talking about those calling for the adoption of the colloquial, Hussein repeated that the problem was how Arabic was being taught in schools, with complex grammar rules and poor choice of literary texts. He believed such teaching methods failed to attract students and stopped them from appreciating the language. He did not underestimate the danger of these calls, however, and warned that if people started turning to the colloquial, then a day would come when Egyptians would need to translate what the Iraqis and Syrians were writing, and the Iraqis and Syrians would not understand what the Egyptians were writing.⁸⁷ "And I don't think," he concluded, "that any lover of the Arabs, Arab life and its history, the Qur'an that the centuries have inherited, or this colossal heritage, could possibly find appealing the absurdity that is being proposed."⁸⁸

Interestingly, Hussein was not only against Egyptians undertaking literary or artistic expression in the vernacular. He did not endorse their writing in foreign languages either. In his review of *L'Égypte dans Mon Miroir*, a book written in French by the Egyptian francophone writer Jeanne Arcache, Hussein complimented her on the book and on her command of the French language, which, he said, made it difficult for any reader to think French was not her mother tongue. The likes of Arcache in Egypt at the time, Egyptian men and women who were totally proficient in French and used that language in literary creation, were not a few, according to Hussein. "I do not know if this is good or bad," he admitted. Even though he saw these writers as honest translators of how Egyptians thought and felt, he considered that they deprived their fellow Egyptians and the Arabic language itself of their work:

> When [these Egyptians] write or compose in a foreign language they deprive Egyptians and easterners in general who are not fluent in foreign languages of the fruits of their effort. They even deprive the Arabic language itself of their effort. Instead, they give these efforts to people who may not actually need them.⁸⁹

Writing this review in 1935, Hussein argued that the state was to blame for not having protected the Arabic language enough, and for not teaching it properly. The state was also to blame for having ignored building schools for so long, forcing parents to send their children to foreign schools.⁹⁰ He found Arcache's book so valuable and full of Egyptian imagery worthy of admiration, as he said, that he could not but feel sorry that the majority of Egyptians would not be able to share his enjoyment of the book.⁹¹

Over several decades, Hussein and others tried to address the problem. His goal was for people to eventually feel more comfortable with the language and engage with the classical tradition more easily. He criticized how grammar was being taught, separately, in the form of dry rules that students found convoluted and unappealing, instead of being experienced through interesting texts that made students curious and addressed their modern lives. He was against teaching grammar as if it were an end in itself:

> Grammar in school textbooks should shake off that inherited disconnect which comes to it because it is presented [to students] as rules that are separate from the language and far from its literature. [Grammar is] taught as if it were an end in itself when it is only a means. Students would stomach it if it were connected to proper words and taught as a means to understanding and appreciating good taste.[92]

As for reforming the writing, he wanted to make it easier and ensure it was a better reflection of accurate pronunciation. Arabic is mostly written using only consonants. Short vowels (*al-tashkil*), which indicate correct pronunciation and determine the case endings based on the role of the word in the sentence, are usually not supplied except in the Qur'an. Hussein was therefore pushing to find a solution that would incorporate *al-tashkil* into the writing of other materials so that words were always fully vocalized.[93] In his view, such accessible, precise vocalization of classical Arabic would help people avoid making mistakes when reading or writing.[94]

> I want the writing to be an honest accurate representation of the pronunciation, not to represent some of [what is pronounced] and not the rest, not to represent half the term [*al-lafz*] and canceling the other half. I want writing to represent what we call the letters and what we call the vocalization [*al-harakat*] in a way that is complete on one hand and easy, quick, and economical in time, effort, and money on the other hand.[95]

When the short vowels were absent, Hussein explained, readers first had to understand the text and see what each word was doing in the sentence before they could deduce the appropriate short vowels and read it correctly. "We should read in order to understand," he said, "not understand in order to read." Properly vocalized texts, he insisted, were necessary so that readers could focus on reading, understanding, and thinking deeply about the text.[96] The current way grammar was being taught and the language was being written meant that students suffered.

> This year I read some of the students' answers on one of the exams of the high school certificate. What I read was odd to the point that it filled me with anger and irritation. I saw how grammar and rhetoric lessons corrupt the taste of young people, in the expressions they use, the imagery, the formulation of terms, and how they relate words to meaning. [Students] say words without fully understanding them, and repeat sentences that they had learnt by heart from their teacher. The teacher did not understand those sentences when he dictated them, and students did not understand those sentences when they heard them. And we did not understand those sentences when we graded them.[97]

With his proposed reforms, Hussein was convinced the Arabic Language Academy would strengthen classical Arabic, not weaken it, and enrich people's knowledge of its vocabulary. He said he would continue to resist calls for the Latinization of the alphabet or the adoption of the colloquial, but he warned that such resistance would be futile if serious measures were not taken to make the language accessible, in which case people would turn away from the classical tongue altogether.[98] By reforming how the language was taught, Hussein wanted to democratize classical Arabic. After having made education universal and compulsory in some of its stages, he believed that simplifying the rules of grammar also became an obligation. For him, democratizing education meant democratizing the language as well. He saw finding ways to make the language accessible as a duty.[99]

> If the writing and the grammar have been simplified, and if teachers have taught literature and the language in a way that is adapted to the minds of the youth by selecting [texts] that agree with modern taste, if all this is done well—and as you know education has been made universal—I have no doubt that one day not far from now . . . strong life will have returned to the language, and it will become not just the language of intellectuals or just the language of literature, but a language of intellectuals and literature which the entire people can understand.[100]

Rendering classical *adab* more accessible was crucial to Hussein, and he tried to do so in many of his books. Perhaps his most famous attempt in that direction was a series of articles published in 1924 in *al-Jihad* and *al-Siyasa*. He later gathered these articles into a three-volume work: *Hadith al-Arba'a'*. In this classic work, Hussein helped contemporary readers understand and appreciate pre-Islamic poetry, or the "old *adab*," as he called it. He admitted that the language of that old *adab* was unfamiliar, and that dictionaries and language references for it were complex and difficult to use. When readers found nothing to help them understand this "unwilling literature" (*adab nafir*), he wrote, especially when some of it was forced on them at school, this only pushed them away from literature and from school itself. Readers then turned to the European literatures, which they found simpler and more accessible.[101] Old literature, he insisted, however, must remain alive in modern times.

> We do not want this old literature to remain today what it was before, for we neither like the old simply because it is old, nor do we long for [the old] out of sentiments of passion and nostalgia. We like old literature [because it should] be the underpinning [*quwam*] of culture and food for thought, because it is the basis of Arab culture. It is the chief element [*muqawwim*] of our personality, the achiever of our nationhood, our guardian against dissolving into the foreign, and what helps us know who we are.[102]

Hadith al-Arbaʿaʾ was born out of Hussein's wish to involve contemporary readers in literary discussions that helped them appreciate the classical literary canon. His work, he argued, proved that those who claimed that old literature had become obsolete, irrelevant, or dead were making such claims out of "ignorance."[103] So, week after week, he selected and analyzed poetry from the pre-Islamic era, followed by the Umayyad and Abbasid periods, and ending with modern poetry. He also reviewed new literary works and responded to his readers and critics.

Finally, in order to improve the abilities of Arabic language teachers, Hussein pushed hard for the Faculty of Arts to take on the responsibility of their training. After receiving their training at the university, he also wanted them to spend time at the institute for teachers to learn more about teaching and pedagogy.[104] He therefore wanted this institute, which was created in 1929, to be annexed to the university. The Ministry of Public Instruction refused, however, as it did not want to relinquish control over the teachers who would later teach in its schools.[105] Hussein believed that the Faculty of Arts was the only institution capable of properly training Arabic language teachers. In 1935, he wrote a report after the annexation of the veterinary school and the schools of engineering, agriculture, and commerce to the university. He called for the annexation of Dar al-ʿUlum to the university as well, and argued that Dar al-ʿUlum, where future Arabic language teachers were trained, should have been the first of these higher colleges to join the university.[106] In his view, some of these teachers should be trained in Semitic languages while others should know Islamic and European languages. In this way, they would collectively gain a better understanding of Arabic literature and other literatures. He believed a comparative approach was necessary to enable teachers to assess the current needs of the language and how to make it more accessible and appealing to youths. Only the university, he insisted, had the technical means to provide such training in terms of teaching methods and materials, especially given its strong ties to academic life in Europe, and the university's young age, which made it less burdened by the traditions weighing on other institutions, like al-Azhar and Dar al-ʿUlum. The "way" of the university, he stressed, was to "preserve the old heritage without being paralyzed by it or forcing it to ossify; to nourish [the old heritage] with the new so that heritage could live, grow, and be active."[107] Similarly, he was against al-Azhar's wish to train Arabic language teachers. He explained that al-Azhar had a "critical religious mission" and should not have to worry about supplying state schools with language teachers. Given its mission, he went on, al-Azhar by definition had to be conservative and extremely careful about change. He also cautioned against the power exerted by al-Azhar's Council of Senior Scholars (Hay'at Kibar al-ʿUlamaʾ) over Azharites, and warned that if that council decided to excommunicate an Azharite teacher, then the minister of public instruction would be forced to remove that teacher from his position, thus compromising both the power of the state and academic freedom.[108]

Getting the Work of the Academy Out There

Despite the efforts of the academy to simplify grammatical rules and writing, Taha Hussein could not hide his disappointment with the results. He explained in 1955 that the academy had tried hard but had been unlucky with delivering its work to the people. In terms of simplifying the writing, he said, the academy did not receive enough support to implement its recommendations in a useful way, and he called for taking these recommendations more seriously. In one of the rare instances in which Hussein admitted his inability to assist in a particular endeavor related to the language, he implicitly referred to his blindness when he asked his audience not to question him on how to simplify the writing. "Do not ask me how to make the writing easier," he pleaded.[109] For years, the academy had examined various propositions for changing the writing, including ʿAbd al-ʿAziz Fahmi's. In 1947, an open competition was announced in newspapers, with a 1,000-pound prize to be awarded to the best proposal for simplifying the writing, and members of the academy were not allowed to participate. The committee received over two hundred proposals and studying these proposals carried on until May 1952. Eventually, however, the committee decided that none of the proposals represented a workable solution, cancelled the prize, and called for further studies.¹¹⁰ Finally, in 1956, the academy participated in a committee organized by the cultural division of the Arab League, to which representatives from various Arab countries had been invited. Collectively, they decided to drop the question of simplifying writing by hand and to focus instead on standardizing writing in print, especially in school textbooks, to ensure students learned correct pronunciation.¹¹¹

On the issue of grammar, Hussein accused those who monopolized the language and its grammar of having resisted the efforts of the academy to simplify it. "Those who monopolize grammar, or those who monopolize the Arabic language, have decided, among themselves one day, that reforming the grammar would be a corruption of the Qur'an."¹¹² He said he could not understand why such a link had been made between grammar and the Qur'an. "When the Qur'an came down, Arabic grammar did not exist. When the Qur'an was recited during the first half of the first century, grammar did not exist. Grammar was created afterward, and so, it did not accompany the Qur'an. The Qur'an had existed without grammar."¹¹³ Hussein explained that classical grammarians wrote down rules for grammar, and then described already existing words or case endings that did not match their rules as exceptions. Nothing, he insisted, forbade the creation of a new simplified grammar that codified the rules of the language without changing it. He admitted that the Arabic grammar was one of the Arabic sciences closest to his heart, as he found "pleasure in reading difficult grammar books, despite the philosophy and the complexity that characterize them." But even if he and other language specialists liked to read and study such complex works, it would be "foolish" to subject hundreds of thousands of young men and women to learning the existing grammar, with its "problems, difficulty and convolution."¹¹⁴ Only with a simplified grammar, he said, could the youth learn the language "with ease and without violence."¹¹⁵ In *The Future of Culture in Egypt*, Hussein had made a similar call for simplifying grammar so that students would not be burdened with its philosophy, and argued that only language specialists needed to go into the expansive details.¹¹⁶ As he explained in one of his reports to the minister of public instruction, he believed it was silly to teach grammar the way it was taught a thousand years ago in Basra and Kufa.¹¹⁷ The reluctance to modify this ancient teaching method, according to Hussein, resulted from an erroneous assumption that grammar *was* the language, and that grammar should not be touched given that it was the language of the Qur'an and the hadith and thus should be preserved. He pointed out that Arabic language had developed and changed several times over the course of its history without having any impact on the Qur'an or the hadith.[118]

Hussein was especially disappointed because the academy had submitted its recommendations for the simplification of grammar in 1944 to the Ministry of Public Instruction, yet these reports, he complained in 1955, were still "asleep" in the drawers of the ministry, waiting to be taken into consideration.[119] According to Ibrahim Bayumi Madkur, who succeeded Hussein as president of the academy, these recommendations were more than enough to facilitate the learning and teaching of grammar and morphology, and Madkur lamented that the ministry had not followed through with rolling out the new curriculum in state schools.[120] He noted how enthusiastic Hussein had been about this task, and how he had offered to write the new grammar book himself.[121]

The lack of cooperation from the Ministry of Public Instruction was not the only difficulty facing the academy. Members of the academy in this early formative period realized they had to agree first among themselves on how to carry out their duties. For example, they had to decide not only on the methods to use for the creation of new terms but also on the ways to disseminate their work to the public. Regarding technical questions, Ibrahim Madkur explained that it was not until 1949 that members of the academy had settled to some extent on what to do with the new words in circulation. They decided that the academy's duty was to record the terms scientists and specialists were using in their respective fields, in addition to words from colloquial speech that had their origin in classical Arabic. Then the respective committees were to decide on the equivalent correct terms for them. This included the Arabization of foreign words if the experts could not agree on equivalent terms from Arabic itself.[122] Part of the problem the academy faced with coining new terms, according to Madkur, was the lack of specialized literary and scientific academies, like the ones that operated in France and worked closely with the Académie Française to standardize scientific terminology.[123]

While the academy could propose various changes to the language—on condition that none of these changes broke any of the standard rules governing correct language usage—it did not have the authority to impose its recommendations and did not seek to do so. Madkur states that members of the academy deliberated on what to do with the various terms that they approved, published, or sent to various organizations. Should writers and researchers be forced to use these terms? "Fortunately," Madkur went on, "[the academy] firmly opposed such an idea, and left writers and researchers free to decide for themselves."

Democratizing the Language   163

By approving certain terms and not others, members of the academy believed that the academy was giving more legitimacy to the correct terms, and this, its members judged, was enough.[124]

Other problems had a more direct impact on widening the gap between the academy's recommendations and the general public. Publishing these recommendations, as well as the academy conference proceedings and its periodical, was a major concern. Forced to rely on the state printing press (al-Matba'a al-Amiriyya) through the Ministry of Public Instruction, the academy was not free to publish systematically or on time. The Second World War and the lack of printing paper only made matters worse and resulted in a severe backlog.[125] As a result, the academy at times had to publish its periodical years after the actual academy meetings had taken place, and its work was not being made available to the public in a consistent manner. Hussein pushed repeatedly for the academy to have its own printing press, but he was unsuccessful.[126]

Furthermore, Madkur admitted that within the academy, addressing the various issues that came up took a long time and resulted in extended debates. He identified two opposing currents within the academy: "one of them is protective of the past and holds on to it, and the other is driven toward the new and is proud of it." As a result, decisions were often postponed, and an issue might be brought up more than once, especially as the number of academy members increased. Still, Madkur praised the debates, the rigor that went into them, and the academy members who fully understood that they were deciding on the future of the language. He described these long discussions as "the way to uncover the truth, and the means to connect the present with the past, moderately, without excess or exaggeration."[127]

Summarizing the accomplishments of the academy from its creation until 1965, a few years before Taha Hussein's death, Ibrahim Madkur explained that the academy had taken over fifty decisions in its effort to standardize the Arabization (ta'rib) of foreign terms and the derivation (ishtiqaq) of new ones. Moreover, the academy had published 3,500 new terms in 1942, then 9,590 terms in 1957, and 2,357 terms in 1960. This in addition to various dictionaries, including *al-Mu'jam al-Wasit*, written along the lines of *Le Petit Larousse* and appearing in its full version in 1960. Several volumes of a dictionary for the words in the Qur'an also found their way to the printing press.[128] Hussein had had many discussions with Sheikh al-Azhar al-Maraghi in order to get the dictionary of the Qur'an sorted historically.[129] The academy also published several volumes of philosophical, geographical, and geological dictionaries.[130] In 1946, the academy decided to start writing a grand dictionary for the Arabic language.[131] In 1948, Hussein was appointed as the rapporteur responsible for creating the model the academy would adopt for this dictionary.[132] According to Madkur, he spent years studying and carefully revising this model before submitting it in five hundred pages for feedback from the academy members in 1956.[133] Over the years, Hussein also insisted on attending all academy meetings, even after his health had deteriorated. He can be seen here, in one of the last meetings he attended, where, too weak to walk, he was accompanied by his wife, Suzanne, and had to be carried in and out of the building.

FIGURE 15. Taha Hussein at an Arabic Language Academy meeting, shortly before his death. Courtesy of the Taha Hussein family.

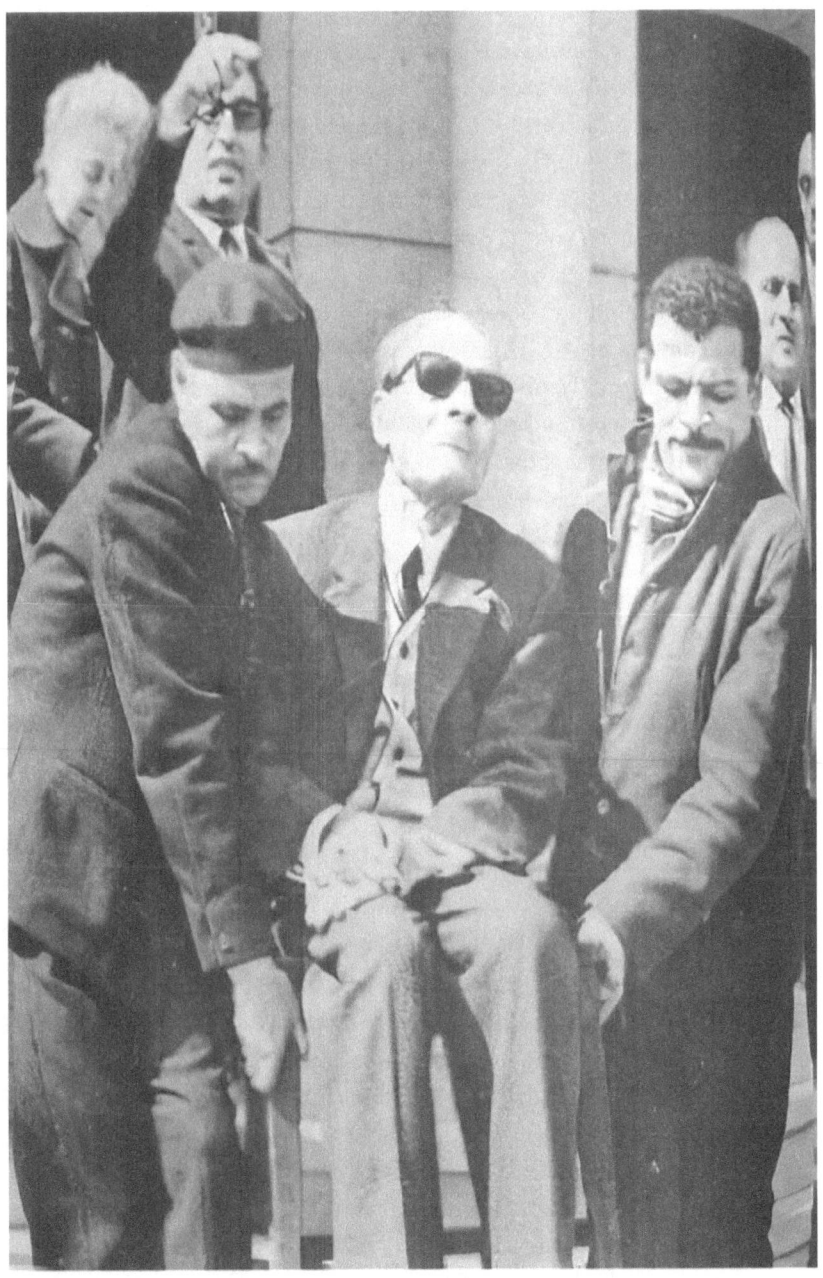

FIGURE 16. Taha Hussein being carried from the Arabic Language Academy after a meeting, shortly before his death. Courtesy of the Taha Hussein family.

Conclusion

Taha Hussein saw classical Arabic as the Arab world's link between past and present, and much of his oeuvre revolved around ensuring that the language remained vibrant and accessible to future generations of Egyptians and Arabs. He believed it would be an irreparable loss if the language became restricted to the religious domain, because for him, the Arab-Islamic heritage was not restricted to religion. He saw the Arabic language as the means by which people could engage with that classical tradition in the larger sense, and as the vehicle by which they could build on and enrich that tradition. He was categorically opposed to any literary or artistic expression in colloquial speech, even as he admitted and fully understood that the colloquial was easier to use. He also resisted radical propositions such as Latinizing the Arabic script and severing ties with the past. Arguing that the language and the heritage it gave access to belonged to the people, his work at the Arabic Language Academy sought to bring "the eloquent language," as he always referred to classical Arabic, closer to them, or to democratize the language as he liked to say.

Hussein's focus on the people was not new. Besides his battle for universal education, he was also intent on keeping the public informed about important ministerial decisions. Similarly, the Arabic Language Academy in its early days was eager to get the public involved in its debates through publications and competitions. Like the university, the academy was a *nahdawi* institution created to revive the old while synthesizing it with the new. It brought experts together from Egypt and abroad to analyze the challenges facing the language and propose careful solutions that did not compromise the rules governing its proper usage. Hussein also advised the Ministry of Public Instruction not take any suggestions for changes to the language into account until they had been broadcast to the public in Egypt and abroad for scrutiny, study, and feedback. Even if a proposed reform had been approved, he was against assigning it immediately to students in textbooks. Instead, he hoped it would first be published and inspire general and professional feedback. Only then could the ministry consider integrating the reform into school textbooks.[134] Even before joining the academy, Hussein had asked the minister of public instruction, Bahiy al-Din Barakat, to invite various people, through a general competition, to submit their ideas on reforming the language, instead of assigning that task to one of the committees at the Ministry of Public Instruction as it was customary to do. Such a committee, he told Barakat, should be formed only to review the submitted proposals.[135]

In practice, however, rolling out the results of these efforts proved difficult. Hussein and others proposed what they believed were much-needed changes to the way the language was being taught in public schools. Their goal was to make the language more engaging to an increasing number of young men and women getting an education and relieve them of the difficulty associated with learning it. But, as Niloofar Haeri has recently pointed out, "both the very authority of Classical Arabic and lack of good public education hamper mass literacy in the official language."[136] This chapter has shown that authority and political will were needed to change the way classical Arabic was being taught. For many reasons, the changes recommended by the Arabic Language Academy were not implemented in the way Hussein and others had hoped. The academy remained tied to the Ministry of Public Instruction in terms of budget and politics. It had neither the means nor the authority to impose its recommendations. Technical reasons to do with the language itself made it difficult for academy members to agree on a workable solution that made the writing correspond more accurately to the correct pronunciation in the full way Hussein and his colleagues had envisaged. Moreover, there was insufficient political will on the part of the successive ministries of public instruction to challenge al-Azhar and roll out a simplified version of grammar fully integrated into engaging literary texts.[137]

5 WINDS OF CHANGE

Taha Hussein and the End of a Political Project

> Allow me to be free in the widest and deepest possible meaning of that word. Rest assured that even if you spoke your minds and said that you would not give me this freedom, then my response to you would be very simple. I will be free whether you accept it or not.
>
> Taha Hussein on committed literature (*iltizam*)[1]

IN THE EARLY HOURS of July 23, 1952, the Free Officers seized power in Egypt, and sent King Farouk into exile three days later. Over the course of the following decade, the military coup, carried out by junior officers without exact goals, became a revolution from above that transformed Egyptian society and changed the old political order. In their grand majority, Egyptians supported the coup and hoped the new regime would succeed where the old one had failed. By 1954, land reform laws and signing an evacuation treaty with Great Britain reassured Egyptians that their long-standing demands for social justice and full independence were being addressed. Yet, also by the end of 1954, outlawing all political parties, revoking press licenses, abrogating the 1923 constitution, and suppressing political opponents made it clear that the officers were not keen on sharing power with civilians. In a few years, Gamal Abdel Nasser had successfully consolidated his power, and until his death in 1970, he was the unrivaled leader of Pan-Arabism and an important hero of anti-colonial struggle.

Taha Hussein welcomed the army coup d'état and cheered the end of the monarchy as the dawn of a new era of freedom, social justice, and real independence. Predicting that the revolution would change not only Egypt but also the neighboring Arab countries, he repeatedly compared the Egyptian revolution to the French revolution in the ideals it sought and the impact he hoped it would have. He supported the overall guiding principles of the revolution and called for a swift return to parliamentary life. Although he remained a vocal supporter of Nasser's anti-colonial foreign policy, Hussein chose not to comment publicly on most of Nasser's domestic policies. Such unusual silence on the part of an intellectual who had shaped, written on, and commented regularly on local politics for decades could not have gone unnoticed by those in power, or by the younger generation of writers and intellectuals who supported those policies. Moreover, by refusing to condone the calls for "literature for life," or "committed literature," made by younger writers who hoped to use literature as a means of social reform, Hussein alienated himself from the younger generation.

While Hussein's silence spoke of his disapproval of the new regime's domestic policies, this chapter shows that Hussein also gave the young officers clear advice in private on where he thought the country should go, and that the Revolutionary Council knew exactly what his views were. As a member of the committee tasked with drawing up a new constitution between December 1952 and August 1954, he made those beliefs clear by calling for the immediate adoption of a parliamentary system and the end of military rule. The decision of the Revolutionary Council to ignore the 1954 constitution and not even publish it for review was a clear indication very early on that Hussein and the young officers had parted ways.

Nevertheless, rapidly escalating political events, including the attempt on Nasser's life in October 1954, the Czech arms deal crisis in 1955, and then the tripartite aggression against Egypt following the nationalization of the Suez Canal in 1956, convinced Taha Hussein that the nation's newly acquired full independence following the Anglo-Egyptian Treaty of 1954 was on shaky ground. During that period of political instability, he chose to fully support Nasser in his fight against the colonial powers. Hussein saw that the situation called for firm unity behind the young leader so that independence would survive. He wrote prolifically during that period, praising Nasser and his courage while deploring the arrogance and double standards of western powers, especially France, which spoke in the name of freedom but denied that same freedom to its colonies and violently suppressed anti-colonial attempts to achieve independence. As the struggle grew stronger in the 1950s and early '60s, Hussein saw the European powers lose all moral ground in the Middle East and the Third World in general.

On the local scene, although it became increasingly difficult for Taha Hussein and others to speak publicly in favor of a return to parliamentary democracy or to defend individual freedoms, Hussein used literary debates as an outlet to voice his opinions. Refusing what he believed were ideological restrictions imposed on Egyptian intellectuals, he used the debate on committed literature to claim freedom for writers and artists in general, warning repeatedly against an overt politicization of literature and calls for aligning it with official ideologies. Nevertheless, his critique was not taken seriously. He was seen as part of an older generation whose failure to address problems in prerevolutionary Egypt had precipitated the intervention of the army in 1952, and his measured words were marginalized by a powerful anti-colonial revolutionary discourse that left no space for serious intellectual opposition. This official discourse monopolized speaking in the name of the people, vilified the west, and dismissed seeking "knowledge for knowledge's sake," while favoring the study of the more practical sciences that were of more immediate benefit for the national struggle.

This chapter examines how Taha Hussein responded to the army coup and its impact, not only on politics but also on the role of literature and of intellectuals, showing that the marginalization of Hussein and his project for culture and education in Egypt was a result of two radically different readings of the success of the 1952 coup. While Hussein believed that the people's support for the army stemmed from the education and culture he and his generation had created between 1919 and 1952, the army leaders and younger writers believed Hussein's generation had failed to bring real change to the people. This latter view, combined with persistent colonial intervention in Egyptian and Arab affairs in the 1950s and '60s and the suppression of all political opposition, made it impossible for Hussein to continue to promote his project of critical thinking in which he called for a natural synthesis of the classical Arab-Islamic tradition and Europe's cultural accomplishments.

A Coup or a Revolution?

Upon learning that the army had taken control of the country, Taha Hussein, then summering in Italy, passed out from excitement.[2] Writing for the daily *al-Ahram* from Italy a few days later, he did not hide his happiness, and declared that with the coup, "Egypt had found itself."[3] He justified the coup by saying that the army intervened because civilians wanted to put an end to widespread corruption but were unable to. He therefore saw the military intervention as a response to a public demand. Without referring directly to the 1948 defeat in Palestine, he believed the army itself had already tasted the dangerous impact of such corruption.

> Since the army has the right to safeguard the nation from the external enemy, then it also has the right to safeguard it from the internal enemy. Corruption

within our borders subjects the army itself to an immense danger, something the army has already tasted before. It has been patient but more patience would have become cowardice and accommodation of humiliation.[4]

In a second article, also written in Italy, he expressed pride in the army, for without violence, it had managed to accomplish its mission, depose King Farouk, and send him to exile on July 26, 1952. In this article, he was the first to call what had happened a revolution and not a coup: "Egypt has set an example to the entire modern world with its *revolution*, which has combined elegant respectful calmness with unwavering resolution. It has destroyed oppression and sent a king to his exile without spilling a drop of blood, all while being patient, careful and wisely cautious."[5] Furthermore, Hussein was optimistic about the impact the revolution was going to have on Egypt and its neighbors. He believed that Egypt's revolution represented in the "east," what the French revolution represented in the "west." Egypt's revolution was even more impressive because it was a "white revolution," and did not result in the killing of millions of people, as had been the case in France.[6] He expressed his support for the six principles of the revolution, which were to liberate the country from colonialism and its agents, liquidate feudalism, eliminate the control of capital, establish social justice, create a strong national army, and lay the foundations for a proper democratic life.[7] Hussein saw the revolution as a glorious moment in Egyptian history, and he saluted the calm and calculated tone of General Commander Muhammad Najib (1901–1984), who was in charge of the coup and the government.

> I have read reports in the papers reiterating what the general commander and the prime minister have said, and I only saw good in them. I do not disapprove of anything that came in these reports, big or small, because they do not accuse, gloat, call for revenge or try to set anyone up. [What they said] explained the principles of the revolution and the expectations of the people and revealed the plan of the army and the government to achieve those expectations.[8]

Taha Hussein had a very specific understanding of why the people embraced the army movement the way they did, and how their reaction transformed what happened in July 1952 from a coup into a revolution. This understanding was diametrically opposed to the way that the leaders of the army read the situation, or at least how they explained it to the people. Whereas army leaders dismissed the contributions of Egyptian intellectuals before the revolution, Hussein saw the Egyptian revolution as the culmination of a culture that he and others had worked hard for decades to produce in educational institutions and on the pages of books and periodicals. He believed this culture and knowledge made the people aware of their rights and motivated them to support the army that promised to give them back those rights. He argued that literature had paved the way for and created the revolution, as it showed the people what their lives should be like and made them understand the values of justice and equality that should dominate those lives.[9] Despite many differences between the French and Egyptian revolutions, he believed there were some similarities. In France, according to Hussein, people had read about freedom, equality, and fraternity in books written by philosophers and litterateurs. Those who could not read, learned about those values from people who could. Finding that their actual lives lagged behind the ideals they had learned about, the French rebelled against a system they believed was unjust.[10] Egyptians did the same in 1952.

> We compared what we had revived from our old, and the new we had taken from Europe, to the life we were leading and the systems we were following. We abhorred what we were in and tried to change an obnoxious life for one that was better. The army allowed us to do that, and it should have done so because it is composed of our sons and brothers, who suffer as much as we do and hope for the [same] dignity that we all hope for. The army had the power that allowed it to liberate the people, so it did not neglect them when it got the chance, and God crowned its efforts with success.[11]

For Hussein, the people's response to the coup was a direct result of the culture he and others had been developing, and the project he had been advocating, which was based on a critical synthesis of the old and the new spearheaded by institutions like the Egyptian University. Readers of Hussein at the time would have understood his words in connection with his career as a professor, civil servant, and writer. They would have made a link between his words and the university and its professors and graduates. They would have also understood that with his references to the philosophers and the litterateurs, he was giving the nod to Egyptian writers, like himself, and the intellectual life they had created over the decades. For Taha Hussein, it was *his* revolution.

Convinced that it was culture, education, and the university that had created the revolution, Hussein wanted the new regime to strengthen the system of higher education. Seeking inspiration again from the French revolution, he argued that just as those revolutionaries had spread their ideals in France, Europe, and the world by supporting scientific research, disseminating knowledge, and creating a "thinking free elite," he was calling on the new Egyptian regime to do the same. He insisted that this new elite should come from all walks of life and not be limited to any social class.[12] Warning against the semi-educated, who relied on what he referred to as "easy knowledge" coming from newspapers, he advised the government to rely on the advice of the "people who have devoted themselves to knowledge, excelled in it, and are producing more of it."[13]

In the summer of 1954, Hussein reminded the army leaders that if the old regime had failed to protect the people from poverty, ignorance, and illness, then the revolution must find ways to provide that protection. He advised them to seek advice from Egypt's "intelligent insightful elite" on how to eradicate those problems.[14] Faithful to the university and his understanding of its role, he wanted the new government to pay attention to secondary, technical, and university education. Fighting illiteracy was not enough, he insisted, and the revolution had to promote higher education to create leaders who understood the problems facing the nation and could offer adequate solutions:

> [Higher] education is Egypt's only way for the formation of an elite that will lead us to glory. Let Egyptians beware the day when illiteracy has disappeared from society but competent capable leaders have become few. Then the nation will look and will find that all its sons know their rights but do not appreciate their duties. [Egyptians] will see their hopes but will not know how to reach them. They will want what is good but will not find those who can lead them to it.[15]

Reading Taha Hussein's Silence on Domestic Policies

Despite his general optimism in the early days of the revolution, Taha Hussein remained cautious. He criticized the existing political parties for not laying their petty differences aside, and he asked them to stop distracting the government with what he considered to be inconsequential arguments. According to him, it was time for the parties to focus on proposing political and social reforms, as well as suggesting concrete ways to limit land ownership, work toward a better distribution of wealth, deal with unemployment, and side with the poor.[16] He also remained critical of the government, out of his conviction that an intellectual should guide and show the way. For example, he declared that he was against the government's decision to abolish the existing constitution on December 10, 1952, without having adopted a new one first. Yet, he was careful in the same article to state his faith in Muhammad Najib and his promise to safeguard Egyptians' rights until the new constitution was put in place.[17]

Hussein also called on intellectuals to turn their full attention to the new constitution that was being drafted and what it should accomplish. He asked them to clarify to Egyptians what rights the new constitution should guarantee for them, and to advise the rulers on what the constitution should and should not include.[18] He believed those writing it should be selected based on their expert knowledge of constitutions and their awareness of people's rights and expectations. He called for finishing the new constitution without delay.[19] He also asked for a quick referendum to decide whether Egypt was to remain a monarchy or whether a republic should be declared, so that the constitution committee could start working according to the result. He did not hide his preference for a republican system, saying that in the early days of Islam, Muslims followed neither the Persians nor the Romans and did not adopt hereditary rule.[20] He repeated his earlier calls for redefining the relationship between Egyptians and their state: "Egyptians must know that [legitimate] rule comes from them and does not descend upon them. They must know that rulers are servants not masters. [Rulers are] appointed by the people so they can carry out political and social tasks for the people."[21]

By the end of December 1952, Taha Hussein had started expressing concern that the various campaigns denigrating prerevolutionary Egypt were excessive, and he warned against the overpromising of reform and change. Responding to critics of the educational system who were dismissing decades of work in an area that he knew all too well, he argued that education, like any other domain in Egypt, had its problems, but it also had its successes. "If education had been pure evil," he said, "Egypt would not have been able to live on that education until today. But Egypt has lived, developed, and made wide steps forward."[22] Such continual criticism, he warned, had a negative impact on students as it shook their faith in the educational system as a whole and in their own self-confidence as well. Students, he argued, should not be reading in various newspapers that they were not learning or benefiting by going to school or university.[23] He was worried that people wanted to see immediate results when change required time and careful planning. He reminded those in charge, especially the leaders of the revolution and the prime minister, that just as the objectives of the French revolution took a long time to accomplish, the objectives of the Egyptian revolution needed time as well.[24]

Prior to the summer of 1954, Taha Hussein responded to the coup of 1952 with unmistakable enthusiasm. He commented regularly on various events and gave his opinion on where the country should be headed. He believed that at such a critical moment in Egyptian history, it was his role, and that of other intellectuals, to offer sincere advice and try to shed light on the way forward.[25] Perhaps the first time Hussein let a major event pass by without any comment was January 16, 1953, when the Revolutionary Council decided to disband all political parties. His unusual silence on this occasion could be attributed to his association with the Wafd Party and his close friendship with its president, Mustafa al-Nahhas. Yet, this first silence, so unusual for Hussein, was only the beginning of a series of silences. As the historian Ahmad Zakariya al-Shalq has observed, Hussein later remained silent in 1954 when Nasser published *Falsafat al-Thawra* (*The Philosophy of the Revolution*) explaining the reasons leading to the army intervention in 1952, such as the corruption of the monarchy and of the various political parties, and his own aspirations to lead the people.[26] Given Hussein's interest and investment in social and political reform since the early 1920s, and his deep optimism about the regime change, he must have read Nasser's work and must have had an opinion on the new leader's vision for the country, but he chose not to comment. He did not react, either, when the constitution he and others had worked on for a year and half was ignored and replaced in 1956 with a different one (as discussed later in this chapter). Hussein was also silent when Nasser created his populist organizations, the Liberation Rally in 1953, the National Union in 1957, and finally the Arab Socialist Union in 1962, to fill the political void left by the ending of the multiparty system.[27] He also did not publicly condemn Egypt's union with Syria in 1958, although he confided to one of the ministers that the union had happened "too soon."[28] Finally, al-Shalq describes another silence, when Hussein responded neither to the socialist decrees nationalizing the press and private property in 1961 nor to the crisis of the intellectuals, also in 1961, during which the regime's spokesperson, Muhammad Hasanayn Haykal, accused Egyptian intellectuals of not supporting the revolution enough. One could add Hussein's silence on the house arrest imposed in 1954 on Muhammad Najib, when, contrary to the wishes of Nasser and other revolutionary officers, Najib insisted on free elections and the return of the army to its barracks. After Najib was ousted, Hussein did not react to the purges targeting journalists, university professors, and judges seen as inimical to the regime. Such a violent clampdown on the opposition must have convinced Hussein that he had to become strategic about what to write and when to voice his disapproval. If he were to continue to write, and probably out of concern for his own safety and that of his family, he understood that he had to avoid direct criticism of the government.[29]

Nevertheless, in matters of foreign policy Hussein was not silent. On the contrary, he continued to share his observations and analyses with fervor on the pages of *al-Jumhuriyya*, the regime's newly created daily. As observed by the Egyptian writer and editor in chief of the magazine *Ruz al-Yusuf*, Ihsan 'Abd al-Quddus, by the early months of 1955, the revolution had entered a new phase in which foreign affairs dominated.[30] Hussein praised this transformation, hailed Nasser's foreign policy, and frequently celebrated the young leader who, Hussein believed, was proving Egypt could finally stand up to the west. Hussein sided with Nasser and criticized the Baghdad Pact in 1955, arguing it was a colonial ruse to keep Arab countries under control.[31] He praised Nasser and his participation in the Bandung Conference, also in 1955, which ensured that Egypt would have its own foreign policy independent of the major powers in the west and the east.[32] Commenting on angry western reactions to Nasser's arms deal with Czechoslovakia in 1955, or what came to be known as the Czech arms crisis, Hussein wrote:

> What is strange about the reaction of the free world, as it likes to call itself, is that it wants to keep Egypt in a situation that only the subservient would accept. [This free world] reassures Egypt that it is free, independent, and noble, and no one should interfere in its affairs from near or from far. [Yet, it] refuses to sell Egypt the arms that it needs and forbids it to buy these arms from anybody else. [And] on its borders, [this free world] has created a puppet that it calls Israel, giving it enough power and strength, enticing it to aggression, tyranny, and injustice, encouraging it to domineer and bully.[33]

While he hailed Nasser for going through with the arms deal, Hussein warned of possible confrontations with the west and dangerous consequences for Egypt and its independence. On the one hand, he said, Nasser's insistence on purchasing the much-needed arms proved Egyptians were finally "adults" who no longer accepted submission to western wishes. On the other hand, this confrontation proved the west's ill intentions toward Egypt, and Hussein predicted—accurately, for in a year the Suez Crisis would break out—that Egyptians would soon have to stand up and fight to protect their independence.[34]

Furthermore, in a series of articles that spanned the 1950s and early '60s, Hussein lashed out at colonial powers, especially France, for their arrogance and violent suppression of independence movements in Africa and Asia. In August 1954, he wrote that France had not learned from its deplorable tragedy in Indochina and was dealing with North Africa with the same shortsightedness and arrogance. France, he went on, was choosing to ignore that it had been forced to leave Syria and Lebanon, and that Great Britain, a stronger colonial power, had had to listen to India, Pakistan, and other countries and give them their independence.[35] Against French accusations that Nasser was turning Tunisians and Moroccans against France, Hussein defended Egypt's foreign policy, as well as the Egyptian press and the Egyptian radio channel Sawt al-ʿArab, which actively supported the independence of the North African countries of Tunisia, Algeria, and Morocco. The French, Hussein said, should accept that weak countries had become stronger, and should therefore accept criticism from the Egyptian press the same way they accepted criticism from the press in European countries like Russia, the UK, and Italy.[36] In another article, he reminded the French government, and its prime minister, Mendès France, that Egypt had supported France when it was under German occupation, received De Gaulle with open arms, and offered its radio service, the same radio service that Mendès France was now complaining about, so that "the voice of Free France could be broadcast from two cities, London and Cairo."[37] Nothing, he warned, would stop Egypt from supporting Tunisians and Moroccans in their rightful demands.[38]

> Not only will Egypt continue to support Tunisians and Moroccans, but it will also support the Algerians in their demand for independence, even if France continues to claim that Algeria is part of France. Egypt does not believe in invasion. Algerians are not part of France, and France is not Algerian in anything [*laysat minhum fi shay*'].[39]

Writing in March 1956, Hussein was happy Morocco had gained its independence, and Sultan Muhammad V had safely returned from exile. He was also happy that Tunisia had gained some of its independence, and that Jordan had refused to join the Baghdad Pact. He saw all these changes taking place in the Arab world as consequences of the Egyptian revolution, which he had hoped would affect events in the region the same way the French revolution had in Europe. The war of independence was then raging in Algeria, and he predicted that Algerians would not stop until their country had gained its full independence from France, and until France "had forgotten," as he said, "this silly myth, which it used as an excuse for more than a century, claiming that Algeria was part of the French homeland. It claimed so to itself [and yet] refused to give the people of Algeria the rights the French enjoyed."[40]

Taha Hussein was proud of Nasser's foreign policy, which in Hussein's view, gave Egypt confidence and allowed it to deal with other countries, including the major powers, on an equal footing without fear or hesitation. This confidence, he wrote in an article in the spring of 1956, was based not just on words but also on action.[41] The western powers, he insisted, were lying when they said they refused to supply Egypt with weapons in order to maintain peace in the region, because at the same time they refused to help Egypt acquire the means to defend itself, they continued to supply Israel with arms at will. Egypt under Nasser, Hussein went on, was not only responding to western manipulation with strong honest words but also managing to obtain necessary arms from Czechoslovakia. He was ecstatic that Egypt was finally making its own decisions even when these decisions went against the wishes of foreign powers, and he gave Egypt's recent recognition of communist China as an example.[42]

Interestingly, the French embassy in Cairo translated many of these articles that Hussein wrote for *al-Jumhuriyya* and sent them to the French Ministry of Foreign Affairs. The French chargé d'affaires described these articles as not only irritating but also "profoundly hurtful," coming as they did from somebody like Taha Hussein, who had traditionally been seen as a friend of France and French culture.[43] In another report that accompanied the translation one of Hussein's articles, the French ambassador tried to explain Hussein's violent criticism of French politics in North Africa. Referring to Hussein's French wife and his son, who was now teaching French literature at Cairo University, the ambassador argued that given Egypt's new anti-colonial foreign policy, Hussein was trying to distance himself from France and maintain his chances of returning to power.[44]

Yet, Taha Hussein was speaking from his own experience, and not just as an observer. Although he did not refer explicitly to his own conflict with the French over the institute of Arabic and Islamic studies in North Africa a few years earlier, he remembered what his own negotiations with them were like.

> We used to see ourselves as lesser than they were and less powerful. We did not have the same power as they did.... This used to force us to think, reconsider, and worry about consequences. [We] held ourselves accountable to every word even before we had said or written it. This awakened their greed, empowered them and lured them into controlling our facilities, establishments, and our future.[45]

In his articles on Egyptian foreign policy under Nasser, Hussein left no doubt that he fully supported the Egyptian leader in all his confrontations with the colonial powers. The revolution, Hussein stressed, had managed to unite Egyptians behind Nasser, allowing Egypt to face those powers. He saw this as a unique success in Egypt's modern history.

> We now know how to stand up when in conflict with [the foreigner], how to face his tricky flattering language with our honest clear language, how to face his hidden disguised action with our honest visible action, how to face his doubt in our faith and his hesitation [to believe in] our perseverance. This has given our foreign policy a success that it had not seen at any time in our modern history.[46]

The British Are Leaving, Finally

For Taha Hussein, the signing of the evacuation treaty with Great Britain, on October 19, 1954, was an extraordinary achievement. It was a success that came after long and painful negotiations for full independence that had been going on since 1922. Hussein had placed high hopes on the 1936 treaty, and his enthusiasm was reflected in *The Future of Culture in Egypt* and the steps he proposed to prove Egypt could handle the responsibilities of its independence. Yet, just like Britain's unilateral declaration of Egypt's independence in 1922, the 1936 treaty was another disappointment. Nothing serious was done to deal with widespread social injustice, and the British still controlled the Suez Canal and intervened in Egyptian politics at will. This was blatantly demonstrated in the incident of February 4, 1942, when, in a glaring breach of sovereignty, British tanks besieged King Farouk in Abdin palace in Cairo, forcing him to appoint the cabinet they thought was necessary to stabilize the country during the Second World War.

After the war, lengthy negotiations with the British resumed, only to fail but then start again, further destabilizing the country and fueling the already divisive partisan politics. This led historian Afaf Lutfi al-Sayyid Marsot to describe these Anglo-Egyptian negotiations before 1952 as "the cancer of Egyptian politics."[47] Handling these negotiations became the heart of political life in the country, and the public measured the performance of various cabinets against the success or failure of their negotiations. Massive demonstrations put the various Egyptian governments under pressure as the public demanded nothing less than an immediate withdrawal of all British troops from the country. Yet the British, according to Hussein, neither took these negotiations seriously nor intended to leave the country. He believed negotiations were a game that they had invented to prolong the occupation and serve their own interests. Writing in May 1953, as the new regime started another round of negotiations with the British, Hussein, understandably, was full of doubt.

> I am surprised Egyptians have not yet gotten bored with these negotiations invented by the British when they ended their protectorate and [which continue]

until now. This, despite all that we have heard on the subject so far and which we have memorized by heart. We have gained nothing from these negotiations except divisions, differences, hatred, jealousy, and corruption.[48]

Hussein had been an insider during many of these negotiations, which continued until the last Wafd government under al-Nahhas. As explained earlier, Hussein was a member of the cabinet that, upon failing to reach any satisfying results with the British, abrogated the 1936 Anglo-Egyptian Treaty in October 1951, thus declaring the presence of the British troops in Egypt illegal. This famous decision was followed by guerrilla warfare, carried out by the fedayeen against British targets in the Suez Canal Zone, and a period of instability and extreme apprehension followed. After October 28, 1951, every meeting at the Council of Ministers started with an update from Minister of Interior Fu'ad Siraj al-Din, who briefed his colleagues, including Hussein, on the escalating tensions and the reprisals of British forces against Egyptian civilians and public facilities.[49]

Right before the violence began, Hussein had been reporting to his colleagues on the positive results of the changes he was making in education. As political events were about to dominate the discussions, the records of the Council of Ministers show various ministers congratulating Hussein on the success of his educational policies, including the success of his ministry in admitting more students to primary schools than in the previous year, and not turning a single student away from secondary and technical education thanks to the large number of schools the ministry was able to build in record time.[50] Likewise, during those last days of Wafdist rule, Hussein was glad parliament had approved his request to create Egypt's first syndicate for teachers on November 3, 1951.[51] Politics, however, soon took over the center stage and his term in office was cut short.

Two weeks after the announcement of the creation of the Teachers' Syndicate, violence erupted in the canal city of Ismailia on November 17 and 18. The British forces killed eight policemen and wounded eighteen more. On November 25, 1951, the council decided to educate the sons and daughters of the killed and wounded policemen for free until their graduation from university, and assigned LE 8,000 in support of each family. In response to these events, Hussein requested the council's approval to dismiss seventy-two British employees working for the Ministry of Public Instruction.[52] The council not only approved Hussein's request but also decided to fire all British employees working in other government ministries and public offices as well.[53] Moreover, the council decided the government would step in and train the militias fighting in the Canal Zone officially.[54] In December, the council assigned LE 500,000 to help relocate Egyptian laborers working in British camps in the Canal Zone.[55] In further response to British retaliations against Egyptian civilians, the Egyptian ambassador to the UK was recalled, the Egyptian Engineering Office in London was relocated to Switzerland, and a new law was to be issued criminalizing all forms of "cooperation or dealings with any foreign military force in the country."[56]

This instability escalated further on January 25, 1952, when British forces raided a police station in Ismailia, killing scores of police officers.[57] When the news reached Cairo, demonstrations broke out denouncing the occupation and the British show of force in Ismailia. These demonstrations deteriorated into uncontrollable riots resulting in the famous Cairo Fire on January 26, 1952, or Black Saturday as it came to be called. Hussein and the other ministers met at al-Nahhas' house at 7 p.m. on the same day for three hours to discuss the events. They agreed to declare martial law and placed al-Nahhas in charge of these exceptional powers, as regulated by Law No. 15 of 1923. Hussein suspended work in all schools, institutes, and universities until further notice.[58] The next day, King Farouk dismissed al-Nahhas and his government. Numerous successive cabinets between January and the coup in July 1952 were unable to restore calm to a country that was boiling with rage and with uncertainty about the future.

Taha Hussein knew the history of negotiations with the British all too well. Their failure, the abrogation of the treaty in 1951, and the British violence in the Canal Zone threw the country into chaos and brought his government career to an end. In his May 1953 article on negotiations, discussed earlier, he was warning the young officers about the danger of these negotiations. He insisted the only solution was a show of unity by all Egyptians behind their leaders: standing firm in front of the British, and accepting nothing short of complete withdrawal of all British troops from the country.[59] Hussein was apprehensive and now skeptical about an old school of thought—led by Muhammad 'Abduh in the late nineteenth century and adopted by Egypt's moderate parties like al-Umma and the Wafd—calling for a measured cooperation with the British and earning independence through reforms and negotiations.

One can therefore imagine Hussein's reaction when Nasser signed the evacuation treaty, which provided that the last British soldier was to leave Egypt in twenty months. He wrote that after those twenty months, on that "promised day":

> Time will turn back to what it was twenty-six centuries ago, when Egypt was free in the widest possible meaning of freedom, dignified, in the most accurate and truthful sense of the word, independent in the most correct and deepest meaning of independence. A time when Egypt was in control of its own affairs,

and power was in the hands of its sons, not shared by any foreigner, from near or far. Back to a time, when Egypt decided, alone, on all its matters, and did not have to defer to any distant capital in the land of the Persians, Greeks, or Romans, or in the land of the Arabs or in Damascus or Baghdad.[60]

Egypt was finally independent. The revolution, according to Hussein, had managed to accomplish much in two years. It had forced the British to give Egypt its independence, abolished the monarchy, and created a republic that was to return power to the people. Regarding the Sudan, he said that after signing an agreement with Britain in February 1953, the new regime could establish a transitional period of Sudanese self-government (which led to the independence of the Sudan in January 1956). In this way, he believed the revolution solved the problem of the Sudan and gave the country back to its people, while also removing an important obstacle that had complicated negotiations between the Egyptians and the British for decades. In Egypt, the new government adopted much-awaited land reform laws, and ended what Hussein described as "class differences while ensuring that Egypt's wealth was no longer monopolized by a select few."[61] The revolution managed to put to an end to divisive partisan politics, strengthened the country, and rebuilt its foreign policy.[62] Hussein cheered the revolution and those behind it, for in two years they had succeeded where others had failed.

Rallying Behind the Leader: Nasser Fights Imperialism

When the British forces were still in Egypt, Hussein believed the situation demanded caution, unity, and support for the new leadership. During the months leading to the evacuation treaty, he was worried the British would use any instability in the country as an excuse to stall negotiations or postpone the actual evacuation of their forces from the Suez Canal. In March 1954, for example, Hussein denounced the hunger strike organized by the feminist Duriyya Shafiq (1908–1975) and her supporters, which gained much coverage from local and international media. Shafiq was disappointed women were not represented on the committee put in place to write the new constitution, and she decided to act at this politically sensitive moment to put pressure on the government and obtain a written promise that the new constitution would give Egyptian women the right to vote.[63] So, on March 12, Shafiq entered the headquarters of the Egyptian Press Syndicate, refused to leave, and was quickly joined by other high-profile Egyptian women. While Shafiq received much support, for example from Samiha Ahmad Mahir, daughter of the assassinated prime minister Ahmad Mahir, the strike caused an uproar in the country, and public opinion was divided.⁶⁴ To Shafiq's utter dismay, Fatima Rashad, president of the National Feminist Union, came out and denounced Shafiq's timing of the strike as inopportune, saying that demanding women's rights at this crucial moment was not in the best interest of the country.⁶⁵ Shafiq was relentless, however, and declared, "We have waited long enough. We want our constitutional rights immediately, and I think it is in keeping with the logic of our revolution."⁶⁶ After eight days, Muhammad Najib intervened and gave Shafiq his word that the new constitution would guarantee women's political rights, and the strike came to an end.⁶⁷ In this debate, Hussein denounced Shafiq and wrote strongly against the strike in an article for *al-Jumhuriyya* that he called "'Abithat" (Irresponsible Women). Like Fatima Rashad, he believed this was not the right moment for such a highly mediatized domestic conflict. He warned the British could use the unrest for their own benefit, and that everybody's effort should focus on putting an end to the current constitutional void (as the 1923 constitution had been abolished before adopting a new one), which in his opinion left the state without any supervision, and this condition had to be resolved as quickly as possible to ensure a swift return to parliamentary life.⁶⁸

Even after the signing of the evacuation treaty, the political situation remained precarious, and British troops were still on Egyptian soil. The attempt on Nasser's life on October 26, 1954, confirmed Hussein's belief that independence was on shaky ground. Speaking in front of a large crowd in Alexandria, Nasser escaped eight bullets fired by a member of the Muslim Brotherhood. Nasser quickly reassured the large crowd that he had not been killed and asked the people to stay put. "I am not dead. I am alive, and even if I die, you are all Gamal Abdel Nasser," he famously shouted.⁶⁹ The Muslim Brothers had announced they opposed the new Anglo-Egyptian Treaty, arguing that it sold Egypt to the British by allowing them to legally reenter the country if Turkey were attacked. Hussein deplored the event in two articles in *al-Jumhuriyya*, published alongside articles by important intellectuals at the time, such as Muhammad al-Tabi'i, 'Ali Amin, and Kamil al-Shinnawi. These articles were later published in a book called *Ha'ula' hum al-Ikhwan!!* (*These Are the Brothers!!*). Hussein described the assassination attempt as a heavy ordeal; if successful, it could have been a catastrophe.

> I think about the possible consequences that could have befallen this country had those criminals succeeded in what they planned to do. . . . The foreigner would have forced order and security in the country and Egypt would have returned to what it used to be, a humiliated country whose matters are managed

by foreigners because it could not bear the responsibility of [its] independence and freedom for a few days.[70]

He saluted Nasser for his courage and for his responsible reaction in front of the crowds.[71] Members of the Muslim Brotherhood had been successful in other recent assassination attempts, killing Prime Ministers Ahmad Mahir (in 1945) and Mahmud al-Nuqrashi (in 1948), as well as President of the Court of Appeal Ahmad al-Khazindar (also in 1948). These assassinations were still fresh in people's minds. The failed attempt on Nasser's life provided further proof that extreme caution was necessary and that stability in the country had to be maintained if the British evacuation was to proceed as planned.

In this tense buildup to the Suez Canal Crisis, Hussein continued his support for Nasser and Egypt's new independence in the face of the old colonial powers, and defended Nasser's decision to nationalize the canal on July 26, 1956. Hussein wrote that the returns on the British and French capital investment had doubled many times during decades of their exclusive control of the canal without any of that profit going to Egypt or Egyptians, who had built the canal with their own hands. Egypt, according to Hussein, had every moral and legal right to nationalize the canal. Despite their overt threats, Hussein hoped France and Great Britain would not wage war on Egypt. For him, Egypt was an independent country that was a member of the United Nations, and nationalizing the canal was a legal action. Speaking of French and British politicians, he said:

> They have turned everything upside down. They believe that they can scare Egypt with their soldiers and their fleets. They think they can wage war whenever they want, however they want, and wherever they want, as if they own the Earth and can do whatever they like to its people. They think Egypt will fear them today as it used to fear them before and will listen to them today the way it used to listen to them before. They think the world will let them launch a war, if they really want to launch a war.[72]

But war happened. The tripartite aggression, as Egyptians call the attack by Israel, Great Britain, and France on Egypt on October 29, 1956, came as a huge shock to Hussein. He had had his own conflicts with France before, notably over the issue of the Egyptian institute in North Africa and then France's brutal show of force in Algeria, but he never imagined France would attack Egypt. For Hussein, this attack from a country traditionally seen as a friend of Egypt's was a deep betrayal. In protest, he returned his Légion d'honneur award to the French government. In her memoirs, his wife, Suzanne, described his bitter disappointment and profound hurt.

> Already, when [France] had forced the Sultan of Morocco out of his own country, Taha was profoundly saddened. He had an idea of France that was very high. He battled to defend it on many occasions and worked hard to spread its culture. He had put so much heart into preserving the French schools [in Egypt] during the [Second World] war. . . . There was the affair of Algiers, hurtful to the extreme. After an official promise from the French government, came a brisk refusal. He could not accept the attack on Suez, and he returned the Légion d'honneur.[73]

In a series of articles in which he attacked colonial powers, especially France, Hussein commented that the Fourth Republic was trying hard to redeem France from its "disgraceful defeat" in the Second World War and that France was trying to prove it was still a strong power, but its disastrous war in Indochina and its "horrible sins" in North Africa were only adding to the shame and disgrace. He described the Suez Canal war as a crime that France committed with Great Britain, and qualified it as yet another consequence of France's defeat in the Second World War.[74] He also said the attack on Egypt was clearly a "conspiracy," one "that no human being could doubt" and that the British, the French, and their "puppet" (as he always described Israel) had put together in order to entrap the Egyptian army.[75]

> No one could dispute that [the conspiracy] was planned during the night or during the day, or during both night and day, and that those who planned it organized it well and started to execute it. [They] neither felt shame nor any semblance of shame in their hearts or conscience, because their hearts and conscience have hardened and have become cruel, feeling no disgrace and knowing no embarrassment, no matter how horrible the guilt.[76]

Hussein was angry and disappointed, and he continued to deplore French actions in Algeria well into the sixties. Commenting on a speech delivered by the French prime minister in early 1958 describing France's brutality in Algeria as necessary to defend the "free world," Hussein wrote:

> What free world requires committing these sins and crimes for its defense while going against the basics of all religions, morals, civilization, and law. What freedom is established or defended by humiliating the free and sentencing women and boys who have not reached adulthood and have never carried arms to their

death. What is this freedom and what value does it have, what does the world need it for, what benefit could the human being, his civilization, his religions and laws derive from such a freedom, which does not exist unless blood has been spilled, people have been killed, and orphans, widows, and infants have been made homeless.[77]

The Suez war, events in North Africa, and vicious attacks against Egypt and Nasser by British and French diplomats and in the western press made it impossible for Hussein to evoke what he usually liked to call a "shared human civilization" to which all nations should contribute through culture and education. International politics had dealt a heavy blow to his project of critical synthesis. As historian Sharif Yunis has remarked, during the sixties, expressing animosity toward the "West" became a sign of independence and patriotism.[78] In this polarized world, Hussein had to take a stand, and he stood with Nasser, Egypt, and other countries fighting for their freedom.

Redefining the Role of the Intellectual

Not only did Taha Hussein feel estranged by the reaction of the "free world" to attempts by weaker nations to become free and independent, but he also felt increasingly alienated at home. During the early years of the revolution, he addressed the nation and the Revolutionary Council through the pages of *al-Jumhuriyya* saying he did not offer his advice and analysis for personal gain, for he was already an old man. Yet, he felt it was his duty as an intellectual to unpack complex situations and give advice on the way forward. By the mid-1950s, however, it became clear that the government's expectations of intellectuals, like Hussein and others, had changed. The regime expected intellectuals to enforce its vision and little more. Moreover, a populist nationalist discourse discredited Hussein's generation, claiming that between the revolutions of 1919 and 1952, his generation had failed to express the needs of the Egyptian people or carry out the necessary social revolution.

In his famous 1961 book *The Crisis of the Intellectuals*, Muhammad Hasanayn Haykal, a journalist and the spokesperson for Nasser, reprinted several articles he had published in Egypt's leading daily, *al-Ahram*, in which he identified what he, and by extension the new ruling elite, found wrong with Egyptian intellectuals. He accused them of not having been loyal enough to the revolution, and explained what their new role should be. While he admitted that they had cooperated with the revolution after July 23, 1952, he belittled that cooperation as mere "political loyalty to the revolution as a regime," and not a genuine "revolutionary loyalty."[79]

By revolutionary loyalty, he explained, he meant that intellectuals should have worked to theorize the mission of the revolution, providing the leadership with the ideas required to make revolutionary changes in society.

> The normal and essential role for intellectuals was not just for them to "cooperate" with the revolution but to interact with it, to "adopt" its cause, to "take" it on and "give" it from their thoughts its "national theory," to formulate revolutionary belief from their conscience and their knowledge . . . that is to say, the revolution's road to fundamental and root changes in Egyptian society.[80]

The root of the problem, according to Haykal, was that intellectuals were ill placed to know what the people wanted, and he believed this problem went back to the time of the monarchy. Through their alliance with the *ancien régime*, Haykal claimed, intellectuals had isolated themselves from the people and were unable to express their grievances or their needs.[81] In July 1952, he went on, the "vanguard of the army" (*al-tali'a*) that carried out the coup took on the leadership role that intellectuals should have normally occupied. He criticized calls by intellectuals for the army to return to its barracks, arguing that such calls provided further proof that intellectuals had not grasped the significance of that historic moment. Reiterating Nasser's thoughts in *The Philosophy of the Revolution*, Haykal said that the goal of the coup was not simply to depose the king, but to change Egyptian society as a whole. Due to the political vacuum created by the coup, he believed it was inevitable for the army to be in total control. According to Haykal, Nasser understood that it was not the army's role to govern, and he offered the solution when he resigned from the army and joined the people as a civilian. In that way, Haykal went on, Nasser the civilian became the country's president, and the army was no longer running the country.[82]

Ignoring a challenging British colonial context and its debilitating failed negotiations, Haykal accused the main political parties before the revolution of having aligned themselves with the interests of large landowners and ignoring social reforms. He used this argument to dismiss the 1954 calls by intellectuals for the reestablishment of a multiparty system as only "theoretical." The existing parties, he explained, and especially the Wafd, which had the people's support, had failed to accomplish any revolution in Egyptian society and proved they were incapable of effecting any change.[83] Given that the army had no philosophy of its own and that in 1954 the revolution had not made enough grassroots changes to allow the creation of new parties, he insisted that the reestablishment of a multiparty system was not a possibility back then.[84] Writing in 1961, Haykal still believed Egyptian society was not ready to develop new political parties capable of carrying out the reforms society needed. In the absence of political parties, he believed the state-run National Union should organize the Egyptian workforce to develop Egypt's national resources.[85] In his analysis of the problems of intellectuals, Haykal put the army and the people on one side and intellectuals on the other. Army officers, he claimed, understood what Egyptians wanted and acted on their behalf, whereas intellectuals were isolated from the people. The solution, according to Haykal, was for intellectuals to unite themselves with what he described as "the revolutionary driving force" and rally behind the regime, which represented Egyptians and their true interests.

This was not Haykal's opinion alone. It was Nasser's too, and both opinions were at odds with how Taha Hussein had interpreted the early success of the revolution, as I showed earlier. Haykal quoted an important passage from Nasser's *Philosophy of the Revolution*, describing the high hopes Nasser had placed on Egyptian intellectuals and his ultimate disappointment.

> I used to think before July 23 that the entire nation was waiting for the vanguard to break the barriers so the nation would follow in back-to-back orderly lines on a holy march toward the great goal. An infinite crowd did come, but how far reality was from imagination. The crowds that came were divided, and the holy march got delayed. I felt, with a sad bitter heart, that the duty of the vanguard was not over yet.[86]

Intellectuals, according to Nasser, were unable to rise to the occasion, set their differences aside, and unite their efforts to back up the army. He was disappointed because those intellectuals could not agree among themselves on one way forward and were thus unable to provide him with the concrete ideas that he needed to unite the nation and start everybody on the "holy march," as he called it. In *The Philosophy of the Revolution*, Nasser not only talked about intellectuals and their failure but also specifically denounced university professors. He undermined their achievements, and condemned their ego and total lack of awareness of the role the country and nation expected them to play. He even claimed they should have found a role model in the young officers.

> Many of [the university professors] spoke to me. . . . Unfortunately, none of them gave me ideas. Each one introduced himself and his qualifications while looking at me as if he was favoring me with the treasures of the earth and the sources of immortality. I remember I could not contain myself and I told them: "Every one of us can do a miracle in his own place. One's first duty is to put all

effort into one's work, and if you, as university professors, thought about your students, and made them your main priority, then you would provide us with an incredible force to build the country."[87]

This dismissal of intellectuals and fear of divisive ideas reappeared in 1962 in another significant document, *al-Mithaq al-Watani* (*The National Pact*). In *al-Mithaq*, Nasser, after explaining the history of the revolution, described his plan of action and the importance of both democracy and socialism working together for the benefit of the people. In this struggle to realize people's dreams and achieve their expectations, he warned against what he described as "an intellectual adolescence." These intellectual adolescents, whom he described as weak and incapable of creative thinking, undermined society by offering ideas and interpretations that "freeze the national struggle" and "spread a spirit of hesitation." These defeatist ideas represented danger, a "moral terrorism," which should be "confronted and eliminated." In this program, Nasser called for a cultural revolution whose motto would be "knowledge for society's sake," and he asked universities and research institutes to develop themselves so they could meet this objective. For Nasser, the old motto of the university, "knowledge for knowledge's sake," was no longer adequate. "Knowledge for knowledge's sake is a responsibility whose burden our national capacity during this phase cannot bear," he insisted.[88]

On May 26, Taha Hussein responded publicly in disagreement with Nasser for the first time. This response, appearing in one of Hussein's last political articles in *al-Jumhuriyya*, could be read not only as a reaction to the *Mithaq*, but also to Haykal's comments on the crisis of the intellectuals a year earlier, which until now Hussein had completely ignored. Diplomatically, Hussein focused on two specific points, saying that he felt encouraged by Nasser's own confirmation in the *Mithaq* that criticism was necessary for any progress. The first issue dealt with history. In the *Mithaq*, Nasser dismissed the 1919 revolution as a failure. Reiterating Haykal's opinion, Nasser said that given their allegiance to wealthy landowners, the political parties in charge failed to bring any social reform to the people in the aftermath of that revolution.[89] He described the 1936 Anglo-Egyptian Treaty as having sealed this failure by accepting an independence that was empty of any value or meaning.[90] He also described the period between 1919 and 1952 as a "setback" (*naksa*), in which those who had led the 1919 revolution lost all revolutionary capabilities when they aligned themselves with landowners to "divide up the booty." This "corrupt partisan atmosphere," as Nasser described it, attracted intellectuals, who should have protected the revolution. Instead, they could not resist temptation, he said, and eventually all those parties threw themselves into the arms of the palace at times and into the arms of colonialism the rest of the time.⁹¹

Taha Hussein was indignant, and possibly saw Nasser's criticism as an attack on him, for Hussein was not only an intellectual but also a former Wafdist minister and member of government. Moreover, as we have seen, he saw culture and education during the period between 1919 and 1952 as the main reasons for the success of the revolution. Nasser's understanding of what happened was therefore radically different from Hussein's, and Hussein responded, defending himself and his generation of intellectuals. It is worth quoting Hussein's response in full.

> Everything the President said about these political parties, their differences, and competition over power was spot on and there is no point in refuting it. But the President also talked about intellectuals and their activities during the period between the 1919 revolution and the current one. It seems to me that he has not been fair to them. They joined these parties, disagreed just like these parties disagreed, and lost much of their effort and time in futile politics. But not all of them succumbed to temptation. These intellectuals created an intellectual awakening that cannot be denied. They woke up the people and taught them using the books they wrote, the literature they authored, and what they published on politics. They were the foundation of education in various schools and institutes. They took on the burden of the three universities: Cairo, Alexandria, and Ain Shams. They graduated thousands of young people who now bear the burdens of life not only in Egypt, but also elsewhere in Arab countries. I would have preferred if the President were fair to them somewhat after he mentioned they joined the political parties and went along with them.⁹²

By asking Nasser to be fair, Hussein might have also been referring to the effort he and others had made when they spent a year and half writing a new constitution for the country after the coup. Although Nasser in *The Philosophy of the Revolution*, and then Haykal in *The Crisis of the Intellectuals*, accused the older generation of intellectuals of having disappointed the revolution by not giving the new leaders the ideas necessary to move forward, both Nasser and Haykal knew this was not entirely true. Hussein had been appointed to the Committee of the Fifty (*Lajnat al-Khamsin*), as it was called, in December 1952, and the committee submitted the new constitution in August 1954.⁹³ This committee represented various intellectual and political currents in Egyptian society at the time. It included four members from the Wafd, two from the

Liberal Constitutionalists, two Saʿdists, three from the Muslim Brotherhood, two from the New National Party, one member from Young Egypt, and one member from the Kutla al-Wafdiyya, as well as the presidents of the Court of Cassation, the State Council, and the Supreme Court, three officers from the army and the police, and professors of constitutional law, in addition to other public figures. Six of the fifty members were Coptic Christians.[94] Hussein and those on the committee gave the Revolutionary Council what they believed was the result of decades of experience in Egyptian public life, culture, and politics. The Revolutionary Council, however, chose to ignore their constitution and it was never discussed publicly.

The intellectual historian Tariq al-Bishri describes the 1954 constitution as having included "very sophisticated" technical and constitutional references.[95] It protected individual and collective liberties within a parliamentary republic.[96] It ensured freedom of publishing and of the press without censorship or control. It stipulated freedom of assembly without the presence of the police if assemblies were for peaceful purposes and unarmed. The constitution also allowed for the creation of organizations and political parties without prior authorization from the government if the laws organizing their creation were respected and as long as they were created peacefully and for peaceful ends.[97] Al-Bishri describes the constitution as a liberal one that avoided all the mishaps of the 1923 constitution.

> The project [of writing the constitution] was just an adjustment of the abolished constitution of 1923. It really created highly sophisticated formulations, which ensured that parliament would become the principal source of power around which all other state authorities would revolve. It also eliminated the gaps which allowed the king to control the institutions of the 1923 constitution. [The new constitution] prevented any [future] attempts by the president of the republic to dominate the authority of the nation, represented by parliament.[98]

According to this constitution, the president of the republic was to be a parliamentary president, elected by an organization composed of members of parliament and some local organizations for one term of five years. To avoid a repetition of the problems with the constitution of 1923, the new constitution said that parliament could not be dissolved for the same reason twice, and if dissolved and no elections had taken place in sixty days, then the old parliament would reconvene the next day.[99]

Yet, those who wrote the constitution did not give the army any role in building the new constitutional order. In his analysis of the new constitution, al-Bishri found it "clear that those who carried out the project aimed with their constitution to exclude the men of July 23 from participating in power and to keep the military away from having any role in politics." Although al-Bishri admitted that those who wrote the constitution were right, theoretically, to exclude the army from ruling the country, they ignored the new political map and that, as they were writing the constitution, the military and the state were already turning into a "coherent regulatory body."[100] By trying to exclude the army, the new constitution was stillborn.[101]

If Taha Hussein's first response to the *Mithaq* was to correct Nasser on history and the role Hussein's generation had played before and after the 1952 revolution, the second was a direct critique of Nasser's vision for knowledge production. It is very likely that Nasser's critique of the university was what prompted Hussein to respond to the popular leader in the first place. Both Nasser and Haykal had discredited Hussein's generation before, in *The Philosophy of the Revolution* and *The Crisis of the Intellectuals*, but Hussein had never responded. This time was different as the original mission of the university was on the line. Again, it is worth quoting Hussein's response in full.

> The President was absolutely right when he said that knowledge should reform life and develop it. But he said that knowledge for knowledge's sake is a responsibility the burden of which our national efforts at this stage cannot bear. I stopped at this sentence because I believe that knowledge for knowledge's sake is a liability that we can bear in this phase of our lives. Universities and higher institutes should provide the youth with a good sound education that allows them to undertake the responsibilities of life and solve its problems, as well as reform life and develop it. If among those many thousands who are seeking knowledge, there was one possessed by the love of knowledge and he wanted to devote his mind and heart to studying, then we should not turn him away from that, and we should not entice him to [take on] practical duties. Instead, we should totally encourage him to carry on with his studying, learning, and going to the depth of scientific truths, for this is what can best serve a nation.[102]

In this rare case of public disagreement with Nasser, Hussein was defending his firm belief in the mission of the university, especially the Faculty of Arts, whose immediate practical impact on society was, and still is, not always obvious.

Zakariya al-Shalq argues that Hussein chose to respond to Nasser on the *Mithaq* because he felt optimistic about Nasser's call for constructive criticism and Nasser's praise of democracy as the political freedom that must accompany socialism, or the "social freedom" as Nasser put it.¹⁰³ Yet, given the history of Hussein at the university and the Faculty of Arts that was discussed in the previous chapters, it is more likely that his critique was to sound the alarm for what he thought was a dangerous transformation of the mission of the project to which he had dedicated decades of his life. Had Hussein been really excited about the *Mithaq*, he would probably have discussed it in more detail, which did not happen. Furthermore, in his response to the *Mithaq*, Hussein did not refer once to "democracy," dear as that word was to him. Nor did he mention that word in the political article that he wrote for *al-Jumhuriyya* a month later, on August 19, 1962, to commemorate the tenth anniversary of the revolution.¹⁰⁴ Hussein had a very different understanding of democracy and the ways to pursue it. Finally, on July 30, 1964, the Dean of Arabic Literature received a letter at home informing him that he had been fired from *al-Jumhuriyya*.¹⁰⁵

Redefining the Role of Literature

Not only did political expectations for what intellectuals could contribute change in the Nasserite period, but expectations for literature did as well. As Sharif Yunis has shown in his book *al-Zahf al-Muqaddas* (*The Holy March*), the new regime controlled the field of culture, including art, literature, the media, and the press, by revoking licenses, nationalizing existing cultural establishments, and creating new establishments run entirely by the state, such as the new Ministry of Public Guidance and State Television. Within this system, job appointments as well as the funding of literature, the arts, and culture in general depended more on the authorities' approval of the message contained in a work of the art rather than public interest in the work itself.¹⁰⁶ Yunis argues that the criteria against which culture was measured were clear in the "Pact of the Intellectuals," a document published in 1965 by the Nationalist Socialist Union, which defined *culture* as a "service rendered by the socialist government to the people in return for the taxes that they pay."¹⁰⁷ The purpose of this service, according to Yunis, was to "support the revolution and make it successful."¹⁰⁸

New expectations for literature, and art in general, also appeared among young writers, who had strong ideas of their own on how literature should change and why. They responded to the political changes happening around them and thought it was their responsibility to seize what they believed was a historic moment to make radical social changes. They engaged creatively with Jean-Paul Sartre's existentialism and his notion of commitment to chart a new role for literature and intellectuals.¹⁰⁹ Many were attracted to socialist realism, and they debated the ways in which they could commit their literature to the revolution and its principles. They called for the end of colonialism and creating a better life for the peasantry and the working class. While these writers respected Taha Hussein for his long career, and indeed most of them had been his students at the university, he increasingly came to be seen as a pillar of the old school of literature and literary criticism that resisted calls for a more explicit commitment to social and political reforms. Hussein, however, saw their calls as an overt politicization of literature, and he remained protective of writers' freedom to choose the form and content of their work. He questioned who was to decide what the needs of the people were and refused the idea that writers should have to answer to a predefined ideology. His debates with the Marxist writers Mahmud Amin al-ʿAlim and ʿAbd al-ʿAzim Anis in Egypt in 1954 and Raʾif Khuri in Lebanon in 1955 demonstrated his concerns and his distance from the ideas of socialist realism that were rapidly gaining ground. In the view of these writers, the literature of the older generation was not committed enough and failed to address the present moment and its struggles. They saw Hussein as a representative of that older generation that could not see that times had changed. This also fits within what Richard Jacquemond describes as a general "operating mode" in the Egyptian literary field. He argues that in these generational conflicts, new writers try to make room for themselves in the field by getting together and defining their mission against that of the older generation, whom they seek to discredit and displace.[110]

For example, on February 5, 1954, Taha Hussein published an article in *al-Jumhuriyya* titled "The Form of Literature and its Content," in which he argued that language (*al-lugha*) was the form of literature, while meaning (*al-maʿani*) was its content, and that the two formed an inseparable one. Al-ʿAlim and Anis responded to Hussein making a case for socialist realism, and a debate ensued, in which ʿAbbas Mahmud al-ʿAqqad also intervened. Hussein responded to the critique calmly but criticized their ideas for being too abstract; "Greek to me" (literally, "Greek that cannot be read"), he said. Moreover, Al-ʿAqqad was offended by their criticism of his work, and in his violent response he accused them of communism. Consequently, both al-ʿAlim and Anis were fired from their teaching positions at Cairo University during the Revolutionary Council's purge of communists in September 1954. In 1989, al-ʿAlim made it clear that the debate was the reason they lost their jobs. As al-ʿAqqad had rightly understood, their critique had been not just literary but also political and social.[111]

Al-ʿAlim and Anis developed their ideas further, adding new chapters to their contribution to the debate, and including everything in *Fi al-Thaqafa al-Misriyya* (*On Egyptian Culture*), which they published in Lebanon in 1955, with a preface by the famous Lebanese Marxist intellectual Husayn Muruwwa. In his preface, Muruwwa argued that the title was a misnomer because al-ʿAlim's and Anis' critique was accurate and applicable to culture, art, and literature not just in Egypt but everywhere in the world, especially in Arab countries that were experiencing the same struggle. That struggle, as he described it, was "the eternal battle between anything new and anything old, between the culture of a category of society whose historical role is disappearing, and another group that has new ideas and is trying to shift society toward a new historical role."[112] In the book itself, ʿAbd al-ʿAzim Anis described realism as a new school of literature that attracted young writers who wanted the connection between literature and society to be "a living connection that made [literature] an honest image and a creative mirror for social life in its anxieties, hopes and expectations."[113] Anis' and al-ʿAlim's main contribution was to insist that examining, revealing, and evaluating the social content of a work of art was an integral part of any serious literary creation or criticism.[114] In that respect, as they clarified in a later article, they were saying that the work of art was not only about form and content but also that content was in fact a "social stand." In their view, their work revealed "the natural interconnection and organic overlap between literary criticism and social criticism, thus uniting two types of study and enlarging literary criticism."[115]

Using this understanding of literature and its purpose, Anis and al-ʿAlim proceeded to condemn the older generation, intellectuals like Taha Hussein, ʿAbbas Mahmud al-ʿAqqad, Tawfiq al-Hakim, Ibrahim al-Mazini, and others. These younger intellectuals dismissed old literature as "ossified and separate from the movement of life."[116] Anis saw the older writers as "bourgeois intellectuals," associated with a political system run by the middle classes and represented by the Wafd Party. These classes, having failed to achieve independence, had to ally themselves with the British by signing the 1936 Anglo-Egyptian Treaty and then, according to Anis, they tried to convince Egyptians that the struggle for independence was over. In Anis' view, Hussein's literature from that period was disconnected from the "feelings of Egyptians." He used Hussein's protagonist Amina, in the novel *Duʿaʾ al-Karawan* (*The Call of the Curlew*), a "servant who learns French and marries the irrigation engineer to avenge her sister," as an example of "emotions far from Egyptian society [that] do not enforce any serious life."¹¹⁷ In another example, he describes Tawfiq al-Hakim's play *Ahl al-Kahf*, as "reactionary literature, which, although reflective of an aspect of Egyptian life, does not share its surging movement, and remains at the feet of its weak and defeated relationships."¹¹⁸ The worst by far, in Anis' view, was Ibrahim al-Mazini. His work *Ibrahim al-Katib*, according to Anis, was a prime example of defeatist literature, as the protagonist was totally removed from his social environment.¹¹⁹ Literature, in the eyes of al-'Alim and Anis, was a political statement, and so it was not surprising to them that someone like al-Mazini, who wrote defeatist literature, ran journals that represented the interests of the monarchy and the rich, who benefited from such literature. Their critique was not only literary, it was also political, social, and personal. A writer was what he wrote.

In his response to al-'Alim and Anis, Hussein remained focused on the literary discussion at hand, and said he was not convinced that a literary work should be only about society, arguing that if such was the case, then no literary work should describe nature, for example.¹²⁰ He spoke more openly of his concerns about the political implications of socialist realism in Beirut a year later. In a discussion session titled "For Whom Does a Writer Write?" Hussein debated with the Lebanese Marxist intellectual Ra'if Khuri over the question of whether an author should write for the public or the elite. The debate was republished, along with reactions from other readers and intellectuals, in the widely read Lebanese periodical *al-Adab*. *Al-Adab*, founded in January 1953, played a major role in disseminating works of socialist realism, or what also came to be known as committed literature.¹²¹

In this debate, Ra'if Khuri defended the position that a writer should write for everybody (*al-kaffa*). By everybody, he specified that he meant factory workers, peasants, students, small merchants, and functionaries. These readers, he explained, not only made up his audience but also provided him with the material from which he created his literary work. More importantly, he argued, he wrote so that his work would guide this large audience, which, he said, formed the basis of any nation or country.¹²² Turning to Taha Hussein, he asked him to specify who the elite (*al-khassa*) that he wrote for were, and why he chose to limit his readership to intellectuals and the rich, excluding peasants from upper Egypt, for example, who, in Khuri's view, would recognize more of themselves in Hussein's work *al-Mu'adhabun fi al-Ard* (*The Wretched of the Earth*) than a mathematician or an astronomer would see of themselves.¹²³ Literature, Ra'if insisted, should be open to life and connected to it, and a writer should be observant and analytical. As opposed to creating literature that solely entertained or focused on the artistic form without paying attention to the content (art for art's sake, as he saw it), Khuri believed that the task of a writer was to make people conscious of their lives and to direct the people, through literature.[124] "Literature," he declared, "must be concerned with topics derived from the important issues of the time and its problems." In his opinion, there were four major concerns in Arab life at that moment: independence, democracy, social justice, and peace. "I believe in guiding and guided literature," without any influence from the state or those in power, he affirmed.[125]

In his response to Khuri, Hussein refused the terms that framed the discussion. He saw that opposing an elite to a public in order to create a debate was "something artificial," and he said he had never accepted the premise that he wrote for the elite. Throughout his life, he explained, he never considered those terms when writing or commenting on literature. He only saw literature and readers of that literature. Some of those readers liked what they read while others did not. He said that literature had always worked like that, long before Europeans started worrying about those new theories that Khuri and others had become so interested in.[126] Why make up such a division and overcomplicate matters; "why split hairs, and why look for noon at 14:00 hours as the French say?" he asked. Right from the start of his response, Hussein was clear that his main worry was the interference of politics in literature. He argued that speaking of "guided and guiding" literature and "committed and uncommitted" writers, as well as distinguishing writing for the "public" from writing for the "elite," stemmed from politicians trying to use literature to achieve their goals.[127]

Hussein explained that no writer wrote exclusively for the few. He believed that writing happened when a certain idea imposed itself on a writer until the writer felt forced to express that idea, in poetry or prose, and then give what he had written to the people.

> Many litterateurs fool themselves and say that they write only for themselves. Nonsense. A writer does not write for himself, and if this were the case, then he would not need to write. It would be enough for him to flirt with his thoughts and ideas as they roam around in his mind and confuse his emotions. He would not need to see them written down.[128]

Given this view of the act of writing, Hussein declared that he was uncomfortable with labels, such as "socialist literature," "communist literature," or "democratic literature." Such doctrines (*madhahib*) should not be forced on literature, he insisted, and the writer should not feel the obligation to write according to this or that doctrine.[129] As he went on, his critique became sharper. Addressing those in favor of a "guided" literature, he asked them if they did not read and enjoy the old literature, which was not guided. This, he maintained, only illustrated the contradiction between what they liked to read in private and what they wanted to create in public. In addition, he said, he was puzzled there were writers who wanted to give up on their own freedom.

> Let's say the truth, say it openly without hesitation or fear. You want to know the truth? It is very simple. Guided literature is the literature whose purpose is to become a literature of propaganda [adab al-da'wa], whose purpose is to drive people to what this or that [political] party wants, so the people become socialist, communist or democratic. I never fool myself and I do not like it for anybody to fool themselves either. I do not like to flatter people in order to subject them to what they should not be subjected to. . . . For if this guidance came from anyone [but the writer himself], be it an individual, a party, the state, a group, then this would have nothing to do with literature.[130]

He said that he read socialist and communist literature often, but seldom did he find sincerity in that kind of committed literature. He also took issue with the increasing criticism of writers who did not write about people's needs. "What is this talk?" he asked. "First, what do the people need? What could these needs be, and who can decide and realize these needs at any time?" He criticized limiting people's needs to material necessities such as food, insisting that the people were "adults" who could distinguish for themselves between what was good for their bodies and what was good for their minds.[131]

Hussein also defended literature against accusations that it was not responding fast enough to the events reshaping Egyptian life. According to him, literature had helped people realize that their lives needed change, and by doing so, it made the revolution possible.[132] He explained that the literature of the revolution itself, however, which writers were impatient to have, needed time and would not come about until new writers had grown up in the new environment created by the revolution. Literature would change when these new writers had become accustomed to their newly found freedom from the oppressive monarchy, corrupt foreign occupation, and the unjust economic system.[133] Responding later in strong words to young writers advocating "literature for life," as they called it, Hussein insisted that they were wasting their time and the time of their readers over "silly" questions that revolved around the responsibility of writers and the authority to which they should hold themselves accountable.[134] People have solved these problems since the "dawn of civilization," he said. Every writer, he argued, was responsible for his literature and the rules governing that literature. Like any adult, a writer answered first to his conscience, then to public law, then to the community of people within which he lived, and finally to humanity as a whole.[135] Hussein did not understand what those young writers meant by "literature for life." What else, he wondered, could any literature be for; "for death?" he asked.[136] He turned again to the political implications of this debate, and said the real question at hand was whether "art, literature included, should become a tool for social reform as decided by the state." Such a question, he went on, was not limited to literature and art, but also included science, indicating that the debate was not "purely literary or artistic" but a "sociopolitical" one. He therefore saw the debate as a choice between two approaches to art and literature, the individual or the social. On one hand, he argued that the individual approach was free. It allowed writers to use literature as a tool for social reform if they wished to do so, or to use it to express the self, society, or nature if they wanted. The social approach, on the other hand, did not accept anything but its own view that literature was a "pure social means." "While literature has the right to intervene in politics if it wants, I would hate it for politics to force itself onto literature," he concluded.[137]

Noticeable in this debate with younger writers, is the absence of Hussein's usual sarcasm, which had characterized his earlier debates with members of his own generation and the previous one. Indeed, he wrote that this debate over committed literature or literature for life was annoying, because it claimed to be about literature when it had nothing to do with literature. Yet, he said, he intervened because he felt the younger writers were confused and were getting caught up in a "futile debate" that prevented them from dedicating themselves to literature.[138] He was clearly frustrated but calmly refuted their arguments and warned repeatedly against intimidating writers into writing according to prescribed ideologies.

Yet, for the younger writers who felt literature must play a direct role in the struggle for freedom and social justice after the revolution, their disagreement with Hussein could not have been more significant. They felt their role was to guide the people and other writers, too. Hussein was telling them exactly what they did not want to hear. By insisting that literature and art in general "should be seen as an end in itself, and that it should not be exploited for this or that purpose," they believed he was excluding literature from the struggle.[139] Like Muruwwa and Jacquemond, literary scholar Ahmad Abu Haqa saw the conflict between Hussein and Khuri as generational. Abu Haqa mentioned Khuri's age of forty-three and Hussein's age of sixty-six at the time to argue that the former represented the younger generation while the latter represented the old. Abu Haqa believed that Khuri was rebelling against existing standards of literary criticism in the hope of a larger social change, whereas Hussein was old and conservative.[140] Yoav Di-Capua has recently taken this further, showing how this debate marginalized the older generation of *udaba'* who refused the ideologization of culture.[141] He points out how Hussein was not even invited to attend Sartre's and Simone de Beauvoir's much anticipated talk at Cairo University in 1967, and only learned about their visit from the newspapers.[142] This was especially ironic given that it was Hussein who introduced Sartre and his philosophy to the Arab world in his periodical *al-Katib al-Misri* in 1946 and was the one who coined the term *iltizam* in the first place.[143]

Interestingly, in all these debates, neither the young writers nor Hussein himself brought up the accusations of communism leveled against him in the late 1940s. In addition to his incessant calls for free universal education, Hussein had published a series of literary works deploring social injustice in Egypt at the time. He had stressed the importance of combating corruption, as well as the poverty, ignorance, and illness rampant among large segments of the population. These works included, for example, *Ahlam Shahrazad* in 1943, *Shajarat al-Bu's* in 1944, *Jannat al-Shawk* in 1945, *al-Qadar* in 1947, *Mir'at al-Damir al-Hadith* in 1948, *al-Wa'd al-Haqq* in 1949, *Jannat al-Hayawan* in 1950, and most importantly, *al-Mu'adhabun fi al-Ard*, which was banned in Egypt and which he had to publish in Lebanon, in 1949. In addition, he published a series of articles between 1945 and 1949 in which he was outspoken about his disappointment in the outcome of the 1936 treaty and how little impact it had had on the poor and the needy. In these articles, he expressed his disapproval of the way public servants ignored the needs of the people, his worry about the spread of corruption under British occupation, and his concern over the absence of a social welfare system to save the dignity of widows and orphans.[144] It was because of all this that Farouk had suspected Hussein of communism and was opposed to Hussein's appointment as minister of public instruction in the new Wafd cabinet of 1950. Farouk relented only after al-Nahhas' persistence. Even though Hussein positioned himself in the debate with young writers solely as an *adib* (man of letters) and made no references to his credentials as a statesman and a politician, his concerns about committed literature and its impact on individual freedoms were a result of his long and deep experience with the state and its institutions.

In retrospect, as Di-Capua implies in his overall assessment of *iltizam*, Hussein's concerns were, after all, justified:

> Being an existentialist effort that sought to alter Arab ontology, the state defined the notion of *iltizam* as commitment to the sacred politics of collective sacrifice and rebirth. In this way, *iltizam* became the subject of Pan-Arabism. Emptied of its original meaning of intellectual commitment to freedom as such, it gradually slipped into the traitorous trap of self-referential commitments to commitment. In this new role, it was used to justify horrendous acts of political terror against a long list of real and maintained internal enemies.[145]

The End of a World

During the 1950s and '60s, many intellectuals of the older generation whom younger writers saw as resistant to new ideas were already disappearing. Moving eulogies were given at the Arabic Language Academy to commemorate their lives and work. Taha Hussein attended many of those events. He bade farewell to his university and academy colleagues Ahmad Amin (1954), 'Abd al-Hamid al-'Abbadi (1956), 'Abd al-Wahab 'Azzam (1959), Mansur Fahmi (1959), and Muhammad Shafiq Ghurbal (1961). He lost close friends, such as Muhammad Husayn Haykal (1956), his mentor Ahmad Lutfi al-Sayyid (1963), 'Ali 'Abd al-Raziq (1966), Ahmad Hasan al-Zayyat (1968), and two Tunisian friends, the scholars Hasan Husni 'Abd al-Wahab (1968) and the Sheikh of the Zaytuna Fadil 'Ashur (1970). 'Abbas Mahmud al-'Aqqad, Hussein's lifelong adversary, died in 1964, and Hussein evoked his memory with much fondness and respect. The jurist 'Abd al-Hamid Badawi, whom Hussein had proudly welcomed to the academy in 1945, passed away in 1965. The academy meetings, which Hussein attended regularly, also missed the presence of his political rival the jurist 'Abd al-Razzaq al-Sanhuri (1971) and the writer and poet Mahmud Taymur (1973), among others.

After Nasser's sudden death, Hussein gave a eulogy for him at the Arabic Language Academy on October 5, 1970.[146] It was a short speech in which he expressed his sadness and praised Nasser's efforts in abolishing class differences and for having always sided with the poor. In a few sentences that seemed out of place, Hussein mentioned that he had brought up the question of political prisoners with Nasser, expressing concern for their families and their suffering in the absence of their fathers and brothers. Nasser had reassured him that the government continued to pay their salaries, and that the Ministry of Waqfs took care of the families of prisoners who did not work for the state. Hussein also evoked his own relationship with Nasser, saying it was strong and dated back to the early days of the revolution. He said he had been particularly grateful when Nasser appointed him to the Order of the Nile in 1965.[147] Nasser had also awarded him the national honors prize for literature in 1959, memorialized in the photograph here. He also hailed Nasser for his role in the 1956 war:

> It is enough that President Gamal Abdel Nasser led the war against England, France, and Israel in 1956, and I will not forget the speech he made at the venerable Azhar when he repeated "We will fight and we will not surrender." The truth is, he did not know how to surrender and never accepted surrender.

As for Egypt's crushing defeat in 1967, about which Hussein had written nothing, he saluted Nasser's courage in a short sentence, saying he endured the defeat the way "a man who knew the rights the people have over him, and the rights the homeland has over the people" should.[148] Hussein knew that siding with the poor and standing up to arrogant colonial powers would go down in history as Nasser's greatest achievements during his eighteen years in power. However, Hussein glossed over the extent of Nasser's involvement in silencing the opposition and his responsibility for the defeat of 1967. These remain the two most controversial aspects of Nasser's legacy, over which Egyptians disagree to this day. Totally missing from Hussein's eulogy was any reference to freedom, democracy, culture, or the university. In commemorating Nasser, whose death sent shock waves across Egypt and the entire Arab world, Hussein, who was almost eighty-one at the time, chose to remain silent on the great leader's impact on the project to which Hussein had dedicated decades of his own life.

Conclusion

Taha Hussein welcomed the army coup of July 23, 1952, with much enthusiasm. He saw the coup and the people's embrace of the "blessed movement" as a result of what he believed was Egypt's "cultural awakening." In his reading of what had happened, he thought this awakening, spearheaded by the university and disseminated through education and works of art and literature, had made the people understand the values of freedom, justice, and equality. He believed they had realized what the corrupt *ancien régime* had failed to provide them, and so they supported the army to change their lives for the better. In his view, the people's overwhelming support of the army transformed the coup into a revolution. Aware of the shortcomings that existed prior to the coup and which

FIGURE 17. Nasser decorating Taha Hussein, 1959. Courtesy of the Taha Hussein family.

he had criticized time and time again, he hoped this new era would manage to eradicate poverty, illness, and ignorance.

Hussein believed that by siding with the army, the people demonstrated that they understood what was good for them and that power should be returned to them as quickly as possible. Through some articles in the early days of the revolution and, more importantly, in a never-realized constitution that gave full power to an elected parliament within a democratic republican system, he called on the army officers to return to their barracks and hand power back to civilians. The new constitution would have empowered individual and collective freedoms, and ensured that previous constitutional oversights, which had allowed the king to manipulate the country's institutions, were remedied. It would have offered more guarantees that the people, through their elected parliament, would always remain the main source of power in the country.

Following the rejection of the constitution and the rise of an official discourse that dismissed the period between the two revolutions (and its intellectuals) as corrupt and alienated from the people, Hussein chose to remain silent on most of Nasser's domestic policies. In the new official discourse, the army vanguard monopolized speaking in the name of the people. With the absence of political parties and of a free press, there was no real space for any serious opposition. The new role for intellectuals, as defined by Haykal, was reduced to supplying the regime with ideas that reinforced its vision. In matters of foreign policy, however, Nasser courageously put Egypt at the heart of anti-colonial struggles, and he had Hussein's full support in his conflicts with western powers. Given Egypt's new and shaky independence between 1954 and 1956, Hussein thought it was necessary for Egyptians to rally behind their leader until that independence was on more solid ground and the British troops had left the country. The tripartite aggression, along with the fierce repression of liberation movements in North Africa and elsewhere by European powers, made the west an enemy that had lost any kind of moral standing.

But Hussein's silence on what was happening inside Egypt was not absolute. He used literature as an outlet to voice his rejection of the ideological restrictions imposed on writers, artists, and intellectuals. For him, *iltizam*, or "committed literature," was a form of political propaganda that used literature for political ends. His resistance, however, alienated him from a generation of young writers who took socialist realism seriously and believed it was morally reprehensible for any writer not to engage in the anti-colonial revolutionary struggle. Finally, it was on behalf of the university that Hussein disagreed publicly with Nasser. Taking issue with Nasser's view that the challenges facing the national struggle made it necessary to forego "knowledge for knowledge's sake" as a luxury Egypt could not afford, Hussein chose to speak out. While he understood that his call would go unheard, Hussein thought it was imperative to defend the university and its mission. Throughout the 1920s, '30s, and '40s, the university was the cornerstone of his entire project for culture and education. He believed that with its modern research and teaching methods, the university, and especially the Faculty of Arts, was the only institution capable of engaging critically with the Arab-Islamic tradition and ideas coming from Europe. He argued that only such knowledge, rooted in the "old" and the "new," could offer the solutions necessary to meet the challenges facing the country in modern times. This public disagreement with Nasser was Hussein's last *cri de cœur* in defense of the study of the humanities in the country.

CONCLUSION

> It was the antagonism between me and the Palace and between me and the Wafd that triggered the enormous reaction against *On Pre-Islamic Poetry* and which kept people busy for an entire year. This antagonism was neither religious nor literary. It was political.
>
> Taha Hussein[1]

RATHER THAN RELY exclusively or primarily on Taha Hussein's published work, this book has made extensive use of government documents, private papers, and other hitherto largely unutilized sources to reconstruct Hussein's role and views as a chief advocate for the Egyptian University, as a government official deeply involved in designing and implementing educational policies, and as a key figure in debates about the place of the Arabic language in Egyptian society and culture during the first half of the twentieth century. More broadly, Hussein's reforms during Egypt's parliamentary period complicate scholars' tendency to focus on the triangular struggle between the monarchy, the British, and the political parties, and then to foreground parliament's inability to end the occupation as leading inevitably to the Free Officers' coup in 1952. Hussein's political work demonstrates that despite difficulties and frustrations, parliament succeeded in enacting enduring institutional reforms and policies, such as providing free pre-university education and expanding Egyptian cultural influence abroad. Although Hussein criticized partisan politics and their detrimental impact on stability and policymaking, he never expressed disillusionment with parliamentary rule as a viable political system. More importantly, until the army takeover in 1952, he never believed his reform project had failed.

In building institutions of culture and education, Taha Hussein, as well as other intellectuals and policymakers of his generation, faced the challenge of the west with self-confidence and believed that embracing what they saw as the new (the secular university, new kinds of knowledge, new teaching and research methods, new social practices) did not mean giving up or diminishing their own traditions and literary heritage but rather engaging in a natural continuation of that heritage. In the spirit of earlier *nahdawis*, they were inspired by the new but felt rooted in the past. They were well aware of the theoretical debate over "authenticity and modernity," but they also understood that theory had to be anchored in people's lives and had to be translated into action to be effective and improve those lives. By working to reform the Ministry of Public Instruction, strengthen the Egyptian University, and create the Arabic Language Academy, they were confidently embarking on a tangible project of natural synthesis based on an active critical appropriation rather than a passive uncritical reception of ideas, institutions, and practices coming from Europe.

Nonetheless, this book neither tries to redeem Hussein and his generation nor claims that they did everything right. Rather, it is an attempt to understand them in their own context and not through the lens of all that has come since. As political events since Nasser's time made their project of natural synthesis impossible, history was rewritten in Egypt itself in a way that lumped these intellectuals together on one side or the other, for example, "modernist" or "traditionalist." Taha Hussein is a prime example of an intellectual who remains trapped in these binaries, which overlook the context in which he wrote and the bureaucratic and institutional constraints in which he made decisions—whether he is being recalled by Islamists who demonize him or by others who worship him. This tendency has also been paralleled by postcolonial literary scholars in the west who draw on select passages in public writings by Hussein and his generation to create an image of them as intellectuals who were "seduced" by European culture.

But Hussein was deeply conscious of culture's politics and education's political potential. For him, culture was never an isolated social-artistic sphere but rather the best means of ensuring the success of Egyptian democracy, achieving intellectual parity with Europe, and fighting the unequal power relations that held the country back from full independence. During the parliamentary period, Hussein was not only an intellectual but a politician and a statesman as well. It is therefore essential that we consider his career in the civil service and his political life in order to produce new, contextually rich readings of his published work. Interestingly, an unexpected acknowledgment of Hussein's deep political action came in a thoughtful text by his adversary in the debate over committed literature, Mahmud Amin al-'Alim. In a short piece published in the late 1960s, al-'Alim starts with a story about a visit he had made with two friends to Hussein's house in 1946 or 1947 to discuss literature. As soon as the conversation turned to the volatile political situation in the country, al-ʿAlim was astonished by Hussein's enthusiasm for politics. He criticized the youth for writing much about "revolution" without mastering "the art of revolutionary action," and insisted they had to study "revolutionary tactics and strategies." Al-ʿAlim describes how this meeting left him and his friends stunned and determined, and how it was one of several factors that changed the course of his life in the following years.[2] In telling this story, al-ʿAlim says he wants to point attention to "an aspect of the Dean of Literature that is still far from study, analysis, interpretation, and evaluation," and he asks himself how best to think about Hussein and make sense of three confusing truths about him: the writer-poet, the thinker-academic, and the practical man. After deep thought, al-ʿAlim writes that in his view, Hussein's philosophy was based on "a capable mind, a working idea, a strong opinion and an effective stand seeking reform and change as much as it can," leading him to conclude that Hussein was a "practical thinker."[3] Al-ʿAlim sees *The Future of Culture in Egypt* as a testament to Hussein's practical thought, as he managed when he became a civil servant to implement many of the theoretical ideas that he had written down in this book. "Addressing the practical life of Dr. Taha Hussein and its implications on his thought deserves a specialized analysis that is beyond the scope of this quick study," al-ʿAlim decides.[4] It is hard to tell why al-ʿAlim was reconsidering his old teacher's project, or whether Hussein's reservations on committed literature made more sense in the late 1960s. In any case, the man al-ʿAlim described in his text could not have been promoting "art for art's sake."

Moving beyond sterile debates about whether Taha Hussein should be classified as either a "westernizing" or a "culturally authentic" intellectual, this book has offered a fuller and more complex understanding of the sociocultural and political project to which he devoted his adult life: building strong educational and cultural institutions that would contribute to the development of a new national leadership and an increasingly educated, modern citizenry, strengthen the country's political independence, and open the way to a versatile and open culture that would be both deeply rooted in the Arab-Islamic tradition and also fully integrated with, and a contributor to, contemporary western culture. Hussein developed his ideas in tandem with concrete policy decisions to implement what he saw as an essential anti-colonial project. With his focus on institutions and their efficient operation in a challenging colonial context, he was engaged in an effort to extend and deepen the *nahda* project by endowing it with what he believed to be an indispensable and sustainable institutional infrastructure.

Partial decontextualized readings of *The Future of Culture in Egypt* and accusations made against Hussein that he was trying to turn Egypt into Europe culturally do not account for his serious engagement with the Arab-Islamic tradition and dedication to preserving classical Arabic through his work at the university and the language academy. Moreover, the details of his project help us make better sense of his complex relationship with al-Azhar. His often vehement critiques of al-Azhar in his autobiography *The Days* and in *The Future of Culture in Egypt*, in which he dismissed al-Azhar's teaching methods and what he saw as the rigidity of its sheikhs, may persuade the reader that Hussein was a staunch enemy of the prestigious mosque university.[5] Yet, those critiques do not explain why he spoke fondly of his memories there as a student, why he credited it with having safeguarded the tradition for centuries, or why he praised it elsewhere as "a treasure of fertile minds, intelligent hearts, and ultimately ready to undertake the greatest of deeds. [Al-Azhar is] a treasure that modern Egypt should neither ignore nor forget."[6] In the context of his political-cultural project for Egypt, Hussein's disagreement with al-Azhar was primarily over giving modern institutions like the university and the language academy the right to engage critically with the Arab-Islamic tradition and making classical Arabic more accessible. Orientalists were already engaging with both, and Hussein refused the idea that he and other Egyptian and Arab scholars should be excluded from these new conversations and scholarly debates. He did not seek to exclude al-Azhar from his reforms, but he understood that the religious establishment's monopoly of the tradition and the language had to be challenged. For Hussein, democratizing the tradition and the language was the only way to keep them alive and relevant to people in their daily lives. This put him on a collision course with al-Azhar, and partisan politics only made it worse.

By the eve of the 1952 Free Officers' coup, Taha Hussein believed the institutional study of the humanities in its Arab-Islamic and European variants had successfully taken the *nahda* forward. He even attributed Egypt's modern awakening, as he called it, to the Faculty of Arts and the scholarship it produced and the knowledge it disseminated in textbooks, lectures, conferences, and public defenses. He had enough confidence in his institutions and the expertise Egyptian scholars had developed within them that he felt Egypt was ready to export this knowledge beyond its borders and push back against French colonial policies in North Africa. Similarly, he believed that the people's embrace of the army coup was further proof of the success of his educational and cultural policies. For him, knowledge produced in the decades preceding the coup informed the people of their rights. They supported the army because it promised to reinstate those rights. In his view, this overwhelming popular support for the coup transformed it into a revolution. Literature, he stressed, had paved the way for revolution by showing the people what their lives should be like and helped them understand that justice and equality should reign. Without undermining the individual effort and creativity of Egyptian writers, artists, and teachers, this book's focus on institutions tells a more nuanced story about the history of Egypt's cultural influence in the Arab world, instead of simply repeating a nationalist myth of a perennial Egyptian cultural domination. While Hussein defended the idea that Egypt had a particularly rich culture that had developed over its long history, he also saw well-functioning and well-financed institutions as the necessary infrastructure by which Egypt could realistically move from consuming culture to producing it and assuming a leadership position.

In the parliamentary context, Hussein's attention to the public goes beyond the trend of *nahdawis* assigning themselves the role of educators of the masses. Rather, Hussein and other educational experts worked within political parties to shape public opinion and win votes by convincing the public of the soundness of their ideas. In content, the debate over free education was a serious discussion between knowledgeable interlocutors expressing different points of view on policies, objectives, and their ramifications. In form, it was a practical exercise in democracy. The public understood that it was addressed to them, and that their vote should settle it. This recalls the remark of the intellectual Luwis 'Awad in the early 1970s that Egyptians had a much clearer understanding of the rule of law and the role of the state before 1952, as well as the difference between duties and rights, be they public or private.[7] Rather than learning abstract European theories of democracy at school, Egyptians came to understand that their votes mattered through political debates on universal education and other issues directly relevant to their lives. Even if they were frustrated with the parliamentary system, they understood that political decisions had an immediate impact on their lives and their children's future and that governments must serve them and be held accountable.

This is not to say that Egypt's parliamentary experiment did not have problems or did not run into difficulties. On the contrary, that system was unable to put an end to the British occupation or social injustice. Parliament was generally dominated by large landowners and their lackeys. With the connivance of the palace and the British, the constitution was repeatedly suspended by authoritarian governments. Elections were often rigged, and the electoral system and oppressive local structures of power largely kept the bulk of the population from having an effective voice. Hussein himself experienced state censorship, and his critics in government repeatedly accused him of being a communist. The state forced him to shut down his periodical *al-Katib al-Misri* in 1948 and banned his book *al-Muʿadhabun fi al-Ard* (*The Wretched of the Earth*) in 1949 for its vivid depiction of poverty. Yet Hussein saw all these as problems of implementation and as a direct result of the ongoing British occupation. He never lost faith in the parliamentary system nor suffered what some critics have referred to as his generation's "crisis of liberalism."[8] As he cheered the fall of the monarchy in 1953, Hussein served on the committee that drafted a new liberal constitution that made parliament Egypt's most authoritative institution. In the months after the coup, he continued to push for general elections and a swift return to civilian rule. But to his disappointment, the new government never put the 1954 constitution to a referendum.

Unsurprisingly, the only time Hussein disagreed publicly with Nasser was to defend the period between the two revolutions and the university. Hussein admitted there had been frustrations, difficulties, and corruption before 1952, but he refused to dismiss the accomplishments that happened in culture and education *despite* all these problems. In this unique public intervention in which he anticipated the negative consequences of Nasser's discourse on the study of the humanities, Hussein warned against ostracizing "knowledge for knowledge's sake" in favor of what Nasser called "knowledge for society's sake." It is unlikely that he expected much from this public intervention, however. State authoritarianism and rising public anger over colonial intervention in Egyptian and Arab affairs made the promotion of his project impossible after 1952. He must have felt betrayed by the outcome of the 1952 revolution, which he had initially welcomed as *his* revolution. He felt betrayed by France and its violent suppression of Algerians in their war of independence, and was disappointed by his own students who, in his view, had willingly sacrificed their freedom and consciously turned their literature into political propaganda for the state.

By the time Hussein received his dismissal letter from *al-Jumhuriyya* in 1964, he had already witnessed the undermining of the two institutions that had been the pillars of his project: the parliament and the university. Historian Omnia El Shakry convincingly proposes an uninterrupted periodization from the 1930s to the 1960s, crossing what is usually considered the 1952 rupture, arguing that Gamal Abdel Nasser built on the ideas, institutions, and modes of knowledge production that he inherited.[9] While Hussein's free education policies and the institutions he established continued under Nasser, a rupture occurred in the relationship between these institutions and the state. Hussein implicitly expected the multiparty system and a free press to regulate the state's involvement in education by holding governments accountable and pushing for transparency in budgetary allocation and decision making. In the transition to a more authoritarian state, the checks and balances of the parliamentary system Hussein had envisaged became untenable. Weeks before his death, when Ghali Shukri asked him about the university and whether he thought it could provide the required "intellectual leadership," Hussein replied:

> They don't know what a university means now. We used to have a university. Now, I don't know. Did we fall behind or did something wrong happen? In our time, the university was a sanctuary for thought; it was freedom's holiest of holies. Now I hear it has been transformed into something akin to secondary schools or intermediate vocational schools. Let's drop this topic. May God help them.[10]

Shukri wished he could ask Hussein to elaborate, but Hussein was visibly upset, and beads of sweat had started to form on his forehead, so Shukri dropped the subject. Shukri then brought up the 1952 revolution, how it sought political and economic independence before turning into a social revolution. Shukri asked Hussein what role he and his generation could play now, after they had fought honorably for the national cause between 1919 and 1952. Again, it became clear to Shukri this was another topic that struck a chord with Hussein. Shukri even noted this was the most upset he had seen Hussein, as his face expressed much aversion to the question. Hussein replied:

> You speak their language: slogans, slogans. The country still seeks liberation, this time from Israel. The country is still behind: poor, ill, and ignorant. The illiteracy rate is the same, the percentage of the half-educated is the same, the percentage of cultured intellectuals is dropping at a worrying rate. It seems to me that what we had fought for is what you still need to fight for, and what the generation after you will need to fight for still. These are my last days, as I told you before, and I bid you farewell with much pain and little hope. Where is my generation? Unfortunately, I have outlived them all. They all died with deep regret in their heart. Salama Musa hid his bitterness behind his overwhelming love for mankind, his Sufi love for Egypt, and his romantic faith in the future. Al-'Aqqad hid his disappointment behind his stubborn pride, self-respect, and his overprotection of his dignity. 'Aqqad fought for freedom, and Salama Musa

FIGURE 18. On October 31, 1973, the funeral procession of the "university's eldest son" departed from the auditorium at Cairo University and made its way to a nearby mosque for the final funeral prayer. Taha Hussein now lies in the grave shown here under a mimosa planted by his wife, Suzanne. Photograph, by Maha Aon, courtesy of the Taha Hussein family.

fought for socialism. Have you achieved either to claim that our role is over, or to magnanimously try to find a new role for us? What is this talk? And who are you talking about? There is nobody left but me. I live in the shadows now. I am collecting my papers and will be gone soon.[11]

Taha Hussein was the last of the *nahdawis* of his generation and the *nahda* as he had imagined it was no more.

Interestingly, nothing in Hussein's disappointment revealed any inherent incompatibility between Islam and the values he fought for: reason, freedom, and political accountability. As the quotation that opens this conclusion shows, he explicitly denied that the crisis over *On Pre-Islamic Poetry* was religious, insisting it was political antagonism at the time, between him and the palace and between him and the Wafd, that stirred the polemic. Similarly, Arab intellectuals critical of what they see as simplistic culturalist explanations for the failure of the *nahda*, like Syrian playwright Saʿdallah Wannus and Palestinian literary critic and philosopher Faysal Darraj, openly accuse postcolonial authoritarianism of having silenced Hussein by putting an end to political life and reason in the country. As committed writers also turned against Hussein, Wannus believes they dealt a heavy blow to his project by depriving him of popular support.[12] Culturalist explanations, Wannus goes on, conveniently avoid engaging with politics and the responsibility of the postcolonial state in bringing the region to a point in which "human beings are worthless."[13] Much has happened since Hussein published *The Future of Culture in Egypt*, but whether we agree or disagree with his ideas, he anchored both his thought and action in the social reality of his people. Likewise, any ambitious political-cultural vision seeking to address the unfolding gloom in the Arab World today needs to consider people's daily lives, their demands and their expectations. If the ongoing protests in various Arab countries are in any way indicative of the social reality of people in the region, then this vision should address their demands for freedom, justice, and human dignity.

NOTES

Introduction

1. Leyla Dakhli, "The Autumn of the Nahda in Light of the Arab Spring: Some Figures in the Carpet," in *Arabic Thought beyond the Liberal Age: Towards an Intellectual History of the Nahda*, ed. Jens Hanssen and Max Weiss (Cambridge: Cambridge University Press, 2016), 357.

2. *Al-Musawwar*, no. 1173 (April 4, 1947): 8, cited in Khaled Fahmy, "Maydan al-Tahrir," *Reflections on Egypt, the Middle East, and History* (blog), last accessed December 24, 2019, https://khaledfahmy.org/ar/2011/09/11/ميدان-التحرير/.

3. ʿUmar Sulayman, "Omar Suleiman on the Crisis," interview by Christiane Amanpour, *ABC News*, February 6, 2011.

4. Thomas Philipp, "From Rule of Law to Constitutionalism: The Ottoman Context of Arabic Political Thought," in *Arabic Thought beyond the Liberal Age*, ed. Jens Hanssen and Max Weiss, 143.

5. Ghali Shukri, *Madha Yabqa min Taha Husayn?* (Beirut: Dar al-Mutawassit, 1974), 6.

6. Ibid., 24.

7. Ibid., 8. In an interview I conducted in Cairo on April 6, 2013, with the late Egyptian novelist Gamal al-Ghitani, he described *al-Katib al-Misri* as a landmark in the history of Egyptian periodicals. He especially praised the books the periodical published regularly, which he described as "exemplary" in terms of content and quality of translation. He said that as editor in chief of *Akhbar al-Adab*, he tried to do as Hussein had done, and asked his friends around the world to write for *Akhbar al-Adab* to provide Egyptian and Arab readers with access to new and different ideas.

8. Shukri, *Madha Yabqa min Taha Husayn?*, 13.

9. ʿAzza Kamil, "Limadha Yakhsha al-Azhariyun Muhammad ʿAbduh wa-Taha Husayn??," *al-Misri al-Yawm*, November 7, 2016.

10. Muhammad Shihta, "Shaykh al-Azhar: Taha Husayn Shadid al-Adab maʿa al-Turath wa-Sahabat al-Nabi," *Sada al-Balad*, November 11, 2016.

11. Samia Mehrez, *Egypt's Culture Wars: Politics and Practice* (New York: Routledge, 2008), 2.

12. Majida al-Jindi, "Al-Tariq ila Misr Qawwiyya kama Khattahu al-ʿAmid," *al-Ahram*, October 28, 2012.

13. Muhammad Ibrahim Abu Sinna, "Tarh Ru'yat Mustaqbal al-Thaqafa fi Misr," *al-Yawm al-Sabiʿ*, December 15, 2016.

14. In a controversial statement, the Egyptian Minister of Education, Tariq Shawqi, announced that education was a "commodity" and that the state should not pay for it. "Wazir al-Taʿlim al-Jadid: Al-Taʿlim Silʿa wa-l-Dawla qad la Tastamir fi Dafʿ Faturatiha," *Mada Misr*, February 16, 2017, last accessed March 3, 2017, http://www.madamasr.com/ar/2017/02/16/news/ سلعة-التعليم-الجديد-التعليم/وزير/سياسة.وا.

15. Britain reserved the right to protect Egypt and all communications vital to the British Empire against foreign aggression, protect minorities living in Egypt, and maintain the status quo of the Anglo-Egyptian Sudan.

16. Nick Salvatore, "Biography and Social History: An Intimate Relationship," *Labor History* 87 (2004): 187.

17. Barbara Taylor, "Separation of Soul: Solitude, Biography, History," *American Historical Review* 114, no. 3 (June 2009): 641.

18. David Nasaw, "AHR Roundtable: Historians and Biography, Introduction," *American Historical Review* 114, no. 3 (June 2009): 573.

19. Barbara Caine, *Biography and History* (New York: Palgrave Macmillan, 2010), 1–5.

20. Salvatore, "Biography and Social History," 187.

21. Ibid., 189.

22. Ibid., 189–91.

23. Sigurdur Magnusson, "The Singularization of History: Social History and Microhistory within the Postmodern State of Knowledge," *Journal of Social History* 36, no. 3 (2003): 718.

24. Hans Renders, "The Limits of Representativeness: Biography, Life Writing and Microhistory," *Storia della Storiografia* 59–60 (2011): 32–42.

25. Laila Parsons, *The Commander: Fawzi al-Qawuqji and the Fight for Arab Independence, 1914–1948* (New York: Farrar, Straus and Giroux, 2016).

26. Laila Parsons, "Some Thoughts on Biography and the Historiography of the Twentieth-Century Arab World," *Journal of the Canadian Historical Association* 21, no. 2 (2009): 16. Parsons also argues that the old-style Orientalist historical accounts with their cold gaze turn young historians away from narrative history, fearing the label "neo-Orientalist."

27. Laila Parsons, "Micro-narrative and the Historiography of the Modern Middle East," *History Compass* 9, no. 1 (2011): 85.

28. Richard Jacquemond, *Entre Scribes et Écrivains: Le Champs Littéraire dans l'Égypte Contemporaine* (Paris: Sindbad/Actes Sud, 2003), 143.

29. Roger Allen, *The Arabic Novel: An Historical and Critical Introduction* (Syracuse, NY: Syracuse University Press, 1982), 36.

30. Donald Reid, *Cairo University and the Making of Modern Egypt* (Cambridge: Cambridge University Press, 1990), 236. Scholars and literary critics continue to debate the exact genre of *The Days* and its resistance to easy classification as either a novel or an autobiography. For example, Yahya ʿAbd al-Dayim argues that it

is not an autobiography because of its lack of names, places, and dates. Ibrahim Yahya 'Abd al-Dayim, *al-Tarjama al-Dhatiyya fi al-Adab al-'Arabi al-Hadith* (Cairo: Maktabat al-Nahda al-Misriyya, 1975), 420. Fedwa Malti-Douglas refuses this approach and argues that despite the overlap of first- and third-person narration, the reader of *The Days* always understands that author, narrator, and protagonist are one and the same, hence meeting Philippe Lejeune's condition for an autobiographical pact. Fedwa Malti-Douglas, *Blindness and Autobiography: Al-Ayyam of Taha Husayn* (Princeton, NJ: Princeton University Press, 1988), 95.

31. Abdelrashid Mahmoudi, *Taha Husain's Education from the Azhar to the Sorbonne* (Richmond, Surrey: Curzon Press, 1998), 1.

32. Pierre Cachia, *Taha Husayn: His Place in the Egyptian Literary Renaissance* (London: Luzac, 1956).

33. Malti-Douglas, *Blindness and Autobiography*.

34. Meftah Tahar, *Taha Husayn: Sa Critique Littéraire et Ses Sources Françaises* (Tunis: Maison Arabe du Livre, 1976); Jabir 'Usfur, *al-Maraya al-Mutajawira: Dirasa fi Naqd Taha Husayn* (Cairo: Al-Hay'a al-Misriyya al-'Amma li-l-Kitab, 1983); and Ahmad Buhasan, *al-Khitab al-Naqdi 'inda Taha Husayn* (Beirut: Dar al-Tanwir, 1985).

35. Taha Hussein, preface to *Tarikh al-Adab al-'Arabiyyah min al-Jahiliyya hatta 'Asr Bani Ummaya: Nusus al-Muhadarat allati Alqaha bi-l-Jami'a al-Misriyya fi Sanat 1910–1911*, by Carlo Nallino, 2nd ed. (Cairo: Dar al-Ma'arif, 1970), 8.

36. Al-Badrawi Zahran, *Uslub Taha Husayn fi Daw' al-Dars al-Lughawi al-Hadith* (Cairo: Dar al-Ma'arif, 1982).

37. Rashida Mahran, *Taha Husayn bayna al-Sira wa-l-Tarjama al-Dhatiyya* (Alexandria: Al-Hay'a al-Misriyya al-'Amma li-l-Kitab, 1979).

38. Omnia El Shakry, *The Great Social Laboratory: Subjects of Knowledge in Colonial and Postcolonial Egypt* (Stanford, CA: Stanford University Press, 2007), 1.

39. Yoav Di-Capua, *Gatekeepers of the Arab Past: Historians and History Writing in Twentieth-Century Egypt* (Berkeley: University of California Press, 2009), 259–60.

40. Jacquemond, *Entre Scribes et Écrivains*, 21.

41. Mahmoudi, *Taha Husain's Education*, 1.

42. Munji al-Shimli, preface to *Taha Husayn Mu'arrikhan*, by 'Umar al-Jumni (Cairo: Al-Hay'a al-Misriyya al-'Amma li-l-Kitab, 2013), 6–7.

43. Munji al-Shimli, introduction to *Sultat al-Kalima: Masalik li-Dirasat Adab Taha Husayn wa-Fikrih*, ed. Munji al-Shimli, 'Umar al-Jumni, and Rashid al-Qarquri (Tunis: Markaz al-Nashr al-Jami'i, 2001), 6.

44. Tahar, *Taha Husayn: Sa Critique Littéraire*, 147.

45. Jabir Rizq, ed., *Taha Husayn: Al-Jarima wa-l-Idana* (Cairo: Dar al-I'tisam, 1985), 6.

46. Muhammad al-Bahtiti, "Taha Husayn Kana Buqan li-l-Mustashriqin," in *Taha Husayn: Al-Jarima wa-l-Idana*, ed. Jabir Rizq (Cairo: Dar al-I'tisam, 1985), 103.

47. Jamal 'Abd al-Hadi, Wafa' Muhammad Rif'at, and 'Ali Ahmad Labn, *al-Zur wa-l-Buhtan fima Katabuh Taha Husayn fi al-Shaykhan wa-Mu'alafat Ukhra Lahu* (Cairo: Dar al-Nashr wa-l-Tawzi' al-Islamiyya, 1991), 5.

48. Ibid., 61–74. Other such books include 'Abd al-Majid al-Muhtasib, *Taha Husayn*

Mufakirran (Amman: Maktabat al-Nahda al-Islamiyya, 1980); Anwar al-Jindi, *Muhakamat Fikr Taha Husayn* (Cairo: Dar al-I'tisam, 1984); and Mahmud al-Istanbuli, *Taha Husayn fi Mizan al-'Ulama' wa-l-Udaba'* (Beirut: Al-Matkab al-Islami, 1983).

49. Stephen Sheehi, *Foundations of Modern Arab Identity* (Gainesville: University Press of Florida, 2004).

50. Shaden Tageldin, *Disarming Words: Empire and the Seductions of Translation in Egypt* (Berkeley: University of California Press, 2011).

51. Joseph Massad, *Desiring Arabs* (Chicago: University of Chicago Press, 2007).

52. Tarek El-Ariss, *Trials of Modernity: Literary Affects and the New Political* (New York: Fordham University Press, 2013), 10.

53. Kamal al-Mallakh, *Taha Husayn: Qahir al-Zalam* (Cairo: Dar al-Kitab al-Jadid, 1973), 19.

54. Mahmud al-Samra, *Sariq al-Nar* (Beirut: Al-Mu'assassa al-'Arabiyya li-l-Dirasat wa-l-Nashr, 2004).

55. Misri Hannura, *Taha Husayn wa-Sikulujiyyat al-Mukhalafa* (Cairo: Dar Gharib, 2006), 7.

56. 'Umar al-Jumni, *Taha Husayn Mu'arrikhan* (Cairo: Al-Hay'a al-Misriyya al-'Amma li-l-Kitab, 2013).

57. Mustafa 'Abd al-Ghani, *Taha Husayn wa-l-Siyasa* (Cairo: Dar al-Mustaqbal al-'Arabi, 1986); and *Taha Husayn wa-Thawrat Yuliu: Su'ud al-Muthaqqaf wa-Suqutuh* (Cairo: Maktabat al-Turath al-Islami, 1989).

58. Mustafa 'Abd al-Ghani, *Taha Husayn kama lam Ya'rifuh Ahad* (Cairo: Dar al-'Alam al-'Arabi, 2010), 130–1.

59. Rashid al-Qarquri, *Taha Husayn: Mufakirran Siyasiyyan* (Tunis: Dar al-Ma'arif li-l-Tiba'a wa-l-Nashr, 2000), 424.

60. Ahmad Zakariya al-Shalq, *Taha Husayn: Jadal al-Fikr wa-l-Siyasa* (Cairo: Al-Hay'a al-Misriyya al-'Amma li-l-Kitab, 2009).

61. 'Abd al-Ghani, *Taha Husayn wa-l-Siyasa*, 6–7.

62. Al-Qarquri, *Taha Husayn: Mufakirran Siyasiyyan*, 17.

63. Taha Hussein, *Mustaqbal al-Thaqafa fi Misr*, vol. 9 of *al-Majmu'a al-Kamila* (Beirut: Dar al-Kitab al-Lubnani, 1974), 8–11.

64. See for example, Ahmed Abdalla, *The Student Movement and National Politics in Egypt, 1923–1973* (London: Al Saqi Books, 1985); and Haggai Erlich, *Students and University in 20th Century Egyptian Politics* (London: Frank Cass, 1989).

65. 'Abd al-'Azim Ramadan, "Mustafa al-Nahhas bayna al-Haqiqa wa-l-Tazyif," in *Misr fi 'Asr al-Sadat*, by 'Abd al-'Azim Ramadan (Beirut: Dar al-Ruqiy, 1986), 39, originally published in *al-Jumhuriyya*, September 15, 1977.

66. Hussein, *Mustaqbal al-Thaqafa*, 54.

67. Ibid., 55. The longest article in the 1936 Anglo-Egyptian Treaty, Article 8, focuses on the defense of the Suez Canal and includes an annex of several pages detailing the arrangements deemed necessary to implement the article.

68. Ibid., 60.

69. Ibid., 14.

70. See the infamous Article 22 of the Covenant of the League of Nations.

71. Muhammad al-Sayyid Dusuqi, *Ayyam ma'a Taha Husayn* (Beirut: Al-Mu'assassa al-'Arabiyya li-l-Dirasat wa-l-Nashr, 1978), 45.

72. Muhammad Salih al-Marakishi, "Al-Mas'ala al-Tarbawiyya wa-l-Thaqafiyya min Khilal Kitab Taha Husayn: *Mustaqbal al-Thaqafa fi Misr*," in *Waqa'i' al-Multaqa al-Qawmi: Al-Tafkir al-Islahi al-'Arabi; Khasa'isahu wa-Hududahu; Khayr al-Din, Muhammad al-Bairam, Taha Husayn* (Tunis: Manshurat al-Ma'had al-Qawmi li-'Ulum al-Tarbiyya, 1991), 139, quoting Hussein, *Mustaqbal al-Thaqafa*, 63.

73. Ibid., quoting Hussein, *Mustaqbal al-Thaqafa*, 71.

74. Ibid.

75. Tahar, *Taha Husayn: Sa Critique Littéraire*, 25. Interestingly, while Ghali Shukri sees *The Future of Culture in Egypt* as a book on democracy, the pedagogue Sa'id Isma'il 'Ali argues the book was the first and most comprehensive assessment of the Egyptian educational system, and says no similar studies have been undertaken since. Shukri, *Madha Yabqa min Taha Husayn*, 8; and Sa'id Isma'il 'Ali, preface to Kamal Hamid Mughith, *Taha Husayn* (Cairo: Markaz al-Dirasat wa-l-Ma'lumat al-Qanuniyya li-Huquq al-Insan, 1997), 10.

76. Mahmud Amin al-'Alim, introduction to *Fi al-Thaqafa al-Misriyya*, by Mahmud Amin Al-'Alim and 'Abd al-Azim Anis, 3rd ed. (Cairo: Dar al-Thaqafa al-Jadida, 1989), 27.

77. Hussein, *Mustaqbal al-Thaqafa*, 491.

78. Muniya al-Hamami, "Munaqashat," in *Waqa'i' al-Multaqa al-Qawmi: Al-Tafkir al-Islahi al-'Arabi; Khasa'isahu wa-Hududahu; Khayr al-Din, Muhammad al-Bairam, Taha Husayn* (Tunis: Manshurat al-Ma'had al-Qawmi li-'Ulum al-Tarbiyya, 1991), 175–6.

79. For example, al-Husri pointed out that while Taha Hussein used the word *sharq* (East) when denying that Egypt was part of the East in the same way China and Japan were, he still used *sharq* when saying that Egypt had a duty toward Arab countries and should disseminate an "eastern Arab culture." From this, and other examples, al-Husri argued that Hussein repeated himself in different ways using new words each time, without "complying with the meaning of those words and their limits using the 'scientific compliance' necessary for this kind of research." Sati' al-Husri, "Hawla Kitab Mustaqbal al-Thaqafa," *al-Risala*, July 11, 1939, quoted in Samih Kurayyim, *Taha Husayn fi Ma'arikihi al-Adabiyya wa-l-Fikriyya* (Cairo: Majallat al-Idha'a wa-l-Tilifizyun, 1974), 115–21.

80. See Susan Pedersen, *The Guardians: The League of Nations and the Crisis of Empire* (Oxford: Oxford University Press, 2015).

81. David Scott, *Conscripts of Modernity: The Tragedy of Colonial Enlightenment* (Durham, NC: Duke University Press, 2004); and C.L.R. James, *The Black Jacobins: Toussaint Louverture and the San Domingo Revolution* (London: Allison & Busby, 1980). I have also drawn on Harvey Neptune's thoughtful analysis of Scott's work in "Romance, Tragedy and, Well, Irony: Some Thoughts on David Scott's *Conscripts of Modernity*," *Social and Economic Studies* 57, no. 1 (March 2008): 165–81.

82. Scott, *Conscripts of Modernity*, 2. For more on the "space of experience" and "ho-

rizon of expectation," see Reinhart Koselleck, *Futures Past: On the Semantics of Historical Time*, trans. Keith Tribe (New York: Columbia University Press, 2004).

83. Elizabeth Thompson, *Justice Interrupted: The Struggle for Constitutional Government in the Middle East* (Cambridge, MA: Harvard University Press, 2013), 115.

84. Neptune, "Romance, Tragedy and, Well, Irony," 169.

85. Hussein, *Mustaqbal al-Thaqafa*, 40–7.

86. Shukri, *Madha Yabqa min Taha Husayn?*, 29.

87. For a discussion of the *nahda*, the term, some of its major thinkers and texts, and its continued relevance in the Arab world, see Hanssen and Weiss, "Introduction," in *Arabic Thought beyond the Liberal Age*, 1–8.

88. Ilham Khuri-Makdisi, *The Eastern Mediterranean and the Making of Global Radicalism, 1860–1914* (Berkeley: University of California Press, 2010), 40–1.

89. Kamran Rastegar, "Introduction," *Middle Eastern Literatures* 16, no. 3 (2013): 227. For discussions of the Chinese, Indian, and Hebrew renaissances, among others, see Brenda Schildgen, Gang Zhou, and Sander Gilman, eds., *Other Renaissances: A New Approach to World Literatures* (New York: Palgrave Macmillan, 2006).

90. Samah Selim, "The People's Entertainments: Translation, Popular Fiction, and the Nahdah in Egypt," in *Other Renaissances*, ed. Schildgen, Zhou, and Gilman, 35.

91. Albert Hourani, *Arabic Thought in the Liberal Age: 1798–1939* (Cambridge: Cambridge University Press, 1983), 325–6.

92. Ibid., 326.

93. Ibid., 337.

94. Ibid.

95. Hourani mentions briefly the creation of Alexandria University in 1942 and the expansion of state schools as two of the measures Hussein worked hard to implement as a civil servant. Ibid., 338.

96. Hourani, preface to the 1983 edition of *Arabic Thought in the Liberal Age*, vii.

97. Dyala Hamzah, "Introduction," in *The Making of the Arab Intellectual (1880–1960): Empire, Public Sphere and the Colonial Coordinates of Selfhood*, ed. Dyala Hamazh (New York: Routledge, 2012), 3.

98. Ibid., 8.

99. Ibid., 2.

100. Dakhli, "The Autumn of the Nahda," 351.

101. Ibid., 354–5.

102. Yoav Di-Capua, *No Exit: Arab Existentialism, Jean-Paul Sartre and Decolonization* (Chicago: University of Chicago Press, 2018), 19.

103. Ibid., 21. Also see Hanna Meretoja, *The Narrative Turn in Fiction and Theory: The Crisis and Return of Storytelling from Robbe-Grillet to Tournier* (London: Palgrave, 2014).

104. Di-Capua, *No Exit*, 22–3.

105. El Shakry shows how local actors focused on proving the "uniqueness and educability of the collective national subject" as they devised the social projects necessary to fix the ills of Egyptian society. El Shakry, *Great Social Laboratory*, 198–9.

106. For example, Talal Asad refers readers to al-Sayyid Marsot's work as the reference on Egypt's pre-1952 liberal politics. Asad, "Thinking about Tradition, Religion, and Politics in Egypt Today," *Critical Inquiry* 42, no. 1 (September 2015): 200n74.

107. Afaf Lutfi al-Sayyid Marsot, *Egypt's Liberal Experiment, 1922–1936* (Berkeley: University of California Press, 1977), 6.

108. Ibid., 244–5.

109. Ibid., 5.

110. Arthur Goldschmidt and Barak A. Salmoni, introduction to *Re-envisioning Egypt 1919–1952*, ed. Arthur Goldschmidt, Amy J. Johnson, and Barak A. Salmoni (Cairo: American University in Cairo Press, 2005), 2–3.

111. Ibid., 7.

112. Ibid., 4.

113. Roger Owen, conclusion to *Re-envisioning Egypt*, ed. Goldschmidt et al., 494–5.

114. Joel Gordon, *Nasser's Blessed Movement: Egypt's Free Officers and the July Revolution* (New York: Oxford University Press, 1992), 4–5.

115. Owen, conclusion to *Re-envisioning Egypt*, 494–5.

116. Roger Owen, "Review of *Egypt's Liberal Experiment: 1922–1936*," *English Historical Review* 95, no. 375 (April 1980): 462.

117. Taha Hussein, "Fi al-Ta'lim," in *Turath Taha Husayn: Al-Maqalat al-Sahafiyya min 1908–1967*, vol. 1 (Cairo: Matba'at Dar al-Kutub wa-l-Watha'iq al-Qawmiyya, 2010), 716–7. Hereinafter, TTH 1. Originally published in *al-Ahram*, April 6, 1953.

118. Owen, conclusion to *Re-envisioning Egypt*, 495–6.

119. Ibid., 496.

120. Ibid., 497.

121. Yunan Labib Rizq, "Suqut al-Tajruba al-Libraliyya fi Misr," in *Arba'un 'Aman 'ala Thawrat Yuliu: Dirasa Tarikhiyya*, ed. Ra'uf 'Abbas (Cairo: Al-Ahram, Markaz al-Dirasat al-Siyasiyya wa-l-Istiratijiyya, 1992), 40–51.

122. 'Abd al-'Azim Ramadan, "Mustafa al-Nahhas al-Za'im alladhi Ta'amar 'alayhi al-Jami'," in *Misr fi 'Asr al-Sadat*, by 'Abd al-'Azim Ramadan (Beirut: Dar al-Ruqiy, 1986), 25, originally published in *al-Katib*, September 1974.

123. Ibid., 25–7.

124. Luwis 'Awad, *Aqni'at al-Nasiriyya al-Sab'a: Munaqashat Tawfiq al-Hakim wa-Muhammad Hasanayn Haykal* (1976; Cairo: Markaz al-Mahrusa, 2014), 9.

125. Ibid., 143.

126. Fu'ad Zakariya, *Kam 'Umr al-Ghadab: Haykal wa-Azmat al-'Aql al-'Arabi* (Cairo: Dar al-Qahira, 1983), 75–8.

127. Ibid., 82.

128. Ibid., 75–7.

129. Ibid., 73. Critics of the Wafd include the Marxist historian Ra'uf 'Abbas, who accused the Wafd of autocracy and of having monopolized speaking on behalf of the people, refusing to see itself as a political party. Ra'uf 'Abbas, "Al-Tariq ila al-Thawra," in *Arba'un 'Aman 'ala Thawrat Yuliu*, ed. Ra'uf 'Abbas, 17.

130. Zakariya, *Kam 'Umr al-Ghadab*, 76.

131. Ra'uf 'Abbas, preface to *Turath Taha Husayn: Al-Maqalat al-Sahafiyya min 1908–1967*, vol. 6 (Cairo: Matba'at Dar al-Kutub wa-l-Watha'iq al-Qawmiyya, 2006), 7–9. Hereinafter, TTH 6.

132. Muhi al-Din Hamdi, "Al-'Ilm wa-l-Din fi Tafkir Taha Husayn," in *Waqa'i' al-Multaqa al-Qawmi: Al-Tafkir al-Islahi al-'Arabi; Khasa'isahu wa-Hududahu; Khayr al-Din, Muhammad al-Bairam, Taha Husayn* (Tunis: Manshurat al-Ma'had al-Qawmi li-'Ulum al-Tarbiyya, 1991), 183.

133. Mahmoudi, *Taha Hussein's Education*, 1.

134. Jacques Berque, introduction to *Au-delà du Nil*, by Taha Hussain, ed. Jacques Berque (Paris: Gallimard, 1990), 31.

135. Al-Jumni, *Taha Husayn Mu'arrikhan*, 8.

136. Shukri Faysal, introduction to *Taqlid wa-Tajdid*, by Taha Husayn (Beirut: Dar al-'Ilm li-l-Malayin, 1978), 8.

137. Ibid., 6.

138. Ibid., 6–7.

139. Taha Hussein, "Ana la Aktub wa-Innama Umli," *Un Effort* 47 (October 1934), quoted in Taha Hussein, *Min al-Shati' al-Akhar: Kitabat Taha Husayn al-Firinsiyya*, ed. Abdelrashid Mahmoudi (Cairo: Al-Markaz al-Qawmi li-l-Tarjama, 2008), 33. This article presents Hussein's responses to a series of questions on how he writes; the title given here was supplied later by Mahmoudi.

140. "M. T-Hussein à Arabies: Mon Père Était Désespéré," *Arabies* 35 (1989): 90–1, quoted in Munji al-Shimli and 'Umar al-Jumni, eds., *Taha Husayn fi Mir'at al-'Asr: Shahadat wa-Dirasat* (Tunis: Al-Majma' al-Tunisi li-l-'Ulum wa-l-Adab wa-l-Funun, 2001), 25. This was confirmed by Hussein's secretary, Muhammad al-Dusuqi, who wrote that Hussein never revised what he wrote, but sent it straight to the publisher. Al-Dusuqi, *Ayyam ma'a Taha Husayn*, 79.

141. See for example, Hisham Sharabi, *Arab Intellectuals and the West* (Baltimore, MD: Johns Hopkins University Press, 1970); Zaki Badawi, *The Reformers of Egypt: A Critique of al-Afghani, 'Abduh, and Ridha* (Slough: Open Press, 1976); and Ibrahim M. Abu-Rabi', *Intellectual Origins of Islamic Resurgence in the Modern Arab World* (Albany: State University of New York Press, 1996); and *Contemporary Arab Thought: Studies in Post-1967 Arab Intellectual History* (London: Pluto Press, 2004). For a recent summary and critique of these binaries, see Abdulrazzak Patel, *The Arab Nahdah: The Making of the Intellectual and Humanist Movement* (Edinburgh: Edinburgh University Press, 2013).

Chapter 1

A version of this chapter has been previously published as "Egyptian Cultural Expansionism: Taha Hussein Confronts the French in North Africa, 1950–1952," *Die Welt des Islams* 58, no. 4 (2018): 409–441. I thank Brill's *Die Welt des Islams* for allowing me to reuse this material.

1. DWQ/RMW/0081-096923: Creation of Farouk I Institute for Islamic Studies in Spain. Telegram from Taha Hussein to Mustafa al-Nahhas (in French), November 11, 1950.

2. PP: Muhammad Husni 'Umar, Confidential Political Report no. 3 to Egypt's acting minister of foreign affairs on the inauguration of Farouk I Institute for Islamic Studies, Madrid, November 21, 1950, pp. 1, 4.

3. Taha Hussein, *Mustaqbal al-Thaqafa fi Misr*, vol. 9 of *al-Majmu'a al-Kamila* (Beirut: Dar al-Kitab al-Lubnani, 1974), 453.

4. The agreement to abolish the Capitulations was signed in Montreux in 1937; it stipulated an interim period of twelve years.

5. For more on the development of Pan-Arab thought in Egypt, see Israel Gershoni and James Jankowski, *Redefining the Egyptian Nation, 1930–1945* (Cambridge: Cambridge University Press, 1995); James Jankowski, "Egyptian Responses to the Palestine Problem in the Interwar Period," *International Journal of Middle East Studies* 12, no. 1 (August 1980): 1–38; Ernest Dawn, "The Formation of Pan-Arab Ideology in the Interwar Years," *International Journal of Middle East Studies* 20, no. 1 (February 1988): 67–91; Reem Abou-El-Fadl, "Early Pan-Arabism in Egypt's July Revolution: The Free Officers' Political Formation and Policy-Making, 1946–54," *Nations and Nationalism* 21, no. 2 (2015): 289–308; and Rami Ginat, "The Egyptian Left and the Roots of Neutralism in the Pre-Nasserite Era," *British Journal of Middle Eastern Studies* 30, no. 1 (May 2003): 5–24.

6. Gershoni and Jankowski, *Redefining the Egyptian Nation*, 200–10; and Dawn, "The Formation of Pan-Arab Ideology in the Interwar Years," 82.

7. For official state policies promoting Pan-Arabism after World War II, see Michael Doran, *Pan-Arabism before Nasser: Egyptian Power Politics and the Palestine Question* (Oxford: Oxford University Press, 1999).

8. For more on Nasser's Pan-Arabism see Israel Gershoni and James Jankowski, *Rethinking Nationalism in the Arab Middle East* (New York: Columbia University Press, 1997); Joseph Lorenz, *Egypt and the Arabs: Foreign Policy and the Search for National Identity* (Boulder, CO: Westview Press, 1990); and Avraham Sela, "Nasser's Regional Politics: A Reassessment," in *Rethinking Nasserism: Revolution and Historical Memory in Egypt*, ed. Elie Podeh and Onn Winckler (Gainesville: Florida University Press, 2004).

9. Gerasimos Tsourapas, "Nasser's Educators and Agitators across al-Watan al-'Arabi: Tracing the Foreign Policy Importance of Egyptian Regional Migration, 1952–1967," *British Journal of Middle Eastern Studies* 43, no. 3 (January 2016): 324–41. Heather Sharkey also talks about the role played by Egyptian teachers in the "Arabization" of Algeria, in "Language and Conflict: The Political History of Arabisation in Sudan and Algeria," *Studies in Ethnicity and Nationalism* 12, no. 3 (2012): 427–49.

10. Tsourapas, "Nasser's Educators and Agitators," 328.

11. David Stenner, "'Bitterness towards Egypt'—the Moroccan Nationalist Movement, Revolutionary Cairo and the Limits of Anti-Colonial Solidarity," *Cold War History* 16, no. 2 (2005): 159–75. Stenner nuances Nasser's involvement in Morocco, showing he was not supportive of Moroccan diplomatic efforts to abolish the French and Spanish protectorates, and instead favored arming the small Moroccan Liberation Army, an alliance of several military groups.

12. Ibid., 164.

13. Hussein stood firm on this position and insisted that a thorough unification of educational systems in Arab countries was necessary before any political unity was possible.

14. Hussein, *Mustaqbal al-Thaqafa*, 481–6.

15. Ibid., 482–9.

16. Ibid., 454–6.

17. Ibid., 18–24, 29–30, 40.

18. For more on the usefulness and limitations of Mediterraneanism as a category of analysis, see W. V. Harris, ed., *Rethinking the Mediterranean* (Oxford: Oxford University Press, 2005). Also see Peregrine Horden and Nicholas Purcell, *The Corrupting Sea: A Study of Mediterranean History* (Oxford: Blackwell, 2000); and David Abulafia, "Mediterranean History as Global History," *History and Theory* 50, no. 2 (May 2011): 220–8.

19. Shaden Tageldin, *Disarming Words: Empire and the Seductions of Translation in Egypt* (Berkeley: University of California Press, 2011), 280.

20. Ibid., 285.

21. Ibid., 273–88.

22. Abu al-Qasim Muhammad Karru, *Taha Husayn wa-l-Maghrib al-'Arabi* (Tunis: Mu'assassat Ibn 'Abdallah li-l-Nashr wa-l-Tawzi', 2001), 11.

23. Karru, *Taha Husayn wa-l-Maghrib*, 56–7.

24. PP: Report by Taha Hussein on his visit to Tunisia, July 9, 1957.

25. PP: 'Umar, Confidential Political Report no. 3, p. 1.

26. DWQ/RMW/0081–096923: Creation of Farouk I Institute for Islamic Studies in Spain/Memorandum by the Minister of Public Instruction Muhammad al-'Ashmawi to the Council of Ministers.

27. AMAE/Relations Culturelles 1945–1961/431. 1948–1959/1948–1951: Telegram from Madrid to the French Ministry of Foreign Affairs on the inauguration of the Farouk I Institute for Islamic Studies in Madrid, March 20, 1950. The same telegram indicates that upon the inauguration of the institute, Taha Hussein also suggested the creation of a Farouk I University in Madrid.

28. Memorandum by the Minister of Public Instruction Muhammad al-'Ashmawi to the Council of Ministers.

29. DWQ/RMW/0081–096923: Creation of Farouk I Institute for Islamic Studies in Spain/Memorandum by the Finance Committee to the Council of Ministers, July 1950.

30. DWQ/RMW/0081–096923: Creation of Farouk I Institute for Islamic Studies in Spain/Telegram from al-Nahhas to Hussein; and telegram from Hussein to al-Nahhas.

31. DWQ/MNW/0075–056781: Session of April 12, 1950. Proposition approved in DWQ/MNW/0075–057859: The Minutes of the Sessions of April 1950/The Minutes of the Session of April 12, 1950.

32. DWQ/MNW/0075–056784: Council of Ministers Pre-session of April 19, 1950. Approval noted in DWQ/MNW/0075–057859: Minutes of the Sessions of April 1950/ Minutes of the Pre-session of April 19, 1950. Among those who gave lectures at the new institute was the historian Shafiq Ghurbal, who gave two lectures in 1951. The writer

Dr. Husayn Fawzi, Professor of Oceanology at Farouk I University, also gave two lectures in Nice. See DWQ/MNW/0075-057866: Minutes of the Sessions of January 1951/ Minutes of the Session of January 21, 1951.

33. DWQ/MNW/0075-057867: Minutes of the Sessions of February–March 1951/ Minutes of the Session of March 11, 1951.

34. DWQ/MNW/0075-057867: Minutes of the Sessions of February-March 1951/ Minutes of the Session of March 18, 1951.

35. DWQ/MNW/0075-057025: Minutes of the Session of March 18, 1951.

36. On attempts by the Wafd to contain the party's disagreements with King Farouk, see Latifa Muhammad Salim, "Al-Wafd wa-l-Qasr: Al-Malik Faruq (1936–1952)," in *Tarikh al-Wafd*, ed. Jamal Badawi and Lam'i al-Mutai'i (Cairo: Dar al-Shuruq, 2010): 325–33.

37. DWQ/Abdin/0069-004681: Papers concerning the creation of a Farouk I Institute for Islamic Studies in North Africa, May 13 and 19, 1951.

38. Ibid.

39. DWQ/MNW/0075-057167: Minutes of the Session of November 18, 1951/ Memorandum on Farouk I Institute for Islamic Culture in London, November 17, 1951.

40. DWQ/MNW/0075-057873: Minutes of the Sessions of October–November 1951/Minutes of the Session of November 18, 1951.

41. DWQ/RMW/0081-021260: Bestowing the title of Pasha on his Excellency Dr. Taha Hussein Pasha, minister of public instruction, January 1, 1951.

42. PP: 'Umar, Confidential Political Report no. 3, p. 2.

43. Ibid., p. 3.

44. Ibid., pp. 2, 5.

45. AMAE/Relations Culturelles 1945–1961/431. 1948–1959/1948–1951: Report from the chargé of the French Delegation to Spain to the French minister of foreign affairs regarding the inauguration of the Institute Farouk I in Madrid, November 21, 1950.

46. DWQ/Abdin/0069-004681: Papers concerning the creation of a Farouk I Institute for Islamic Studies in North Africa, May 13 and 19, 1951.

47. Ibid.

48. AMAE/Relations Culturelles 1945–1961/431. 1948–1959/1948–1951: Report from the Direction d'Afrique-Levant to the Direction Générale des Relations Culturelles on the mission of April–May 1946 regarding a possible intellectual cooperation between Egypt and France, August 18, 1948, 32.

49. AMAE/Relations Culturelles 1945–1961/431. 1948–1959/1948–1951: Report from the governor-general of Algeria to the French minister of foreign affairs regarding the Franco-Egyptian cultural exchange, February 9, 1948.

50. AMAE/Relations Culturelles 1945–1961/431. 1948–1959/1948–1951: Memorandum from the Direction Générale des Relations Culturelles to the Direction d'Afrique-Levant regarding a project for Franco-Egyptian cultural exchange, July 20, 1948.

51. Ibid.

52. AMAE/Relations Culturelles 1945–1961/431. 1948–1959/1948–1951: Report from the Direction d'Afrique-Levant to the Direction Générale des Relations Culturel-

les regarding a possible intellectual cooperation between Egypt and France, August 18, 1948, 32.

53. Ibid., 5–6.
54. Ibid., 6.
55. Ibid., 7.
56. Ibid., 11.
57. Ibid., 38.
58. Ibid., 32.
59. Ibid., 2, 11.
60. Ibid., 6.
61. Ibid., 40.
62. Ibid., 1.
63. Ibid., 39.
64. Ibid., 15.
65. Ibid., 41.
66. Ibid., 16–7.
67. Ibid., 12.
68. PP: Letter from Muhammad Shaniq, Grand Tunisian Vizir, to Taha Hussein, December 18, 1950.
69. AMAE/Relations Culturelles 1945–1961/431. 1948–1959/1948–1951: Telegram from the French ambassador in Cairo to the French Ministry of Foreign Affairs. January 22, 1950.
70. AMAE/Relations Culturelles 1945–1961/431. 1948–1959/1948–1951: Report from the French ambassador in Cairo to the minister of foreign affairs on the new minister of public instruction, January 26, 1950.
71. Ibid.
72. AMAE/Relations Culturelles 1945–1961/431. 1948–1959/1948–1951: Report from the resident-general of France in Tunis to the French minister of foreign affairs regarding sending a mission of Egyptian professors to Tunis, January 28, 1950.
73. A renowned theologian, Sheikh al-Khidr Husayn was Grand Sheikh of al-Azhar from 1952 to 1954. He also sympathized with the old Tunisian Liberal Constitutional Party, founded in 1920, which fought against the French protectorate and called for the independence of Tunisia. The new Dustur Party, however, was created in 1934 by Habib Bourguiba.
74. For more on the bureau, see Attillio Gaudio, *Guerre et Paix au Maroc: Reportages: 1950–1990* (Paris: Éditions Karthala, 1991).
75. AMAE/Relations Culturelles 1945–1961/431. 1948–1959/1948–1951: Intelligence report on the trip of Fadil ibn ʿAshur of the Zaytuna Mosque to Egypt, January 23, 1950.
76. Ibid.
77. AMAE/Relations Culturelles 1945–1961/431. 1948–1959/1948–1951: Response from the French minister of foreign affairs to the resident-general in Tunis on sending Egyptian professors to Tunis, February 14, 1950.
78. DWQ/MNW/0075–057866: Agenda of January 1951, the Pre-session of February 4, 1951.

79. Ibid.

80. For an account of Freemasonry in Egypt and the various lodges in their British and French variants, see Karim Wissa, "Freemasonry in Egypt 1798-1921: A Study in Cultural and Political Encounters," *British Society for Middle Eastern Studies Bulletin* 16, no. 2 (1989): 143-61. For a more recent work on the history of Freemasonry during the Ottoman period, see Dorothe Sommer, *Freemasonry in the Ottoman Empire: A History of the Fraternity and Its Influence in Syria and the Levant* (London: I. B. Tauris, 2013).

81. AMAE/Relations Culturelles 1945-1961/431. 1948-1959/1948-1951: Letter from the minister of France in Syria to the French ambassador in Egypt regarding the direction of the Egyptian politics in the Maghrib, February 18, 1950.

82. AMAE/Relations Culturelles 1945-1961/431. 1948-1959/1948-1951: Report from the French ambassador in Egypt to the French minister of foreign affairs regarding the Egyptian politics in North Africa, March 7, 1950. My emphasis.

83. AMAE/Relations Culturelles 1945-1961/431. 1948-1959/1948-1951: Letter from the Direction d'Afrique-Levant to Tunis and Rabat regarding the meeting with Taha Hussein, March 9, 1950.

84. AMAE/Relations Culturelles 1945-1961/431. 1948-1959/1948-1951: Report from the French ambassador in Egypt to the French minister of foreign affairs regarding the Egyptian politics in North Africa, March 7, 1950.

85. AMAE/Relations Culturelles 1945-1961/431. 1948-1959/1948-1951: Report from the French ambassador in Egypt to the French minister of foreign affairs on the Second Conference for Arab Culture in Egypt, September 5, 1950.

86. AMAE/Relations Culturelles 1945-1961/431. 1948-1959/1948-1951: Report from the French ambassador in Egypt to the French minister of foreign affairs regarding the Egyptian politics in North Africa, March 7, 1950.

87. AMAE/Relations Culturelles 1945-1961/431. 1948-1959/1948-1951: Telegram from the French chargé d'affaires to the French Ministry of Foreign Affairs, September 17, 1950.

88. AMAE/Relations Culturelles 1945-1961/431. 1948-1959/1948-1951: Report from the French ambassador in the United States to the French minister of foreign affairs, September 20, 1950.

89. AMAE/Relations Culturelles 1945-1961/431. 1948-1959/1948-1951: Marchandage relatif à l'institut français d'archéologie lié à la création d'un institut égyptien à Alger/Telegram from A. Juin to the French Ministry of Foreign Affairs, June 11, 1951.

90. AMAE/Relations Culturelles 1945-1961/431. 1948-1959/1948-1951: Marchandage relatif à l'institut français d'archéologie lié à la création d'un institut égyptien à Alger/Telegram from A. Juin Resident-General of Morocco to the French Ministry of Foreign Affairs, May 23, 1951. Algeria was departmentalized in 1848 into civil zones (*départements*), similar to metropolitan France.

91. AMAE/Relations Culturelles 1945-1961/431. 1948-1959/1948-1951: Telegram from the French embassy in Cairo to the French Ministry of Foreign Affairs on a statement made by Taha Hussein, June 7, 1951.

92. AMAE/Relations Culturelles 1945-1961/431. 1948-1959/1948-1951: Letter

from the French minister of foreign affairs to the minister of interior regarding the creation of an Egyptian institute in Algiers, September 20, 1951.

93. AMAE/Relations Culturelles 1945–1961/431. 1948–1959/1948–1951: Letter from the French minister of foreign affairs to the minister of interior regarding the creation of an Egyptian institute in Algiers, October 24, 1951.

94. AMAE/Relations Culturelles 1945–1961/431. 1948–1959/1948–1951: Telegram from French Ambassador Couve de Murville, in Egypt, to the French Ministry of Foreign Affairs, November 14, 1951.

95. AMAE/Relations Culturelles 1945–1961/431. 1948–1959/1948–1951: Memorandum to the French minister of foreign affairs regarding the Egyptian request to create an institute in North Africa, November 26, 1951.

96. AMAE/Relations Culturelles 1945–1961/431. 1948–1959/1948–1951: Marchandage relatif à l'institut français d'archéologie lié à la création d'un institut Égyptien à Alger/Report from the French ambassador in Egypt to the French minister of foreign affairs on Yahya al-Khashshab, October 25, 1951.

97. AMAE/Relations Culturelles 1945–1961/431. 1948–1959/1948–1951: Marchandage relatif à l'institut français d'archéologie lié à la création d'un institut égyptien à Alger/Letter from the French ambassador to the French minister of foreign affairs regarding Taha Hussein's measures against the French archeological missions, December 7, 1951.

98. AMAE/Relations Culturelles 1945–1961/431. 1948–1959/1952–1961: Report on the situation of the Egyptian institute in Algiers, May 2, 1952.

99. AMAE/Relations Culturelles 1945–1961/431. 1948–1959/1948–1951: Report from the French ambassador in Egypt to the French Ministry of Foreign Affairs, December 13, 1951.

100. Letter from the French ambassador to the French minister of foreign affairs regarding Taha Hussein's measures, December 7, 1951.

101. See Nancy Reynolds, *A City Consumed: Urban Commerce, the Cairo Fire, and the Politics of Decolonization in Egypt* (Stanford, CA: Stanford University Press, 2012).

102. AMAE/Relations Culturelles 1945–1961/431. 1948–1959/1952–1961: A French translation of an *al-Ahram* article on the Algiers institute, May 2, 1952.

103. AMAE/Relations Culturelles 1945–1961/431. 1948–1959/1952–1961: Telegram from the French ambassador to the French Ministry of Foreign Affairs, June 23, 1952.

104. AMAE/Relations Culturelles 1945–1961/431. 1948–1959/1952–1961: Telegram from the French Ministry of Foreign Affairs to the French ambassador, August 30, 1952.

105. Muhammad Hasan al-Zayyat, *Ma Ba'da al-Ayyam* (Cairo: Dar al-Hilal, 1986), 153.

Chapter 2

1. Taha Hussein, "Kulliyat al-Adab," in TTH 1:315–6, originally published in *al-Musawwar*, March 4, 1932.

2. Donald Reid, *Cairo University and the Making of Modern Egypt* (Cambridge: Cambridge University Press, 1990), 4.

3. Abdulrazzak Patel, *The Arab Nahdah: The Making of the Intellectual and Humanist Movement* (Edinburgh: Edinburgh University Press, 2013), 198.

4. Ibid., 190.

5. Ibid., 2–15.

6. George Makdisi, *The Rise of Humanism in Classical Islam and the Christian West: With Special Reference to Scholasticism* (Edinburgh: Edinburgh University Press, 1990), 120–1, 332. Also, George Makdisi, "Inquiry into the Origins of Humanism," in *Humanism, Culture, and Language in the Near East*, ed. Asma Afsaruddin and A. H. Mathias Zahniser (Winona Lake, IN: Eisenbrauns, 1997), 18–9, quoted in Patel, *Arab Nahdah*, 9.

7. Patel, *Arab Nahdah*, 6–7.

8. Ibid., 9.

9. Ibid., 26.

10. Ibid., 23. See Ibrahim Abu Rabi', *Intellectual Origins of Islamic Resurgence in the Modern Arab World* (Albany: State University of New York Press, 1996); and Zaki Badawi, *The Reformers of Egypt: A Critique of al-Afghani, 'Abduh, and Ridha* (Slough: Open Press, 1976).

11. Muhammad 'Abd al-Ghani Hasan, "Husayn al-Marsafi," in *A'lam al-Nahda al-Haditha, al-Halaqa al-Uwla* (Beirut: Dar al-Hamra, 1990), 285–6, quoted in Patel, *Arab Nahdah*, 183–6.

12. Patel, *Arab Nahdah*,184.

13. J. Brugman, *An Introduction to the History of Modern Arabic Literature in Egypt* (Leiden: Brill, 1984), 326, quoted in Patel, *Arab Nahdah*,184.

14. Patel, *Arab Nahdah*, 192.

15. Muhammad Rashid Rida, *Tarikh al-Ustadh al-Imam al-Shaykh Muhammad 'Abduh* (Cairo: Matba'at al-Manar, 1906–1931, repr., Cairo: Dar al-Fadila, 2003), vol. 2, 427–9, 503, quoted in Patel, *Arab Nahdah*, 193.

16. 'Abd al-Mun'im Ibrahim al-Dusuqi al-Jumay'i, *al-Jami'a al-Misriyya al-Qadima: Nash'atuha wa-Dawruha fi al-Mujtama' (1908–1925)* (Cairo: Dar al-Kitab al-Jami'i, 1980), 14.

17. Patel, *Arab Nahdah*, 229–30.

18. Shafiq Ghurbal, preface to Ahmad 'Abd al-Fattah Budayr, *al-Amir Ahmad Fu'ad wa-Nash'at al-Jami'a al-Misriyya* (Cairo: Matba'at Jami'at Fu'ad al-Awwal, 1950, repr., Cairo: Dar al-Kutub wa-l-Watha'iq al-Qawmiyya, 2008) xiv (*nun*).

19. Reid, *Cairo University*, 4.

20. In 1908, the university founders must have felt encouraged by Japan's recent victory over Russia in 1905. As French scholar Alain Roussillon has shown, for Egyptian nationalists and intellectuals at the time, like Mustafa Kamil, Japan represented an inspiring model for successful modernization without compromising the country's proper identity. See Alain Roussillon, *Identité et Modernité: Les Voyageurs Égyptiens au Japon (xixe—xxe Siècle)* (Arles: Actes Sud, 2005).

21. Robert Tignor, *Modernization and British Colonial Rule in Egypt 1882–1914* (Princeton, NJ: Princeton University Press 1966), 337. As Roger Owen has shown,

Cromer did not believe the state should invest in education and thought it was better to educate a small elite instead of producing "overeducated underemployed agitators." He was also skeptical that the natives, as a different race, in his view, could benefit from a British kind of education. As a result, education under Cromer received only about 1% of the annual budget. He imposed tuition fees in state schools and was in favor of investing in existing *katatib* rather than higher education. See Roger Owen, *Lord Cromer: Victorian Imperialist, Edwardian Preconsul* (Oxford: Oxford University Press, 2004), 313–5.

22. Ahmad Lutfi al-Sayyid, *Qissat Hayati*, in *Turath Ahmad Lutfi al-Sayyid* (Cairo: Dar al-Kutub wa-l-Watha'iq al-Qawmiyya, 2008), 231–2.

23. *Ibid.*, 223.

24. Ghurbal, preface to Budayr, *al-Amir Ahmad Fu'ad*, xiii (*mim*) and xiv (*nun*).

25. Yacoub Artin, *Considérations sur l'Instruction Publique en Égypte* (Paris, 1894).

26. Amina Hijazi, "Aba' al-Jami'a al-Ahliyya," in *Mi'at 'am 'ala al-Jami'a al-Misriyya*, ed. Ahmad Zakariya al-Shalq (Cairo: Dar al-Kutub wa-l-Watha'iq al-Qawmiyya, 2011), 95; and Samia Ibrahim, *al-Jami'a al-Ahliyya bayna al-Nash'a wa-l-Tatawwur* (Cairo: Dar al-Kutub wa-l-Watha'iq al-Qawmiyya, 2011), 14.

27. 'Ali Barakat, "Jami'at al-Qahira wa-Takwin Misr al-Mu'asira: Mi'at 'Am 'ala Nash'at al-Jami'a al-Misriyya," in *Mi'at 'Am 'ala al-Jami'a al-Misriyya*, ed. Ahmad Zakariya al-Shalq, 53.

28. Hasan Nasr al-Din, *al-Ajanib fi al-Jami'a al-Misriyya* (Cairo: Dar al-Kutub wa-l-Watha'iq al-Qawmiyya, 2011).

29. Muhammad Husayn Haykal, *Tarajim Misriyya wa-Gharbiyya* (Cairo: Kitab Ruz al-Yusuf), 61, quoted in al-Jumay'i, *al-Jami'a al-Misriyya*, 19.

30. See for example, 'Abd al-Rahman al-Rafi'i, *Mustafa Kamil: Ba'ith al-Nahda al-Wataniyya* (Cairo: Dar al-Hilal, 1957).

31. Budayr, *al-Amir Ahmad Fu'ad*, 15–6.

32. Muhammad Rashid Rida, *Tarikh al-Ustadh al-Imam al-Shaykh Muhammad 'Abduh* (Cairo: Matba'at al-Manar, 1931), 1066, quoted in al-Jumay'i, *al-Jami'a al-Misriyya*, 15.

33. Ibrahim, *al-Jami'a al-Ahliyya*, 26.

34. *Al-Jami'a al-Misriyya: La'ihat Ijra'atiha al-Dakhiliyya wa Tarikh Mashru'iha* (Cairo: Maktabat al-Wa'iz), 8–9, quoted in al-Jumay'i, *al-Jami'a al-Misriyya*, 17.

35. "A University, or a College; Literary or Natural Sciences," *al-Hilal* 9 (Year 16), June 1, 1908, quoted in al-Jumay'i, *al-Jami'a al-Misriyya*, 19.

36. Zaydan learned in October 1910, from *al-Mu'ayyad*, that he had been replaced. The following day a delegation from the university went to see him, and explained that fearing strong public sentiments, the University Council had decided to assign his course to a Muslim. He was offered LE 100 in compensation for the material he had prepared and the maps he had printed. The following year the university awarded him a prize for his book *The History of Arabic Literature*, perhaps as a consolation and in recognition of his competence. For the details of the story, see Anne-Laure Dupont, *Gurgi*

Zaydan 1861–1914: Écrivain Réformiste et Témoin de la Renaissance Arabe (Damascus: Institut Français du Proche-Orient, 2006), 629–42.

37. Budayr, *al-Amir Ahmad Fu'ad*, 19.

38. Ibid., 19–26.

39. Fouad's speech to the University Council on March 15, 1911, repr., Budayr, *al-Amir Ahmad Fu'ad*, 90. For more on the international missions of French and German professors between 1880 and 1930, see Christophe Charle, "Ambassadeurs ou Chercheurs? Les Relations Internationales des Professeurs de la Sorbonne sous la IIIe République," *Genèses* 14 (1994): 8–19.

40. Budayr, *al-Amir Ahmad Fu'ad*, 83.

41. Ibid., 84. For example, Fouad accepted the invitation extended by the German Emperor to attend the centennial of the University of Berlin on behalf of the Egyptian University in 1910, and also attended similar events at the Universities of Geneva and Edinburgh.

42. DWQ/Abdin/0069-004479: Report to the General Assembly on the academic year 1911–1912.

43. Fourth Annual Report 1911–1912, repr., *al-Jami'a al-Ahliyya (1908–1925): Safahat min Dhakirat al-Sahafa* (Cairo: Dar al-Kutub wa-l-Watha'iq al-Qawmiyya, 2010), 131. Zaki's and Najib's disagreement with Fouad was reported in *The Gazette*. DWQ/Abdin/0069-004481: Notes on the University/1912/The Egyptian University and the Egyptian Gazette. Budayr mentions that they resigned because they were unsatisfied with how Fouad was running the university. Budayr, *al-Amir Ahmad Fu'ad*, 291.

44. Yunan Labib Rizq, "al-Jami'a al-Misriyya min al-Tawr al-Ahli ila al-Tawr al-Hukumi," in *Mi'at 'Am 'ala al-Jami'a al-Misriyya*, ed. Ahmad Zakariya al-Shalq, 29.

45. DWQ/Abdin/0069-004610: Memorandum on the Egyptian University/Note: Université Égyptienne 1933–34. This memorandum also explained that besides the annual grant of LE 2,000 from the Ministry of Public Instruction, the university received LE 5,000 from the Ministry of Waqfs, in addition to other donations from members of the Royal Family, such as Princess Fatima Ismail, sister of Prince Fouad, and from other notables. In 1923, King Fouad instructed his minister of public instruction to reorganize the university. The old private university (l'Université Libre) would thus become the Faculty of Arts in the new state university. The old law and medical schools would be incorporated into the new university as the Faculties of Law and Medicine, and a Faculty of Science would be created. Budayr agrees that it was Fouad who asked the minister of public instruction to create a new state university and merge the old one into it. See Budayr, *al-Amir Ahmad Fu'ad*, 308.

46. *Al-Mu'ayyad*, no. 5444, April 18, 1908, quoted in Budayr, *al-Amir Ahmad Fu'ad*, 29–38.

47. Budayr, *al-Amir Ahmad Fu'ad*, 34–6.

48. Communiqué from the University Committee to the press upon the creation of the Egyptian University, repr., Budayr, *al-Amir Ahmad Fu'ad*, 54–5.

49. Ibid.

50. "The Regulations of the Educational Missions," repr., Budayr, *al-Amir Ahmad Fu'ad*, 41–2.

51. Communiqué from the University Committee to the press upon the creation of the Egyptian University, repr., Budayr, *al-Amir Ahmad Fu'ad*, 55.

52. DWQ/Abdin/0069-004476: Minutes of the Sessions of the University/December 2, 1910-1913/Règlements de la Faculté des Lettres/December 2, 1910. Here it is called the Conseil d'Administration. The University Council included the professors, while the University Administrative Council met without them.

53. For more on the history of the university in Europe, see Walter Rüegg and Hilde de Ridder-Symoens, eds., *A History of the University in Europe*, 4 vols. (Cambridge: Cambridge University Press, 1991–2011).

54. Minutes of the Technical Committee meeting of the Egyptian University/Session of April 19, 1910/Prince Fouad to the Committee members, repr., Budayr, *al-Amir Ahmad Fu'ad*, 121–2.

55. Fouad's speech to the University Council on March 15, 1911, repr., Budayr, *al-Amir Ahmad Fu'ad*, 87–8. The University Administrative Council expressed the same idea again in 1912. DWQ/Abdin/0069-004482: Report of the University Administrative Council to the General Assembly, March 14, 1912.

56. Fouad's speech to the University Council in 1912, repr., Budayr, *al-Amir Ahmad Fu'ad*, 93.

57. Fouad to the University Council session on April 19, 1910, on the creation of a Faculty of Arts, repr., Budayr, *al-Amir Ahmad Fu'ad*, 121.

58. Stephen Sheehi, *Foundations of Modern Arab Identity* (Gainesville: University Press of Florida, 2004), 36. For Sheehi's analysis of Bustani, see 15–36.

59. Minutes of the Session of the Technical Committee of the Egyptian University, April 19, 1910/Prince Fouad to the committee members, repr., Budayr, *al-Amir Ahmad Fu'ad*, 121–2. The Académie des Inscriptions et Belles-lettres is dedicated to the humanities and was founded in 1663 as part of the Institut de France.

60. "Partie Antique" with "Section Orientale" and "Section Occidentale," and "Partie Moderne" with "Section Orientale" and "Section Occidentale." DWQ/Abdin/0069-004481: Gaston Maspero, Note sur l'Établissement d'une Faculté des Lettres, February 26, 1910.

61. Donald Reid shows that Maspero always defended French interests at the university, against the British and even the Italians, until his retirement in 1914. See Reid, *Cairo University*, 39–40.

62. Here Maspero was exaggerating, as Italian was the dominant European language used in Egypt before 1798 and during the early years of the rule of Muhammad Ali.

63. Maspero, Note sur l'Établissement d'une Faculté des Lettres.

64. Ibid.

65. Ibid.

66. DWQ/Abdin/0069-004529: Correspondence of Ahmed Fouad/Courses for the academic year 1910–1911, July 30, 1910.

67. Reid mentions two cases of student reactions. The first occurred when Ignazio

Guidi compared the Syriac accounts of the "People of the Cave" story with the version in the Qur'an, after which students from al-Azhar and Dar al-'Ulum protested. The second arose after David Santillana's lectures about the Greek influence on Islamic theology, which also solicited a strong reaction from students. See Reid, *Cairo University*, 58.

68. Taha Hussein, *The Days*, vol. 2, trans. Hilary Wayment (Cairo: American University in Cairo, 2001), 114.

69. Hussein, *The Days*, 2:118.

70. Taha Hussein, *The Days*, vol. 3, trans. Kenneth Cragg (Cairo: American University in Cairo, 2001), 247.

71. Ibid., 248.

72. Ibid., 275–6.

73. Ibid., 248. Cragg uses *qanqala*, but the Arabic is *fanqala*, which Abdelrashid Mahmoudi describes as a dialectical skill, from the Arabic *fanaqulu* meaning "then we would say." Mahmoudi goes on to say that *fanqala* "stands for the Azhari form of dialectic involving objection and counter-objection. 'If you say so and so, then I would say such and such.'" Abdelrashid Mahmoudi, *Taha Husain's Education: From the Azhar to the Sorbonne* (Richmond, Surrey: Curzon, 1998), 38.

74. Hussein, *The Days*, 3:282.

75. Reid, *Cairo University*, 58–9. In 1913, Hussein came first in class, with a 30/30 in History of Arabic Literature, Arabic Literature, Arabic Philosophy, History of Philosophy Schools, and History of the Islamic Nations. In Geography and Ethnography, he got 28/30, but it was still the highest grade in his class. Cairo University Archives/B15/F452: Exam Results/April 1913, quoted in Reid, *Cairo University*, 60–1.

76. Taha Hussein, "al-Marhum al-Ustadh Innu Litman," *Majallat Majma' al-Lugha al-'Arabiyya* 14 (1962): 335–6. The eulogy was given on October 9, 1958.

77. Ibid., 336–7.

78. 'Abd al-Wahab 'Azzam, *Sahifat al-Jami'a al-Misriyya* 2 (1931): 83–4, cited in Reid, *Cairo University*, 60.

79. Ahmad Amin, *My Life: The Autobiography of an Egyptian Scholar, Writer, and Cultural Leader*, trans. Issa Boulatta (Leiden: Brill, 1978), 45, 52, cited in Reid, *Cairo University*, 58–9. Reid also cites the Arabic original: Ahmad Amin, *Hayati* (Cairo, Dar Maktabat al-Nahda al-Misriyya, 1961), 65, 77.

80. Amin, *Hayati*, 101, cited in Reid, *Cairo University*, 59.

81. Amin, *My Life*, 73, 149–50, cited in Reid, *Cairo University*, 60. Reid also cites *Hayati*, 109; 223–4.

82. Mahmoudi, *Taha Husain's Education*, 18. The full sentence reads: "It was precisely at the Azhar that Taha learnt to question the so-called "traditional" culture, and to discern beneath this layer of ossified tradition, the primary sources of Arab creativity." While Hussein shared Muhammad 'Abduh's wish to return to the primary sources, recent scholarship has shown that writers of such commentaries and supercommentaries were seriously engaging with the scholarship that came before them and were keeping the tradition alive through their own scholarly contributions in the form of these commentaries and supercommentaries. I disagree that it was an "ossified" tradition. See for example, Robert

Wisnovsky, "The Nature and Scope of Arabic Philosophical Commentary in Postclassical (ca. 1100–1900 AD) Islamic Intellectual History: Some Preliminary Observations," *Bulletin of the Institute of Classical Studies* 47, no. 1 (February 2004): 149–91. Wisnovsky explains that roughly half of the philosophical activity in postclassical Islamic intellectual history was "some form of exegetical work," and he disagrees with scholars who have dismissed this form of contribution as evidence of decline or ossification.

83. Pierre Cachia, *Taha Husayn: His Place in the Egyptian Literary Renaissance* (London: Luzac, 1956), 50.

84. Taha Hussein, "La Grande Figure du Cheikh Mohammed Abdo," *Un Effort* (June 1934): 4, translated and cited in Mahmoudi, *Taha Husain's Education*, 28–9.

85. Ibid.

86. Mahmoudi, *Taha Husain's Education*, 22–3, 30–1.

87. Hussein, *The Days*, 2:115.

88. Mahmoudi, *Taha Husain's Education*, 33.

89. Hussein, *The Days*, 2:217–8.

90. Timothy Mitchell, *Colonising Egypt* (London: University of California Press, 1991).

91. Mahmoudi, *Taha Husain's Education*, 22–3.

92. Bahiy al-Din Barakat, "Abu al-Jami'a Ahmad Lutfi al-Sayyid," *al-Hilal* (January 1951): 14–8. Hasan al-Zayyat, too, referred to Taha Hussein as the university's eldest son: "Al-Ibn al-bikr li-l-jami'a howa Taha Husayn." Hasan al-Zayyat, "Tahiyya li-Jami'at Fu'ad fi Yubiliha al-Fiddi," *al-Risala*, December 25, 1950.

93. This incident is discussed in more detail in the next chapter.

94. Taha Hussein, "Hadith al-Massa': La'ib," TTH 1: 351, originally published in *Kawkab al-Sharq*, May 22, 1933.

95. DWQ/Abdin/0069–004482: Report of the University Administrative Council to the General Assembly, March 14, 1912.

96. DWQ/Abdin/0069–004479: Report on the University in the academic year 1911–1912 to be presented to the General Assembly. That year the university had a total of 112 students (76 men and 36 women).

97. DWQ/Abdin/0069–004482: Report of the Administrative Council on the University/1912; and Draft letter from the Egyptian University Council to the minister of public instruction, January 1911.

98. Minutes of Majlis al-Nuwwab, Session of April 19, 1924, cited in Ibrahim, *al-Jami'a al-Ahliyya*, 140.

99. Notes on the University/1912/The Egyptian University and the Egyptian Gazette.

100. DWQ/Abdin/0069–004482: Report of the Administrative Council on the University/1912/Université Égyptienne: Rapport de 1910–1911; présenté à Sir Eldon Gorst.

101. Notes on the University/1912/The Egyptian University and the Egyptian Gazette. The response is neither signed nor dated, but the dossier is dated 1912, which matches the contents of the response and the details provided in it. The response is written in English but is a translation from French.

Notes to Chapters 2 and 3   235

102. Report of the University Administrative Council on the academic year 1914–1915 to the General Assembly on June 17, 1915, quoted in al-Jumayʿi, *al-Jamiʿa al-Misriyya*, 37.

103. Report of the University Administrative Council on the academic year 1916–1917 to the General Assembly on October 15, 1917, quoted in al-Jumayʿi, *al-Jamiʿa al-Misriyya*, 53. Reid cites the same numbers and ties the budget cut to the war as well. He adds that a donation from Sultan Husayn Kamil enabled the university to allow Taha Hussein and other students to continue their studies in Europe. See Reid, *Cairo University*, 62–3; Budayr, *al-Amir Ahmad Fuʾad*, 200; 273; and Hussein, *The Days*, 3:85–94.

104. Report of the University Administrative Council on the academic year 1915–1916 to the General Assembly on June 29, 1916, quoted in al-Jumayʿi, *al-Jamiʿa al-Misriyya*, 53–4. Students were also able to return to Europe after the Ministry of Waqfs raised its annual support to LE 2,000. Furthermore, the university professors gave up a quarter of their salaries, and some even taught without any remuneration. Report of the University Administrative Council on the academic year 1914–1915, quoted in al-Jumayʿi, *al-Jamiʿa al-Misriyya*, 54–5.

105. Al-Jumayʿi, *al-Jamiʿa al-Misriyya*, 58. Also, the university no longer had the means to invite European professors to teach in Cairo and was forced to cut down on its educational missions in Europe. Cairo University Archives/Folder Number 3: A report from the professors of the Faculty of Arts raised to the University Administrative Council; quoted in Ibrahim, *al-Jamiʿa al-Ahliyya*, 138–9.

106. Reid, *Cairo University*, 72.

107. DWQ/Abdin/0069-004494: The University and the Egyptian Government/Note explicative sur le projet de décret-loi portant création de l'Université d'État, March 3, 1925. The minister stressed that the majority of the members of the University Council would be academics and not representatives from the ministry.

Chapter 3

A version of this chapter was previously published as "The *Nahda* in Parliament: Taha Husayn's Career Building Knowledge Production Institutions, 1922–1952," *The Arab Studies Journal* 16, no. 1 (2018): 8–32. I thank *The Arab Studies Journal* for allowing me to reuse this material.

1. Taha Hussein, "Tabaʿat al-Taʿlim," TTH 1:729, originally published in *al-Jumhuriyya*, August 14, 1954.

2. DWQ/MNW/0075-057861: Minutes of the Sessions of June 1950/Minutes of the Session of June 25, 1950.

3. DWQ/MNW/0075-056819: Minutes of the Session of June 25, 1950/Memorandum for the Creation of a Supreme Council of the Egyptian Universities.

4. Ibid.

5. DWQ/MNW/0075-057066: Minutes of the Pre-session of June 3, 1951/Memorandum for the Annulment of the Supreme Council of the Universities.

6. Ibid. After the regime change, Law No. 508 of 1954 stipulated the re-creation of

the Supreme Council of the Universities. The first council session took place on October 2, 1954, after the purge of the universities (during which faculty considered a threat to the regime were fired). The president of Cairo University, Muhammad Kamal Mursi, oversaw the first session. In 1958, according to Law No. 184, the president of Cairo University was to be the president of the SCU. In 1963, however, this was changed so that the minister of higher education (the ministry itself had been created in 1961) was to automatically become the president of the SCU. In 1972, Law No. 49 forced all Egyptian universities to comply with all decisions made by the council. See Mahmud Munawi, *Jami'at al-Qahira fi 'Idiha al-Mi'awi* (Giza: Al-Maktaba al-Akadimiyya, 2007), 196–7.

7. Bahiy al-Din Barakat, "Abu al-Jami'a Ahmad Lutfi al-Sayyid," *al-Hilal* (January 1951): 14–8. Barakat (1889–1972) was an Egyptian statesman, and minister of public instruction from January 1, 1930, to June 19, 1930, and from December 30, 1937, to April 26, 1938. He had been a professor of law before turning to politics. See Wizarat al-Tarbiyya wa-l-Ta'lim, *Mi'a wa-Situn 'Aman min al-Ta'lim fi Misr: Wuzara' al-Ta'lim wa-Abraz Injazatihim (1837–1997)* (Cairo: Matbu'at Wizarat al-Tarbiyya wa-l-Ta'lim, 2000), 181–2.

8. Lutfi al-Sayyid submitted his resignation on March 9, which is now celebrated as Independence Day for all Egyptian universities.

9. Ahmad 'Ulabi, *Taha Husayn: Sirat Mukafih 'Anid* (Beirut: Dar al-Farabi, 1990), 120.

10. For the clash between Sidqi and Taha Hussein, see Donald Reid, *Cairo University and the Making of Modern Egypt* (Cambridge: Cambridge University Press, 1990), 120–5; and Ahmad Zakariya al-Shalq, "Taha Husayn wa-Istiqlal al-Jami'a," in *Mi'at 'Am 'ala al-Jami'a al-Misriyya*, ed. Ahmad Zakariya al-Shalq (Cairo: Dar al-Kutub wa-l-Watha'iq al-Qawmiyya, 2011), 109–24.

11. Barakat, "Abu al-Jami'a," 14–8.

12. DWQ/MNW/0075-054705: The session of December 9, 1939/Memorandum from the Ministry of Finance to the Council of Ministers regarding the appointment of Dr. Taha Husayn as supervisor of the Directorate of General Culture.

13. Ibid.

14. DWQ/MNW/0075-057763: Minutes of the Sessions of September–December 1940/Minutes of the Session of November 25, 1940, A year later, Hussein was appointed to the consulting committee for the fine arts, for three renewable years.

15. DWQ/MNW/0075-057771: Minutes of the Sessions of May–July 1942/The Sessions of May 12, 14, and 16, 1942.

16. Cairo University/Archives of the Faculty of Arts: Taha Hussein's File/The Ministry of Public Instruction ministerial decree number 5590, May 26, 1942.

17. Taha Hussein was a vocal supporter of his friend Mustafa al-Nahhas when al-Nahhas signed the 1936 Egyptian-Anglo Treaty and also when he abrogated that treaty in 1951, after negotiations with the British had come to a stalemate. When the Wafd Party won reelection in 1950, Hussein declined the position of minister of public instruction, fearing the reaction of other Wafdists since he was not a party member. Nahhas refused Hussein's resignation and said this was a question of nation and

not party: "Taha avait offert sa démission à Nahas qui la refusa, alléguant—et le lui écrivant—que ce n'était pas une question de parti, mais de Patrie." Suzanne Taha Hussein, *Avec Toi: De la France à l'Égypte: "Une Extraordinaire Amour"; Suzanne et Taha Hussein (1915–1973)* (Paris: Les Éditions du Cerf, 2011), 213.

18. Second Annual Report 1909–10, repr., *al-Jamiʻa al-Ahliyya (1908–1925): Safahat min Dhakirat al-Sahafa* (Cairo: Dar al-Kutub wa-l-Wathaʾiq al-Qawmiyya, 2010), 103.

19. In the academic year 1911–1912, the university administration was happy to increase the number of lectures offered to women. Lectures in French discussed morality and raising children, while lectures in Arabic focused on ancient Egyptian history, the history of Islam in Egypt, the French wars, and famous women in all these historical periods. There were also lectures on home economics. DWQ/Abdin/0069–004479: Report on the University in the academic year 1911–1912. These lectures were stopped in 1912–13, however. The reason given in the annual report was that these courses would stop until the creation of a system that addressed the needs of Egyptian women. Fifth Annual Report 1912–1913, repr., *al-Jamiʻa al-Ahliyya*, 171. Historian Latifa Salim has argued, however, that the section was closed due to the male opposition to offering such education to women. See Latifa Salim, "al-Marʾa fi Rihab al-Jamiʻa," in *Miʾat ʻAm ʻala al-Jamiʻa al-Misriyya*, ed. Ahmad Zakariya al-Shalq, 44. For more on the "Women's Section," also see Reid, *Cairo University*, 51–6.

20. Robert Blum, "La Mode des Conférences," *Images*, December 12, 1931, 5.

21. These publications were made available in public bookshops, like al-Maʻarif and al-Hilal bookshops on Faggalah street. Their prices ranged between 12 and 40 piasters. DWQ/Abdin/0069–004479: Report on the University in the academic year 1911–1912.

22. Taha Hussein, "Kulliyat al-Adab," in TTH 1:314, originally published in *al-Musawwar*, March 4, 1932.

23. Ibid., 313.

24. Ibid., 314.

25. Anthony Gorman, *Historians, State and Politics in Twentieth-Century Egypt: Contesting the Nation* (New York: RoutledgeCurzon, 2003), 23.

26. Yoav Di-Capua, *Gatekeepers of the Arab Past: Historians and History Writing in Twentieth-Century Egypt* (Berkeley: University of California Press, 2009), 196–9.

27. Ibid., 159.

28. Ibid., 203.

29. Taha Hussein's wife, Suzanne, was friends with Huda Shaʻrawi, and was on the board of the Egyptian Feminist Union. See Bahija Sidki Rashid et al., eds., *The Egyptian Feminist Union* (Cairo: 1963), cited in Reid, *Cairo University*, 104. Hussein himself lectured at the Egyptian Feminist Union headquarters and was appointed to the union's formal advisory committee when it was created in 1929, along with such others as Husayn Haykal, Ahmad Lutfi al-Sayyid, and Mustafa ʻAbd al-Raziq. See Samia Sharawi Lanfranchi, *Casting Off the Veil: The Life of Huda Shaarawi, Egypt's First Feminist* (London: I. B. Tauris, 2012), 202, 175.

30. Reid, *Cairo University*, 105–6. Reid had interviewed Suhayr al-Qalamawi in Cairo, on February 16, 1983.

31. Salim, "al-Mar'a fi Rihab al-Jami'a," 46.

32. Suhayr al-Qalamawi, preface to *Taha Husayn fi Ma'arikihi al-Adabiyya wa-l-Fikriyya*, by Samih Kurayyim (Cairo: Majallat al-Idha'a wa-l-Tilifizyun, 1974), 4.

33. Reid, *Cairo University*, 108–9.

34. Taha Hussein, "Fawz," in TTH 1:380, originally published in *Kawkab al-Sharq*, June 26, 1933.

35. Taha Hussein, "al-Ta'lim al-Dini wa-Ikhtilat al-Jinsayn fi Kuliyyat al-Jami'a al-Misriyya," in TTH 1:434–6, originally published in *al-Misri*, March 10, 1937.

36. Taha Hussein, "Ayna Kanat Hadhihi al-Ghira fi al-'Uhud al-Sabiqa?," in TTH 1:439, originally published in *al-Misri*, March 13, 1937.

37. "Muzaharat al-Jami'iyn fi Haram al-Jami'a al-Misriyya," in TTH 1:449, originally published in *al-Misri*, March 17, 1937.

38. Salim, "al-Mar'a fi Rihab al-Jami'a," 47.

39. Taha Hussein, "Kulliyat al-Adab," in TTH 1:315–6, originally published in *al-Musawwar*, March 4, 1932.

40. Taha Hussein, "Hadith al-Duktur Taha Husayn Bey 'ann Kulliyat al-Adab," in TTH 1:431, originally published in *al-Muqtataf*, January 1937.

41. Ibid., 428.

42. 'Azzam studied at al-Azhar and then at the School of Judges before earning a degree in literature and philosophy from the old Egyptian University. He then earned a master's degree in Persian literature from the School of Oriental and African Studies in London in 1927, and a doctorate from the Egyptian University in 1932, writing on the *Shahnameh*. He became dean of arts at Fouad I University in 1945 and was the first president of Riyadh University (later King Saud University) from 1957 until his death in 1959.

43. Ibid., 428–30.

44. Ibid., 429.

45. Cairo University/Archives of the Faculty of Arts: Faculty Meetings/Minutes of November 27, 1939.

46. DWQ/Abdin/0069-004610: Memorandum on the Egyptian University, 1933–34.

47. DWQ/Abdin/0069-004500: Documents pertaining to the university and the Ministry of Public Instruction/The Egyptian University Council/Minutes of the Session of August 28, 1938/Faculty of Arts/Decree Project for the Creation of an Institute for Oriental Languages and Literatures.

48. Hussein, "Hadith al-Duktur Taha Husayn Bey," 429. For the development of the social sciences in Egypt, see Omnia El Shakry, *The Great Social Laboratory: Subjects of Knowledge in Colonial and Postcolonial Egypt* (Stanford, CA: Stanford University Press, 2007).

49. DWQ/Abdin/0069-004610: Memorandum on the Egyptian University, 1933–34.

50. Hussein, "Hadith al-Duktur Taha Husayn Bey," 430.

51. Taha Hussein, "Athar al-Jami'a al-Misriyya al-Qadima fi Hayat Misr al-Haditha," in TTH 1:763–4, originally published in *Watan*, January 25, 1959.

52. Ibid., 764.

53. Ibid.

54. Mustafa Sadiq al-Rafiʿi, "al-Adab al-ʿArabi fi al-Jamiʿa," in TTH 1:278–9, originally published in *Kawkab al-Sharq*, July 28, 1926.

55. Ghali Shukri, *Madha Yabqa min Taha Husayn?* (Beirut: Dar al-Mutawassit, 1974), 62–4.

56. Hussein, "Athar al-Jamiʿa al-Misriyya al-Qadima," 764–5.

57. Taha Hussein, "Hadith al-Duktur Taha Husayn Bey," 431. For example, in 1937, the ministry assigned *Naqd al-Nathr* by Abi al-Faraj Qudama al-Baghdadi to high school students, in an edition revised and edited by Taha Hussein and ʿAbd al-Hamid al-ʿAbbadi (1892–1956). Cairo University/Archives of the Faculty of Arts: Taha Hussein's File/Letter from the assistant undersecretary of the ministry of public instruction to Taha Hussein, September 30, 1937; and Cairo University/Archives of the Faculty of Arts: Taha Hussein's File/Letter from Taha Hussein to the undersecretary of the Ministry of Public Instruction, November 20, 1937.

58. Cairo University/Archives of the Faculty of Arts: Taha Hussein's File/Letter from the undersecretary of the Ministry of Public Instruction to Taha Hussein, July 19, 1938.

59. DWQ/Abdin/0069-004477: Papers relevant to education, January 22, 1909–April 12, 1939/Agenda for the Session of March 22, 1938, of the University Administrative Council.

60. Cairo University/Archives of the Faculty of Arts: Faculty Meetings/Minutes of the Session of January 2, 1940.

61. Taha Hussein, "al-Dimuqratiyya Laysat illa al-ʿIlm wa-l-Maʿrifa," in TTH 1:535, originally published in *al-Wafd al-Misri*, June 9, 1944.

62. Elizabeth Suzanne Kassab, *Contemporary Arab Thought: Cultural Critique in Comparative Perspective* (New York: Columbia University Press, 2010), 24.

63. Taha Hussein, *Mustaqbal al-Thaqafa fi Misr*, vol. 9 of *al-Majmuʿa al-Kamila* (Beirut: Dar al-Kitab al-Lubnani, 1974), 12–4.

64. Taha Hussein, "Yawman," in TTH 1:264, originally published in *al-Siyasa*, August 25, 1924.

65. Ibid., 266–7.

66. Ibid., 264.

67. Ibid., 263–9.

68. Taha Hussein, "Fi Wizarat al-Maʿarif: Al-ʿAbath bi-l-ʿIlm wa-l-Muʿalimin," in TTH 1:168, originally published in *al-Siyasa*, July 31, 1923.

69. Taha Hussein, "Thaqafa," in TTH 1:326, originally published in *al-Siyasa*, July 25, 1932.

70. Taha Hussein, "Siyasat al-Taʿlim," in TTH 1:194, originally published in *al-Siyasa*, November 2, 1923.

71. Ibid.

72. Hussein, "Fi Wizarat al-Maʿarif," 169.

73. Ibid.," 169–70.

74. Taha Hussein, "Tanzim al-Ta'lim," in TTH 1:200–1, originally published in *al-Siyasa*, September 18, 1923.

75. Ibid.

76. DWQ/MNW/0075-057867: Minutes of the Session of March 11, 1951/ Memorandum for the Reorganization of the Supreme Council of Education. Taha Hussein also created the Teachers' Syndicate in 1951 and was elected by its members as its first president.

77. Hussein, "Tanzim al-Ta'lim," 205.

78. Ibid.

79. Taha Hussein, "Hadith al-Yawm: Tahqiq," in TTH 1:319, originally published in *al-Siyasa*, July 17, 1932.

80. Ibid.

81. Taha Hussein, "Hadith al-Massa': Insaf," in TTH 1:373, originally published in *Kawkab al-Sharq*, June 6, 1933.

82. Taha Hussein, "Hadith al-Massa': Tawassu'," in TTH 1:345, originally published in *Kawkab al-Sharq*, April 5, 1933.

83. Hussein, "Fi Wizarat al-Ma'arif," 168.

84. Taha Hussein, "Harakat al-Islah," in TTH 1:209, originally published in *al-Siyasa*, October 10, 1923.

85. Taha Hussein, "Hadith al-Yawm: Al-Azhar wa-Madrasat al-Qada' al-Shar'i," in TTH 1:164–6, originally published in *al-Siyasa*, July 20, 1923. Also see Taha Hussein, "Madrasat al-Qada' al-Shar'i," in TTH 1:177, originally published in *al-Siyasa*, August 26, 1923.

86. Hussein, "al-Dimuqratiyya laysat illa al-'Ilm wa-l-Ma'rifa," 536.

87. Ibid., 535.

88. Ibid., 535–40.

89. Taha Husayn, "Tasrihat Hamma li-l-Duktur Taha Husayn," in TTH 1:493, originally published in *al-Misri*, 21 December 1942.

90. For example, in September 1942, the proportion of registered students receiving scholarships increased from 1% to 3%. In October 1942, the ministry raised this proportion to 10%. In a memorandum, the ministry stated: "Current circumstances have made it impossible for many parents to meet the required tuition fees and thus their girls and boys are now liable to dismissal from schools and being cut off from education.... It should be indicated here that primary education in most civilized countries, and even secondary education in England, France, and Turkey, is for free.... There are also countries like Iraq where the gratuity percentage in primary and secondary schools is almost 30%, while Egypt has not reached any worthy number despite all the efforts spent in increasing the percentage of scholarships." DWQ/MNW/0075-057772: For the memorandum, see Minutes of the Session of October 26, 1942; and for the increase from 1% to 3%, see Minutes of the Sessions of August-September 1942/Minutes of the Session of September 15, 1942. The minister of public instruction at the time, Najib al-Hilali, made a further request, to increase the percentage of scholarships by 5%, on December 2, 1942, saying that the previous increase had not been enough, and that given how

the public had reacted favorably to the previous increase, he was requesting the council's approval for more scholarships. DWQ/MNW/0075-055365: Minutes of the Session of December 2, 1942. Then on February 10, 1943, he made yet another request for another increase, of 3%. He argued that the ministry had exhausted the 15% already given, yet there were still thousands of students incapable of paying their tuition fees, despite warnings of dismissal, which, al-Hilali argued, "destabilized students psychologically, distracted them from their lessons, and embarrassed them and their parents." DWQ/MNW/0075-055402: Minutes of the Session of February 10, 1943.

91. Taha Hussein, "Fi al-Taʿlim," in TTH 1:717, originally published in *al-Ahram*, April 6, 1953. For more on the writer as an educator and "the conscience of the nation," see Richard Jacquemond, *Entre Scribes et Écrivains: Le Champs Littéraire dans l'Égypte Contemporaine* (Paris: Sindbad/Actes Sud, 2003), 23–5.

92. Taha Hussein, "Duktur Taha Husayn Yaqul: Al-Taʿlim Haqq Iktasabahu al-Shaʿb wa-la Yastatiʿ ayy Fard ann Yaslubahu minh," in TTH 1:533, originally published in *al-Wafd al-Misri*, January 14, 1944.

93. Taha Hussein, "Haʾulaʾ al-Muʿalimun al-Mudribun!" in TTH 1:590, originally published in al-*Musawwar*, April 11, 1947.

94. Ibid.

95. See Ismaʿil Mahmud al-Qabbani, *Dirasat fi Tanzim al-Taʿlim bi-Misr* (Cairo: Makatabat al-Nahda, 1958).

96. Ibid., 103.

97. Taha Hussein, "al-Nush al-Daʾiʿ," in TTH 1:556–7, originally published in *al-Balagh*, June 7, 1945.

98. Taha Hussein, "Dimuqratiyyat al-Taʿlim bayna al-Wafd wa-l-Hukumat al-Ukhra," in TTH 1:549, originally published in *al-Wafd al-Misri*, June 7, 1945.

99. Sanhuri was minister of public instruction from January 15, 1945, to February 15, 1946, and from December 9, 1946, to February 27, 1949.

100. Hussein, "Dimuqratiyyat al-Taʿlim bayna al-Wafd wa-l-Hukumat al-Ukhra," 551.

101. Misako Ikeda, "Toward the Democratization of Public Education: The Debate in Late Parliamentary Egypt, 1943–52," in *Re-envisioning Egypt 1919–1952*, ed. Arthur Goldschmidt, Amy J. Johnson, and Barak A. Salmoni (Cairo: American University in Cairo Press), 218–48.

102. Muhammad Farid Abu Hadid, "The Story of Water and Air," *al-Thaqafa* 56 (November 21, 1949): 5–6, cited in Ikeda, "Toward the Democratization of Public Education," 237. I am using Ikeda's translation here.

103. Ikeda, "Toward the Democratization of Public Education," 234.

104. Ibid.

105. Taha Hussein, "Birnamaj," in TTH 1:644, originally published in *al-Ahram*, November 7, 1949.

106. Taha Hussein, "Nadwat al-Hilal: Mashakil al-Shabab, Kayfa Nahiluha?" in TTH 1:620, originally published in *al-Hilal*, January 1948.

107. Hussein, "Birnamaj," 644.

108. Taha Hussein, [Untitled article], in TTH 1:626–7, originally published in *al-Ahram*, July 11, 1949.

109. Taha Hussein, "al-Haqq al-Murr," in TTH 1:640, originally published in *al-Ahram*, October 28, 1949.

110. Taha Hussein, "Taha Husayn Bey Yaqul," in TTH 1:646, originally published in *al-Nida'*, February 28, 1950.

111. DWQ/MNW/0075-057863: Minutes of the Sessions of September and October 1950/Minutes of the Session of October 15, 1950.

112. Taha Hussein, "Hadith li-Wazir al-Ma'arif," in TTH 1:691, originally published in *al-Assas*, June 7, 1951.

113. Taha Hussein, "Nadhir!" in TTH 1:592–6, originally published in *Musamarat al-Jayb*, November 2, 1947.

114. In a television interview years later, Hussein explained that as minister he also tried to make higher education free, but King Farouk refused and accused Hussein of wanting to spread communism in the country. Taha Hussein, "Katib wa Qissa," interview by Samira al-Kilani, *al-Tilifizyun al-'Arabi*, 1970, last accessed July 23, 2020, https://www.youtube.com/watch?v=6W4YhZonH-8.

115. Taha Hussein, "Iftitah Mu'tamar al-Thaqafa al-'Arabi al-Thani-Kalimat al-Iftitah: Khutbat Wazir al-Ma'arif," in TTH 1:653, originally published in *al-Assas*, August 23, 1950.

116. Ibid.

Chapter 4

1. Taha Hussein, "Mushkilat al-I'rab," *Majallat Majma' al-Lugha al-'Arabiyya* 11 (1959): 100.

2. Debates over language reform were not specific to the Arab world. In the second half of the eighteenth century, Greek intellectuals engaged with similar questions over the proper form Modern Greek should take so it would be reflective of both Ancient Greek with its prestigious history and spoken Demotic Greek. This resulted in Katharevousa, a form of modern Greek that was developed in the early nineteenth century and was used primarily for literary and official purposes until it was replaced by Demotic Greek by an act of parliament in 1976. For the history of these Greek language debates, see Peter Mackridge, *Language and National Identity in Greece, 1766–1976* (Oxford: Oxford University Press, 2009). The famous linguist Charles Ferguson used both Greek and Arabic as examples of *diglossia*, a term he developed to describe the complex sociolinguistic situation in which two forms of the same language coexist, and the usage of each form depends on the social setting and function. See Charles Ferguson, "Diglossia," *Word* 15 (1959): 325–40. Mackridge takes issue with Ferguson's binary, and argues that in the Greek case, the situation was never that simple as "diglossia is as much a matter of speakers' perceptions as of the actual sociolinguistic situation, which is always more messy; actual language used in Greece covered a continuum of linguistic registers ranging from 'pure' demotic to 'extreme' Katharevousa, with hybrid varieties in between." Mackridge, *Language and National Identity in Greece*, 29.

3. Adrian John Gully, "Arabic Linguistic Issues and Controversies of the Late Nineteenth and Early Twentieth Centuries," *Journal of Semitic Studies* 42, no. 1 (1997): 76-7, cited in Abdulrazzak Patel, *The Arab Nahdah: The Making of the Intellectual and Humanist Movement* (Edinburgh: Edinburgh University Press, 2013), 103.

4. Niloofar Haeri, *Sacred Language, Ordinary People: Dilemmas of Culture and Politics in Egypt* (New York: Palgrave Macmillan, 2003), 9.

5. 'Isa M. Saba, *al-Shaykh Ibrahim al-Yaziji* (Beirut, 1955), 83, cited in Anwar Chejne, *The Arabic Language: Its Role in History* (Minneapolis: University of Minnesota Press, 1969), 135.

6. Patel, *Arab Nahdah*, 113-4.

7. Haeri, *Sacred Language, Ordinary People*, 80.

8. Ibid., 11.

9. Salama Musa, *al-Balagha al-'Asriyya wa-l-Lugha al-'Arabiyya* (Cairo: Al-Matba'a al-'Asriyya, 1953): v (*ha'*).

10. Ibid., 23.

11. Ibid., 62.

12. Ibid., v (*ha'*). The preface was written in 1945.

13. Ibid., vi (*waw*).

14. Ibid., vii (*zay*).

15. Ibid., 92-3.

16. Haeri, *Sacred Language, Ordinary People*, 82-4; and 'Abd al-'Aziz Sami al-Kumi, *al-Sahafa al-Islamiyya fi Misr fi al-Qarn al-Tasi' 'Ashar* (Mansura: Dar al-Wafa li-l-Tiba'a wa-l-Nashr wa-l-Tawzi', 1992), 212, cited in Haeri, *Sacred Language, Ordinary People*, 84. The debate was also covered in Yusuf Qazma Khuri, *Najah al-Umma al-'Arabiyya fi Lughatiha al-Asliyya* (Beirut: Dar al-Hamra, 1991), 35-65, cited in Yasir Suleiman, *A War of Words: Language and Conflict in the Middle East* (Cambridge: Cambridge University Press, 2004), 47.

17. Haeri, *Sacred Language, Ordinary People*, 84.

18. Suleiman uses the work of these Orientalists to substantiate an argument put forward by the Egyptian historian Naffusa Zakariya Sa'id in her book *Tarikh al-Da'wa ila al-'Ammiyya wa-Athariha fi Misr* (Cairo: Dar al-Ma'arif, 1964), in which she argued that calls for replacing classical Arabic with the colloquial were the work of Europeans for colonial political ends. See Suleiman, *A War of Words*, 63.

19. Suleiman, *A War of Words*, 62-72.

20. Haeri, *Sacred Language, Ordinary People*, 84. Suleiman explains that Arab intellectuals who support various dialects are sometimes considered to be continuing the work of Orientalists and colonialists, and sometimes their calls are interpreted according to their religious or political affiliations. For example, Suleiman shows that Umar Farrukh accused Sa'id 'Aql and Anis Frayha of supporting the Lebanese dialect because of their Christian background. Suleiman, *A War of Words*, 73-4. Similarly, in Egypt, Salama Musa and Luwis 'Awad were accused of supporting Egyptian colloquial Arabic because they were Christians. 'Abbas al-'Aqqad opposed Musa's appointment to the Arabic Language Academy because of the latter's negative view of classical Arabic, while 'Awad's

book *Muqadimma fi Fiqh al-Lugha al-'Arabiyya* (1980) was banned. Suleiman, *A War of Words*, 78–80.

21. Musa, *al-Balagha al-'Asriyya*, 90. Haeri defines case endings as "short vowels that are indicated orthographically with diacritics placed above and below letters." Haeri, *Sacred Language, Ordinary People*, 44.

22. Suleiman, *A War of Words*, 80–1. Musa explains that both Lutfi al-Sayyid and Bahiy al-Din Barakat were trying to reform the language. Musa, *al-Balagha al-'Asriyya*, 93.

23. Musa, *al-Balagha al-'Asriyya*, 99. The Turkish Republic adopted the Latin script in 1928. Anis Frayha, professor of Arabic at the American University of Beirut also supported 'Abd al-'Aziz Fahmi's call. See Chejne, *Arabic Language*, 158.

24. Haeri, *Sacred Language, Ordinary People*, 3.

25. Ibid., 14.

26. Ibid., 66.

27. Ibid., 67.

28. Ibid.

29. Ibid., 66–7.

30. Haeri concludes that "in the 'tastes and contexts' of the 'socially-charged' life of classical Arabic, religion dominates." Ibid., 17.

31. Taha Hussein, *Mustaqbal al-Thaqafa fi Misr*, vol. 9 of *al-Majmu'a al-Kamila* (Beirut: Dar al-Kitab al-Lubnani, 1974), 298. I am using Haeri's translation here.

32. Haeri, *Sacred Language, Ordinary People*, 70.

33. Hussein, *Mustaqbal al-Thaqafa*, 290-1.

34. Ibid., 291.

35. Ibid., 292–3.

36. Ibid., 293.

37. Hussein uses strong language to make his point: "Al-Azhar knows nothing about the development of foreign languages, old or new. It hardly even knows anything about those languages and is completely ignorant in Semitic languages. Al-Azhar hardly goes beyond its known barren books to the books the ancients wrote on the Arabic language, its literature and sciences. And despite all this, it wants to supervise the sciences of the Arabic language, prevent its reform and monopolize its teaching, and finds among officials those who pretend to agree with it, not because they believe this would actually benefit the language, or that going against the wishes of al-Azhar is to infringe on religion, but because they are afraid [of being accused of going against religion] or they desire [al-Azhar's support in the name of religion]." Ibid., 293–4.

38. Ibid., 312.

39. As discussed in the previous chapter, Muhammad 'Abduh introduced the study of literature to al-Azhar curriculum but only as an elective that students did not have to study and were not examined in.

40. Mansur Fahmi, dean of arts, was one of the first academy members, appointed in 1933. He was editor of the academy's periodical and was elected to be its secretary (*katib al-sirr*) until his death on May 11, 1959. "Qararat al-Majma': Al-Qararat al-Idariyya,

Qarar Intikhab Katib Sirr al-Majma'," *Majallat Majma' al-Lugha al-'Arabiyya* 1 (October 1934): 28. On that day, upon arriving at the academy, Fahmi's driver opened the car door to discover Fahmi had died on the way to the academy.

41. Mansur Fahmi, "Tarikh al-Majami'," *Majallat Majma' al-Lugha al-'Arabiyya* 1 (October 1934): 173.

42. Ibid., 174–5.

43. Ibrahim Bayumi Madkur, "Ta'bin Ahmad Lutfi al-Sayyid," *Majallat Majma' al-Lugha al-'Arabiyya* 16 (1963): 118.

44. Fahmi, "Tarikh al-Majami'," 174–5.

45. Ibid.

46. Madkur, "Ta'bin Ahmad Lutfi al-Sayyid," 118.

47. Fahmi, "Tarikh al-Majami'," 174–5.

48. Madkur, "Ta'bin Ahmad Lutfi al-Sayyid," 118. Following the death of Taha Hussein, Madkur became president of the academy in 1974.

49. Ibid., 119–20. For the Dar al-Kutub Academy, al-Sayyid had wanted to have 28 members: 25 Arabs and 3 more members knowledgeable in Iranian, Syriac, and Hebrew. Ibid., 118. Al-Sayyid was not appointed to the Arabic Language Academy until 1940. He was elected by the academy members as president in April 1941, but the official appointment did not come until March 1945. Madkur believes that was for political reasons. Ibid., 119–20.

50. Fahmi, "Tarikh al-Majami'," 175–6.

51. "Marsum bi-Insha' Majma' Malaki li-l-Lugha al-'Arabiyya," *Majallat Majma' al-Lugha al-'Arabiyya* 1 (October 1934): 6.

52. "Mahdar Jalsat al-Iftitah: Kalimat Ma'ali Ra'is al-Majma' al-Duktur Muhammad Tawfiq Rif'at Basha," *Majallat Majma' al-Lugha al-'Arabiyya* 5 (1948): 4–5. (For Arabic Language Academy session 5, December 18, 1937, to January 27, 1938. The delay in publication was due to the eruption of the Second World War and the backlog that ensued.)

53. "La'iha li-Majma' al-Lugha al-'Arabiyya al-Malaki," *Majallat Majma' al-Lugha al-'Arabiyya* 1 (October 1934): 22.

54. "Marsum bi-Insha' Majma' Malaki li-l-Lugha al-'Arabiyya," 6–7.

55. Ibid., 10–1.

56. "Marsum bi-Ta'iyn al-A'da' al-'Amilin li-Majma' al-Lugha al-'Arabiyya," *Majallat Majma' al-Lugha al-'Arabiyya* 1 (October 1934): 12–3.

57. "Qararat al-Majma': Al-Qararat al-Idariyya, Qarar Intikhab Ra'is al-Majma'," *Majallat Majma' al-Lugha al-'Arabiyya* 1 (October 1934): 28. Among the decisions taken was the creation of committees for Mathematics, Physics and Chemistry, Biology and Medicine, Social Sciences and Philosophy, Belles-Lettres and Fine Arts, Dictionaries, Dialects, the Library, the Budget, and the General Principles. "Qararat al-Majma': Al-Qararat al-Idariyya, Qarar Tasmiyyat al-Lijan," *Majallat Majma' al-Lugha al-'Arabiyya* 1 (October 1934): 29–33.

58. "Iftitah Dawr al-In'iqad al-Thalith," *Majallat Majma' al-Lugha al-'Arabiyya* 3 (October 1936): 1; and "Jalsat Iftitah al-Dawra al-Khamisa: Mahdar Jalsat al-Iftitah,"

Majallat Majma' al-Lugha al-'Arabiyya 5 (1948): 3. Marsum bi-Ta'iyn A'da' 'Amilin bi-Majma' Fu'ad al-Awwal lil-Lugha al-'Arabiyya," *Majallat Majma' al-Lugha al-'Arabiyya* 5 (1948): 174.

59. "Marsum bi-Insha' Majma' Malaki li-l-Lugha al-'Arabiyya," 10–1.

60. "Jalsat al-Iftitah: Kalimat Hadrat Sahib al-Ma'ali al-Duktur Muhammad Tawfiq Rif'at Basha Ra'is al-Majlis," *Majallat Majma' al-Lugha al-'Arabiyya* 5 (1948): 86. (For Arabic Language Academy session 6, December 17, 1938, to January 28, 1939.)

61. "Qararat al-Majma' fi Hadhihi al-Dawra," *Majallat Majma' al-Lugha al-'Arabiyya* 5 (1948): 88.

62. Ibid.

63. "Marsum bi-Ta'iyn A'da' 'Amilin bi-Majma' Fu'ad al-Awwal lil-Lugha al-'Arabiyya," 174.

64. "Jalsat al-Iftitah li-Majlis al-Majma': Kalimat Ma'ali Ra'is al-Majma' al-Duktur Muhammad Tawfiq Rif'at Basha," *Majallat Majma' al-Lugha al-'Arabiyya* 5 (1948): 181. (For Arabic Language Academy session 7, December 3, 1940, to April 22, 1941.)

65. "Marsum bi-Ta'dil ba'd Ahkam al-Marsum al-Sadir bi-Insha' Majma' Fu'ad al-Awwal li-l-Lugha al-'Arabiyya," *Majallat Majma' al-Lugha al-'Arabiyya* 5 (1948): 171–3. Taha Hussein was elected and then appointed a member of this office on December 19, 1940, along with Mansur Fahmi, Ahmad Amin, and Ibrahim Hamrush. "Qarar Wizari Raqam 5425 bi-Tarikh 19 December 1940 bi-Sha'n Ta'lif Maktab Majma' Fu'ad al-Awwal lil-Lugha al-'Arabiyya," *Majallat Majma' al-Lugha al-'Arabiyya* 5 (1948): 178.

66. Later, Law No. 434 of 1955 was issued to reorganize the academy, and in that law, the name Academy Office was changed to Academy Board, or Majlis Idarat al-Majma'. This board was composed of the president, the undersecretary of the Ministry of Education, the undersecretary of the Ministry of Economy and Finance, the secretary of the academy, and three academy members to be elected by the Academy Council (the Academy Council was composed of the Egyptian members, who served for a period of three years). "Qanun Raqam 434 li-Sanat 1955 bi-Sha'n Tanzim Majma' al-Lugha al-'Arabiyya," *Majallat Majma' al-Lugha al-'Arabiyya* 8 (1955): v (*ha'*), vi (*waw*), and vii (*zay*). Interestingly, the new law stipulated that the academy was to become an independent organization, not part of the Ministry of Education, but the same law indicated that the minister of education was to remain the higher president of the academy. Ibid., v (*ha'*).

67. "Qarar Wizari Raqam 5434 bi-Tarikh 6 February 1941 bi-Taysir al-Kitaba wal-Qawa'id wa-Tashji' al-'Amal al-Adabi al-Hadith," *Majallat Majma' al-Lugha al-'Arabiyya* 5 (1948): 179.

68. "Musabaqat Wizarat al-Ma'arif li-l-Qissa al-Misriyya," *Majallat Majma' al-Lugha al-'Arabiyya* 5 (1948): 209–10. The letter was dated March 7, 1942.

69. "Qarar Wizari Raqam 5434 bi-Tarikh 6 February 1941 bi-Taysir al-Kitaba wal-Qawa'id wa-Tashji' al-'Amal al-Adabi al-Hadith," *Majallat Majma' al-Lugha al-'Arabiyya* 5 (1948): 179; and "Qararat al-Majlis wa-l-Mu'tamar," *Majallat Majma' al-Lugha al-'Arabiyya* 5 (1948): 194–5.

70. "Qararat Majlis al-Majma fi Hadhihi al-Dawra: Musabaqat Wizarat al-Ma'arif

li-l-Qissa al-Misriyya," *Majallat Majmaʿ al-Lugha al-ʿArabiyya* 5 (1948): 209–13. (For Arabic Language Academy session 8, February 8, 1942 to July 1, 1942.)

71. "Ja'izat Faruq al-Awwal lil-Shʿir al-ʿArabi wal-Qissa al-Misriyya," and "Ja'iza li-Dirasat Harakat al-Tarjama," *Majallat Majmaʿ al-Lugha al-ʿArabiyya* 6 (1951): 19–20.

72. "Jawa'iz al-Majmaʿ al-Adabiyya fi Musabaqat 1945–1947," *Majallat Majmaʿ al-Lugha al-ʿArabiyya* 7 (1953): 58–9. (For Arabic Language Academy session 13: October 14, 1946, to May 26, 1947.)

73. *Majallat Majmaʿ al-Lugha al-ʿArabiyya* 12 (1960): 322.

74. "Qararat al-Majlis wal-Mu'tamar," *Majallat Majmaʿ al-Lugha al-ʿArabiyya* 5 (1948): 194.

75. "Qararat Mu'tamar al-Majmaʿ fi Taysir Qawaʿid al-Lugha al-ʿArabiyya [February and March 1945]," *Majallat Majmaʿ al-Lugha al-ʿArabiyya* 6 (1951): 180–1. (For Arabic Language Academy session 11, November 23, 1944, to May 28, 1945.)

76. Salama Musa must have written his book *al-Balagha al-ʿAsriyya*, mentioned earlier, in response to Fahmi's suggestion and the public debate that followed.

77. Hussein, *Mustaqbal al-Thaqafa*, 288–9.

78. Hussein, "Mushkilat al-Iʿrab," 93.

79. For example, Hussein criticized the Egyptianization of a French play, which he attended at the Opera House, because it was in colloquial Arabic. "I have to admit, that I grew very impatient with the story and the opera as soon as I heard part of the dialogue, for the entire performance was in the colloquial, and people know that I grow impatient with the colloquial when it is used as a tool for artistic creation, and I hate it if a writer depended on it unless there was an urgent need or absolute necessity." Taha Hussein, "Tamsir," TTH 1:407, originally published in *Majallati*, December 15, 1934.)

80. Hussein, *Mustaqbal al-Thaqafa*, 297–8.

81. Hussein, "Mushkilat al-Iʿrab," 90.

82. Ibid., 93.

83. Ibid., 94.

84. PP: Report draft from Taha Hussein to the president of the Egyptian University (n.d.).

85. PP: Report draft from Taha Hussein to the minister of public instruction (n.d.).

86. PP: Report draft (n.d.).

87. Hussein, "Mushkilat al-Iʿrab," 99.

88. Ibid., 100.

89. Taha Hussein, "Kitab Akhar ʿan Misr bi-Qalam al-Anisa Jann Arqash," *Majallati* 7 (March 1, 1935): 614.

90. Ibid., 614–5. Taha Hussein sent his own children, Amina and Moenis, to French schools in Cairo, and the shortage of schools at the time could have been a reason for that choice. Their mother, Suzanne, must have also preferred sending her children to French schools. In an interview I carried out in Cairo on October 20, 2013, with Taha Hussein's granddaughter, Sawsan, she explained to me that her grandmother Suzanne wanted to send Sawsan and her siblings to French schools, while Taha Hussein advised his daughter Amina to send them to public schools.

91. Ibid., 615.
92. PP: Report draft (n.d.).
93. PP: Report draft from Taha Hussein to the minister of public instruction (n.d.).
94. Hussein, *Mustaqbal al-Thaqafa*, 307.
95. Ibid., 308.
96. Hussein, "Mushkilat al-I'rab," 95.
97. Hussein, *Mustaqbal al-Thaqafa*, 313–5.
98. Ibid., 309–10.
99. Ibid., 306.
100. Hussein, "Mushkilat al-I'rab," 99.
101. Taha Hussein, *Hadith al-Arba'a'*, vol. 2 of *al-Majmu'a al-Kamila* (Beirut: Dar al-Kitab al-Lubnani, 1974), 15–6.
102. Ibid., 17.
103. Ibid., 20.
104. Hussein, *Mustaqbal al-Thaqafa*, 327–8.
105. Ibid., 331, 336.
106. Ibid., 360.
107. Ibid., 363–5.
108. Ibid., 366–7.
109. Hussein, "Mushkilat al-I'rab," 95. In the lecture transcript, "*Wa-la tas'aluni ana 'an taysir al-kitaba kaifa yakun*," is in a separate paragraph. Reading this line, I initially thought Hussein was excluding himself from the task because of his annoyance with how it was being handled. Most likely, however, he was referring subtly to his blindness.
110. "Taqrirat wa-Akhbar," *Majallat Majma' al-Lugha al-'Arabiyya* 9 (1957): 283–5.
111. Ibrahim Bayumi Madkur, *Majma' al-Lugha al-'Arabiyya fi Thalathin 'Aman, 1932-1962, Madih wa-Hadiruh* (Cairo: al-Matba'a al-Amiriyya, 1964), 87.
112. Hussein, "Mushkilat al-I'rab," 98.
113. Ibid. Abdulrazzak Patel refers to other serious attempts to simplify grammar that were also met with resistance: Jirmanus Farhat's *Bahth al-Matalib* (1707) and Faris al-Shidyaq's *Ghunyat al-Talib wa-Munyat al-Raghib* (1872); in the latter, the author offered abridgements of the classical grammar books. Patel also mentions the Andalusian scholar Ibn Madda' al-Qurtubi (d. 1194), who, in his book *al-Radd 'ala al-Nuha*, was the first to start what Patel describes as the "unpopular drive toward simplification of grammar." See Patel, *Arab Nahdah*, 108–9.
114. Hussein, "Mushkilat al-I'rab," 98–9.
115. Ibid., 99.
116. Hussein, *Mustaqbal al-Thaqafa*, 311.
117. PP: Report draft from Taha Hussein to the minister of public instruction (n.d.).
118. Ibid. In another report draft, to the undersecretary of the Ministry of Public Instruction, Hussein believed the modified and simplified Arabic language curriculum could be ready without delay for the school year 1935–1936, so we may assume the first report was written prior to 1935. PP: Report draft from Taha Hussein to the undersecretary of the minister of public instruction (n.d.).

119. Hussein, "Mushkilat al-Iʻrab," 102.

120. Ibrahim Bayumi Madkur, "al-Majmaʻ fi Rubʻ Qarn," *Majallat Majmaʻ al-Lugha al-ʻArabiyya* 15 (1962): 115–9; and "al-Majmaʻ fi Khidmat al-Lugha al-ʻArabiyya," *Majallat Majmaʻ al-Lugha al-ʻArabiyya* 22 (1967): 23–4.

121. Ibrahim Bayumi Madkur, "Taha Husayn Mukafihan," *Majallat Majmaʻ al-Lugha al-ʻArabiyya* 33 (May 1974): 256.

122. Ibrahim Bayumi Madkur, "Majmaʻ al-Lugha al-ʻArabiyya fi Ahad ʻAshar ʻAman," *Majallat Majmaʻ al-Lugha al-ʻArabiyya* 8 (1955): 12.

123. Ibid.

124. Ibid., 13.

125. Ibid.

126. Madkur, "Taha Husayn Mukafihan," 256.

127. Madkur, "Majmaʻ al-Lugha al-ʻArabiyya fi Ahad ʻAshar ʻAman," 15.

128. Madkur, "al-Majmaʻ fi Rubʻ Qarn," 115–9; and "al-Majmaʻ fi Khidmat al-Lugha al-ʻArabiyya," 23–4.

129. Madkur, "Taha Husayn Mukafihan," 256.

130. Madkur, "al-Majmaʻ fi Rubʻ Qarn," 115–9; and "al-Majmaʻ fi Khidmat al-Lugha al-ʻArabiyya," 23–4.

131. Ibid.

132. "Mudhakirra bi-Raʼi al-Maktab fi Ikhtiyar Muqarrir lil-Muʻjam al-Lughawi al-Kabir," *Majallat Majmaʻ al-Lugha al-ʻArabiyya* 7 (1953): 181–4. (For Arabic Language Academy session 14, October 6, 1947, to May 31, 1948.)

133. Madkur, "Taha Husayn Mukafihan," 256; "al-Majmaʻ fi Rubʻ Qarn," 115–9; and "al-Majmaʻ fi Khidmat al-Lugha al-ʻArabiyya," 23–4.

134. Hussein, *Mustaqbal al-Thaqafa*, 304.

135. Ibid., 308.

136. Haeri, *Sacred Language, Ordinary People*, 72.

137. Teaching classical Arabic in Egyptian schools remains a difficult endeavor. Haeri remarks: "Every time I asked about what specifically people found difficult [about grammar], they would give examples of problems with case endings. It is difficult to exaggerate Egyptians' attention to and fear of the case system. There is an ever present and an all-pervasive consciousness about them." Haeri, *Sacred Language, Ordinary People*, 42.

Chapter 5

1. Taha Hussein, "al-Adib Yaktub li-l-Khassa," *al-Adab* 5 (May 1955): 9.

2. Ahmad Zakariya al-Shalq, preface to TTH 6, 20.

3. Taha Hussein, "Sura," TTH 6:45, originally published in *al-Ahram*, August 2, 1952.

4. Ibid., 48.

5. Taha Hussein, "Min Baʻid," TTH 6:49, originally published in *al-Balagh*, August 5, 1952. My emphasis.

6. Ibid., 52.

7. Taha Hussein, "Nasayan al-Nafs," TTH 6:54, originally published in *al-Balagh*, August 25, 1952.

8. Ibid., 54. Muhammad Najib was Egypt's first president, in office from the declaration of the Republic on June 18, 1953, until he was placed under house arrest on November 14, 1954.

9. Taha Hussein, "Adab al-Thawra," in *Turath Taha Husayn: Al-Maqalat al-Sahafiyya min 1908–1967*, vol. 2 (Cairo: Matba'at Dar al-Kutub wa-l-Watha'iq al-Qawmiyya, 2007), 437, originally published in *al-Jumhuriyya*, October 23, 1954.

10. Taha Hussein, "Min Ba'id: Thawratuna," in TTH 6:128–9, originally published in *al-Jumhuriyya*, July 17, 1954.

11. Ibid., 129.

12. Ibid., 130.

13. Taha Hussein, "Min Ba'id: Thawratuna," in TTH 6:134, originally published in *al-Jumhuriyya*, August 1, 1954.

14. Taha Hussein, "Thawratuna min Ba'id," in TTH 6:123, originally published in *al-Jumhuriyya*, July 16, 1954.

15. Ibid., 127.

16. Taha Hussein, "Hazal wa-Jad," in TTH 6:65, originally published in *al-Ahram*, September 6, 1952.

17. Taha Hussein, "Thumma Madha?," in TTH 6:67, originally published in *al-Ahram*, December 13, 1952.

18. Ibid., 67–8.

19. Ibid., 69.

20. Ibid., 69–70.

21. Ibid., 69.

22. Taha Hussein, "Bayna al-Rida wa-l-Sukht," in TTH 6:72, originally published in *al-Ahram*, December 27, 1952.

23. Ibid., 73.

24. Taha Hussein, "Min Ba'id: Thawratuna," in TTH 6:115–6, originally published in *al-Jumhuriyya*, July 14, 1954.

25. Ibid., 115.

26. Al-Shalq, preface to TTH 6:35.

27. As Joel Gordon discusses, through this system of centralized mass parties, Nasser "refined a system that maintained rigid control of the polity behind a face of popular participation." Joel Gordon, *Nasser's Blessed Movement: Egypt's Free Officers and the July Revolution* (New York: Oxford University Press, 1992), 197.

28. Taha Hussein, "Batar," in TTH 6:249, originally published in *al-Jumhuriyya*, October 7, 1961.

29. The Revolutionary Council absolved Taha Hussein from appearing before the "Treachery Court," created in December 1952 to investigate corruption charges raised against former ministers and parliamentarians. Fu'ad Siraj al-Din, the Wafdist minister of interior, however, was sentenced to fifteen years in prison for collaborating with the palace and the British, while Mahmud Abu al-Fath, editor in chief of *al-Misri*, who

supported a return to civilian rule, was sentenced to ten years for "anti-revolutionary propaganda."

30. Ihsan 'Abd al-Quddus, *Ruz al-Yusuf*, February 7, 1955, 3, cited in Gordon, *Nasser's Blessed Movement*, 196.

31. Taha Hussein, "Bayna al-Jadd wa-l-La'ib," in TTH 6:186, originally published in *al-Jumhuriyya*, April 2, 1955; and "Kha'ifun Mukhawifun," in TTH 6:179–82, originally published in *al-Jumhuriyya*, March 30, 1955. The Baghdad Pact formed in 1955 committed the countries of Turkey, Iraq, Pakistan, Iran, and the United Kingdom to cooperation and mutual protection.

32. Taha Hussein, "Mawqif," in TTH 6:187, originally published in *al-Jumhuriyya*, May 7, 1955. Taking place in Bandung, Indonesia, in 1955, this conference brought together twenty-nine African and Asian countries, mostly newly independent, and was seen as an important step toward the creation of the Non-Aligned Movement.

33. Taha Hussein, "Mawqif," in TTH 6:205, originally published in *al-Jumhuriyya*, October 6, 1955.

34. Ibid., 206.

35. Taha Hussein, "Faransa wa-l-Islam," in TTH 6:146–7, originally published in *al-Jumhuriyya*, August 24, 1954.

36. Taha Hussein, "Ihtijaj," in TTH 6:150–3, originally published in *al-Jumhuriyya*, September 1, 1954.

37. Taha Hussein, "Wa-law," in TTH 6:156, originally published in *al-Jumhuriyya*, October 1, 1954.

38. Hussein, "Ihtijaj," 150–3.

39. Hussein, "Wa-law," 159.

40. Taha Hussein, "Iradat Sha'b," in TTH 6:222–4, originally published in *al-Jumhuriyya*, March 5, 1956.

41. Taha Hussein, "Lughatan," in TTH 6:234–7, originally published in *al-Jumhuriyya*, May 18, 1956.

42. Hussein, "Lughatan," 235.

43. AMAE/Relations Culturelles/1945–1961/431. 1948–1959/1948–1961: Letter from the chargé d'affaires of France to the Minister of Foreign Affairs Mendès France, "On the Subject of Taha Hussein's Article," November 26, 1954

44. AMAE/Relations Culturelles/1945–1961/431. 1948–1959/1948–1961: Letter from the French ambassador to the Minister of Foreign Affairs Antoine Pinay, "On the Subject of Taha Hussein's Article," October 7, 1955.

45. Hussein, "Lughatan," 234.

46. Ibid., 235.

47. Afaf Lutfi al-Sayyid Marsot, *Egypt's Liberal Experiment, 1922–1936* (Berkeley: University of California Press, 1977), 145.

48. Taha Hussein, "al-Hadith al-Mu'ad," in TTH 6:86, originally published in *al-Ahram*, May 1, 1953.

49. DWQ/MNW/0075–057873: Sessions of October and November 1951/Session of October 28, 1951.

50. Ibid.

51. DWQ/MNW/0075-057873: Sessions of October and November 1951/Session of November 8, 1951.

52. DWQ/MNW/0075-057873: Sessions of October and November 1951/Session of November 25, 1951. While several memoirs evoke the sudden disappearance of British and French teachers from Egyptian schools after the Suez Crisis, this shows that the first to use this measure was Taha Hussein. See for example, Leila Ahmed, *A Border Passage: From Cairo to America—A Woman's Journey* (New York: Farrar, Straus & Giroux, 1999); and Robert Solé, *L'Égypte Passion Française* (Paris: Éditions du Seuil, 1997).

53. DWQ/MNW/0075-057874: Sessions of December 1951/Session of December 9, 1951. It was also decided, upon the request of Taha Hussein, that the respective ministries would pay the cost of the relocation of the British teachers back to their country, in addition to three months of severance pay. Ibid.

54. DWQ/MNW/0075-057873: Sessions of October and November 1951/Session of November 25, 1951.

55. DWQ/MNW/0075-057874: Sessions of December 1951/Session of December 2, 1951.

56. DWQ/MNW/0075-057874: Sessions of December 1951/Session of December 23, 1951.

57. Haykal mentioned that more than 80 policemen were killed. See Muhammad Husayn Haykal, *Mudhakkirat fi al-Siyasa al-Misriyya*, vol. 2 (Cairo: Dar al-Ma'arif, 1990), 311. January 25 is celebrated annually as national police day. In 2011, decrying the police brutality of the postcolonial state, demonstrators went out on that day, and by February 11, they had put an end to Husni Mubarak's long reign (1981–2011).

58. DWQ/MNW/0075-057875: Sessions of January and February 1952/Session of January 26, 1952.

59. Hussein, "al-Hadith al-Mu'ad," 86–9.

60. Taha Hussein, "al-Yawm al-Maw'ud," in TTH 6:137, originally published in *al-Jumhuriyya*, August 6, 1954.

61. Ibid., 138–9.

62. Hussein, "Lughatan," 235.

63. Cynthia Nelson, *Doria Shafiq, Egyptian Feminist: A Woman Apart* (Gainesville: University Press of Florida, 1996), 196.

64. Ibid., 197, 200.

65. Ibid., 200.

66. "Prime Minister Meets with Shafiq," *al-Ahram*, March 14, 1954, cited in Nelson, *Doria Shafiq*, 199.

67. Nelson, *Doria Shafiq*, 204. Later, in February 1957, Shafiq went into the Indian Embassy in Cairo and declared she was going on another hunger strike in protest of the Israeli occupation of Egyptian land after the Suez Crisis in 1956, and she also demanded an end to what she described as Nasser's "dictatorial rule that is driving our country towards bankruptcy and chaos." After eleven days, she ended her fast. Nasser then placed her under house arrest, and the press was ordered not to mention her name again. See

Nelson, *Doria Shafik*, 238–50. Shafiq fell into a depression and committed suicide on September 20, 1975.

68. Taha Hussein, "'Abithat," *al-Jumhuriyya*, March 16, 1954. What followed was an intense debate, in which other intellectuals like Ahmad Baha' al-Din and Shafiq herself attacked Hussein, whom they had expected to support women's rights, given his previous support for women in general and women's university education in particular. See Ahmad Baha' al-Din, "al-Sa'imat," *Ruz al-Yusuf*, March 22, 1954; and Duriyya Shafiq, "Taha Husayn wa-'Aja'iz al-Farah," *Ruz al-Yusuf*, March 22, 1954. Ironically, it was Hussein who had made it possible for Shafiq to study philosophy at the Sorbonne in 1928. After she had registered to specialize in history and geography "as one of the branches of feminine education," she failed to convince the head of the educational mission in Paris that she preferred to study philosophy. She wrote to Hussein, then dean of arts, and asked for his help. "Within days, the director received a telegram from the Ministry of Education in Cairo advising him to change Doria's program at her pleasure." Nelson, *Doria Shafik*, 36.

69. Muhammad Hasanayn Haykal, *The Cairo Documents* (New York: Doubleday, 1973), 25.

70. Taha Hussein, "Fitna," in *Ha'ula' hum al-Ikhwan!!* (Cairo: 1954), 19–20.

71. Ibid., 20.

72. Taha Hussein, "'Ubbad al-Dhahab," in TTH 6 :249, originally published in *al-Jumhuriyya*, August 11, 1956.

73. Suzanne Taha Hussein, *Avec Toi: De la France à l'Égypte: "Un Extraordinaire Amour"; Suzanne et Taha Hussein (1915–1973)* (Paris: Les Éditions du Cerf, 2011), 216.

74. Taha Hussein, "Majnun," in TTH 6:256–7, originally published in *al-Jumhuriyya*, November 12, 1956.

75. The release of the Protocol of Sèvres revealed the collusion of Great Britain, France, and Israel against Egypt, and Hussein's qualification of the aggression as a "conspiracy" was indeed accurate. See Avi Shlaim, "The Protocol of Sèvres, 1956: The Anatomy of a World Plot," in *The 1956 War: Collusion and Rivalry in the Middle East*, ed. David Tal (London: Frank Cass, 2001): 119–43.

76. Taha Hussein, "Mu'amaratan," in TTH 6:259, originally published in *al-Jumhuriyya*, November 23, 1956.

77. Taha Hussein, "Ahl al-Kahf," in TTH 6:307, originally published in *al-Jumhuriyya*, March 26, 1958.

78. Sharif Yunis, *al-Zahf al-Muqaddas*, 2nd ed. (Beirut: Dar al-Tanwir, 2012), 105.

79. Muhammad Hasanayn Haykal, *Azmat al-Muthaqqafin: Nazra ila Mashakilina al-Dakhiliyya* (Cairo: Al-Sharika al-'Arabiyya al-Muttahida li-l-Tawzi', 1961), 48–9.

80. Ibid., 50.

81. Ibid., 16–9.

82. Ibid., 24–5.

83. Ibid., 40–1.

84. Ibid., 65.

85. Ibid., 76.

86. Ibid., 85–6.

Notes to Chapter 5

87. Gamal Abdel Nasser, *Falsafat al-Thawra wa-l-Mithaq* (Beirut: Dar al-Qalam, 1970), 31–2.
88. Ibid., 222–3.
89. Ibid., 144–5.
90. Ibid., 147.
91. Ibid., 148–50.
92. Taha Hussein, "Juhd Ha'il," in TTH 6:363, originally published in *al-Jumhuriyya*, May 26, 1962.
93. Al-Shalq, preface to TTH 6:22.
94. See Tariq al-Bishri, *al-Dimuqratiyya wa-Nizam Thalatha wa-'Ishrin Yuliu: 1952–1970* (Beirut: Mu'assassat al-Abhath al-'Arabiyya, 1987), 98.
95. Ibid., 103. Al-Bishri explains that he was able to find a typewritten copy of the constitution in the library of the Institute of Arab Studies (Ma'had al-Dirasat al-'Arabiyya).
96. Ibid., 98.
97. Ibid., 98–9.
98. Ibid., 101.
99. Ibid., 99.
100. Ibid., 102.
101. Ibid., 98.
102. Hussein, "Juhd Ha'il," 363–4.
103. Abdel Nasser, *Falsafat al-Thawra wa-l-Mithaq*, 162; and al-Shalq, preface to TTH 6:37.
104. Taha Hussein, "Yawm al-Thawra," in TTH 6:365–70, originally published in *al-Jumhuriyya*, August 19, 1962.
105. According to al-Shalq, Hussein was deeply hurt by the decision, especially by the way he was informed of his dismissal after eleven years of writing regularly for *al-Jumhuriyya*. Al-Shalq, preface to TTH 6:26.
106. Yunis, *al-Zahf al-Muqaddas*, 59. For a similar discussion on Nasser's institutional control of writers and intellectuals, see Richard Jacquemond, *Entre Scribes et Écrivains: Le Champs Littéraire dans l'Égypte Contemporaine* (Paris: Sindbad/Actes Sud, 2003), 31–2.
107. Ibid., 60.
108. Ibid.
109. For more on Arab existentialism and Arab intellectuals' engagement with Jean-Paul Sartre and his ideas in their pursuit of intellectual decolonization in the 1950s and '60s see Yoav Di-Capua's extensive analysis in his recent *No Exit: Arab Existentialism, Jean-Paul Sartre and Decolonization* (Chicago: The University of Chicago Press, 2018).
110. Jacquemond, *Entre Scribes et Écrivains*, 203–6.
111. Mahmud Amin al-'Alim, introduction to *Fi al-Thaqafa al-Misriyya*, by Mahmud Amin al-'Alim and 'Abd al-'Azim Anis, 3rd ed. (Cairo: Dar al-Thaqafa al-Jadida, 1989), 16–7. Al-'Alim taught philosophy, while Anis taught mathematics.
112. Husayn Muruwwa, preface to *Fi al-Thaqafa al-Misriyya*, by al-'Alim and Anis, 3–5.

113. Al-ʿAlim and Anis, *Fi al-Thaqafa al-Misriyya*, 31.
114. Ibid., 44.
115. Ibid., 49.
116. Ibid., 39.
117. Ibid., 111.
118. Ibid., 66.
119. Ibid., 61.
120. Taha Hussein, "Yunani fala Yuqra'," *al-Jumhuriyya*, March 5, 1954, cited in al-ʿAlim and Anis, *Fi al-Thaqafa al-Misriyya*, 55.
121. Suhayl Idris, "Risalat al-Adab," *al-Adab* 1 (January 1953): 1.
122. Ra'if Khuri, "al-Adib Yaktub li-l-Kaffa," *al-Adab* 5 (May 1955): 2.
123. Ibid., 4–5.
124. Ibid., 5.
125. Ibid., 6–7.
126. In reference to Jean-Paul Sartre and his writings on committed literature.
127. Hussein, "al-Adib Yaktub li-l-Khassa," 9.
128. Ibid., 12.
129. Ibid., 13.
130. Ibid., 13–4.
131. Ibid., 14–5.
132. Hussein, "Adab al-Thawra," 437.
133. Ibid., 440–1.
134. Taha Hussein, "As'ila," in TTH 6:659, originally published in *al-Jumhuriyya*, February 28, 1956.
135. Ibid., 660.
136. Ibid., 661.
137. Ibid., 662–4.
138. Ibid., 664.
139. Hussein, "al-Adib Yaktub li-l-Khassa," 15.
140. Ahmad Abu Haqa, *al-Iltizam fi al-Shiʿr al-ʿArabi* (Beirut: Dar al-ʿIlm li-l-Malayin, 1979), 361–2.
141. Di-Capua, *No Exit*, 77–107.
142. "Al-Duktur Taha Husayn Yatahaddath ila al-Jumhuriyya," *al-Jumhuriyya*, March 14, 1967, 12, cited in Di-Capua, *No Exit*, 200.
143. Taha Hussein, "al-Adab bayna al-Ittisal wa-l-Infisal," *al-Katib al-Misri*, August 1946, 373–88.
144. Taha Hussein discussed these ideas in "ʿId," *al-Balagh*, August 26, 1945; "Junun," *al-Musawwar*, May 23, 1947; "al-Qalaq al-Khatar," *Musamarat al-Jayb*, December 21, 1947; "al-Thawb al-Dayyiq," *al-Musawwar*, January 9, 1948; "Azma," *al-Musawwar*, February 20, 1948; and "Junud al-Shaytan," *al-Musawwar*, January 12, 1949.
145. Di-Capua, *No Exit*, 252.
146. Nasser died on September 28, 1970.
147. The Order of the Nile is Egypt's highest state honor, awarded in recognition of

exceptional services to the country. Nasser decorated Taha Hussein on the Day of Science (*id al-ʿilm*), December 21, in 1965.

148. Taha Hussein, "Raʾis al-Majmaʿ Yuʾabbin al-Rahil al-ʿAzim," *Majallat Majmaʿ al-Lugha al-ʿArabiyya* 27 (1971): 254–5. In the wake of Egypt's dramatic defeat in 1967, Israel captured the Sinai Peninsula, the Golan Heights, the Gaza Strip, the West Bank, and Old Jerusalem. On June 9, Nasser admitted the defeat, took full responsibility for it, and resigned. After massive demonstrations in Egypt and the Arab world calling for his reinstatement, he retracted his resignation.

Conclusion

1. Taha Hussein, "Katib wa Qissa," interview by Samira al-Kilani, *al-Tilifizyun al-ʿArabi*, 1970, last accessed July 23, 2020, https://www.youtube.com/watch?v=6W4YhZonH-8.

2. Mahmud Amin al-ʿAlim, "Taha Husayn Mufakirran," in *Taha Husayn kama Yaʿrifuhu Kuttab ʿAsrihi*, ed. Ibrahim al-Ibyari et al. (Cairo: Dar al-Hilal, [1968?]), 122–3.

3. Ibid., 130, 124.

4. Ibid., 134.

5. For Hussein's critique of al-Azhar, see for example, *The Days*, vol. 3, trans. Kenneth Cragg (Cairo: American University in Cairo, 2001), 248; and *Mustaqbal al-Thaqafa fi Misr*, vol. 9 of *al-Majmuʿa al-Kamila* (Beirut: Dar al-Kitab al-Lubnani, 1974), 366–7.

6. Taha Hussein, preface to *al-Azhar wa-Atharuhu fi al-Nahda al-Adabiyya al-Haditha*, by Muhammad Kamil al-Fiqi (Cairo: Al-Matbaʿa al-Muniriyya bi-l-Azhar, 1956), vii (*zay*).

7. Luwis ʿAwad, *Aqniʿat al-Nasiriyya al-Sabʿa: Munaqashat Tawfiq al-Hakim wa-Muhammad Hasanayn Haykal* (Cairo: Markaz al-Mahrusa, 2014 [1976]), 120.

8. Ghali Shukri considers that Hussein's and Muhammad Husayn Haykal's Islamic writings in the 1930s signaled the end of attempts by the "liberal bourgeois democracy" to achieve the objectives of the 1919 revolution. Shukri, *Madha Yabqa min Taha Husayn?*, 24. See also Mahmud Amin al-ʿAlim and ʿAbd al-ʿAzim Anis, *Fi al-Thaqafa al-Misriyya*, 3rd ed. (Cairo: Dar al-Thaqafa al-Jadida, 1989), 109–10. Historian Israel Gershoni has written about the Orientalist "crisis narrative" when H.A.R. Gibb and other Orientalists were furious with Hussein and Haykal for writing on Islamic topics in the 1930s, seeing it as a serious relapse in their commitment to rational and liberal principles. Albert Hourani refused to accept that the Islamiyyat were a setback, and supported Hussein's biographer Pierre Cachia in his interpretation that Hussein wished to rewrite aspects of the Islamic tradition in a way that appealed to the sensibility of modern readers, Israel Gershoni, "The Theory of Crisis and the Crisis in a Theory: Intellectual History in Twentieth-Century Middle Eastern Studies," in *Middle East Historiographies: Narrating the Twentieth Century*, ed. Israel Gershoni, Amy Singer, and Hakan Erdem (Seattle: University of Washington Press, 2006): 131–82.

9. Omnia El Shakry, *The Great Social Laboratory: Subjects of Knowledge in Colonial and Postcolonial Egypt* (Stanford, CA: Stanford University Press, 2007), 5, 19.

10. Shukri, *Madha Yabqa min Taha Husayn?*, 72.
11. Ibid., 74.
12. Elizabeth Suzanne Kassab, *Enlightenment on the Eve of Revolution: The Egyptian and Syrian Debates* (New York: Columbia University Press, 2019), 109–10.
13. Ibid., 111.

BIBLIOGRAPHY

Archives and Libraries

CAIRO—EGYPT

The Egyptian National Archives—Dar al-Watha'iq al-Qawmiyya bi-l-Qahira (DWQ)
    Abdin Archival Unit (Abdin 0069)
    Majlis al-Nuzzar wa-l-Wuzara' (Council of Ministers) Archival Unit (MNW 0075)
    Ri'asat Majlis al-Wuzara' (Prime Minister's Office) Archival Unit (RMW 0081)
The Egyptian Registry and Property Records Archive—Dar al-Mahfuzat al-'Umumiyya (DMZ)
Cairo University—Archives of the Faculty of Arts
Taha Hussein Private Papers (PP)
The Egyptian National Library—Dar al-Kutub
Cairo University Central Library
The American University in Cairo Library
The Library of the Dominican Institute for Oriental Studies

PARIS—FRANCE
Archives du Ministère des Affaires Étrangères—(AMAE)
La Bibliothèque Nationale de France
La Bibliothèque Sainte-Geneviève

Periodicals
Al-Adab
Al-Ahram
Al-Akhbar
Al-Assas
Al-Balagh
Un Effort
Al-Hilal
Images
Al-Jumhuriyya
Al-Katib al-Misri
Kawkab al-Sharq

Kul Shayʾ wa-l-Dunya
Majallati
Majallat Majmaʿ al-Lugha al-ʿArabiyya
Al-Misri
Al-Muʾayyad
Al-Mujallad
Al-Muqtataf
Musamarat al-Jayb
Al-Musawwar
Al-Nidaʾ
Al-Risala
Ruz al-Yusuf
Al-Siyasa
Al-Thaqafa
Al-Wafd al-Misri
Watan

Select Works by Taha Hussein

AL-MAJMUʿA AL-KAMILA, "THE BOOKS COLLECTION" (BEIRUT: 1974)

Husayn, Taha. *Al-Majmuʿa al-Kamila li-Muʾallafat al-Duktur Taha Husayn*. 16 vols. Beirut: Dar al-Kitab al-Lubnani, 1974.

Titles in this collection.

    Adib. 1935. Vol. 12, no. 2 of *al-Majmuʿa al-Kamila*.
    Ahadith. 1959. Vol. 12, no. 2 of *al-Majmuʿa al-Kamila*.
    Ahlam Shahrazd. 1943. Vol. 14, no. 2 of *al-Majmuʿa al-Kamila*.
    ʿAla Hamish al-Sira. 3 vols. 1933, 1937, 1938. Vol. 3 of *al-Majmuʿa al-Kamila*.
    Alwan. 1952. Vol. 6 of *al-Majmuʿa al-Kamila*.
    Al-Ayyam. 3 vols. 1929, 1940, 1967. Vol. 1 of *al-Majmuʿa al-Kamila*.
    Bayna Bayna. 1953. Vol. 14, no. 2 of *al-Majmuʿa al-Kamila*.
    Duʿaʾ al-Karawan. 1934. Vol. 13, no. 2 of *al-Majmuʿa al-Kamila*.
    Falsafat ibn Khaldun al-Ijtimaʿiyya. 1925. Vol. 8 of *al-Majmuʿa al-Kamila*.
    Fi al-Adab al-Jahili. 1927. Vol. 5 of *al-Majmuʿa al-Kamila*.
    Al-Fitna al-Kubra. 2 vols. 1952, 1961. Vol. 4 of *al-Majmuʿa al-Kamila*.
    Fusul fi al-Adab wa-l-Naqd. 1945. Vol. 5 of *al-Majmuʿa al-Kamila*.
    Hadith al-Arabaʿaʾ. 3 vols. 1925, 1926, 1945. Vol. 2 of *al-Majmuʿa al-Kamila*.
    Hafiz wa-Shawqi. 1933. Vol. 12, no. 1 of *al-Majmuʿa al-Kamila*.
    Al-Hubb al-Daʾiʿ. 1942. Vol. 13, no. 2 of *al-Majmuʿa al-Kamila*.
    Jannat al-Hayawan. 1950. Vol. 13, no. 1 of *al-Majmuʿa al-Kamila*.
    Jannat al-Shawk. 1945. Vol. 11 of *al-Majmuʿa al-Kamila*.
    Khisam wa-Naqd. 1955. Vol. 11 of *al-Majmuʿa al-Kamila*.
    Kutub wa-Muʾalifun. 1980. Vol. 16 of *al-Majmuʿa al-Kamila*.
    Lahazat. 2 vols. 1942. Vol. 11 of *al-Majmuʿa al-Kamila*.

Ma'a Abi al-'Ala' fi Sijnih. 1939. Vol. 10 of *al-Majmu'a al-Kamila*.
Ma'a al-Mutanabbi. 2 vols. 1936. Vol. 6 *al-Majmu'a al-Kamila*.
Min Ba'id. 1935. Vol. 12, no. 1 of *al-Majmu'a al-Kamila*.
Min Hadith al-Shi'r wa-l-Nathr. 1936. Vol. 5 of *al-Majmu'a al-Kamila*.
Min Laghu al-Sayf ila Jadd al-Shita'. 1959. Vol. 14, no. 2 of *al-Majmu'a al-Kamila*.
Mir'at al-Damir al-Hadith. 1949. Vol. 11 of *al-Majmu'a al-Kamila*.
Mir'at al-Islam. 1959. Vol. 7 of *al-Majmu'a al-Kamila*.
Al-Mu'adhabun fi al-Ard. 1949. Vol. 12, no.2 of *al-Majmu'a al-Kamila*.
Mustaqbal al-Thaqafa fi Misr. 1938. Vol. 9 of *al-Majmu'a al-Kamila*.
Nizam al-Athiniyyin. 1921. Vol. 8 of *al-Majmu'a al-Kamila*.
Qadat al-Fikr. 1925. Vol. 8 of *al-Majmu'a al-Kamila*.
Al-Qasr al-Mashur. 1936. Vol. 14, no. 1 of *al-Majmu'a al-Kamila*.
Sawt Abi al-'Ala'. 1944. Vol. 10 of *al-Majmu'a al-Kamila*.
Sawt Baris. 2 vols. 1943. Vol. 13, no. 1 of *al-Majmu'a al-Kamila*.
Shajarat al-Bu's. 1943. Vol. 13, no. 2 of *al-Majmu'a al-Kamila*.
Al-Shaykhan. 1960. Vol. 4 of *al-Majmu'a al-Kamila*.
Tajdid Dhikra Abi al-'Ala'. 1915. Vol. 4 of *al-Majmu'a al-Kamila*.
Al-Wa'd al-Haqq. 1950. Vol. 7 of *al-Majmu'a al-Kamila*.

TURATH TAHA HUSAYN, "THE ARTICLES COLLECTION" (CAIRO: 2003-2010)

Husayn, Taha. *Turath Taha Husayn: Al-Maqalat al-Sahafiyya min 1908 ila 1967*. 6 vols. Cairo: Matba'at Dar al-Kutub wa-l-Watha'iq al-Qawmiyya, 2003-2010.
Titles in this collection.
Al-Ta'lim. Vol. 1 of *Turath Taha Husayn*, 2010.
Al-Islamiyyat. Vol. 2 of *Turath Taha Husayn*, 2006.
Al-Siyasa al-Misriyya. Vol. 3 of *Turath Taha Husayn*, 2004.
Azmat al-Nizam al-Siyasi al-Misri. Vol. 4 of *Turath Taha Husayn*, 2003.
Maqalat al-Arba'iniyyat. Vol. 5 of *Turath Taha Husayn*, 2005.
Thawrat Yuliu. Vol. 6 of *Turath Taha Husayn*, 2006.

OTHER WORKS

Husayn, Taha. *Ara' Hurra*. Cairo: Al-Matba'a al-'Asriyya, n.d.
———. *Au-delà du Nil*. Edited by Jacques Berque. Translated by Michel Hayek et al. Paris: Gallimard, 1977.
———. *The Days*. Translated by E. H. Paxton, Hilary Wayment, and Kenneth Cragg, 3 vols. Cairo: American University Press, 1987.
———. "L'Écrivain dans la Société Moderne." In *L'Artiste dans la Société Contemporaine: Témoignages Recueillis par l'UNESCO*. Paris: UNESCO, 1954.
———. *Étude Analytique et Critique de la Philosophie Sociale d'Ibn Khaldoun*. Paris: 1917.
———. "La Grande Figure du Cheikh Mohammed Abdo." *Un Effort* (June 1934): 3-5.
———. *Le Livre des Jours*. Paris: Gallimard, 1984.

———. "Kitab Akhar 'an Misr." *Majallati* 7 (March 1, 1935): 613–20.
———. *Min al-Shati' al-Akhar: Kitabat Taha Husayn al-Firinsiyya*. Edited by Abdelrashid Mahmoudi. Cairo: Al-Markaz al-Qawmi li-l-Tarjama, 2008.
———. "La Renaissance Poétique de l'Irak au Ie Siècle de l'Hégire." *Bulletin de l'Institut d'Égypte* 34 (1941–1942): 90–106.
———. *Taqlid wa-Tajdid*. Beirut: Dar al-'Ilm li-l-Malayin, 1978.
———. "Tendances Religieuses de la Littérature Égyptienne d'Aujourd'hui." *Cahiers du Sud* (1947): 235–41.

Select Works on Taha Hussein

'Abd al-Ghani, Mustafa. *Taha Husayn kama lam Ya'rifuhu Ahad*. Cairo: Dar al-'Alam al-'Arabi, 2010.
———. *Taha Husayn wa-l-Siyasa*. Cairo: Dar al-Mustaqbal al-'Arabi, 1986.
———. *Taha Husayn wa-Thawrat Yuliu: Su'ud al-Muthaqqaf wa-Suqutuh*. Cairo: Maktabat al-Turath al-Islami, 1989.
'Abd al-Hadi, Jamal, Wafa' Muhammad Rif'at, and 'Ali Ahmad Labn. *Al-Zur wa-l-Buhtan fima Katabuh Taha Husayn fi al-Shaykhan wa-Mu'alafat Ukhra Lahu*. Cairo: Dar al-Nashr wa-l-Tawzi' al-Islamiyya, 1991.
Awad, Mahmud. *Taha Husayn*. Cairo: Dar al-Ma'arif, 1980.
Badawi, 'Abd al-Rahmn. *Ila Taha Husayn fi 'Id Miladih al-Sab'in: Dirasat Muhdah min Asdiqa'ih wa-Talamidhih*. Cairo: Dar al-Ma'arif, 1962.
Buhasan, Ahmad. *Al-Khitab al-Naqdi 'inda Taha Husayn*. Beirut: Dar al-Tanwir, 1985.
Cachia, Pierre. *Taha Husayn: His Place in the Egyptian Literary Renaissance*. London: Luzac, 1956.
Dusuqi, Muhammad al-Sayyid. *Ayyam ma'a Taha Husayn*. Beirut: Al-Mu'assassa al-'Arabiyya li-l-Dirasat wa-l-Nashr, 1978.
Francis, Raymond. *Taha Hussein Romancier*. Cairo: Dar al-Ma'arif, 1945.
Al-Hamami, Muniya. "Munaqashat." In *Waqa'i' al-Multaqa al-Qawmi: Al-Tafkir al-Islahi al-'Arabi; Khasa'isahu wa-Hududahu; Khayr al-Din, Muhammad al-Bairam, Taha Husayn*. Tunis: Manshurat al-Ma'had al-Qawmi li-'Ulum al-Tarbiyya, 1991.
Hamdi, Muhi al-Din. "Al-'Ilm wa-l-Din fi Tafkir Taha Husayn." In *Waqa'i' al-Multaqa al-Qawmi: Al-Tafkir al-Islahi al-'Arabi; Khasa'isahu wa-Hududahu; Khayr al-Din, Muhammad al-Bairam, Taha Husayn*. Tunis: Manshurat al-Ma'had al-Qawmi li-'Ulum al-Tarbiyya, 1991.
Hannura, Misri. *Taha Husayn wa-Sikulujiyyat al-Mukhalafa*. Cairo: Dar Gharib, 2006.
Al-Ibyari, Ibrahim et al. *Taha Husayn kama Ya'rifuhu Kuttab 'Asrihi*. Cairo: Dar al-Hilal, [1968?].
Al-Istanbuli, Mahmud. *Taha Husayn fi Mizan al-'Ulama' wa-l-Udaba'*. Beirut: Al-Matkab al-Islami, 1983.
Al-Jindi, Anwar. *Muhakamat Fikr Taha Husayn*. Cairo: Dar al-I'tisam, 1984.
Al-Jumni, 'Umar. *Taha Husayn Mu'arrikhan*. Cairo: Al-Hay'a al-Misriyya al-'Amma li-l-Kitab, 2013.
Karru, Abu al-Qasim Muhammad. *Taha Husayn wa-l-Maghrib al-'Arabi*. Tunis: Mu'assassat Ibn 'Abdalla li-l-Nashr wa-l-Tawzi', 2001.

Al-Kashif, Muhammad Sadiq. *Taha Husayn Basiran*. Cairo: Maktabat al-Khanji, 1987.
Kayyali, Sami. *Maʿa Taha Husayn*. Cairo: Dar al-Maʿarif, 1952, 1968.
Kilani, Muhammad Sayyid. *Taha Husayn al-Shaʿir al-Katib*. Cairo: Dar al-Qawmiyya al-ʿArabiyya li-l-Tibaʿa, 1963.
Kurayyim, Samih. *Taha Husayn fi Maʿarikihi al-Adabiyya wa-l-Fikriyya*. Cairo: Majallat al-Idhaʿa wa-l-Tilifizyun, 1974.
Louca, Anouar. *L'autre Égypte: De Bonaparte à Taha Hussein*. Cairo: Institut Français d'Archéologie Orientale, 2006.
———. "Taha Hussein et l'Occident." *Cultures* 2 (1975): 118–42.
Louca, Leila. "Le Discours Autobiographique de Taha Hussein selon la Clôture du *Livre des Jours*." *Arabica* 39, no. 3 (1992): 346–57.
Mahmoudi, Abdelrashid. *Taha Husain's Education from the Azhar to the Sorbonne*. Richmond, Surrey: Curzon Press, 1998.
Mahran, Rashida. *Taha Husayn bayna al-Sira wa-l-Tarjama al-Dhatiyya*. Alexandria: Al-Hayʾa al-Misriyya al-ʿAmma li-l-Kitab, 1979.
Mallakh, Kamal. *Taha Husayn: Qahir al-Zalam*. Cairo: Dar al-Kitab al-Jadid, 1973.
Malti-Douglas, Fedwa. *Blindness and Autobiography: Al-Ayyam of Taha Husayn*. Princeton, NJ: Princeton University Press, 1988.
Al-Marakishi, Muhammad Salih. "Al-Masʿala al-Tarbawiyya wa-l-Thaqafiyya min Khilal Kitab Taha Husayn: *Mustaqbal al-Thaqafa fi Misr*." In *Waqaʾiʿ al-Multaqa al-Qawmi: Al-Tafkir al-Islahi al-ʿArabi; Khasaʾisahu wa-Hududahu; Khayr al-Din, Muhammad al-Bairam, Taha Husayn*. Tunis: Manshurat al-Maʿhad al-Qawmi li-ʿUlum al-Tarbiyya, 1991.
Mughith, Kamal Hamid. *Taha Husayn*. Cairo: Markaz al-Dirasat wa-l-Maʿlumat al-Qanuniyya li-Huquq al-Insan, 1997.
Al-Muhtasib, ʿAbd al-Majid. *Taha Husayn Mufakirran*. Amman: Maktabat al-Nahda al-Islamiyya, 1980.
Qabbani, ʿAbd al-ʿAlim. *Taha Husayn fi al-Duha min Shababih 1908–1913*. Cairo: Al-Hayʾa al-Misriyya al-ʿAmma li-l-Kitab, 1976.
Qalamawi, Suhayr. *Dhikra Taha Husayn*. Cairo: Dar al-Maʿarif, 1974.
Al-Qarquri, Rashid. *Taha Husayn: Mufakirran Siyasiyyan*. Tunis: Dar al-Maʿarif li-l-Tibaʿa wa-l-Nashr, 2000.
Qulta, Kamal. *Taha Husayn wa-Athar al-Thaqafa al-Firinsiyya fi Adabih*. Cairo: Dar al-Maʿarif, 1973.
Rizq, Jabir, ed. *Taha Husayn: Al-Jarima wa-l-Idana*. Cairo: Dar al-Iʿtisam, 1985.
Al-Sakkut, Hamdi, and Marsden Jones. *Aʿlam al-Adab al-Muʿasir fi Misr: Taha Husayn*. Cairo: Markaz al-Dirasat al-ʿArabiyya bi-l-Jamiʿa al-Amrikiyya, 1982.
Al-Samra, Mahmud. *Sariq al-Nar*. Beirut: Al-Muʾassassa al-ʿArabiyya li-l-Dirasat wa-l-Nashr, 2004.
Al-Shalq, Ahmad Zakariya. *Taha Husayn: Jadal al-Fikr wa-l-Siyasa*. Cairo: Al-Hayʾa al-Misriyya al-ʿAmma li-l-Kitab, 2009.
Sharaf, ʿAbd al-ʿAziz. *Taha Husayn wa-Zawal al-Mujtamaʿ al-Taqlidi*. Cairo: Al-Hayʾa al-Misriyya al-ʿAmma li-l-Kitab, 1977.

Al-Shimli, Munji, 'Umar al-Jumni, and Rashid al-Qarquri, eds. *Sultat al-Kalima: Masalik li-Dirasat Adab Taha Husayn wa-Fikrih*. Tunis: Markaz al-Nashr al-Jami'i, 2001.

Al-Shimli, Munji, and 'Umar al-Jumni, eds. *Taha Husayn fi Mir'at al-'Asr: Shahadat wa-Dirasat*. Tunis: Al-Majma' al-Tunisi li-l-'Ulum wa-l-Adab wa-l-Funun, 2001.

Shukri, Ghali. *Madha Yabqa min Taha Husayn?* Beirut: Dar al-Mutawassit, 1974.

Taha Hussein, Suzanne. *Avec Toi: De la France à l'Égypte: "Un Extraordinaire Amour"; Suzanne et Taha Hussein (1915–1973)*. Paris: Les Éditions du Cerf, 2011.

Tahar, Meftah. *Taha Husayn: Sa Critique littéraire et Ses Sources Françaises*. Tunis: Maison Arabe du Livre, 1982.

'Ulabi, Ahmad. *Taha Husayn: Sirat Mukafih 'Anid*. Beirut : Dar al-Farabi, 1990.

'Umar, Najah. *Taha Husayn: Ayyam wa-Ma'arik*. Beirut: Al-Maktaba al-'Asriyya, 1970.

'Usfur, Jabir. *Al-Maraya al-Mutajawira: Dirasa fi Naqd Taha Husayn*. Cairo: Al-Hay'a al-Misriyya al-'Amma li-l-Kitab, 1983.

Zahran, al-Badrawi. *Uslub Taha Husayn fi Daw' al-Dars al-Lughawi al-Hadith*. Cairo: Dar al-Ma'arif, 1982.

Al-Zayyat, Muhammad Hasan. *Ma Ba'da al-Ayyam*. Cairo: Dar al-Hilal, 1986.

Other Sources

'Abbas, Ra'uf. *Al-Ahzab al-Misriyya 1922–1953*. Cairo: Al-Ahram, Markaz al-Dirasat al-Siyasiyya wa-l-Istiratijiyya, 1995.

———, ed. *Arba'un 'Aman 'ala Thawrat Yuliu: Dirasa Tarikhiyya*. Cairo: Al-Ahram, Markaz al-Dirasat al-Siyasiyya wa-l-Istiratijiyya, 1992.

'Abd al-Dayim, Yahya Ibrahim. *Al-Tarjama al-Dhatiyya fi al-Adab al-'Arabi al-Hadith*. Cairo: Maktabat al-Nahda al-Misriyya, 1975.

Abdalla, Ahmed. *The Student Movement and National Politics in Egypt: 1923–1973*. London: Al Saqi Books, 1985.

Abdel-Malek, Anouar. *L'Égypte Moderne: Idéologie et Renaissance Nationale*. Paris: L'Harmattan, 2004.

Abdel Nasser, Gamal. *Falsafat al-Thawra wa-l-Mithaq*. Beirut: Dar al-Qalam, 1970.

Abou-El-Fadl, Reem. "Early Pan-Arabism in Egypt's July Revolution: The Free Officers' Political Formation and Policy-Making, 1946–54." *Nations and Nationalism* 21, no. 2 (2015): 289–308.

Abu Haqa, Ahmad. *Al-Iltizam fi al-Shi'r al-'Arabi*. Beirut: Dar al-'Ilm li-l-Malayin, 1979.

Abu-Rabi', Ibrahim M. *Contemporary Arab Thought: Studies in Post-1967 Arab Intellectual History*. London: Pluto Press, 2004.

———. *Intellectual Origins of Islamic Resurgence in the Modern Arab World*. Albany: State University of New York Press, 1996.

Abulafia, David. "Mediterranean History as Global History." *History and Theory* 50, no. 2 (May 2011): 220–8.

Ahmed, Leila. *A Border Passage: From Cairo to America—A Woman's Journey*. New York: Farrar, Straus & Giroux, 1999.

———. *Women and Gender in Islam: Historical Roots of a Modern Debate*. New Haven, CT: Yale University Press, 1992.
Al-ʿAlim, Mahmud Amin, and ʿAbd al-Azim Anis. *Fi al-Thaqafa al-Misriyya*. 3rd ed. Cairo: Dar al-Thaqafa al-Jadida, 1989.
Ali, Samer. *Arabic Literary Salons in the Islamic Middle Ages: Poetry, Public Performance, and the Presentation of the Past*. Notre Dame, Ind.: University of Notre Dame Press, 2010.
Allen, Roger. *The Arabic Novel: An Historical and Critical Introduction*. Syracuse, NY: Syracuse University Press, 1995.
Amin, Ahmad. *Hayati*. Cairo: Dar Maktabat al-Nahda al-Misriyya, 1978.
Armbrust, Walter. *Mass Culture and Modernism in Egypt*. Cambridge: Cambridge University Press, 1996.
Artin, Yacoub. *Considérations sur l'Instruction Publique en Égypte*. Paris, 1894.
ʿAwad, Luwis. *Aqniʿat al-Nasiriyya al-Sabʿa: Munaqashat Tawfiq al-Hakim wa-Muhammad Hasanayn Haykal*. Cairo: Markaz al-Mahrusa, 2014 [1976].
———. *Al-Huriyya wa-Naqd al-Huriyya*. Cairo: Al-Hayʾa al-ʿAmma li-l-Taʾlif wa-l-Nashr, 1971.
———. *Muqadimma fi Fiqh al-Lugha al-ʿArabiyya*. 1980. Cairo: Ruʾya li-l-Nashr wa-l-Tawziʿ, 2006.
Ayalon, Ami. *The Press in the Arab Middle East: A History*. New York: Oxford University Press, 1995.
Badawi, Jamal, and Lamʿi al-Mutaiʿi, eds. *Tarikh al-Wafd*. Cairo: Dar al-Shuruq, 2010.
Badawi, Muhammad. *Al-Riwaya al-Jadida fi Misr: Dirasa, al-Tashkil wa-l-Idiyulujiyya*. Beirut: Al-Muʾassassa al-Jamiʿiyya li-l-Dirasat wa-l-Nashr wa-l-Tawziʿ, 1993.
Badawi, Mustafa. *A Short History of Modern Arabic Literature*. Oxford: Clarendon Press, 1993.
Badawi, Zaki. *The Reformers of Egypt: A Critique of al-Afghani, ʿAbduh, and Ridha*. Slough: Open Press, 1976.
Badr, ʿAbd al-Muhsin Taha. *Tatawwur al-Riwaya al-ʿArabiyya al-Haditha fi Misr 1870–1938*. Cairo: Dar al-Maʿarif, 1963.
Badrawi, Malak. *Political Violence in Egypt 1910–1924: Secret Societies, Plots, Assassinations*. Richmond, UK: Curzon Press, 2000.
Banner, Lois. "AHR Roundtable: Biography as History." *American Historical Review* 114, no. 3 (June 2009): 579–86.
Baraka, Magda. *The Egyptian Upper Class between Revolutions, 1919–1952*. Reading: Ithaca Press, 1998.
Baron, Beth. *Egypt as a Woman: Nationalism, Gender, and Politics*. Berkeley: University of California Press, 2005.
———. *The Orphan Scandal: Christian Missionaries and the Rise of the Muslim Brotherhood*. Stanford, CA: Stanford University Press, 2014.
———. *The Women's Awakening in Egypt: Culture, Society, and the Press*. London: Yale University Press, 1994.

Beinin, Joel, and Zachary Lockman. *Workers on the Nile: Nationalism, Communism, Islam and the Egyptian Working Class, 1882–1954*. London: I. B. Tauris, 1988.

Booth, Marilyn. *May Her Likes Be Multiplied: Biography and Gender Politics in Egypt*. Berkeley: University of California Press, 2001.

Al-Biqa'i, Shafiq. *Adab 'Asr al-Nahda*. Beirut: Dar al-'Ilm li-l-Malayin, 1990.

Al-Bishri, Tariq. *Al-Dimuqratiyya wa-Nizam Thalatha wa-'Ishrin Yuliu: 1952–1970*. Beirut: Mu'assassat al-Abhath al-'Arabiyya, 1987.

Boyle, Helen. *Quranic Schools: Agents of Preservation and Change*. New York: RoutledgeFalmer, 2004.

Brown, Daniel. *Rethinking Tradition in Modern Islamic Thought*. Cambridge: Cambridge University Press, 1999.

Brown, Judith. "AHR Roundtable: 'Life Histories' and the History of Modern South Asia." *American Historical Review* 114, no. 3 (June 2009): 587–95.

Brown, Kate. "AHR Roundtable: A Place in Biography for Oneself." *American Historical Review* 114, no. 3 (June 2009): 596–605.

Budayr, Ahmad 'Abd al-Fattah. *Al-Amir Ahmad Fu'ad wa-Nash'at al-Jami'a al-Misriyya*. Cairo: Matba'at Jami'at Fu'ad al-Awwal, 1950, repr. Cairo: Dar al-Kutub wa-l-Watha'iq al-Qawmiyya, 2008.

Cachia, Pierre. *An Overview of Modern Arabic Literature*. Edinburgh: Edinburgh University Press, 1990.

Caine, Barbara. *Biography and History*. New York: Palgrave Macmillan, 2010.

Chafik, Ahmed. *L'Égypte Moderne et les Influences Étrangères*. Cairo: Imprimerie Misr, 1931.

Charle, Christophe. "Ambassadeurs ou Chercheurs? Les Relations Internationales des Professeurs de la Sorbonne sous la IIIe République." *Genèses* 14 (1994): 8–19.

Chejne, Anwar. *The Arabic Language: Its Role in History*. Minneapolis: University of Minnesota Press, 1969.

Chin, Chuanfei. "Margins and Monsters: How Some Micro Cases Lead to Macro Claims." *History and Theory* 5 (October 2011): 341–57.

Choueiri, Youssef. *Arab History and the Nation-State: A Study in Modern Arab Historiography 1820–1980*. London: Routledge, 1989.

Cole, Juan Ricardo. *Colonialism and Revolution in the Middle East: Social and Cultural Origins of Egypt's 'Urabi Movement*. Princeton, NJ: Princeton University Press, 1993.

Coury, Ralph M. *The Making of an Egyptian Arab Nationalist: The Early Years of Azzam Pasha, 1893–1936*. Reading: Ithaca Press, 1998.

Cuno, Kenneth. *Modernizing Marriage Family, Ideology, and Law in Nineteenth and Early Twentieth Century Egypt*. New York: Syracuse University Press, 2015.

Dar al-Kutub wa-l-Watha'iq al-Qawmiya. *Al-Jami'a al-Ahliyya (1908–1925): Safahat min Dhakirat al-Sahafa*. Cairo: Dar al-Kutub wa-l-Watha'iq al-Qawmiyya, 2010.

Darwiche Jabbour, Zahida. *Littératures Francophones du Moyen-Orient: Égypte, Liban, Syrie*. Aix-en-Provence: Edisud, 2007.

Dawn, Ernest. "The Formation of Pan-Arab Ideology in the Interwar Years." *International Journal of Middle East Studies* 20, no. 1 (February 1988): 67–91.
Denzin, Norman. *Interpretive Biography*. Newbury Park, CA: Sage, 1989.
Di-Capua, Yoav. *Gatekeepers of the Arab Past: Historians and History Writing in Twentieth-Century Egypt*. Berkeley: University of California Press, 2009.
———. *No Exit: Arab Existentialism, Jean-Paul Sartre and Decolonization*. Chicago: University of Chicago Press, 2018.
Dib, Mariyus Kamil. *Al-Siyasa al-Hizbiyya fi Misr: Al-Wafd wa-Khusumuh, 1919–1939*. Beirut: Mu'assassat al-Abhath al-'Arabiyya, 1987.
Diyab, 'Abd al-Hayy. *Al-Turath al-Naqdi Qabl Madrasat al-Jil al-Jadid*. Cairo: Dar al-Katib al-'Arabi, 1968.
Dodge, Bayard. *Al-Azhar: A Millennium of Muslim Learning*. Washington, DC: Middle East Institute, 1961.
Doran, Michael. *Pan-Arabism before Nasser: Egyptian Power Politics and the Palestine Question*. Oxford: Oxford University Press, 1999.
Douglas, Mary. *How Institutions Think*. Syracuse, NY: Syracuse University Press, 1986.
Dupont, Anne-Laure. *Gurgi Zaydan 1861–1914: Écrivain Réformiste et Témoin de la Renaissance Arabe*. Damascus: Institut Français du Proche-Orient, 2006.
Egger, Vernon. *A Fabian in Egypt: Salamah Musa and the Rise of the Professional Classes in Egypt, 1909–1939*. Lanham, MD: University Press of America, 1986.
El-Ariss, Tarek. *Trials of Modernity: Literary Affects and the New Political*. New York: Fordham University Press, 2013.
El-Enany, Rasheed. *Arab Representations of the Occident: East-West Encounters in Arabic Fiction*. New York: Routledge, 2006.
El Shakry, Omnia. *The Great Social Laboratory: Subjects of Knowledge in Colonial and Postcolonial Egypt*. Stanford, CA: Stanford University Press, 2007.
Erlich, Haggai. *Students and University in 20th Century Egyptian Politics*. London: Frank Cass, 1989.
Fahmy, Khaled. *All the Pasha's Men: Mehmed Ali, his Army, and the Making of Modern Egypt*. Cambridge: Cambridge University Press, 1997.
Fahmy, Ziad. *Ordinary Egyptians: Creating the Modern Nation through Popular Culture*. Stanford, CA: Stanford University Press, 2011.
Faksh, Mahmoud A. "The Consequences of the Introduction and Spread of Modern Education: Education and National Integration in Egypt." *Middle Eastern Studies* 16, no. 2 (1980): 42–55.
Fay, Mary Ann. "From Warrior-Grandees to Domesticated Bourgeoisie: The Transformation of the Elite Egyptian Household into a Western-Style Nuclear Family." In *Family History in The Middle East: Household, Property, and Gender*, edited by Beshara Doumani, 77–98. Albany: State University of New York Press, 2003.
Al-Fiqi, Muhammad Kamil. *Al-Azhar wa-Atharuhu fi al-Nahda al-Adabiyya al-Haditha*. Cairo: Al-Matba'a al-Muniriyya bi-l-Azhar, 1956.
Fleming, Robin. "AHR Roundtable: Writing Biography at the Edge of History." *American Historical Review* 114, no. 3 (June 2009): 606–14.

Gasper, Michael. *The Power of Representation: Publics, Peasants, and Islam in Egypt.* Stanford, CA: Stanford University Press, 2009.
Gaudio, Attillio. *Guerre et Paix au Maroc: Reportages: 1950–1990.* Paris: Éditions Karthala, 1991.
Gershoni, Israel, Amy Singer, and Hakan Erdem, eds. *Middle East Historiographies: Narrating the Twentieth Century.* Seattle: University of Washington Press, 2006.
Gershoni, Israel, and James Jankowski. *Egypt, Islam, and the Arabs: The Search for Egyptian Nationhood, 1900–1930.* New York: Oxford University Press, 1986, 1987.
———. *Redefining the Egyptian Nation, 1930–1945.* Cambridge: Cambridge University Press, 1995.
———. *Rethinking Nationalism in the Arab Middle East.* New York: Columbia University Press, 1997.
Ghazoul, Ferial, and Barbara Harlow, eds. *The View from Within: Writers and Critics on Contemporary Arabic Literature.* Cairo: American University in Cairo Press, 1994.
Ginat, Rami. "The Egyptian Left and the Roots of Neutralism in the Pre-Nasserite Era." *British Journal of Middle Eastern Studies* 30, no. 1 (May 2003): 5–24.
Goldberg, Ellis. *Tinker, Tailor, and Textile Worker: Class and Politics in Egypt, 1930–1952.* Berkeley: University of California Press, 1986.
Goldschmidt, Arthur, Amy J. Johnson, and Barak A. Salmoni, eds. *Re-envisioning Egypt 1919–1952.* Cairo: American University in Cairo Press, 2005.
Gordon, Joel. *Nasser's Blessed Movement: Egypt's Free Officers and the July Revolution.* New York: Oxford University Press, 1992.
Gorman, Anthony. *Historians, State and Politics in Twentieth-Century Egypt: Contesting the Nation.* New York: RoutledgeCurzon, 2003.
Gran, Peter. *Islamic Roots of Capitalism: Egypt, 1760–1840.* Austin: University of Texas Press, 1979.
Haeri, Niloofar. *Sacred Language, Ordinary People: Dilemmas of Culture and Politics in Egypt.* New York: Palgrave Macmillan, 2003.
Hafiz, Sabri. *The Genesis of Arabic Narrative Discourse: A Study in the Sociology of Modern Arabic Literature.* London: Saqi Books, 1993.
Al-Hakim, Tawfiq. *'Awdat al-Wa'y.* Cairo: Maktabat Misr, 1974.
Hamilton, Nigel. *Biography: A Brief History.* Cambridge, MA: Harvard University Press, 2007.
Hamzah, Dyala, ed. *The Making of the Arab Intellectual (1880–1960): Empire, Public Sphere and the Colonial Coordinates of Selfhood.* New York: Routledge, 2012.
Hanley, Will. *Identifying with Nationality: Europeans, Ottomans, and Egyptians in Alexandria.* New York: Columbia University, 2017.
Hanssen, Jens, and Max Weiss, eds. *Arabic Thought beyond the Liberal Age: Towards an Intellectual History of the Nahda.* Cambridge: Cambridge University Press, 2016.
Harris, W. V., ed. *Rethinking the Mediterranean.* Oxford: Oxford University Press, 2005.
Haykal, Muhammad Hasanayn. *Azmat al-Muthaqqafin: Nazra ila Mashakilina al-Dakhiliyya.* Cairo: Al-Sharika al-'Arabiyya al-Muttahida li-l-Tawzi', 1961.
———. *The Cairo Documents.* New York: Doubleday, 1973.

Haykal, Muhammad Husayn. *Mudhakkirat fi al-Siyasa al-Misriyya.* 3 vols. Cairo: Dar al-Ma'arif, 1990.
Hellbeck, Jochen. "AHR Roundtable: Galaxy of Black Stars: The Power of Soviet Biography." *American Historical Review* 114, no. 3 (June 2009): 615–24.
Heyworth-Dunne, J. *An Introduction to the History of Education in Modern Egypt.* London: Luzac, 1938.
Hopkins, Nicholas, and Nathalie Bernard-Maugiron. *Political and Social Protest in Egypt.* Cairo: American University in Cairo Press, 2009.
Horden, Peregrine, and Nicholas Purcell. *The Corrupting Sea: A Study of Mediterranean History.* Oxford: Blackwell, 2000.
Hourani, Albert. *Arabic Thought in the Liberal Age, 1798–1939.* Cambridge: Cambridge University Press, 1983.
Hunter, Robert. *Egypt under the Khedives: From Household Government to Modern Bureaucracy.* Pittsburgh, PA: University of Pittsburgh Press, 1984.
Hyde, Georgie. *Education in Modern Egypt: Ideals and Realities.* London: Routledge & Kegan Paul, 1978.
Ibrahim, Samia. *Al-Jami'a al-Ahliyya bayna al-Nash'a wa-l-Tatawwur.* Cairo: Dar al-Kutub wa-l-Watha'iq al-Qawmiyya, 2011.
Jacquemond, Richard. *Entre Scribes et Écrivains: Le Champs Littéraire dans l'Égypte Contemporaine.* Paris: Sindbad/Actes Sud, 2003.
Jacob, Wilson. *Working out Egypt: Effendi Masculinity and Subject Formation in Colonial Modernity, 1870–1940.* Durham, NC: Duke University Press, 2011.
James, C.L.R. *The Black Jacobins: Toussaint Louverture and the San Domingo Revolution.* London: Allison & Busby, 1980.
Al-Jumay'i, 'Abd al-Mun'im Ibrahim al-Dusuqi. *Al-Jami'a al-Misriyya al-Qadima: Nash'atuha wa-Dawruha fi al-Mujtama' (1908–1925).* Cairo: Dar al-Kitab al-Jami'i, 1980.
Jankowski, James. "Egyptian Responses to the Palestine Problem in the Interwar Period." *International Journal of Middle East Studies* 12, no. 1 (August 1980): 1–38.
Kane, Patrick. *The Politics of Art in Modern Egypt: Aesthetics, Ideology and Nation-Building.* New York: I. B. Tauris, 2013.
Kassab, Elizabeth Suzanne. *Contemporary Arab Thought: Cultural Critique in Comparative Perspective.* New York: Columbia University Press, 2010.
——. *Enlightenment on the Eve of Revolution: The Egyptian and Syrian Debates* (New York: Columbia University Press, 2019.
Kazamias, Andreas. *Education and the Quest for Modernity in Turkey.* London: Allen & Unwin, 1966.
Kazziha, Walid. "The Jarida-Umma Group and Egyptian Politics." *Middle Eastern Studies* 13, no. 3 (1977): 373–85.
Kessler-Harris, Alice. "AHR Roundtable: Why Biography?" *American Historical Review* 114, no. 3 (June 2009): 625–30.
Kholoussy, Hanan. *For Better, for Worse: The Marriage Crisis That Made Modern Egypt.* Stanford, CA: Stanford University Press, 2010.

Khuri, Ra'if. *Al-Fikr al-'Arabi al-Hadith: Athar al-Thawra al-Firinsiyya fi Tawjihihi al-Siyasi wa-l-Ijtima'i*. 1943. Beirut: Dar al-Saqi, 2013.

Khuri-Makdisi, Ilham. *The Eastern Mediterranean and the Making of Global Radicalism, 1860–1914*. Berkeley: University of California Press, 2010.

Lanfranchi, Samia Sharawi. *Casting Off the Veil: The Life of Huda Shaarawi, Egypt's First Feminist*. London: I. B. Tauris, 2012.

Lia, Brynjar. *The Society of the Muslim Brothers in Egypt: The Rise of an Islamic Mass Movement, 1928–1942*. Reading: Ithaca Press, 1998.

Lockman, Zachary. *Contending Visions of the Middle East: The History and Politics of Orientalism*. New York: Cambridge University Press, 2010.

———. "La Gauche et le Mouvement Ouvrier au Début des Années 1920." *Cahiers d'Histoire* 105–106 (2008): 65–83.

———. "Imagining the Working Class: Culture, Nationalism, and Class Formation in Egypt, 1899–1914." *Poetics Today* 15, no. 2 (1994): 157–90.

———, ed. *Workers and Working Classes in the Middle East: Struggles, Histories, Historiographies*. Albany: State University of New York Press, 1994.

Lorenz, Joseph. *Egypt and the Arabs: Foreign Policy and the Search for National Identity*. Boulder, CO: Westview Press, 1990.

Mackridge, Peter. *Language and National Identity in Greece, 1766–1976*. Oxford: Oxford University Press, 2009.

Madkur, Ibrahim Bayumi. *Majma' al-Lugha al-'Arabiyya fi Thalathin 'Aman, 1932–1962, Madih wa-Hadiruh*. Cairo: Al-Matba'a al-Amiriyya, 1964.

Magnusson, Sigurdur. "The Singularization of History: Social History and Microhistory within the Postmodern State of Knowledge." *Journal of Social History* 36, no. 3 (2003): 701–35.

———. "Social History as 'Sites of Memory'? The Institutionalization of History: Microhistory and the Grand Narrative." *Journal of Social History* 39, no. 3 (Spring 2006): 891–913.

Makarius, Raoul. *La Jeunesse Intellectuelle d'Égypte au Lendemain de la Deuxième Guerre Mondiale*. Paris: Mouton, 1960.

Makdisi, George. *The Rise of Humanism in Classical Islam and the Christian West: With Special Reference to Scholasticism*. Edinburgh: Edinburgh University Press, 1990.

Mann, Susan. "AHR Roundtable: Scene Setting: Writing Biography in Chinese History." *American Historical Review* 114, no. 3 (June 2009): 631–39.

Massad, Joseph. *Desiring Arabs*. Chicago: University of Chicago Press, 2007.

Mehrez, Samia. *Egypt's Culture Wars: Politics and Practice*. New York: Routledge, 2008.

———. *Egyptian Writers between History and Fiction: Essays on Naguib Mahfouz, Sonallah Ibrahim, and Gamal al-Ghitani*. Cairo: American University in Cairo Press, 1994.

Meijer, Roel. *The Quest for Modernity: Secular Liberal and Left-wing Political Thought in Egypt, 1945–1958*. London: RoutledgeCurzon, 2002.

Meretoja, Hanna. *The Narrative Turn in Fiction and Theory: The Crisis and Return of Storytelling from Robbe-Grillet to Tournier*. London: Palgrave, 2014.

Meriwether, Margaret L., and Judith E. Tucker, eds. *Social History of Women and Gender in the Modern Middle East*. Boulder, CO: Westview Press, 1999.

Mikhail, Alan. *Nature and Empire in Ottoman Egypt: An Environmental History*. Cambridge: Cambridge University Press, 2011.

Mitchell, Richard. *The Society of the Muslim Brothers*. New York: Oxford University Press, 1993.

Mitchell, Timothy. *Colonising Egypt*. London: University of California Press, 1991.

———. *Rule of Experts: Egypt, Techno-Politics, Modernity*. Berkeley: University of California Press, 2002.

Morewood, Steven. "Appeasement from Strength: The Making of the 1936 Anglo-Egyptian Treaty of Friendship and Alliance." *Diplomacy & Statecraft* 7, no. 3 (1996): 530–62.

———. *The British Defence of Egypt, 1935–1940: Conflict and Crisis in the Eastern Mediterranean*. London: Frank Cass, 2005.

Morsy, Laila. "Britain's Wartime Policy in Egypt, 1940–42." *Middle Eastern Studies* 25, no. 1 (1989): 64–94.

———. "Indicative Cases of Britain's Wartime Policy in Egypt, 1942–44." *Middle Eastern Studies* 30, no. 1 (1994): 91–122.

———. "The Military Clauses of the Anglo-Egyptian Treaty of Friendship and Alliance, 1936." *International Journal of Middle East Studies* 16, no. 1 (1984): 67–97.

Munawi, Mahmud. *Jamiʿat al-Qahira fi ʿIdiha al-Miʾawi*. Giza: Al-Maktaba al-Akadimiyya, 2007.

Musa, Salama. *Al-Balagha al-ʿAsriyya wa-l-Lugha al-ʿArabiyya*. Cairo: Al-Matbaʿa al-ʿAsriyya, 1953.

Nasaw, David. "AHR Roundtable: Historians and Biography, Introduction." *American Historical Review* 114, no. 3 (June 2009): 573–78.

Nasim, Sulayman. *Siyaghat al-Taʿlim al-Misri al-Hadith: Dawr al-Quwa al-Siyasiyya wa-l-Ijtimaʿiyya wa-l-Fikriyya, 1923–1952*. Cairo: Al-Hayʾa al-Misriyya al-ʿAmma li-l-Kitab, 1984.

Nasr al-Din, Hasan. *Al-Ajanib fi al-Jamiʿa al-Misriyya*. Cairo: Dar al-Kutub wa-l-Wathaʾiq al-Qawmiyya, 2011.

Nelson, Cynthia. *Doria Shafik, Egyptian Feminist: A Woman Apart*. Gainesville: University Press of Florida, 1996.

Neptune Harvey. "Romance, Tragedy and, Well, Irony: Some Thoughts on David Scott's Conscripts of Modernity." *Social and Economic Studies* 57, no. 1 (March 2008): 165–81.

Ostle, Robin, Ed de Moor, and Stefan Wild, eds. *Writing the Self: Autobiographical Writing in Modern Arabic Literature*. London: Saqi Books, 1998.

Owen, Roger. *Lord Cromer: Victorian Imperialist, Edwardian Preconsul*. Oxford: Oxford University Press, 2004.

Parsons, Laila. *The Commander: Fawzi al-Qawuqji and the Fight for Arab Independence, 1914–1948*. New York: Farrar, Straus and Giroux, 2016.

———. "Micro-narrative and the Historiography of the Modern Middle East." *History Compass* 9, no. 1 (2011): 84–96.

———. "Some Thoughts on Biography and the Historiography of the Twentieth-Century Arab World." *Journal of the Canadian Historical Association* 21, no. 2 (2010): 5–20.

Patel, Abdulrazzak. *The Arab Nahdah: The Making of the Intellectual and Humanist Movement*. Edinburgh: Edinburgh University Press, 2013.

Pedersen, Susan. *The Guardians: The League of Nations and the Crisis of Empire*. Oxford: Oxford University Press, 2015.

Podeh, Elie, and Onn Winckler, eds. *Rethinking Nasserism: Revolution and Historical Memory in Egypt*. Gainesville: Florida University Press, 2004.

Pollard, Lisa. *Nurturing the Nation: The Family Politics of Modernizing, Colonizing, and Liberating Egypt, 1805–1923*. Berkeley: University of California Press, 2005.

Popkin, Jeremy. *History, Historians, and Autobiography*. Chicago: University of Chicago Press, 2005.

Powell, Eve M. Troutt. *A Different Shade of Colonialism: Egypt, Great Britain, and the Mastery of the Sudan*. Berkeley: University of California Press, 2003.

Al-Qabbani, Isma'il Mahmud. *Dirasat fi Tanzim al-Ta'lim bi-Misr*. Cairo: Makatabat al-Nahda, 1958.

Al-Rafi'i, 'Abd al-Rahman. *Mustafa Kamil: Ba'ith al-Nahda al-Wataniyya*. Cairo: Dar al-Hilal, 1957.

———. *Thawrat 1919: Tarikh Misr al-Qawmi min Sanat 1914 ila Sanat 1921*. Cairo: Mu'assassat Dar al-Sha'b, 1968.

Ramadan, 'Abd al-'Azim. *Misr fi 'Asr al-Sadat*. Beirut: Dar al-Ruqiy, 1986.

———. *Mudhakkirat al-Siyasiyyin wa-l-Zu'ama' fi Misr 1891–1981*. Cairo: Maktabat Madbuli, 1984.

———. *Tatawwur al-Haraka al-Wataniyya fi Misr min Sanat 1918 ila Sanat 1936*. (2 vols.) Cairo: Maktabat Madbuli, 1983.

———. *Tatawwur al-Haraka al-Wataniyya fi Misr min Sanat 1937 ila Sanat 1948*. Cairo: Al-Hay'a al-Misriyya al-'Amma li-l-Kitab, 1989.

Rastegar, Kamran. "Introduction." *Middle Eastern Literatures* 16, no. 3 (2013): 227–31.

Reid, Donald. *Cairo University and the Making of Modern Egypt*. Cambridge: Cambridge University Press, 1990.

———. *Whose Pharaohs?: Archaeology, Museums, and Egyptian National Identity from Napoleon to World War I*. Berkeley: University of California Press, 2002.

Renders, Hans. "The Limits of Representativeness: Biography, Life Writing and Microhistory." *Storia della Storiografia* 59–60 (2011): 32–42.

Reynolds, Dwight, ed. *Interpreting the Self: Autobiography in the Arabic Literary Tradition*. Berkeley: University of California Press, 2001.

Reynolds, Nancy. *A City Consumed: Urban Commerce, the Cairo Fire, and the Politics of Decolonization in Egypt*. Stanford, CA: Stanford University Press, 2012.

Rizq, Yunan Labib. *Al-Ahzab al-Siyasiyya fi Misr 1907–1984*. Cairo: Dar al-Hilal, 1984.

———. *Tarikh al-Wizarat al-Misriyya, 1878–1953*. Cairo: Markaz al-Dirasat al-Siyasiyya wa-l-Istratijiyya bi-l-Ahram, 1975.
Roussillon, Alain. *Identité et Modernité: Les Voyageurs Égyptiens au Japon (xixe–xxe Siècle)*. Arles: Actes Sud, 2005.
Rüegg, Walter, and Hilde de Ridder-Symoens, eds. *A History of the University in Europe*. 4 vols. Cambridge: Cambridge University Press, 1991–2011.
Russell, Mona. "Competing, Overlapping, and Contradictory Agendas: Egyptian Education under British Occupation, 1882–1922." *Comparative Studies of South Asia, Africa and the Middle East* 21, no. 1–2 (2001): 50–60.
———. *Creating the New Egyptian Woman: Consumerism, Education and National Identity, 1863–1922*. New York: Palgrave Macmillan, 2004.
Said, Edward. *Humanism and Democratic Criticism*. New York: Columbia University Press, 2004.
Salama, Jirjis. *Tarikh al-Ta'lim al-Ajnabi fi Misr fi al-Qarnayn al-Tasi' 'Ashar wa-l-'Ishrin*. Cairo: Al-Majlis al-A'la li-Ri'ayat al-Funun wa-l-Adab wa-l-'Ulum al-Ijtima'iyya, 1963.
Salvatore, Armando, and Mark Lavine, eds. *Religion, Social Practice, and Contested Hegemonies: Reconstructing the Public Sphere in Muslim Majority Societies*. New York: Palgrave Macmillan, 2005.
Salvatore, Nick. "Biography and Social History: An Intimate Relationship." *Labor History* 87 (2004): 187–92.
Al-Sayyid, Ahmad Lutfi. *Turath Ahmad Lutfi al-Sayyid*. Cairo: Dar al-Kutub wa-l-Watha'iq al-Qawmiyya, 2008.
Sayyid Marsot, Afaf Lutfi. *Egypt and Cromer: A Study in Anglo-Egyptian Relations*. London: Murray, 1968.
———. *Egypt's Liberal Experiment, 1922–1936*. Berkeley: University of California Press, 1977.
Schildgen, Brenda, Gang Zhou, and Sander Gilman (eds.). *Other Renaissances: A New Approach to World Literatures*. New York: Palgrave Macmillan, 2006.
Scott, David. *Conscripts of Modernity: The Tragedy of Colonial Enlightenment*. Durham, NC: Duke University Press, 2004.
Selim, Samah. *The Novel and the Rural Imaginary in Egypt, 1880–1985*. New York: RoutledgeCurzon, 2004.
Shafiq, Ahmad. *Mudhakkirati fi Nisf Qarn*. Cairo: 1936.
Al-Shalq, Ahmad Zakariya, ed. *Mi'at 'Am 'ala al-Jami'a al-Misriyya*. Cairo: Dar al-Kutub wa-l-Watha'iq al-Qawmiyya, 2011.
Sharabi, Hisham. *Arab Intellectuals and the West*. Baltimore, MD: Johns Hopkins University Press, 1970.
Sharkey, Heather. "Language and Conflict: The Political History of Arabisation in Sudan and Algeria." *Studies in Ethnicity and Nationalism* 12, no. 3 (2012): 427–49.
Sheehi, Stephen. *Foundations of Modern Arab Identity*. Gainesville: University Press of Florida, 2004.

Siddiq, Muhammad. *Arab Culture and the Novel: Genre, Identity and Agency in Egyptian Fiction*. London: Routledge, 2007.
Smith, Charles. *Islam and the Search for Social Order in Modern Egypt: A Biography of Muhammad Husayn Haykal*. Albany: State University of New York Press, 1983.
Solé, Robert. *L'Égypte Passion Française*. Paris: Éditions du Seuil, 1997.
Sommer, Dorothe. *Freemasonry in the Ottoman Empire: A History of the Fraternity and Its Influence in Syria and the Levant*. London: I. B. Tauris, 2013.
Starkey, Paul. *Modern Arabic Literature*. Edinburgh: Edinburgh University Press, 2006.
Starr, Deborah. *Remembering Cosmopolitan Egypt: Literature, Culture, and Empire*. London: Routledge, 2009.
Stenner, David. "'Bitterness towards Egypt'—The Moroccan Nationalist Movement, Revolutionary Cairo and the Limits of Anti-Colonial Solidarity." *Cold War History* 16, no. 2 (2005): 159–75.
Suleiman, Yasir. *A War of Words: Language and Conflict in the Middle East*. Cambridge: Cambridge University Press, 2004.
Tageldin, Shaden. *Disarming Words: Empire and the Seductions of Translation in Egypt*. Berkeley: University of California Press, 2011.
Tal, David, ed. *The 1956 War: Collusion and Rivalry in the Middle East*. London: Frank Cass, 2001.
Tarabishi, Georges. *Min al-Nahda ila al-Ridda: Tamazuqat al-Thaqafa al-ʿArabiyya fi ʿAsr al-ʿAwlama*. Beirut: Dar al-Saqi, 2009.
Taylor, Barbara. "AHR Roundtable: Separations of Soul: Solitude, Biography, History." *American Historical Review* 114, no. 3 (June 2009): 640–50.
Thompson, Elizabeth. *Justice Interrupted: The Struggle for Constitutional Government in the Middle East*. Cambridge, MA: Harvard University Press, 2013.
Tignor, Robert. *Modernization and British Colonial Rule in Egypt 1882–1914*. Princeton, NJ: Princeton University Press 1966.
———. *State, Private Enterprise, and Economic Change in Egypt, 1918–1952*. Princeton, NJ: Princeton University Press, 1984.
Tomiche, Nada. *Histoire de la Littérature Romanesque de l'Égypte Moderne*. Paris: G.-P. Maisonneuve et Larose, 1981.
Tripp, Charles. "Ali Mahir and the Politics of the Egyptian Army, 1936–1942." In *Contemporary Egypt: Through Egyptian Eyes: Essays in Honor of Professor P. J. Vatikiotis*, edited by Charles Tripp and P. J. Vatikiotis, 45–71. London: Routledge, 1993.
Tsourapas, Gerasimos. "Nasser's Educators and Agitators across al-Watan al-ʿArabi: Tracing the Foreign Policy Importance of Egyptian Regional Migration, 1952–1967." *British Journal of Middle Eastern Studies* 43, no. 3 (January 2016): 324–41.
ʿUkasha, Tharwat. *Mudhakkirati fi al-Siyasa wa-l-Thaqafa*. Cairo: Maktabat Madbuli, 1987–1988.
Vardi, Liana. "AHR Roundtable: Re-writing the Lives of Eighteenth-Century Economists." *American Historical Review* 114, no. 3 (June 2009): 652–61.
Waqaʾiʿ al-Multaqa al-Qawmi: Al-Tafkir al-Islahi al-ʿArabi; Khasaʾisahu wa-Hududahu:

Khayr al-Din, Muhammad al-Bairam, Taha Husayn. Sfax, Tunisia, 1990. Tunis: Manshurat al-Maʿhad al-Qawmi li-ʿUlum al-Tarbiyya, 1991.

Wisnovsky, Robert. "The Nature and Scope of Arabic Philosophical Commentary in Postclassical (ca. 1100–1900 AD) Islamic Intellectual History: Some Preliminary Observations." *Bulletin of the Institute of Classical Studies* 47, no. 1 (February 2004): 149–91.

Wissa, Karim. "Freemasonry in Egypt 1798–1921: A Study in Cultural and Political Encounters." *British Society for Middle Eastern Studies Bulletin* 16, no. 2 (1989): 143–61.

Wizarat al-Tarbiyya wa-l-Taʿlim. *Miʾa wa-Situn ʿAman min al-Taʿlim fi Misr: Wuzaraʾ al-Taʿlim wa-Abraz Injazatihim (1837–1997)*. Cairo: Matbuʿat Wizarat al-Tarbiyya wa-l-Taʿlim, 2000.

Yousef, Hoda. *Composing Egypt: Reading, Writing, and the Emergence of a Modern Nation, 1870–1930*. Stanford, CA: Stanford University Press, 2016.

Yunis, Sharif. *Al-Zahf al-Muqaddas*. Beirut: Dar al-Tanwir, 2012.

Zakariya, Fu'ad. *Kam ʿUmr al-Ghadab: Haykal wa-Azmat al-ʿAql al-ʿArabi*. Cairo: Dar al-Qahira, 1983.

INDEX

1919 Revolution: Egyptian independence after the, 10; eruption of the, 146; the university and the, 73, 80, 101, 119; unrealized objectives of the, 7, 189-90, 256n8
1922 independence, 4, 10, 26, 41, 73, 83, 141, 179
1923 constitution, 10, 20, 108, 126, 141, 168, 183, 191
1930 constitution, 20, 108
1954 constitution, 169, 191, 211
Al-'Abbadi, 'Abd al-Hamid, 201, 239n57
Abbas II, Khedive, 77, 100
'Abbas, Ra'uf, 37, 221n129
'Abd al-Quddus, Ihsan, 176
'Abd al-Raziq, 'Ali, 76, 119, 201
'Abd al-Raziq, Mustafa, 150, 237n29
'Abd al-Wahab, Hasan Husni, 63, 148, 201
'Abduh, Muhammad: the Arabic Language Academy and, 146; al-Azhar reforms and, 5, 7-8, 75-7, 90, 94-6, 144, 233n82; the colonial threat and, 77, 181; Sayyid 'Ali al-Marsafi and, 13, 95; the secular university and, 77, 81-2
Abu Bakr, Caliph, 8, 16
Abu al-Fath, Mahmud, 56, 250n29
Abu Hadid, Muhammad Farid, 130
Académie Française, 146, 162
Académie des Inscriptions et Belles-lettres, 88, 232n59

Academy Office (Arabic Language Academy), 27, 150-1, 246n65, 246n66
Adab: nahdawi interest in, 73-6, 103, 146-7, 151; study of, 86, 96, 103; Taha Hussein's interest in, 76, 96, 103, 137, 143, 151, 158-9
Al-Adab, 196
Administrative Council, 82, 88, 99-100, 232n52
Ahlam Shahrazad, 200
Al-Ahram, 69-70, 130-1, 140, 152, 170, 186
Ain Shams University, 106, 122, 190
Alexandria University, 46, 48, 52, 106, 220n25, 224n32
Algeria: Egyptian cultural presence in, 57-58, 64; Egyptian institute in, 67-68, 70; French rule in, 153, 227n90; Nasser's involvement in, 43, 45, 177; war of independence, 48, 177, 184, 185, 211. *See also* Algiers
Algerian People's Party, 63
Algiers: Egyptian cultural presence in, 64; Egyptian institute in, 43, 48, 67-71, 185; exchange of professors between Cairo and, 57
Al-'Alim, Mahmud Amin: 254n111; debate on committed literature and, 7, 194-6; on *The Future of Culture in Egypt* 23, 208; on Taha Hussein's political action, 207-8. See also *Iltizam*
Amin, Ahmad, 90, 93-94, 117, 141, 150-2, 201, 246n65

Amin, 'Ali, 183
Amin, Qasim, 77, 81-82, 84, 141
Amis de la Culture Française en Égypte, 112
'Ammiyya, 139, 141, 153. *See also* Colloquial
Anglo-Egyptian Treaty (1936): abrogation of the, 27, 38, 180-1; Egyptian cultural diplomacy and the, 43, 45, 50, 70; the futility of the, 27, 189, 195; *The Future of Culture in Egypt* and the, 20, 24, 110, 218n67; as a positive step, 20, 33. *See also* The Capitulations.
Anglo-Egyptian Treaty (1954), 169, 183
Anis, 'Abd al-'Azim, 7, 194-6, 254n111
Anti-colonial: discourse, 170; figures, 25, 28; foreign policy, 169, 178; goal, 44, 72; project, 19, 208; resistance, 45; struggle, 7, 24, 168-9, 204
Antun, Farah, 76
Al-'Aqqad, Mahmud 'Abbas: in the Arabic Language Academy 150-2; debate between Salama Musa and, 139, 243n20; debate between Taha Hussein and, 47; debate on *iltizam* and, 194-5; disappointment of, 212; eulogy for, 201; influence of, 5
Arab Conference on Culture (Alexandria), 66, 132
Arab League, 2, 45, 63, 64, 66, 161
Arab Monuments Institute, 51
Arab Socialist Union, 175, 193, 250n27
Arab Spring, 1
Arabic and Islamic studies, 27, 43-45, 47, 50, 70, 178
Arabic Language Academy: as institution of knowledge production, 29, 70, 105, 145-6, 207; journal of the, 37; members of the, 9, 26, 63, 92, 103, 141, 201, 243n20, 245n49; Taha Hussein and the, 9, 26, 40, 103, 158, 166; tasks of the, 136-7, 144, 151, 166-7. *See also* Academy office
Arabic Language Department, 114

Arabic studies, 53, 55
Arabization, 58, 148, 162-3, 223n9
Arcache, Jeanne, 156
Art for art's sake, 7-8, 197. *See also Iltizam*
Artin, Yacoub, 81
Al-'Ashmawi, Muhammad, 50, 130
Asín Palacios Institute, 55
Assiut University, 106, 121
Association des Étudiants Nord-Africains, 63
Athens, 47, 52, 67-68, 71, 145
'Awad, Luwis, 35, 210, 243n20
Al-Ayyam. See *The Days*
'Azzam, 'Abd al-Wahab, 90, 93, 117-8, 201, 238n42
Azhar: the blind at the, 5, 91; curriculum of the, 51, 96, 142, 144, 154, 233n73, 233n82, 244n39; Nasser and the, 202; North Africa and the, 61, 63, 65, 70; plan to merge the School of Judges with the, 126; scholars and students of the, 75-77, 89-90, 94, 96, 114, 116, 119, 121, 146-50, 163, 226n73, 232n67, 238n42; Taha Hussein's conflict with the, 120, 209; Taha Hussein critique of the, 7, 16, 40, 90, 96, 137, 143-4, 154, 160, 167, 209, 244n37; Taha Hussein's praise for the, 133, 137, 144, 209; Taha Hussein's study at the, 5, 13, 19, 92-96

Badawi, 'Abd al-Hamid, 201
Baghdad Pact, 176-7, 251n31
Baha' al-Din, Ahmad, 253n68
Al-Balagha al-'Asriyya wa-l-Lugha al-'Arabiyya, 139, 247n76. *See also* Salama Musa
Bandung Conference, 176, 251n32
Barakat, Bahiy al-Din, 107-9, 152, 166, 236n7, 224n22
Beauvoir, Simone de, 200
Ben Bella, Ahmed, 45, 63
Berque, Jacques, 38
Black Saturday, 69, 111, 181
Blum, Robert, 122

Bourguiba, Habib, 45, 63, 226n73
Bresseau, Suzanne. *See* Taha Hussein, Suzanne
Britain: the Anglo-Egyptian Treaty (1936) and, 20-21; the Anglo-Egyptian Treaty (1954) and, 168, 179; Egypt's 1922 independence and, 4, 10, 73, 179, 216n15; Egypt's occupation and, 105; Egyptian interest in North Africa and, 64; the Egyptian University and, 78, 85; Indian and Pakistani independence and, 177; the return of Qasr al-Nil barracks and, 2; the Sudan and, 182; Suez and, 184-5, 253n75
Bureau of the Arab Maghrib. *See* Maktab al-Maghrib al-'Arabi
Bureaucracy/bureaucratic, 29, 32, 53, 105, 109, 139, 207
Al-Bustani, Butrus, 17, 87, 138, 145, 232n58

Cairo Fire. *See* Black Saturday
Call of the Curlew, 195
Camus, Albert, 7
The Capitulations, 20-1, 24, 43,57-8, 116, 223n4. *See also* The Anglo-Egyptian Treaty (1936)
Center for Islamic Culture (London), 53
Centre de Coopération Intellectuelle, 60
Chair for Arabic Language and Literature (University of Athens), 43, 52, 72
Chair for Hellenic Studies (Alexandria University), 46, 52
China, 178, 219n79
Civil service/servant, 2, 9-10, 22, 31, 39-40, 74, 105, 172, 109, 207-8, 220n95. *See also* Controller of general culture; Technical advisor to the minister; Minister of public instruction
Collège de France, 88
Colloquial: adoption of the, 139-41, 154, 156, 158, 243n18, 243n20, 247n79; against the, 76, 136, 154, 156, 166; the Arabic Language Academy and the,

148-9, 162; introducing into written Arabic, 146
Colonialism: British, 49, 141, 190, 194; European, 12, 26, 72, 119, 138, 171; French, 48-49;
Committed literature. *See Iltizam*
Committee of the Fifty, 174, 190
Conscript, 25-26, 124
Controller of general culture, 9, 22, 110, 150-1
Council of Senior Scholars, 160
Crisis of the Intellectuals, 175, 186, 189-90, 192
Cromer, Evelyn Baring, 78, 82, 123, 229n21
Czech arms deal, 169, 176

Dar al-Kutub, 146
Dar al-Kutub Academy, 146, 245n49
Dar al-Mahfuzat al-'Umumiyya, x, 36
Dar al-'Ulum, 75-76, 89, 92, 140, 146-8, 159-60, 232n67
Dar al-Watha'iq al-Qawmiyya, x, 36, 83
Darb al-Jamamiz, 81
Darraj, Faysal, 214
The Days, 12-13, 16, 90-91, 95-96, 209, 216n30
Dean of arts: 'Abd al-Wahab Azzam as, 238n42; Mansur Fahmi as, 148, 244n40; Shafiq Ghurbal as, 113; Taha Hussein as: 9, 97-98, 108, 110-2, 116-8, 253n68
Democracy: debate on free education and, 32, 210; demonstrations calling for, 2; Egypt inhospitable to, 4; *iltizam* and, 197; the Islamiyyat and, 256n8; the *National Pact* and, 189, 192; Taha Hussein and, 19, 22, 25, 37, 104, 121-3, 126-7, 134, 169, 193, 202, 207, 219n75
Dhikra Abi al-Tayyib ba'd Alf 'Am, 118. *See also* 'Abd al-Wahab 'Azzam
Direction Afrique-Levant, 57-58, 68
Direction Générale de Relations Culturelles, 57-58

Directorate of Elementary Education, 108
Directorate of General Culture, 110
Diwan al-Madaris, 81
Du'a' al-Karawan. See Call of the Curlew
Duha al-Islam, 117. *See* Ahmad Amin
Dunlop, Douglas, 122-3

École Française de Droit, 57-58
Un Effort, 95, 222n139
Egyptian Council of Ministers: abrogating the 1936 Anglo-Egyptian Treaty, 180; the Arabic Language Academy and the, 148, 150; archives of the, 36-38; free education and the, 132, 180; headquarters of the, 2; promoting a new cultural diplomacy, 50-51, 53, 64; the Supreme Council of the Universities and the, 106-7
On Egyptian Culture, 23, 195
Egyptian Feminist Union, 152, 183, 237n29
Egyptian Gazette, 100, 231n43, 234n101
Egyptian Hight School Certificate, 99, 114, 158
Egyptian Institute (London), 50
Egyptian Institute (Washington), 50
Egyptian Institute for Arab Culture (Tangier), 43, 51, 53, 66-67
Egyptian Institute for Arabic and Islamic Studies (North Africa), 43-44, 46, 48-49, 56-57, 65, 67-72, 178, 184
Egyptian National Archives, 35-37, 44. *See also* Dar al-Watha'iq al-Qawmiyya
Egyptian Registry and Property Records Archive. *See* Dar al-Mahfuzat al-'Umumiyya
Egyptian University: from al-Azhar to the, 5, 13; Egyptian women at the, 115-6; the *nahdawi* mission of the, 73, 120-1, 145-7, 172; national role of the, 20, 70; as a private initiative, 83-84, 146, 102-3, 112, 231n41; professors of the, 5, 19, 73, 93, 97, 110, 113, 148, 155,

238n42; Taha Hussein's project and the, 26, 105, 206-7. *See also* Faculty of Arts
Elementary education, 123-5, 129
Essayistes, 112

Fabianism, 139. *See also* Salama Musa
Faculty of Arts: academic freedom and the, 108; archives of the, 36; from al-Azhar to the, 89; Egyptian women and the, 114, 116; the *nahdawi* mission of the, 87, 97, 117, 143-4, 192, 205; as a private initiative, 86, 88-89, 99, 231n45; professors of the, 5, 73, 145; as a state initiative, 83, 102; Taha Hussein's project and the, 26, 40, 73, 97, 105, 111-4, 117-21, 137, 143-4, 159, 192-3, 205, 209. *See also* Egyptian University
Faculty of Law, 108, 115-6
Faculty of the Principles of Religion, 7, 121
Faculty of Science, 114, 116, 231
Fahmi, 'Abd al-'Aziz, 101, 141, 150, 153, 160, 244n23, 247n76
Fajr al-Islam, 117. *See* Ahmad Amin
Falsafat al-Thawra. See Philosophy of the Revolution
Farid, Muhammad, 82
Farouk, King: the 1952 revolution and, 168, 171; the British and, 179; the French government and, 44, 56, 69; Taha Hussein and, 18, 40, 51, 53-4, 56, 71, 200, 242n114; the Wafd party and, 69, 71, 111, 181
Farouk I Institute for Arab Culture (Tangier). *See also* Egyptian Institute for Arab Culture (Tangier)
Farouk I Institute for Arabic Studies (Istanbul), 53
Farouk I Institute for Arabic Studies (North Africa). *See also* Egyptian Institute for Arabic and Islamic Studies (North Africa)
Farouk I Institute of Islamic Culture

Index 281

(London), 54. *See also* Center for Islamic Culture (London)
Farouk I Institute of Islamic Studies (Madrid), 42-43, 50-51, 53-54, 72
Farouk I Prize for Arabic poetry and the Egyptian Story, 152
Farouk I University. *See* Alexandria University
Farouk I University in Madrid, 224n27
Fi al-Adab al-Jahili. *See On Pre-Islamic Literature*
Fi al-Shi'r al-Jahili. *See On Pre-Islamic Poetry*
Fi al-Thaqafa al-Misriyya. *See On Egyptian Culture*
First World War, 101
Al-Fitna al-Kubra, 18
Fouad I, King: and the Arabic Language Academy 145-6; and the Egyptian University, 78, 82-4, 86-8, 100, 231n41, 231n43, 231n45; punishing Taha Hussein, 108, 150; the triangular struggle over power and, 20, 32-3
Fouad I Academy for the Arabic Language. *See* Arabic Language Academy
Fouad I University, 68, 77, 82, 106-7, 238n42. *See also* Egyptian University
France: the Arabic Language Academy and, 162; Baccalauréat des territoires de la, 62; Collège de, 88; colonialism and, 48, 153, 169, 176-7, 185, 227n90; Egyptian cultural diplomacy and, 55, 57-60, 64-65; Egyptian press and, 59; Egyptian University and, 79, 83, 85, 88; free education and, 240n90; Institut de, 232n59; Masonic lodges in, 64; Ministry of Foreign Affairs in, x, 37; the revolution in, 171-2; Suez and, 184-5, 202, 253n75; Taha Hussein's institutes and, 40, 44, 46, 56-57, 67, 69; Taha Hussein's ties with, ix, 5, 18, 40, 55, 57, 61, 65, 73-74, 98, 122, 178, 211; Tangier incident between Egypt and, 56; the Wafd and, 65
France, Mendès, 177

Franco-Oriental Center of Cooperation, 57. *See also* Centre de Coopération Intellectuelle
Free education: introducing 34-35, 105, 128, 131-4, 210; opposition to 40, 128; Taha Hussein's project and, 111, 135, 211; viability of, 8. *See also* Gratuity
Free Officers, 27, 35, 168-9, 175, 206, 209
French Council of Ministers, 67-68
French Revolution, 168, 171-2, 174, 177
Front de Défense de l'Afrique du Nord, 63
Future of Culture in Egypt: critiques of the, 8, 23-24, 29-30, 32, 38, 208-9, 219n75; interwar context of the, 20, 179; Taha Hussein's ideas in the, 19, 26-27, 46-47, 110, 143, 152-3, 161, 209, 214

Gaulle, Charles de, 177
Al-Ghitani, Gamal, 215n7
Ghurbal, Shafiq, 80, 113-4, 201, 224n32
Goichon, Anne-Marie, 57-58
Gómez, Emilio García, 42, 54
Gratuity, 131-3, 240n90
Guidi, Ignazio, 83, 232n67

Hadith al-Arba'a', 158-9
Al-Hakim, Tawfiq, 10, 195-6
Hay'at Kibar al-'Ulama'. *See* Council of Senior Scholars
Haykal, Muhammad Hasanayn, 35-6, 175, 186-90, 192, 204
Haykal, Muhammad Husayn, 150-1, 201, 237n29, 252n57, 256n8
Hebrew, 93, 220n89, 245n49
Higher education: access to, 127, 133; design of, 21, 26, 46, 110, 122-4, 155, 172-3, 192, 229n21; institutions of, 58, 74, 80-81, 84-5, 98-9, 113, 121, 139, 159
Higher Teachers' College, 113
Al-Hilal, 82, 108, 138
Al-Hilali, Najib, 50, 108, 111, 240n90
Hourani, Albert, 29-30, 33-4, 220n95, 256n8
Humanism, 73-7, 87-8, 90, 96, 98-100, 103. *See also* Adab

282 *Index*

Husayn, Muhammad al-Khidr, 63, 148, 226n73
Al-Husri, Sati', 24, 219n79

Ibn 'Ashur, Fadil, 62-63, 201
Ibn Khaldun, 5, 18, 128
Ibrahim Pasha University. *See* Ain Shams University.
Iltizam: 168, 200-1, 204
Imitation and Renewal, 38
Indochina, 176, 185
Institut d'Études Méditerranéennes, 51-2, 72
Institut Français d'Archéologie Orientale (IFAO), 56, 67, 69
Institute of Arabic Studies (Granada), 55
Institute of Egyptian and Islamic Archaeology, 118
Institute of Oriental Languages and Literatures, 118
I'rab, 141, 154
Iraq, 119, 156, 240n90, 251n31
Iran, 119, 245n49, 251n31
Islam and the Principles of Governing, 119. *See also* 'Ali 'Abd al-Raziq
Al-Islam wa-Usul al-Hukm. *See Islam and the Principles of Governing*
Islamic Monuments Institute, 51
Islamic studies, 42-43, 50, 54, 56
Islamist, 14-17, 207
Islamiyyat, 120, 256n8
Ismail, Khedive, 82, 145
Israel, 176, 178, 184-5, 202, 212, 253n75, 256n148
'Issa, Hilmi, 108, 149-50

James, C.L.R., 24-25
Jannat al-Hayawan, 200
Jannat al-Shawk, 200
Japan, 85, 219n79, 229n20
Al-Jarim, 'Ali, 148, 151-2
Al-Jimayil, Antun, 152
Al-Jinan, 138
Al-Jisr, Husayn, 75

Al-Jumhuriyya, 176, 178, 183, 186, 189, 193-4, 211

Kafka, Franz, 7
Kamil, Husayn, 235n103
Kamil, Mustafa, 81, 229n20
Al-Katib al-Misri, 7, 200, 211, 215n7
Al-Khalduniyya, 63
Al-Khashshab, Yahya, 68-69
Al-Khattabi, Muhammad Ibn 'Abd al-Karim, 66
Al-Khazindar, Ahmad, 184
Khuri, Ra'if, 7, 194, 196-7, 200. *See also Iltizam*
Khutba fi Adab al-'Arab, 87. *See also* Al-Bustani, Butrus
Knowledge for knowledge's sake, 79, 84-85, 97-98, 170, 189, 192, 204, 211
Knowledge for society's sake, 189, 211
Al-Kutla al-Wafdiyya, 191
Kuttab, 5, 26, 76, 113, 229n21

Lajnat al-Adab. *See* Literature Committee
Lajnat al-Khamsin. *See* Committee of the Fifty
Lajnat al-Usual. *See* Principles Committee
Latinization: as a means of reform, 136, 139; resisting, 153, 158 166; support for, 140-1, 150, 153, 244n23
League of Nations, 21-2, 24, 116, 219n70. *See also* The Anglo-Egyptian Treaty (1936)
Lebanon, 28, 46, 64, 138, 177, 194-5, 200
Lévi-Provençal, Évariste, 68
Liberal Constitutionalist party, 19, 108, 191
Liberation Rally, 175, 250n27
Literature Committee, 151-2
Littman, Enno, 83, 92-93, 148
London, 50, 53, 141, 177, 181, 238n42
Lycée Farouk, 61

Ma'a al-Mutanabbi, 118

Al-Ma'arri, Abu al-'Ala', 4, 54
Madkur, Ibrahim Bayumi, 146, 162-4, 245n48, 245n49
Madrasat al-Qada' al-Shar'i. *See* School of Judges
Al-Madrasa al-Wataniyya al-Islamiyya, 75
Madrid, 42-43, 50, 54-56
Madrid Institute. *See* Farouk I Institute of Islamic Studies (in Madrid)
Maghrib. *See* North Africa
Mahfouz, Naguib, 152
Mahir, Ahmad, 182-4
Mahmud, Muhammad, 35, 101
Al-Majlis al-A'la li-l-Jami'at. *See* Supreme Council of the Universities
Majlis al-Dawla. *See* State Council
Majlis al-Ma'arif al-A'la. *See* Supreme Council of Education
Majma' Dar al-Kutub. *See* Dar al-Kutub Academy
Al-Majma' al-Malaki li-l-Lugha al-'Arabiyya. *See* Arabic Language Academy
Maktab al-Maghrib al-'Arabi, 45, 63
Manuscripts, 29, 50, 53-54, 76, 112
Al-Maraghi, Muhammad Mustafa, 116, 149-50, 163
Al-Marsafi, Husayn, 75-76
Al-Marsafi, Sayyid 'Ali, 5, 13, 94-95
Mashriq: Egyptian cultural diplomacy and the, 43-45, 61, 63-65, 70; European educational missions in the, 46; France and the, 59-60; *Future of Culture in Egypt* and the, 46
Maspero, Gaston, 88-89, 232n61, 232n62
Massé, Henri, 68
Massignon, Louis, 68
Al-Matba'a al-'Amiriyya, 163
Al-Mazini, Ibrahim, 5, 10, 152, 195-6
Mediterranean: Egyptian cultural diplomacy in the, 27, 43, 46-7, 51, 64; Taha Hussein's thoughts on the, 20, 24, 47
Mediterraneanism, 47, 224n18

El Mekki, Chadli, 63
Minister of public instruction: 'Abd al-Razzaq al-Sanhuri as, 129, 241n99; Bahiy al-Din Barakat as, 107, 166, 236n7; as higher president of the Arabic Language Academy, 148; as higher president of the university, 79, 83, 98, 102, 109, 231n45; Hilmi 'Issa as, 108, 148-50; Husayn Haykal as, 151; Lutfi al-Sayyid as, 146; Muhammad 'Ashmawi as, 50; Najib al-Hilali as, 108, 240n90; as president of the Supreme Council of the Universities, 107; Sa'd Zaghlul as, 82; Taha Hussein as, 2, 9, 26, 37, 42-44, 46, 51, 57, 61, 64-65, 106, 111, 125, 131-2, 200, 236n17; Yacoub Artin as, 81
Ministry of Education, 9, 16, 36, 41, 130, 246n66, 253n68
Ministry of Finance, 51, 53, 113, 130
Ministry of Foreign Affairs: Egyptian, 2; French, xi, 36-37, 44, 68, 70, 178; Spanish, 54
Ministry of Higher Education, 80
Ministry of Public Guidance, 193
Ministry of Public Instruction: the Arabic Language Academy and the, 145-6, 148-9, 151, 162-3, 166-7, 248n118; Egyptian cultural diplomacy and the, 65, 70; free education and the, 128, 131; reform of the, 26, 122-4, 126, 159, 207; Taha Hussein civil servant in the, 9, 22, 30, 36, 105-6, 109-10, 132, 180; Taha Hussein's reports and memos to the, 20, 64; the university and the, 79, 89, 98-101, 106, 108-9, 113, 118, 121, 231n45
Al-Miniya, 4
Mir'at al-Damir al-Hadith, 200
Al-Mithaq al-Watani. *See* National Pact
Modernity, 12, 17, 25-26, 28-29, 207
Morocco: French-controlled, 67; Spanish-controlled, 55-56, 61

284 Index

Al-Mu'adhabun fi al-Ard. See Wretched of the Earth
Mubarak, 'Ali, 81
Mubarak, Husni, 1, 4, 8, 252n57
Muhammad V, Sultan, 66, 177
Muhammad Ali al-Kabir Chair for Arabic Language and Literature (Nice), 43, 51-52, 72
Muhammad Ali University. See Assiut University
Al-Mu'jam al-Wasit, 163
Multiparty system, 44, 103, 105-6, 175, 187, 212
Al-Muqtataf, 117, 138, 140
Muraqabat al-Thaqafa al-'Amma. See Directorate of General Culture
Mursi, Muhammad, 1, 4
Muruwwa, Husayn, 195, 199
Musa, Salama, 10, 76, 139-41, 153, 212, 247n76
Al-Musawwar, 112-3, 117
Mustaqbal al-Thaqafa fi Misr. See Future of Culture in Egypt
Al-Mustashar al-fanni li-wazir al-ma'arif. See Technical advisor to the minister
Al-Mutannabi, 117

Nahda: the Arabic language and the, 136, 138, 144, 147; Arabic Language Academy and the, 144-5, 147, 166, 207; defining and debating the, 16-17, 28-31, 74, 87, 121, 214, 220n87; Egypt and the, 42, 46-7, 50, 61; humanism and the, 74-75, 77; parliament and the, 28, 105; Taha Hussein and the, 14, 29, 32, 40-2, 46-7, 73, 76, 112, 123, 128, 137, 208-10, 214; the university and the, 73, 77, 81-82, 85-87, 103, 113, 117, 123, 144
Nahdawi(s): critique of, 16-17, 30-1; humanism and the, 74-7; institutions, 77, 81, 86-87, 103, 117, 144-5, 147, 166; reforms, 28, 32, 73, 87, 136, 138, 144-5, 207; Taha Hussein as a, 40-1, 73, 128, 137, 210, 214. See also Nahda
Al-Nahhas, Mustafa: the Anglo-Egyptian Treaty (1936) and, 27, 38, 180, 236n17; foreign policy of, 45, 51; the last Wafd government and, 50, 71, 107, 111, 180-1, 200, 236n17; the national struggle and, 35; Taha Hussein's friendship with, 111, 175, 236n17
Najib, Muhammad, 171, 173, 175, 183, 250n8
Naksa, 189
Nallino, Carlo Alfonso, 13, 148
Nasif, Hifni, 146
Nasser, Gamal Abdel: 1967 defeat and, 202, 256n148; assassination attempt of, 169, 183-4; authoritarianism and, 4, 19, 175, 250n27, 252n67, 254n106; death of, 35, 201-2, 255n146; domestic policy of, 19, 169, 175, 186-7, 189, 204; foreign policy of, 45, 168-9, 175, 176-8, 181, 184, 186, 204; "knowledge for society's sake" and, 189, 211; lack of scholarly biographies on, 35; Muhammad Hasanayn Haykal and, 186-8; The National Pact and, 189, 192-3; Pan-Arabism and, 39, 44-45, 168, 177, 223n11; the period between 1919 and 1952 and, 34-35, 43, 45, 70, 189; Philosophy of the Revolution and, 175, 187-8, 190; Suez and, 184, 202; Taha Hussein and, 49, 255n147; Taha Hussein critical of, 18-9, 189-90, 192-3, 204-5, 211-2; Taha Hussein's eulogy for, 201-2; Taha Hussein silent on,19, 169, 175, 204; Taha Hussein supportive of, 19, 27, 168-9, 176-8, 181, 183-4, 186, 204
Nasserite period, 3, 19, 43, 134, 193
Nassim, Muhammad, 108
National Pact, 189, 192-3
National Party, 81-82, 191
National Union, 175, 187, 250n27
Nationalism, 12, 55-56
Al-Nida', 131

North Africa: Egyptian cultural diplomacy in, 37, 39-40, 42-46, 57-62, 64-66, 68, 70-71, 178, 184; French colonialism in, 28, 48, 138, 153, 176-8, 185-6, 204, 209; opposition movements, 45, 63
Al-Nuqrashi, Mahmud, 184

Ottoman, 53, 81, 227n80

Palestine, 44-46, 131, 170
Pan-Arabism, 39, 43-45, 47, 168, 201
Paris: academy in, 145; cultural exchange between Egypt and, 57, 59-61, 64; Egyptian delegation to, 141; Egyptian educational mission in, 253n68; Egyptian embassy in, 70; University of, 55, 77; response to creating Egyptian cultural institutes, 56, 60, 67-68, 70-71; Taha Hussein in, 5, 20, 42, 55-56
Parliament: 1954 constitution and, 191, 203-4, 211; building of, 2; challenges to, 122, 210; educational reform and, 124-6, 129-31, 180, 206; free education and, 105; *On Pre-Islamic Poetry* and, 19, 120; Taha Hussein's project and, 4, 211, 105-6, 206-7. *See also* Parliamentary
Parliamentary: context, 210; debates, 34, 126; democracy, 169; discussions, 27; Egypt, 3, 28, 32, 39, 134; elections, 122; era, 10, 41, 133; experiment, 7, 210; life, 10, 126, 168, 183; majority, 111; politics, 104; president, 191; republic, 191; rule, 206; session, 100. *See also* Parliamentary period; Parliamentary system
Parliamentary period: beginning and end of the, 4, 10, 41, 126; education in the, 105; players and debates in, 34-35; Taha Hussein's project and the, 4, 19, 40-41, 206-7
Parliamentary system: Egypt's unstable, 29, 39-41, 210; Taha Hussein's project and the, 4, 22, 32, 134-5, 169
Partisan politics: divisive, 7, 29, 105, 125, 129, 179, 182, 206, 209; resisting, 27, 40-41, 125, 133-4, 151
Philosophy of the Revolution, 175, 187-8, 190, 192
Postcolonial state, 3, 15, 25, 34, 214, 252n57
On Pre-Islamic Literature, 14, 120
On Pre-Islamic Poetry, 14, 19, 119, 206, 214
Primary education: design of, 21, 104, 124, 127, 155; free, 104, 111, 126, 128-9, 132, 134, 180, 240n90
Principles Committee, 152-3
Private University: birth of the, 78, 84; mission of the, 74, 103, 119; state takeover of the, 73, 79, 98, 102, 109, 231n45; as a struggling initiative, 79, 83, 89, 99-101, 103, 123
Le Progrès Egyptien, 69

Al-Qabbani, Isma'il, 128-9
Al-Qadar, 200
Al-Qalamawi, Suhayr, 114-5, 152, 237n30
The Qur'an, 5, 16, 116, 120, 136, 142, 154, 156-7, 161-3, 232n 67

Rabat, 43, 64, 66-67, 71
Al-Rafi'i, 'Abd al-Rahman, 113-4
Al-Rafi'i, Mustafa Sadiq, 120
Ramadan, Sa'id, 56
Revolutionary Council, 169, 175, 186, 191, 194, 250n29
Rida, Muhammad Rashid, 82
Rif'at, Muhammad Tawfiq, 147-8, 150
Al-Risala, 24
Rome, 47, 67-68, 71
Royal Academy for the Arabic Language, 144-5. *See* Arabic Language Academy
Royal Geographical Society, 128
Royal Historical Society, 114

Rushdi, Husayn, 101
Ruz al-Yusuf, 176

Sa'dist party, 40, 129, 191
Al-Sanhuri, 'Abd al-Razzaq, 129-30, 150, 201, 241n99
Sarruf, Ya'qub, 76, 138
Sartre, Jean-Paul, 7, 193, 200, 254n109, 255n126
Al-Sayyid, Ahmad Lutfi: co-education debate and, 115-6; Egyptian Feminist Union and, 237n29; Egyptian University and, 77, 79, 8, 101, 120; on language reform and the Arabic Language Academy, 141, 145-6, 148, 150-2, 244n22; resignations of, 78, 108, 236n8; Taha Hussein and, 19, 111, 201
Sawt al-'Arab, 45, 177
School of Fine Arts, 51
School of Judges, 90, 126, 238n42
School of Languages, 75
Second World War, 27, 37, 45, 53, 163, 179, 185
Secondary education: design of, 21, 104 124, 127, 155, 173; free, 2, 111, 129, 131-2, 134, 180, 240n90; schools, 64, 89, 99, 121, 212
Shafiq, Duriyya, 182-3, 252n67, 253n68
Shahnameh, 118. See also 'Abd al-Wahab 'Azzam
Shajarat al-Bu's, 200
Shaniq, Muhammad, 61
Sha'rawi, Huda, 152, 237n29
Al-Sharif, Muhammad Hanafi, 130
Al-Shartuni, Rashid, 77
Al-Shartuni, Sa'id, 77
Al-Shinnawi, Kamil, 183
Shukri, Ghali: on *Future of Culture in Egypt*, 219n75; interview with Taha Hussein, 28, 120, 212; on the Islamiyyat, 256n8; on Taha Hussein's influence, 5, 7
Sidqi, Isma'il, 33, 35, 108, 236n10
Siraj al-Din, Fu'ad, 180, 250n29

Al-Sisi, 'Abd al-Fattah, 1
Al-Siyasa, 158
Social biography, 10-12, 31
Sorbonne, 5, 19, 55, 68, 96, 253n68
Spain, 42, 46, 50-51, 54-56, 145
Spanish Academy of History, 54-55
Spanish Directorate of Cultural Relations, 55
State Council, 107, 191
Statesman: Bahiy al-Din Barakat as, 236n7; Taha Hussein as, 10, 29, 37, 39-40, 56, 200, 207
Studia adabiyya, 75
Studia humanitatis, 75
Sudan, 182, 216n15
Suez Canal: and the British, 20, 27, 38, 64, 179-80, 182, 218n67; Crisis (1956), 43, 169, 176, 184-6, 252n52n67, the tripartite aggression, 169, 184, 204, 253n75
Sulayman, 'Umar, 4
Supreme Council of Education, 27, 124-5, 132
Supreme Council of the Universities (SCU), 27, 80, 106-7, 109, 124, 134, 235n6
Syria, 46, 64, 119, 156, 175, 177

Al-Tabi'i, Muhammad, 183
Taha Hussein, Amina-Marguerite, 5, 16, 111, 247n90
Taha Hussein, Moenis-Claude, 5, 16, 39, 52, 247n90
Taha Hussein, Suzanne (née Bresseau), 5, 43, 164, 185, 213, 237n29, 247n90
Tahrir Square, 1, 3, 101
Al-Tahtawi, Rifa'a, 17, 75
Tangier, 55-56, 61, 64-67
Tangier Institute. *See* Farouk I Institute for Arab Culture (Tangier)
Taqlid wa-Tajdid. *See Imitation and Renewal*.
Taymur, Mahmud, 152, 201
Al-Tayyib, Ahmad, 8

Teachers' Syndicate, 180, 240n76
Technical advisor to the minister, 9, 50, 110, 129
Technical councils, 3, 27, 29, 105, 124-5, 133-4, 151. *See also* Supreme Council of Education; Supreme Council of the Universities; Academy Office
Technical education, 111, 131, 134, 180
Tharwat, 'Abd al-Khaliq, 101
Toynbee, Arnold, 113
Tunis, 43, 49, 61-64, 71
Tunisia: academy, 14, 18, 22-23, 38; Arab League and, 63; Arab Spring and, 1; Baccalauréat des territoires de la France d'outre-mer et de l'étranger, 62; communications between Egypt and, 61-64; creation of an Egyptian institute in, 64, 67-68; French resident-general in, 58; independence of, 45, 177, 226n73; Taha Hussein's visit to, 48
Turkey, 53, 141, 183, 240n90, 251n31

'Umar, Caliph, 8, 16
'Umar, Muhammad Husni, 42, 54-55
Université d'Aix-Marseille, 51. *See also* Institut d'Études Méditerranéennes
University Committee, 82, 85
University Council: challenges facing the, 82, 99, 101; duties of, 89, 98, 106, 107, 125, 230n36; Fouad I and the, 83, 86; members of the, 84, 98, 101, 232n52, 235n107

'Uthman, Caliph, 8

Al-Wa'd al-Haqq, 200
Wafd: Committee of the Fifty and the, 190; Egyptian cultural diplomacy and the, 45, 50, 61, 65, 70; last government of the, 44, 50, 69, 111, 180; Mustafa al-Nahhas and the, 35, 45; opposition to the, 129-30, 187, 195, 221n129; popularity of the, 35-36, 71, 105, 110, 126, 129, 131, 134; Taha Hussein and the, 2, 10, 19, 43, 108, 111, 116, 129, 134, 175, 190, 200, 206, 214, 236n17; tension between Farouk and the, 44, 53, 69, 225n36; triangular struggle over power and the, 32, 34
Waqfs, 83, 100-1, 201, 231, 235n104
Wannus, Sa'dallah, 214
Washington, 50
Al-Wasila al-Adabiyya ila al-'Ulum al-'Arabiyya, 76
Wilcox, William, 140-1
Wretched of the Earth, 196, 211

Al-Yaziji, Ibrahim, 77, 138
Young Egypt, 191

Zaghlul, Sa'd, 35, 77, 81-82, 101, 141
Zakariya, Fu'ad, 36
Zaydan, Jirji, 81-82, 138 (Jurji), 230n36
Al-Zaytuna, 61-64, 201
Al-Zayyat, Ahmad Hasan, 201, 234n92
Zionism, 16

The authorized representative in the EU for product safety and compliance is:
Mare Nostrum Group
B.V Doelen 72
4831 GR Breda
The Netherlands

www.ingramcontent.com/pod-product-compliance
Lightning Source LLC
Chambersburg PA
CBHW021958220426
43663CB00007B/862